EVERYDAY *crafting*

Knitting TOYS & DOLLS

LOUISE CROWTHER, LAURA LONG
& CLAIRE GARLAND

sewandso

www.sewandso.co.uk

Contents

Knit & Purl Pets........... 218

Index..................... 335

My Knitted Doll

LOUISE CROWTHER

I'm delighted to introduce you to twelve adorable little people who are bound to make the little people in *your* life very happy indeed. I think we all had a doll or a teddy, or something similar, that we thought of as a best friend when we were growing up—someone to share adventures and make up stories with. The great thing about Penny, Grace, Anna, Ralph, and the whole gang is that they are full of personality and have plenty of features like clothes, bags and hats that can enhance play and add to the fun. I've designed them all with play in mind and have given complete instructions to make knitting them a breeze.

The inspiration for my dolls comes mainly from all the beautiful children's clothes available on the high street, the gorgeous little dresses and trendy outfits I would love to buy and dress my little girl in ... if only I'd had one!

I created my first doll back in 2010, after looking for a pattern to knit a gift for a friend's daughter. There is something very special and satisfying about seeing a child all snuggled up with a toy that you have lovingly made. I wanted something different, something other than the traditional knitted dolls I remembered from my childhood, something that was stylish and cute rather than brash and garish. Unable to find anything suitable, I decided to have a go at making my own pattern, with the contemporary look I had in mind. The resulting doll was a resounding success, and I soon became inundated with requests for more dolls.

Each pattern is written in a straightforward, easy-to-follow manner with row by row instructions, so that even the less-experienced knitter will find them easy to follow. The patterns in this book are designed for you and your friends and family to enjoy and for private use only.

Finally, please look at the section on personalising your knitted doll. You can treat any of the dolls as a starting point and adapt the hair, clothing, colors and features to make the perfect doll for you. I look forward to seeing photos of your knitted dolls! Share them using the hashtag #myknitteddoll and you can see everyone else's, too.

Hope you enjoy knitting these dolls as much as I have enjoyed creating them,

Louise

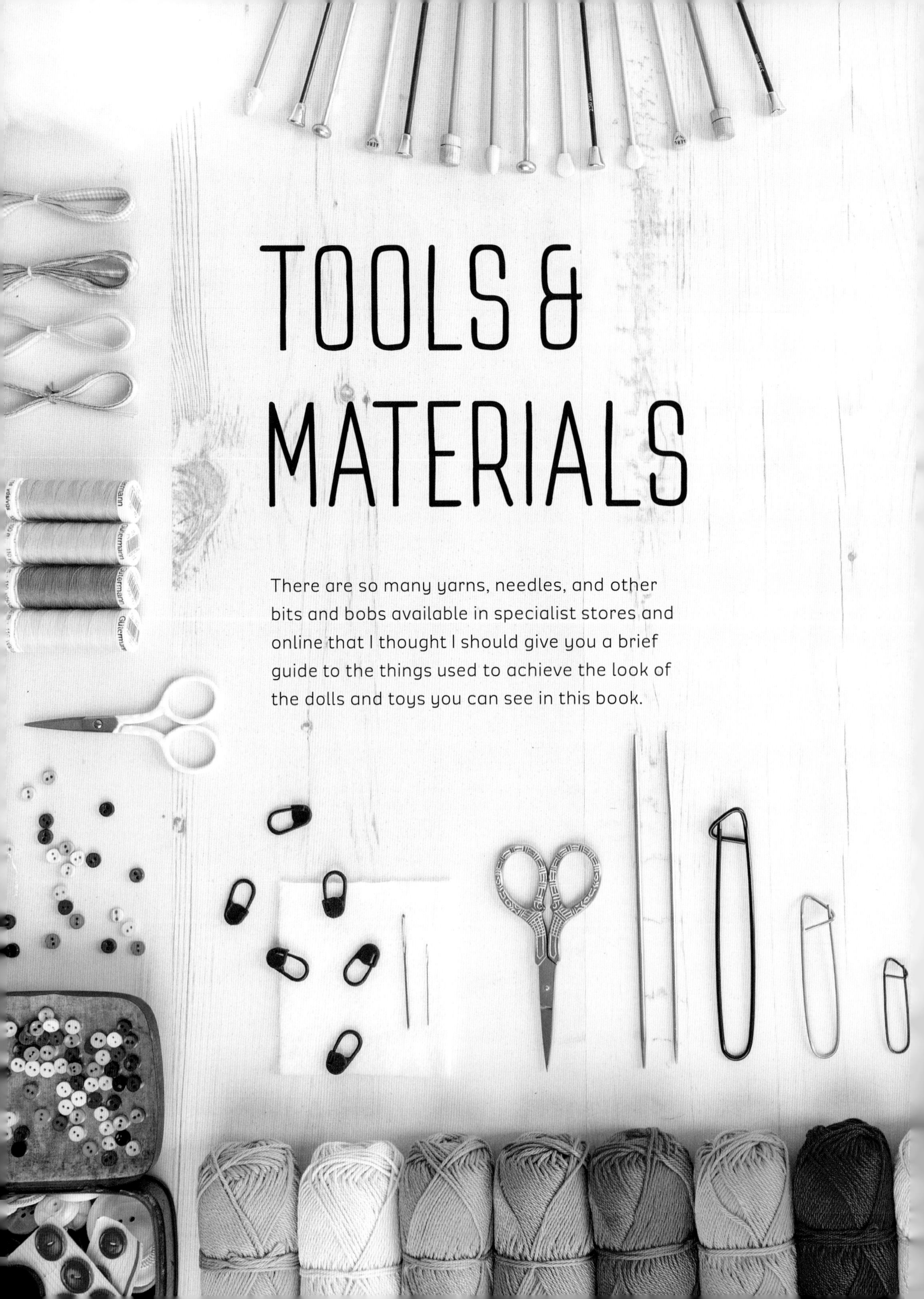

TOOLS & MATERIALS

There are so many yarns, needles, and other bits and bobs available in specialist stores and online that I thought I should give you a brief guide to the things used to achieve the look of the dolls and toys you can see in this book.

YARN

The dolls in the first section of this book have been made using fingering-weight (4-ply) yarn in 100% cotton. I love the crisp, clean look of 100% cotton yarn. It is non-allergenic for most people, incredibly robust and stands up well to being played with.

Various brands of cotton yarn have been used for these dolls, mainly Patons 100% cotton 4-ply, Puppets Lyric 4-ply, Anchor Creativa Fino Cotton and Scheepjes Catona (please refer to Suppliers on page 111).

Although I recommend using 100% cotton yarn to achieve the same look and feel as my dolls, the patterns will work just as well with any fingering-weight (4-ply) non-fancy spun yarn.

Tip

BECAUSE THE DOLLS ARE RELATIVELY SMALL YOU'LL ONLY NEED A SMALL AMOUNT OF EACH COLOR OF YARN— ½ X 1¾OZ (50G) BALL OF YARN IN EACH WOULD EASILY BE ENOUGH.

NEEDLES

You'll need a pair of each of Size 1½ (2.5mm) and Size 2½ (3mm) knitting needles and two Size 1½ (2.5mm) double-pointed needles to complete each doll.

You may need to adjust your needle sizes to accommodate your own personal tension. I am quite a tight knitter, but many of you may knit loosely and therefore will need to adjust your needle size to achieve the correct gauge.

All the dolls in this section should have the same gauge: 35 sts and 48 rows to 4in (10cm) in stockinette stitch (also known as stocking stitch by European knitters) on Size 1½ (2.5mm) needles.

STUFFING

I recommend a synthetic high-loft polyester toy filling for stuffing these dolls. It is lovely and soft, holds its shape well and is hand or machine washable on a cool delicate cycle.

When stuffing your doll use small pieces. Roll and manipulate the body parts in your hands to spread the stuffing evenly and ensure a smooth shape. Tease out any lumps using a blunt tapestry needle carefully inserted through the knitting in the gap between stitches.

YOU WILL ALSO NEED

White felt

Small circles of white felt (roughly ½in (15mm) diameter) are used to strengthen the knitted fabric behind the facial features and prevent the knotted ends showing through to the right side.

Basic kit and embellishments

The other items you need to complete each doll are listed at the beginning of each project. The following is a basic guide:

- Tapestry needle
- Stitch holder
- Stitch markers
- Small buttons, ¼in (6mm) diameter
- Sewing needle and thread
- Ribbon, small lengths 3⁄16in (5mm) wide
- Scissors

WASHING

If made in 100% cotton yarn and stuffed with synthetic toy filling, these dolls can either be washed by hand or on a gentle cool machine cycle. I would recommend reshaping the dolls and their clothing while still damp.

Safety note

DO NOT USE SAFETY EYES, BUTTONS, BEADS OR GLASS EYES ON TOYS INTENDED FOR CHILDREN UNDER THREE YEARS OLD AS THEY ARE A POTENTIAL CHOKING HAZARD.

ABBREVIATIONS

dpn	Double-pointed needle
K	Knit
K2tog	Knit two stitches together
K3tog	Knit three stitches together
Kfb	Knit one stitch through front loop, then knit through back loop
Ktbl	Knit stitch through back loop
kw	Knitwise
M1	Make one stitch: from the front, lift loop between stitches with left needle, knit into back of loop
m1l	Make one left: from the front, lift loop between stitches with left needle, knit into back of loop
m1r	Make one right: from the back, lift loop between stitches with left needle, knit into front of loop
P	Purl
P2tog	Purl two stitches together
Pfb	Purl one stitch through front loop, then purl through back loop
pm	Place marker
PSSO	Pass slipped stitch/stitches over
pw	Purlwise
rpt	Repeat
sl1	Slip one stitch
sl2tog	Slip two stitches together
sm	Slip marker
SSK	Slip two stitches knitwise one at a time, knit together through back loops
SSP	Slip two stitches knitwise one at a time, purl together through back loops
SSSK	Slip 3 stitches knitwise one at a time, knit together through back loops
st(s)	Stitch(es)
St st	Stockinette stitch (stocking stitch). Knit all stitches on right side rows, purl all stitches on wrong side rows
ws	Wrong side
wyif	With yarn in front
YO	Yarn over

Naomi

She's reached the sweet shop, but Naomi's sure she's forgotten something. Whatever it is, perhaps it's in her little flower bag, or maybe she dropped it when she was admiring the fact that the paper bags are striped like her tights? Naomi's a bit of a daydreamer. She wears her bobble hat all year round, otherwise she might lose that, too.

You Will Need

Yarn

- **Yarn A** Beige
- **Yarn B** Pale Yellow
- **Yarn C** Navy
- **Yarn D** Pink
- **Yarn E** Cerise
- **Yarn F** Cream
- **Yarn G** Moss Green
- **Yarn H** Burgundy
- Oddments of black and red for eyes and mouth

Finished size

- 11in (28cm) tall

You will also need

- Size 2½ (3mm) knitting needles
- Size 1½ (2.5mm) knitting needles
- Size 1½ (2.5mm) double-pointed needles
- Stitch holder
- Tapestry needle
- 3 x ½in (15mm) circles of white felt
- Toy stuffing
- 5 x ¼in (6mm) buttons
- 1 x 2½in (6.5cm) long piece of card

Pattern

Cast on using the Long-tail (double cast-on) method (see Techniques, page 102) unless otherwise indicated. Where possible leave long tails when you cast on and bind off and use these for the sewing up.

Head

Using Yarn A and Size 1½ (2.5mm) needles cast on 13 sts.

Starting at neck:

Row 1 (ws): Purl.

Row 2: [K1, M1] 12 times, K1. (25 sts)

Row 3: Purl.

Row 4: K3, [K1, M1] 7 times, K4, [K1, M1] 7 times, K4. (39 sts)

Rows 5–7: St st 3 rows.

Row 8: K3, [K3, M1] 4 times, K6, [K3, M1] 4 times, K6. (47 sts)

Cut yarn.

Rows 9–31: Using intarsia method (see Techniques, page 109) and working in st st, work Hair Chart. Start with a purl row (ws) at the bottom left-hand corner of chart, read purl rows (ws) from left to right and knit rows (rs) from right to left.

For top of head continue in Yarn B.

Row 32: K8, K2tog, K4, SSK, K15, K2tog, K4, SSK, K8. (43 sts)

Row 33: Purl.

Row 34: K8, K2tog, K2, SSK, K15, K2tog, K2, SSK, K8. (39 sts)

Row 35: Purl.

Row 36: K8, K2tog, SSK, K15, K2tog, SSK, K8. (35 sts)

Cut yarn, transfer the stitches onto a stitch holder.

Body

T-SHIRT

Using Yarn D and Size 1½ (2.5mm) needles cast on 9 sts.

Starting at neck:

Row 1 (ws): Purl.

Row 2: K1, [K1, M1] 6 times, K2. (15 sts)

Row 3: Purl.

Row 4: K2, [K1, M1] 3 times, K4, [K1, M1] 3 times, K3. (21 sts)

Row 5: Purl.

Row 6: K3, [K1, M1] 4 times, K6, [K1, M1] 4 times, K4. (29 sts)

Rows 7–9: St st 3 rows.

Row 10: K4, [K1, M1] 6 times, K8, [K1, M1] 6 times, K5. (41 sts)

Rows 11–15: St st 5 rows.

Row 16: K3, [K3, M1] 4 times, K8, [K3, M1] 4 times, K6. (49 sts)

Rows 17–25: St st 9 rows.

Rows 26–27: Knit 2 rows.

TOP OF TIGHTS

Continue working the 49 sts on needle.

Change to Yarn F.

Rows 28–29: Starting with a knit row, st st 2 rows.

Change to Yarn D.

Rows 30–33: St st 4 rows.

Change to Yarn F.

Rows 34–35: St st 2 rows.

Change to Yarn D.

Rows 36–37: St st 2 rows.

Change to Yarn F.

Rows 38–39: St st 2 rows.

Change to Yarn D.

Rows 40–43: St st 4 rows.

Bind off.

Arms

(make 2)

Using Yarn A and Size 1½ (2.5mm) needles cast on 12 sts.

Rows 1–3: Starting with a purl row (ws), st st 3 rows.

Row 4: Cast on 3 sts using Knit cast-on method (see Techniques, page 103), knit to end. (15 sts)

Row 5: Cast on 3 sts using Purl cast-on method (see Techniques, page 103), purl to end. (18 sts)

Rows 6–7: St st 2 rows.

Row 8: SSK, K14, K2tog. (16 sts)

Row 9: Purl.

Row 10: SSK, K12, K2tog. (14 sts)

Row 11: Purl.

Row 12: SSK, K10, K2tog. (12 sts)

Rows 13–31: St st 19 rows.

Change to Yarn D.

Rows 32–33: Knit 2 rows.

Rows 34–47: Starting with a knit row, st st 14 rows.

Row 48: SSK, K8, K2tog. (10 sts)

Row 49: Purl.

Row 50: SSK, K6, K2tog. (8 sts)

Row 51: Purl.

Row 52: SSK, K4, K2tog. (6 sts)

Row 53: Purl.

Row 54: SSK, K2, K2tog. (4 sts)

Row 55: Purl.

Bind off.

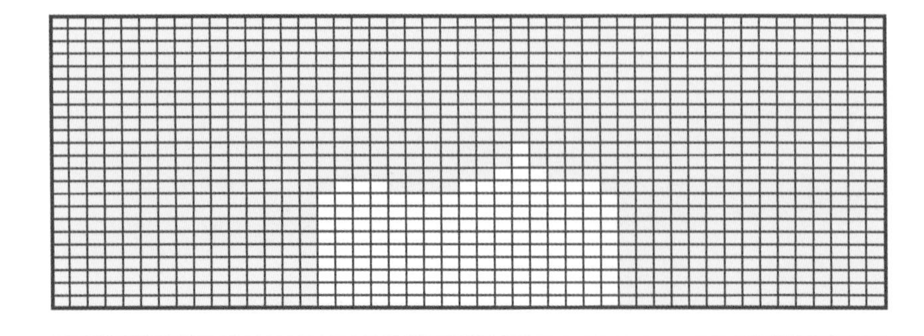

Hair Chart

□ = Yarn A □ = Yarn B

Legs

(make 2)

Using Yarn F and Size 1½ (2.5mm) needles cast on 16 sts.

Starting at top of leg:

Row 1 (ws): Purl.

Change to Yarn D.

Rows 2–3: St st 2 rows.

Change to Yarn F.

Rows 4–5: St st 2 rows.

Change to Yarn D.

Rows 6–9: St st 4 rows.

Change to Yarn F.

Rows 10–11: St st 2 rows.

From this point onwards, the legs are worked in stripe pattern of 2 rows Yarn D, 2 rows Yarn F, 4 rows Yarn D and 2 rows Yarn F throughout leg.

Rows 12–55: Continue in st st 44 rows.

TOP OF FOOT

Row 56: Bind off 5 sts, knit to end. (11 sts)

Row 57: Bind off 5 sts pw, purl to end. (6 sts)

Rows 58–75: St st 18 rows.

Bind-off row: SSK, K2, K2tog (bind off all sts as you work them).

Mary Jane shoes

(make 2)

Using Yarn C and Size 1½ (2.5mm) needles cast on 12 sts.

Row 1 (ws): Purl.

Row 2: K1, M1, K3, [K1, M1] 3 times, K4, M1, K1. (17 sts)

Row 3: Purl.

Row 4: [K1, M1] 2 times, K3, [K1, M1] 2 times, K2, [K1, M1] 2 times, K3, [K1, M1] 2 times, K1. (25 sts)

Row 5: Purl.

Row 6: [K2, M1] 2 times, K2, [K2, M1] 2 times, K3, [K2, M1] 2 times, K2, [K2, M1] 2 times, K2. (33 sts)

Row 7: Purl.

Row 8: [K3, M1] 2 times, K1, [K3, M1] 2 times, K4, [K3, M1] 2 times, K1, [K3, M1] 2 times, K3. (41 sts)

Rows 9–13: St st 5 rows.

Row 14: K15, SSK, K7, K2tog, K15. (39 sts)

Row 15: Purl.

Row 16: K15, SSK, K5, K2tog, K15. (37 sts)

Row 17: Purl.

Bind-off row: K15, SSK, K3, K2tog, K15 (bind off all sts as you work them).

Shoe straps

(make 2)

Using Yarn C and Size 1½ (2.5mm) needles cast on 10 sts.

Row 1 (ws): K7, P3.

Row 2: K3, turn.

Row 3: P3.

Bind off kw.

Dress

Front of dress

Using Yarn C and Size 2½ (3mm) needles cast on 37 sts.

Row 1 (ws): Knit.

Row 2: Knit.

Row 3: Purl.

Rows 4–5: Knit 2 rows.

Rows 6–7: Starting with a knit row, st st 2 rows.

Rows 8–20: Using Fair Isle method (see Techniques, page 108) and working in st st, work Dress Chart across the stitches, start with a knit row (rs) at the bottom right-hand corner of the chart. Read knit rows (rs) from right to left and purl rows (ws) from left to right.

Rows 21–37: St st 17 rows.

Row 38: [K1, K2tog] to last st, K1. (25 sts)

Row 39: Purl.

Row 40: K1, SSK, K19, K2tog, K1. (23 sts)

Row 41: Purl.

Row 42: K1, SSK, K17, K2tog, K1. (21 sts)

Row 43: Purl.

Row 44: K1, SSK, K15, K2tog, K1. (19 sts)

Rows 45–53: St st 9 rows.

Bind off.

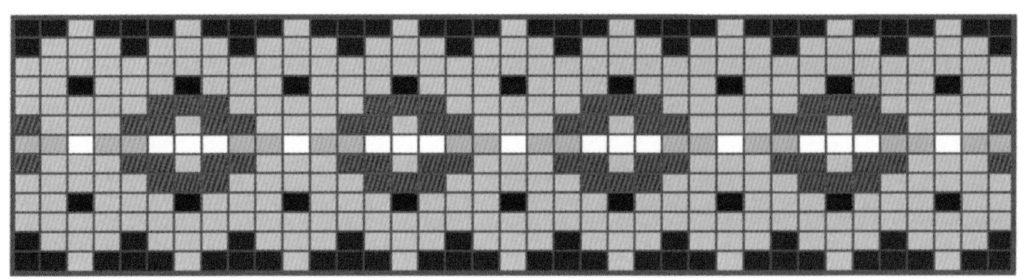

Dress Chart

■ = Yarn C
▨ = Yarn D
▩ = Yarn E
□ = Yarn F
▨ = Yarn G
■ = Yarn H

Back of dress

Using Yarn C and Size 2½ (3mm) needles cast on 37 sts.

Row 1 (ws): Knit.

Row 2: Knit.

Row 3: Purl.

Rows 4–5: Knit 2 rows.

Row 6–7: Starting with a knit row, st st 2 rows.

Rows 8–20: Work Dress Chart (see Front of dress).

Rows 21–37: St st 17 rows.

Row 38: [K1, K2tog] to last st, K1. (25 sts)

Row 39: Purl.

RIGHT BUTTON PLACKET

Row 40: K1, SSK, K11, turn. (13 sts)

Row 41: K3, P10.

Row 42: K1, SSK, K10, turn. (12 sts)

Row 43: K3, P9.

Row 44: K1, SSK, K7, YO, K2tog, turn. (11 sts)

Row 45: K1, Ktbl, K1, P8.

Row 46: K11, turn.

Row 47: K3, P8.

Rows 48–51: Rpt last 2 rows, 2 more times.

Row 52: K9, YO, K2tog, turn.

Row 53: K1, Ktbl, K1, P8.

Bind off 11 sts, cut yarn.

LEFT BUTTON PLACKET

Row 1: Returning to stitches still on needle, rejoin Yarn C and pick up and knit 3 sts from behind the first row of right button placket (see Techniques, page 104: Picking Up Stitches), knit across stitches on Left-hand needle to last 3 sts, K2tog, K1. (13 sts)

Row 2: P10, K3.

Row 3: Knit to last 3 sts, K2tog, K1. (12 sts)

Row 4: P9, K3.

Row 5: Knit to last 3 sts, K2tog, K1. (11 sts)

Row 6: P8, K3.

Row 7: Knit.

Rows 8–13: Rpt last 2 rows, 3 more times.

Row 14: P8, K3.

Bind off.

Bolero jacket

Bolero front right side

Using Yarn E and Size 2½ (3mm) needles cast on 6 sts.

Row 1 (ws): Knit.

Row 2: K2, Kfb, K3. (7 sts)

Row 3: P4, Pfb, K2. (8 sts)

Row 4: K2, Kfb, K5. (9 sts)

Row 5: P7, K2.

Row 6: K2, Kfb, K6. (10 sts)

Row 7: P8, K2.

Row 8: K2, Kfb, K7. (11 sts)

Row 9: P9, K2.

Row 10: Knit.

Rows 11–14: Rpt last 2 rows, 2 more times.

Row 15: P9, K2.

Row 16: K2, SSK, K7. (10 sts)

Row 17: P8, K2.

Row 18: K2, SSK, K6. (9 sts)

Row 19: P7, K2.

Row 20: K2, SSK, K5. (8 sts)

Row 21: P4, SSP, K2. (7 sts)

Row 22: K2, SSK, K3. (6 sts)

Row 23: P4, K2.

Bind off.

Bolero front left side

Using Yarn E and Size 2½ (3mm) needles cast on 6 sts.

Row 1 (ws): Knit.

Row 2: K2, Kfb, K3. (7 sts)

Row 3: K2, P1, Pfb, P3. (8sts)

Row 4: K4, Kfb, K3. (9 sts)

Row 5: K2, P7.

Row 6: K5, Kfb, K3. (10 sts)

Row 7: K2, P8.

Row 8: K6, Kfb, K3. (11 sts)

Row 9: K2, P9.

Row 10: Knit.

Rows 11–14: Rpt last 2 rows, 2 more times.

Row 15: K2, P9.

Row 16: K7, K2tog, K2. (10 sts)

Row 17: K2, P8.

Row 18: K6, K2tog, K2. (9 sts)

Row 19: K2, P7.

Row 20: K5, K2tog, K2. (8 sts)

Row 21: K2, P2tog, P4. (7 sts)

Row 22: K3, K2tog, K2. (6 sts)

Row 23: K2, P4.

Bind off.

Bolero back

Using Yarn E and Size 2½ (3mm) needles cast on 25 sts.

Row 1 (ws): Knit.

Rows 2–23: Starting with a knit row, st st 22 rows.

Bind off.

Sleeves

(make 2)

Using Yarn E and Size 2½ (3mm) needles cast on 14 sts.

Row 1 (ws): Knit.

Row 2: [K1, Kfb] to last 2 sts, K2. (20 sts)

Rows 3–21: St st 19 rows.

Bind off.

Bobble hat

Using Yarn C and Size 1½ (2.5mm) needles cast on 51 sts.

Row 1 (ws): P1, [K1, P2] to last 2 sts, K1, P1.

Row 2: K1, [P1, K2] to last 2 sts, P1, K1.

Rows 3–16: Rpt last 2 rows, 7 more times.

Row 17: P1, [K1, P2] to last 2 sts, K1, P1.

Row 18: K1, P1, [K2tog, P1] to last st, K1. (35 sts)

Row 19: [P1, K1] to last st, P1.

Row 20: [K1, P1] to last st, K1.

Rows 21–22: Rpt last 2 rows.

Row 23: [P1, K1] to last st, P1.

Row 24: K1, [K2tog] to end. (18 sts)

Rows 25–27: Starting with a purl row, st st 3 rows.

Row 28: K1, [K2tog] rep to last st, K1. (10 sts)

Cut yarn leaving a long tail. Using a tapestry needle thread tail through the stitches left on needle and draw up.

Bobble

Using Yarn D and Size 2½ (3mm) needles cast on 4 sts.

Row 1 (ws): Pfb, P2, Pfb. (6 sts)

Rows 2–5: Starting with a knit row, st st 4 rows.

Row 6: SSK, K2, K2tog. (4 sts)

Row 7: P2tog, P2tog, pass 1st stitch over last, cut yarn leaving a long tail and pull through remaining stitch. Using the yarn tail, sew a running stitch around the outer edge of bobble and pull tightly. Knot both tail ends together to secure.

Flower bag

Using Yarn G and Size 2½ (3mm) needles cast on 24 sts.

Row 1 (ws): Purl.

Row 2: [K1, M1] 2 times, K7, [K1, M1] 2 times, K1, [K1, M1] 2 times, K7, [K1, M1] 2 times, K1. (32 sts)

Rows 3–4: Knit 2 rows.

Row 5: [P2, K1] to last 2 sts, P2.

Row 6–8: Knit 3 rows.

Rows 9–16: Rep rows 5–8, 2 more times.

Row 17: Rep row 5.

Rows 18–19: Knit 2 rows.

Row 20: K5, bind off 6 sts, K10, bind off 6 sts, Knit to end. (20 sts)

Row 21: K4, *Kfb, pass knitted front-loop stitch over knitted back-loop stitch and pull yarn tight, turn, cast on 13 sts, turn, slip last cast on stitch onto left needle, K2tog and pull yarn tight*, K8; rpt from * to *, K4.

Bind off kw.

Flower

Using Yarn D and Size 1½ (2.5mm) needles cast on 31 sts.

FIRST PETAL

Row 1 (ws): Slip 1 pw, P5, turn.

Row 2: K5, turn.

Row 3: P5, turn.

Row 4: K6, turn.

Row 5: [P2tog] 3 times.

REMAINING PETALS

Rpt rows 1-5, 4 more times until 1 st remains, P1.

Next row: K1, [slip 2 together kw, K1, PSSO] to end.

Cut yarn leaving a long tail. Using a tapestry needle, thread the tail through the stitches left on needle and draw up.

Making Up

Doll

See Making Up Your Doll in Techniques, page 96.

Plaits

(make 2)

1. See Making up Plaits in Techniques, page 101.
2. Sew the plaits in place on either side of the completed head **(A)**.

Clothing & accessories

Bolero jacket

1. Block all the pieces of the bolero before making up.
2. Start by sewing up the shoulder seams, then sew the arms to the front and back pieces, lining up the center of the arms to the shoulder seams.
3. Sew up the arm and body edge seams to finish.

Dress

1. Block all the pieces of the dress before making up.
2. Start by sewing the buttons into place on the back of the dress, matching them up with the button holes **(B)**.
3. Sew up the shoulder seams making sure you leave a big enough gap to fit around Naomi's neck.
4. Matching up the Fair Isle pattern sew up the edge seams, leaving a 1in (2.5cm) gap at the top for the arm holes.

Bobble hat

1. Block the hat before you begin.
2. Sew the side edges together.
3. Stitch the bobble in place on the top of the hat.

Flower bag

1. Block the bag piece before making up.
2. Start by sewing the side and bottom edges together.
3. Join the first and last petals of the flower together at the 'cast on' edge with a small stitch.
4. Sew onto the front of the bag, then add a contrasting button in the center of the flower to finish.

A

B

Grace

Some people wear their heart on their sleeve, but Grace prefers to wear hers on her pinafore. Friendship bracelets, hair bobbles, and making slightly lop-sided gifts for granny are just a few of her favorite things. Being a caring crusader means getting through a lot of beads, glitter, and sparkly stickers, but it's worth it to make people smile.

You Will Need

Yarn

- **Yarn A** Beige
- **Yarn B** Orange
- **Yarn C** Aqua
- **Yarn D** Turquoise
- **Yarn E** Bright Red
- **Yarn F** Cream
- Oddments of black and red for eyes and mouth

Finished size

- 11in (28cm) tall

You will also need

- Size 2½ (3mm) knitting needles
- Size 1½ (2.5mm) straight needles
- Size 1½ (2.5mm) double-pointed needles
- Stitch holder
- Tapestry needle
- 3 x ½in (15mm) circles of white felt
- Toy stuffing
- 5 x ¼in (6mm) buttons

Pattern

Cast on using the Long-tail (double cast-on) method (see Techniques, page 102) unless otherwise indicated. Where possible leave long tails when you cast on and bind off and use these for the sewing up.

Head

Using Yarn A and Size 1½ (2.5mm) needles cast on 13 sts.

Starting at neck:

Row 1 (ws): Purl.

Row 2: [K1, M1] 12 times, K1. (25 sts)

Row 3: Purl.

Row 4: K3, [K1, M1] 7 times, K4, [K1, M1] 7 times, K4. (39 sts)

Rows 5–7: St st 3 rows.

Row 8: K3, [K3, M1] 4 times, K6, [K3, M1] 4 times, K6. (47 sts)

Cut yarn.

Rows 9–31: Using intarsia method (see Techniques, page 109) and working in st st, work Hair Chart. Start with a purl row (ws) at the bottom left-hand corner of chart, read purl rows (ws) from left to right and knit rows (rs) from right to left.

For top of head continue in Yarn B.

Row 32: K8, K2tog, K4, SSK, K15, K2tog, K4, SSK, K8. (43 sts)

Row 33: Purl.

Row 34: K8, K2tog, K2, SSK, K15, K2tog, K2, SSK, K8. (39 sts)

Row 35: Purl.

Row 36: K8, K2tog, SSK, K15, K2tog, SSK, K8. (35 sts)

Cut yarn, transfer the stitches onto a stitch holder.

Pigtails

(make 2)

Using Yarn B and Size 1½ (2.5mm) needles cast on 10 sts.

Row 1 (ws): Purl.

Row 2: K4, M1, [K1, M1] 2 times, K4. (13 sts)

Row 3: Purl.

Row 4: K6, M1, K1, M1, K6. (15 sts)

Row 5: Purl

Row 6: K7, M1, K1, M1, K7. (17 sts)

Row 7: Purl.

Row 8: SSK, K13, K2tog. (15 sts)

Row 9: Purl.

Row 10: K5, bind off 5 sts, K to end. (10 sts)

Row 11: P4, P2tog, P4. (9 sts)

Row 12: SSK, K5, K2tog. (7 sts)

Rows 13–15: St st 3 rows.

Row 16: K1, SSK, K1, K2tog, K1. (5 sts)

Row 17: Purl.

Cut yarn leaving a long tail, use a tapestry needle to thread tail through the stitches left on needle and draw up.

Hair scrunchies

(make 2)

Using Size 1½ (2.5mm) dpns and Yarn D, cast on 3 sts and make an i-cord of 8 rows (see Techniques, page 104).

Body

Using Yarn A and Size 1½ (2.5mm) needles cast on 9 sts.

Starting at neck:

Row 1 (ws): Purl.

Row 2: K1, [K1, M1] 6 times, K2. (15 sts)

Row 3: Purl.

Row 4: K2, [K1, M1] 3 times, K4, [K1, M1] 3 times, K3. (21 sts)

Row 5: Purl.

Row 6: K3, [K1, M1] 4 times, K6, [K1, M1] 4 times, K4. (29 sts)

Rows 7–9: St st 3 rows.

Row 10: K4, [K1, M1] 6 times, K8, [K1, M1] 6 times, K5. (41 sts)

Rows 11–15: St st 5 rows.

Row 16: K3, [K3, M1] 4 times, K8, [K3, M1] 4 times, K6. (49 sts)

Rows 17–27: St st 11 rows.

TOP OF TIGHTS

Continue working the 49 sts on needle.

Starting with Yarn C, the tights are worked in a stripe pattern of 2 rows Yarn C and 2 rows Yarn F throughout.

Rows 28–29: Knit 2 rows.

Rows 30–43: Starting with a knit row, st st 14 rows.

Bind off using Yarn C.

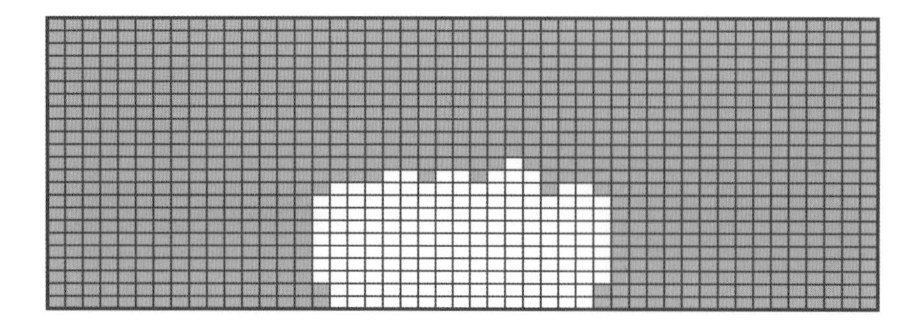

Hair Chart

□ = Yarn A
■ = Yarn B

Arms

Left arm

Using Yarn A and Size 1½ (2.5mm) needles cast on 12 sts.

Rows 1–3: Starting with a purl row (ws), st st 3 rows.

Row 4: Cast on 3 sts using Knit cast-on method (see Techniques, page 103), knit to end. (15 sts)

Row 5: Cast on 3 sts using Purl cast-on method (see Techniques, page 103), purl to end. (18 sts)

Rows 6–7: St st 2 rows.

Row 8: SSK, K14, K2tog. (16 sts)

Row 9: Purl.

Row 10: SSK, K12, K2tog. (14 sts)

Row 11: Purl.

Row 12: SSK, K10, K2tog. (12 sts)

Row 13: Purl.

BRACELET

The next 4 rows form the bracelet.

Change to Yarn E.

Row 14: Knit.

Change to Size 2½ (3mm) needles for next 2 rows.

Row 15: Purl

Row 16: K1, [YO, K2tog] to last st, K1.

Change to Size 1½ (2.5mm) needles.

Row 17: Purl.

Change to Yarn A.

Rows 18–47: St st 30 rows.

Row 48: SSK, K8, K2tog. (10 sts)

Row 49: Purl.

Row 50: SSK, K6, K2tog. (8 sts)

Row 51: Purl.

Row 52: SSK, K4, K2tog. (6 sts)

Row 53: Purl.

Row 54: SSK, K2, K2tog. (4 sts)

Row 55: Purl.

Bind off.

Right arm

Rows 1–12: Work as Left Arm rows 1–12.

Rows 13–47: St st 35 rows.

Row 48: SSK, K8, K2tog. (10 sts)

Row 49: Purl.

Row 50: SSK, K6, K2tog. (8 sts)

Row 51: Purl.

Row 52: SSK, K4, K2tog. (6 sts)

Row 53: Purl.

Row 54: SSK, K2, K2tog. (4 sts)

Row 55: Purl.

Bind off.

Legs

(make 2)

Starting at top of leg:

Using Yarn C and Size 1½ (2.5mm) needles cast on 16 sts.

Row 1 (ws): Purl.

From this point onwards the legs are worked in stripe pattern of 2 rows Yarn F and 2 rows Yarn C, starting with Yarn F.

Rows 2–55: Continue in st st for a further 54 rows.

TOP OF FOOT

Row 56: Bind off 5 sts, knit to end. (11 sts)

Row 57: Bind off 5 sts pw, purl to end. (6 sts)

Rows 58–75: St st 18 rows.

Bind-off row: SSK, K2, K2tog (bind off all sts as you work them).

T-bar shoes

(make 2)

Using Yarn E and Size 1½ (2.5mm) needles cast on 12 sts.

Row 1 (ws): Purl.

Row 2: K1, M1, K3, [K1, M1] 3 times, K4, M1, K1. (17 sts)

Row 3: Purl.

Row 4: [K1, M1] 2 times, K3, [K1, M1] 2 times, K2, [K1, M1] 2 times, K3, [K1, M1] 2 times, K1. (25 sts)

Row 5: Purl.

Row 6: [K2, M1] 2 times, K2, [K2, M1] 2 times, K3, [K2, M1] 2 times, K2, [K2, M1] 2 times, K2. (33 sts)

Row 7: Purl.

Row 8: [K3, M1] 2 times, K1, [K3, M1] 2 times, K4, [K3, M1] 2 times, K1, [K3, M1] 2 times, K3. (41 sts)

Rows 9–13: St st 5 rows.

Row 14: K15, SSK, K7, K2tog, K15. (39 sts)

Row 15: Purl.

Row 16: K15, SSK, K5, K2tog, K15. (37 sts)

Row 17: Purl.

Row 18: Bind off 15 sts, SSK, K3, k2tog, knit to end. (20 sts)

Row 19: Bind off 15 sts pw, purl to end. (5 sts)

Row 20: SSK, K1, K2tog.

Row 21: K1, P1, K1.

Row 22: Knit.

Rows 23–29: Rpt last 2 rows, 3 more times, then rpt row 21 once more.

Row 30: K1, sl1 pw with yarn at back, K1.

Row 31: K1, sl1 pw with yarn at front, K1.

Bind off.

Shoe straps

(make 2)

Using Yarn E and Size 1½ (2.5mm) needles cast on 10 sts.

Row 1 (ws): K7, P3.

Row 2: K3, turn.

Row 3: P3.

Bind off kw.

Dress

Front of dress

Using Yarn D and Size 1½ (2.5mm) needles cast on 35 sts.

Rows 1–3: Starting with a purl row (ws), st st 3 rows.

Row 4: K1, [YO, K2tog] to end. (35 sts)

Change to Size 2½ (3mm) needles.

Rows 5–9: St st 5 rows.

The next 36 rows are worked in a stripe pattern of 6 rows Yarn C and 6 rows Yarn D, starting with Yarn C.

Rows 10–12: St st 3 rows.

The Dress Chart is placed in the following rows using Intarsia method (see Techniques, page 109) and worked in st st. Starting at the bottom left corner, read purl (ws) rows from left to right and knit (rs) rows from right to left.

Row 13: P16, work Dress Chart, P4.

Row 14: K4, work Dress Chart, K16.

Row 15–28: Repeat the last 2 rows, 7 more times.

Rows 29–43: Continue in st st for a further 15 rows.

Row 44: [K2tog, K1] to last 2 sts, K2tog. (23 sts)

Row 45: Purl.

Change to Yarn C.

Row 46: K1, SSK, K17, K2tog, K1. (21 sts)

Row 47: Purl.

Row 48: K1, SSK, K15, K2tog, K1. (19 sts)

Row 49: Purl.

Row 50: K1, SSK, K13, K2tog, K1. (17 sts)

Rows 51–59: St st 9 rows.

Bind off.

Back of dress

Using Yarn D and Size 1½ (2.5mm) needles cast on 35 sts.

Rows 1–3: Starting with a purl row (ws), st st 3 rows.

Row 4: K1, [YO, K2tog] to end. (35 sts).

Change to Size 2½ (3mm) needles.

Rows 5–9: St st 5 rows.

The next 36 rows are worked in a stripe pattern of 6 rows Yarn C and 6 rows Yarn D, starting with Yarn C.

Rows 10–43: Continue in st st for a further 34 rows.

Row 44: [K2tog, K1] to last 2 sts, K2tog. (23 sts)

Row 45: Purl.

RIGHT BUTTON PLACKET

Change to Yarn C.

Row 46: K1, SSK, K10, turn. (12 sts)

Row 47: K3, P9.

Row 48: K1, SSK, K9, turn. (11 sts)

Row 49: K3, P8.

Row 50: K1, SSK, K6, YO, K2tog, turn. (10 sts)

Row 51: K1, Ktbl, K1, P7.

Row 52: K10, turn.

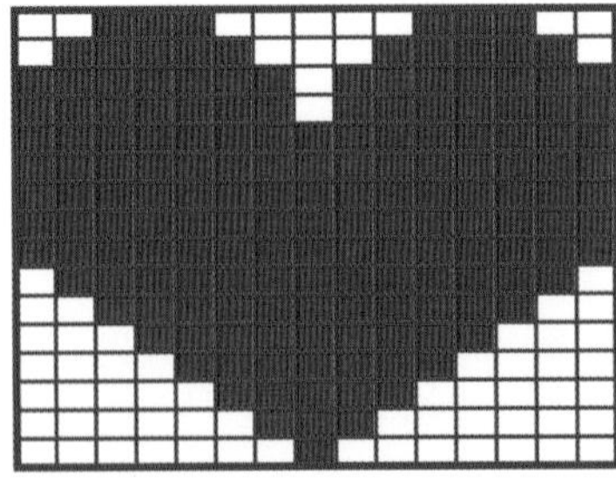

Dress Chart

□ = Yarn C/D (stripe pattern)

■ = Yarn E

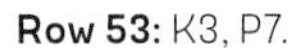

Row 53: K3, P7.

Rows 54–57: Rpt last 2 rows, 2 more times.

Row 58: K8, YO, K2tog, turn.

Row 59: K1, Ktbl, K1, P7.

Bind off 10 sts, cut yarn.

LEFT BUTTON PLACKET

Row 1: Returning to stitches still on needle, rejoin Yarn C and pick up and knit 3 sts from BEHIND the first row of Right button placket (see Techniques, page 104: Picking Up Stitches), knit across stitches on Left-hand needle to last 3 sts, K2tog, K1. (12 sts)

Row 2: P9, K3.

Row 3: K9, K2tog, K1. (11 sts)

Row 4: P8, K3.

Row 5: K8, K2tog, K1. (10 sts)

Row 6: P7, K3.

Row 7: Knit.

Rows 8–13: Rpt last 2 rows, 3 more times.

Row 14: P7, K3.

Bind off.

Shrug

Right front of shrug

Using Yarn F and Size 2½ (3mm) needles cast on 6 sts.

Row 1 (ws): Knit.

Row 2: K2, Kfb, K3. (7 sts)

Row 3: P4, Pfb, K2. (8 sts)

Row 4: K2, Kfb, K5. (9 sts)

Row 5: P7, K2.

Row 6: K2, Kfb, K6. (10 sts)

Row 7: P8, K2.

Row 8: K2, Kfb, K7. (11 sts)

Row 9: P9, K2.

Row 10: Knit.

Rows 11–14: Rpt last 2 rows, 2 more times.

Row 15: P9, K2.

Row 16: K2, SSK, K7. (10 sts)

Row 17: P8, K2.

Row 18: K2, SSK, K6. (9 sts)

Row 19: P7, K2.

Row 20: K2, SSK, K5. (8 sts)

Row 21: P4, SSP, K2. (7 sts)

Row 22: K2, SSK, K3. (6 sts)

Row 23: P4, K2.

Bind off.

Left front of shrug

Using Yarn F and Size 2½ (3mm) needles cast on 6 sts.

Row 1 (ws): Knit.

Row 2: K2, Kfb, K3. (7 sts)

Row 3: K2, P1, Pfb, P3. (8 sts)

Row 4: K4, Kfb, K3. (9 sts)

Row 5: K2, P7.

Row 6: K5, Kfb, K3. (10 sts)

Row 7: K2, P8.

Row 8: K6, Kfb, K3. (11 sts)

Row 9: K2, P9.

Row 10: Knit.

Rows 11–14: Rpt last 2 rows, 2 more times.

Row 15: K2, P9.

Row 16: K7, K2tog, K2. (10 sts)

Row 17: K2, P8.

Row 18: K6, K2tog, K2. (9 sts)

Row 19: K2, P7.

Row 20: K5, K2tog, K2. (8 sts)

Row 21: K2, P2tog, P4. (7 sts)

Row 22: K3, K2tog, K2. (6 sts)

Row 23: K2, P4.

Bind off.

Back of shrug

Using Yarn F and Size 2½ (3mm) needles cast on 25 sts.

Row 1 (ws): Knit.

Rows 2–23: Starting with a knit row, st st 22 rows.

Bind off.

Sleeves

(make 2)

Using Yarn F and Size 2½ (3mm) needles cast on 20 sts.

Row 1 (ws): Knit.

Rows 2–11: Starting with a knit row, st st 10 rows.

Bind off.

Making Up

Doll

See Making Up Your Doll in Techniques, page 96. Please follow the Bracelet instructions below before sewing up the left arm.

Bracelet

Stitch together (on ws), the first and last rows of Yarn E using an over stitch through the back loops **(A)**. Fasten off ends of Yarn E.

Pigtails

1. Sew together the small bind off edges using whip stitch (see Techniques, page 107).Thread the cast on tail through cast on stitches at bottom of pigtails and draw up. Sew side edges together, stuffing lightly as you go.
2. Sew pigtails onto each side of head and bury loose ends in head (see **B** for position of pigtails).

Hair scrunchie

Loop the i-cord over top of pigtail and secure ends with a couple of stitches **(B)**.

Clothing

Shrug

1. Block all the pieces of the shrug before making up.
2. Start by sewing up the shoulder seams, then sew the sleeves to the front and back pieces, lining up the center of the sleeves to the shoulder seams.
3. Sew up the sleeve and body edge seams to finish.

Dress

1. Block all the pieces of the dress before making up.
2. Start by sewing the buttons into place on the back of the dress, matching them up with the button holes.
3. Sew up the shoulder seams, make sure you leave a big enough gap to fit around Grace's neck.
4. Matching up the stripes, sew up the edge seams, leaving a 1in (2.5cm) gap at the top for the armholes.
5. Picot hem: fold the hem back along the eyelet holes with wrong sides together, making sure stitches are in line. Working from the wrong side sew in place as follows: secure a length of Yarn C to back of work, insert needle through a backstitch loop **(C)**, then through its vertically matching cast-on loop **(D)** and then down through the next cast on loop **(E)**. Pull yarn through and repeat until hem is complete.

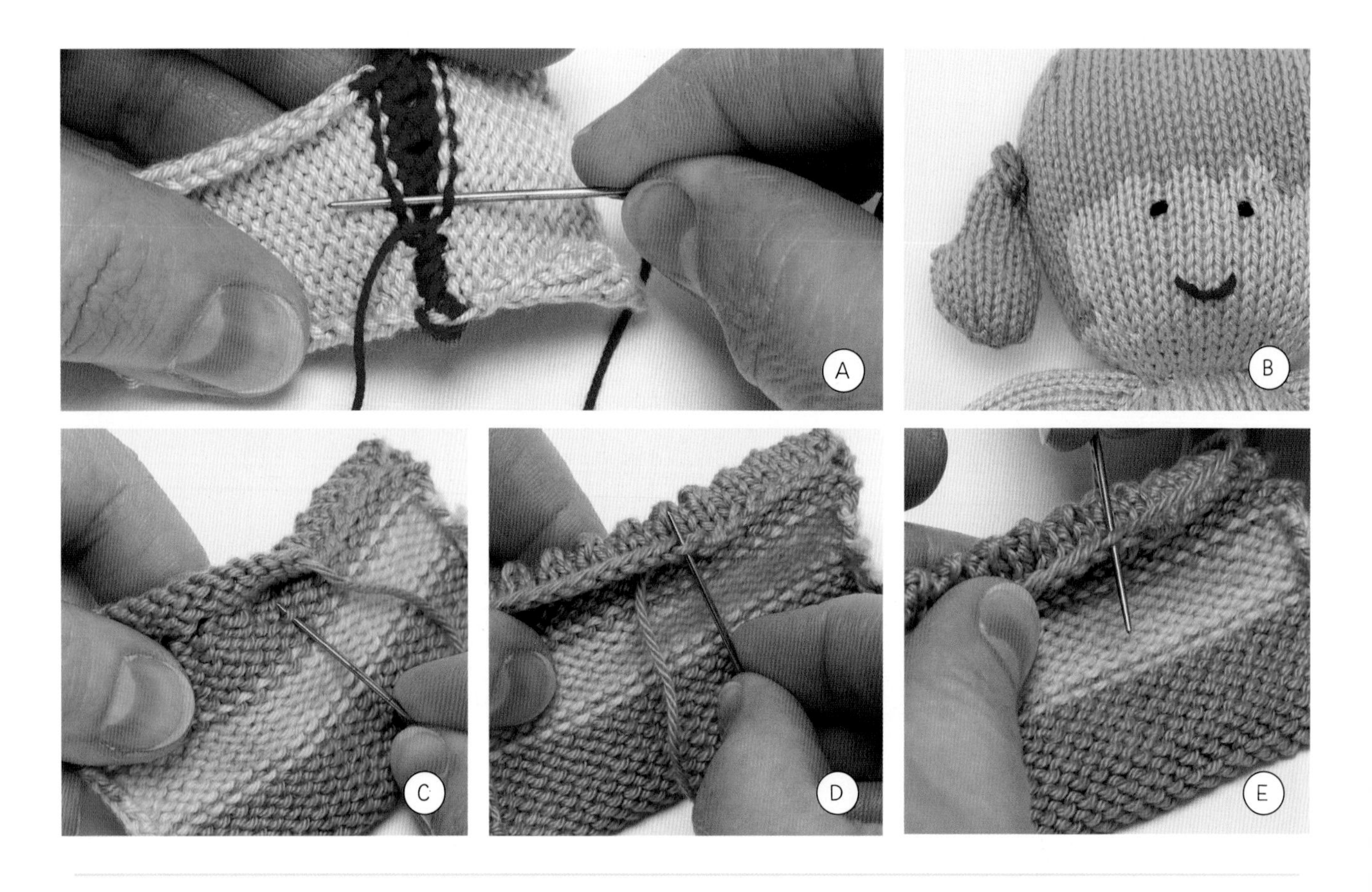

306

Ralph

A lot of little boys like trains, but Ralph absolutely loves them. If he's not pushing wooden toy ones around a track, he's yearning to travel the rails on the real thing. A practical little chap, he wears dungarees with a handy pocket for tickets, timetables and the occasional sweetie. He likes to keep those smart little knee socks pulled up, but no-one can quite manage to tame that unruly tuft of hair.

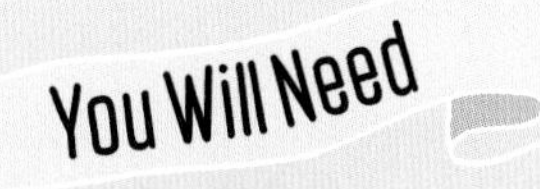

Yarn

- **Yarn A** Beige
- **Yarn B** Brown
- **Yarn C** Petrol Blue
- **Yarn D** White
- **Yarn E** Pale Grey
- **Yarn F** Red
- **Yarn G** Camel
- Oddments of black and red for eyes and mouth

Finished Size

- 11in (28cm) tall

You will also need

- Size 2½ (3mm) knitting needles
- Size 1½ (2.5mm) knitting needles
- Size 1½ (2.5mm) double-pointed needles
- Stitch holder
- Tapestry needle
- 3 x ½in (15mm) circles of white felt
- Toy stuffing
- 3 x ¼in (6mm) buttons

Pattern

Cast on using the Long-tail (double cast-on) method (see Techniques, page 102) unless otherwise indicated. Where possible leave long tails when you cast on and bind off and use these for the sewing up.

Head

Using Yarn A and Size 1½ (2.5mm) needles cast on 13 sts.

Starting at neck:

Row 1 (ws): Purl.

Row 2: [K1, M1] 12 times, K1. (25 sts)

Row 3: Purl.

Row 4: K3, [K1, M1] 7 times, K4, [K1, M1] 7 times, K4. (39 sts)

Rows 5–7: St st 3 rows.

Row 8: K3, [K3, M1] 4 times, K6, [K3, M1] 4 times, K6. (47 sts)

Cut yarn.

Rows 9–31: Using intarsia method (see Techniques, page 109) and working in st st, work Hair Chart. Start with a purl row (ws) at the bottom left-hand corner of chart, read purl rows (ws) from left to right and knit rows (rs) from right to left.

For top of head continue in Yarn B.

Row 32: K8, K2tog, K4, SSK, K15, K2tog, K4, SSK, K8. (43 sts)

Row 33: Purl.

Row 34: K8, K2tog, K2, SSK, K15, K2tog, K2, SSK, K8. (39 sts)

Row 35: Purl.

Row 36: K8, K2tog, SSK, K15, K2tog, SSK, K8. (35 sts)

Cut yarn, transfer the stitches onto a stitch holder.

Hair tufts

(make 3)

Using Size 1½ (2.5mm) dpns and Yarn B cast on 3 sts and make an i-cord of 3 rows (see Techniques, page 107).

Body

T-SHIRT

Using Yarn D and Size 1½ (2.5mm) needles cast on 9 sts.

Starting at neck:

Row 1 (ws): Purl.

Change to Yarn E.

Row 2: K1, [K1, M1] 6 times, K2. (15 sts)

Row 3: Purl.

Change to Yarn D.

Row 4: K2, [K1, M1] 3 times, K4, [K1, M1] 3 times, K3. (21 sts)

Row 5: Purl.

Continue working in stripe pattern of 2 rows Yarn E and 2 rows Yarn D for the next 22 rows.

Row 6: K3, [K1, M1] 4 times, K6, [K1, M1] 4 times, K4. (29 sts)

Rows 7–9: St st 3 rows.

Row 10: K4, [K1, M1] 6 times, K8, [K1, M1] 6 times, K5. (41 sts)

Rows 11–15: St st 5 rows.

Row 16: K3, [K3, M1] 4 times, K8, [K3, M1] 4 times, K6. (49 sts)

Rows 17–27: St st 11 rows.

BOXER SHORTS

Continue working the 49 sts on needle.

Change to Yarn F.

Rows 28–30: Knit 3 rows.

Row 31: P22, K1, P2, K1, P23.

Row 32: Knit.

Rows 33–36: Rpt last 2 rows, 2 more times.

Row 37: P23, K3, P23.

Row 38: Knit.

Row 39: P25, K1, P23.

Row 40: Knit.

Rows 41–42: Rpt last 2 rows.

Row 43: P25, K1, P23.

Bind off.

Arms

(make 2)

Using Yarn A and Size 1½ (2.5mm) needles cast on 12 sts.

Rows 1–3: Starting with a purl row (ws), st st 3 rows.

Row 4: Cast on 3 sts using Knit cast-on method (see Techniques, page 103), knit to end. (15 sts)

Row 5: Cast on 3 sts using Purl cast-on method (see Techniques, page 103), purl to end. (18 sts)

Rows 6–7: St st 2 rows.

Row 8: SSK, K14, K2tog. (16 sts)

Row 9: Purl.

Row 10: SSK, K12, K2tog. (14 sts)

Row 11: Purl.

Row 12: SSK, K10, K2tog. (12 sts)

Row 13: Purl.

SLEEVES

Continue working the 12 sts on needle.

Change to Yarn F.

Rows 14–15: Knit 2 rows.

Change to Yarn D.

Rows 16–17: St st 2 rows.

Change to Yarn E.

Rows 18–19: St st 2 rows.

Continue in stripe pattern of 2 rows Yarn D and 2 rows Yarn E for remainder of arm.

Rows 20–47: St st 28 rows.

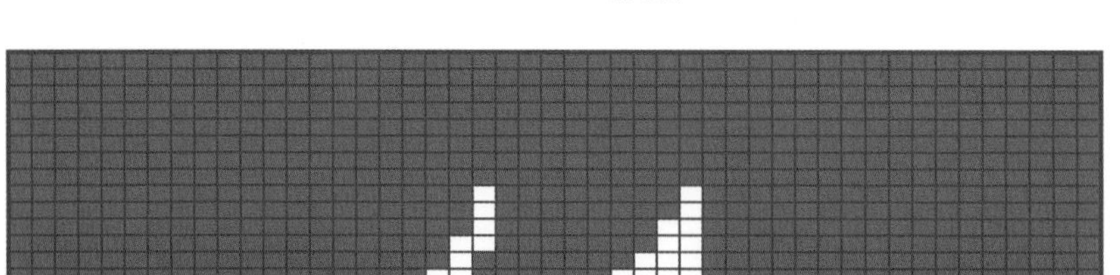

Hair Chart

□ = Yarn A
■ = Yarn B

Row 48: SSK, K8, K2tog. (10 sts)

Row 49: Purl.

Row 50: SSK, K6, K2tog. (8 sts)

Row 51: Purl.

Row 52: SSK, K4, K2tog. (6 sts)

Row 53: Purl.

Row 54: SSK, K2, K2tog. (4 sts)

Row 55: Purl.

Bind off.

Legs and sneakers

(make 2)

Start at base of sneaker.

Using Yarn G and Size 1½ (2.5mm) needles cast on 12 sts.

Row 1 (ws): Purl.

Row 2: K1, M1, K3, [K1, M1] 3 times, K4, M1, K1. (17 sts)

Row 3: Purl.

Row 4: [K1, M1] 2 times, K3, [K1, M1] 2 times, K2, [K1, M1] 2 times, K3, [K1, M1] 2 times, K1. (25 sts)

Row 5: Purl.

Row 6: [K2, M1] 2 times, K2, [K2, M1] 2 times, K3, [K2, M1] 2 times, K2, [K2, M1] 2 times, K2. (33 sts)

Row 7: Purl.

Change to Yarn D.

Row 8: [K3, M1] 2 times, K1, [K3, M1] 2 times, K4, [K3, M1] 2 times, K1, [K3, M1] 2 times, K3. (41 sts)

Row 9: Knit.

Row 10: Purl.

Use Intarsia method (see Techniques, page 109) for changing yarn across the next 8 rows:

(D) = Use Yarn D.

(F) = Use Yarn F.

Row 11: (F) P14, (D) P13, (F) P14.

Row 12: (F) K14, (D) K13, (F) K14.

Row 13: (F) P14, (D) P13, (F) P14.

Row 14: (F) K14, (D) K1, SSK, K7, K2tog, K1, (F) K14. (39 sts)

Row 15: (F) P14, (D) P11, (F) P14.

Row 16: (F) K14, (D) K1, SSK, K5, K2tog, K1, (F) K14. (37 sts)

Row 17: (F) P14, (D) P9, (F) P14.

Row 18: (F) K7, (D) K8, SSK, K3, K2tog, K8, (F) K7. (35 sts)

Change to Yarn D.

Row 19: Purl.

Row 20: P8, [K7, SSK, K1, K2tog, K7] bind off these middle 17 sts as you work them, P to end. (16 sts)

Row 21: K7, P2tog, K7. (15 sts)

SOCKS

Continue working the 15 sts on needle.

Change to Yarn E.

Rows 22–33: St st 12 rows.

Change to Yarn D.

Row 34: Knit.

Change to Yarn C.

Row 35: Purl.

Change to Yarn D.

Row 36: Knit.

Change to Yarn E.

Row 37: Purl.

Rows 38–41: Knit 4 rows.

TOP OF LEG

Continue working the 15 sts on needle.

Change to Yarn A.

Rows 42–71: St st 30 rows.

BOXER SHORTS LEG

Continue working the 15 sts on needle.

Change to Yarn F.

Row 72: Knit.

Row 73: Knit.

Rows 74–77: St st 4 rows.

Bind off.

Dungarees

Made in one piece and seamed at the inside leg and back of body.

Left leg of dungarees

Using Yarn C and Size 2½ (3mm) needles cast on 29 sts.

Start at bottom of left leg:

Rows 1–18: Starting with a purl row (ws), st st 18 rows.

Slip all stitches onto stitch holder.

Cut yarn.

Right leg of dungarees

Starting at bottom of right leg.

Using Yarn C and Size 2½ (3mm) needles cast on 29 sts.

Rows 1–18: Starting with a purl row (ws), st st 18 rows.

Row 19: Purl.

Leave these stitches on the right-hand needle and do not cut yarn.

JOIN LEGS OF DUNGAREES

Slip the stitches from stitch holder back onto left-hand knitting needle, purl to end of the row. You should now have 58 sts on one needle.

Row 20: Knit.

Rows 21–34: Starting with a purl row (ws), st st 14 rows.

Row 35: P1, [K1, P2] 7 times, K2, P10, K2, [P2, K1] 7 times, P1. (58 sts)

Row 36: K1, [P1, K2] 7 times, K14, [K2, P1] 7 times, K1. (58 sts)

Rows 37–38: Rpt last 2 rows.

Row 39: P1, [K1, P2] 7 times, K2, P10, K2, [P2, K1] 7 times, P1. (58 sts)

Row 40: Bind off 22 sts in pattern, K14, Bind off 22 sts in pattern. (14 sts)

Cut yarn.

DUNGAREE BIB

Working on remaining 14 sts, rejoin yarn.

Row 41: K2, P10, K2.

Row 42: Knit.

Rows 43–52: Rpt last 2 rows, 5 more times.

Row 53: Knit.

Bind off kw.

Dungaree strap

(make 2)

Using Yarn C and Size 2½ (3mm) needles cast on 28 sts.

Row 1 (ws): K25, P3.

Row 2: K3, turn.

Row 3: P3.

Bind off kw.

Pocket

Using Yarn C and Size 2½ (3mm) needles cast on 8 sts.

Rows 1–5: Starting with a purl row (ws), st st 5 rows.

Row 6: Purl.

Bind off kw.

Making up

Doll

See Making Up Your Doll in Techniques, page 96. Please note:

1. Sew a small button onto the fly of the boxer shorts before sewing up the body (see **A** for position).
2. Using Duplicate stitch (see Techniques, p108) embroider three white stripes onto each side of the sneakers before sewing up **(B)**.

Hair tufts

Sew the hair tufts onto the top corner of the completed head **(C)**.

Clothing

Dungarees

1. Before sewing together, block all the parts of the dungarees.
2. Sew the pocket onto the front of the bib, making sure it's central **(D)**.
3. Then sew up the inside leg seams to crotch, followed by the back seam.
4. Sew the straps onto the back edge of the dungarees, around ¾in (2cm) either side of the back seam **(E)**. Sew the other end of the straps to the top corners of the bib and then sew on the buttons.

Penny

She's at her happiest in the park. Whether it's swinging so high that her sun hat blows off or playing football with her friends, Penny would spend all day outdoors if she could. Her practical jeggings make climbing trees a breeze, and she can get to the highest branches, which is handy if you're trying to spot where on earth your hat landed.

Yarn

Yarn A Mocha

Yarn B Dark Brown

Yarn C Cream

Yarn D Pale Grey

Yarn E White

Yarn F Watermelon

Yarn G Denim

Oddments of black and red for eyes and mouth

Finished size

11in (28cm) tall

You will also need

Size 2½ (3mm) knitting needles

Size 1½ (2.5mm) knitting needles

Size 1½ (2.5mm) double-pointed needles

Stitch holder

Tapestry needle

3 x ½in (15mm) circles of white felt

Toy stuffing

5 x ¼in (6mm) buttons

Small piece of ribbon

Pattern

Cast on using the Long-tail (double cast-on) method (see Techniques, page 102) unless otherwise indicated. Where possible leave long tails when you cast on and bind off and use these for the sewing up.

Head

Using Yarn A and Size 1½ (2.5mm) needles cast on 13 sts.

Starting at neck:

Row 1 (ws): Purl.

Row 2: [K1, M1] 12 times, K1. (25 sts)

Row 3: Purl.

Row 4: K3, [K1, M1] 7 times, K4, [K1, M1] 7 times, K4. (39 sts)

Rows 5–7: St st 3 rows.

Row 8: K3, [K3, M1] 4 times, K6, [K3, M1] 4 times, K6. (47 sts)

Cut yarn.

Rows 9–31: Using intarsia method (see Techniques, page 109) and working in st st, work Hair Chart. Start with a purl row (ws) at the bottom left-hand corner of chart, read purl rows (ws) from left to right and knit rows (rs) from right to left.

For top of head continue in Yarn B.

Row 32: K8, K2tog, K4, SSK, K15, K2tog, K4, SSK, K8. (43 sts)

Row 33: Purl.

Row 34: K8, K2tog, K2, SSK, K15, K2tog, K2, SSK, K8. (39 sts)

Row 35: Purl.

Row 36: K8, K2tog, SSK, K15, K2tog, SSK, K8. (35 sts)

Cut yarn, transfer the stitches onto a stitch holder.

Body

Using Yarn A and Size 1½ (2.5mm) needles cast on 9 sts.

Starting at neck:

Row 1 (ws): Purl.

Row 2: K1, [K1, M1] 6 times, K2. (15 sts)

Row 3: Purl.

Row 4: K2, [K1, M1] 3 times, K4, [K1, M1] 3 times, K3. (21 sts)

Row 5: Purl.

Row 6: K3, [K1, M1] 4 times, K6, [K1, M1] 4 times, K4. (29 sts)

Rows 7–9: St st 3 rows.

Row 10: K4, [K1, M1] 6 times, K8, [K1, M1] 6 times, K5. (41 sts)

Rows 11–15: St st 5 rows.

Row 16: K3, [K3, M1] 4 times, K8, [K3, M1] 4 times, K6. (49 sts)

Rows 17–27: St st 11 rows.

TOP OF JEGGINGS

Continue working the 49 sts on needle.

Change to Yarn G.

Rows 28–29: Knit 2 rows.

Rows 30–43: Starting with a knit row, st st 14 rows.

Bind off.

Arms

(make 2)

Using Yarn A and Size 1½ (2.5mm) needles cast on 12 sts.

Rows 1–3: Starting with a purl row (ws), st st 3 rows.

Row 4: Cast on 3 sts using Knit cast-on method (see Techniques, page 103), knit to end. (15 sts)

Row 5: Cast on 3 sts using Purl cast-on method (see Techniques, page 103), purl to end. (18 sts)

Rows 6–7: St st 2 rows.

Row 8: SSK, K14, K2tog. (16 sts)

Row 9: Purl.

Row 10: SSK, K12, K2tog. (14 sts)

Row 11: Purl.

Row 12: SSK, K10, K2tog. (12 sts)

Rows 13–47: St st 35 rows.

Row 48: SSK, K8, K2tog. (10 sts)

Row 49: Purl.

Row 50: SSK, K6, K2tog. (8 sts)

Row 51: Purl.

Row 52: SSK, K4, K2tog. (6 sts)

Row 53: Purl.

Row 54: SSK, K2, K2tog. (4 sts)

Row 55: Purl.

Bind off.

Legs and sneakers

(make 2)

Starting at base of sneaker:

Using Yarn D and Size 1½ (2.5mm) needles cast on 12 sts.

Row 1 (ws): Purl.

Row 2: K1, M1, K3, [K1, M1] 3 times, K4, M1, K1. (17 sts)

Row 3: Purl.

Row 4: [K1, M1] 2 times, K3, [K1, M1] 2 times, K2, [K1, M1] 2 times, K3, [K1, M1] 2 times, K1. (25 sts)

Row 5: Purl.

Row 6: [K2, M1] 2 times, K2, [K2, M1] 2 times, K3, [K2, M1] 2 times, K2, [K2, M1] 2 times, K2. (33 sts)

Row 7: Purl.

Change to Yarn E.

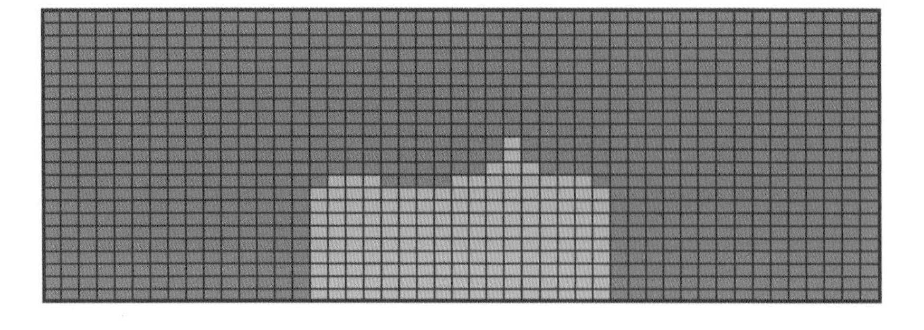

Hair Chart

■ = Yarn A ■ = Yarn B

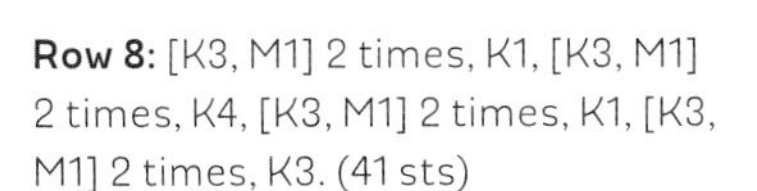

Row 8: [K3, M1] 2 times, K1, [K3, M1] 2 times, K4, [K3, M1] 2 times, K1, [K3, M1] 2 times, K3. (41 sts)

Row 9: Knit.

Row 10: Purl.

The next 8 rows use Intarsia technique (see Techniques) for changing yarns: (E) = Use Yarn E. (F) = Use Yarn F.

Row 11: (F) P14, (E) P13, (F) P14.

Row 12: (F) K14, (E) K13, (F) K14.

Row 13: (F) P14, (E) P13, (F) P14.

Row 14: (F) K14, (E) K1, SSK, K7, K2tog, K1, (F) K14. (39 sts)

Row 15: (F) P14, (E) P11, (F) P14.

Row 16: (F) K14, (E) K1, SSK, K5, K2tog, K1, (F) K14. (37 sts)

Row 17: (F) P14, (E) P9, (F) P14.

Row 18: (F) K7, (E) K8, SSK, K3, K2tog, K8, (F) K7. (35 sts)

Change to Yarn E.

Row 19: Purl.

Row 20: P8, [K7, SSK, K1, K2tog, K7] bind off these middle 17 sts as you work them, P to end. (16 sts)

Row 21: K7, P2tog, K7. (15 sts)

LEGS AND JEGGINGS

Continue working the 15 sts on needle.

Change to Yarn A.

Row 22–27: St st 6 rows.

Change to Yarn G.

Rows 28–29: Knit 2 rows.

Row 30–77: Starting with a knit row, st st 48 rows.

Bind off.

Dress

Front

Using Yarn E and Size 2½ (3mm) needles cast on 55 sts.

Row 1 (ws): Purl.

Row 2: K1, [YO, SSK, K1, K2tog, YO, K1] to end.

Row 3: Purl.

Row 4: K2, [YO, sl1, K2tog, PSSO, YO, K3] to last 5 sts, YO, sl1, K2tog, PSSO, YO, K2.

Rows 5–7: St st 3 rows.

Row 8: [K1, K2tog] to last st, K1. (37 sts)

Change to Yarn C.

Rows 9–10: Purl 2 rows.

Starting with Yarn D, the dress is now worked in a stripe pattern of 2 rows Yarn D and 4 rows Yarn C, throughout.

Rows 11–39: Starting with a purl row, st st 29 rows.

Row 40: [K1, K2tog] to last st, K1. (25 sts)

Row 41: Purl.

Row 42: K1, SSK, K19, K2tog, K1. (23 sts)

Row 43: Purl.

Row 44: K1, SSK, K17, K2tog, K1. (21 sts)

Row 45: Purl.

Row 46: K1, SSK, K15, K2tog, K1. (19 sts)

Rows 47–57: St st 11 rows.

Bind off.

Back

Using Yarn E and Size 2½ (3mm) needles cast on 55 sts.

Row 1 (ws): Purl.

Row 2: K1, [YO, SSK, K1, K2tog, YO, K1] to end.

Row 3: Purl.

Row 4: K2, [YO, sl1, K2tog, PSSO, YO, K3] to last 5 sts, YO, sl1, K2tog, PSSO, YO, K2.

Rows 5–7: St st 3 rows.

Row 8: [K1, K2tog] to last st, K1. (37 sts)

Change to Yarn C.

Rows 9–10: Purl 2 rows.

Rows 11–43 are worked in a stripe pattern of 2 rows Yarn D and 4 rows Yarn C, starting with Yarn D.

Rows 11–39: St st 29 rows.

Row 40: [K1, K2tog] to last st, K1. (25 sts)

Row 41: Purl.

Row 42: K1, SSK, K19, K2tog, K1. (23 sts)

Row 43: Purl.

RIGHT BUTTON PLACKET

Continue in Yarn C.

Row 44: K1, SSK, K10, turn. (12 sts)

Row 45: K3, P9.

Row 46: K1, SSK, K9, turn. (11 sts)

Row 47: K3, P8.

Row 48: K9, YO, K2tog, turn.

Row 49: K1, Ktbl, K1, P8.

Row 50: K11, turn.

Row 51: K3, P8.

Rows 52–55: Rpt last 2 rows, 2 more times.

Row 56: K9, YO, K2tog, turn.

Row 57: K1, Ktbl, K1, P8.

Bind off 11 sts, cut yarn.

LEFT BUTTON PLACKET

Row 1: Returning to stitches still on needle, rejoin Yarn C and pick up and knit 3 sts from BEHIND the first row of Right button placket (see Techniques, page 104: Picking Up Stitches), knit across stitches on Left-hand needle to last 3 sts, K2tog, K1. (12 sts)

Row 2: P9, K3.

Row 3: K9, K2tog, K1. (11 sts)

Row 4: P8, K3.

Row 5: Knit.

Rows 6–13: Rpt last 2 rows, 4 more times.

Row 14: P8, K3.

Bind off.

Sleeves

(make 2)

Using Yarn F and Size 2½ (3mm) needles cast on 20 sts.

Row 1 (ws): Knit.

Starting with Yarn C, the sleeves are now worked in a stripe pattern of 4 rows Yarn C and 2 rows Yarn D throughout.

Rows 2–15: Starting with a knit row, st st 14 rows.

Bind off.

Pocket

Using Yarn F and Size 2½ (3mm) needles cast on 7 sts.

Row 1 (ws): Purl.

Rows 2–6: St st 5 rows.

Row 7: Knit.

Bind off.

Hat

Using Yarn D and Size 2½ (3mm) needles cast on 75 sts.

Row 1 (ws): Knit.

Rows 2–7: Starting with a knit row, st st 6 rows.

Row 8: [K1, K2tog] to end. (50 sts)

Row 9: Knit.

Rows 10–21: St st 12 rows.

Row 22: [K3, K2tog] to end. (40 sts)

Row 23: Purl.

Row 24: [K2, K2tog] to end. (30 sts)

Row 25: Purl.

Row 26: [K1, K2tog] to end. (20 sts)

Row 27: Purl.

Row 28: [K2tog] to end. (10 sts)

Cut yarn leaving a long tail, using a tapestry needle thread tail through the stitches left on needle and draw up.

Making Up

Doll

See Making Up Your Doll in Techniques, page 96.

Plaits

(make 2)

1. See Making up Plaits in Techniques, page 101.
2. Sew plaits to each side of the head and finish of with a small piece of ribbon **(A)**.

Clothing & Accessories

Dress

1. Block all the pieces of the dress before making up.
2. Start by sewing the buttons into place on the back of the dress, matching them up with the button holes **(B)**.
3. Sew the pocket onto the front of dress **(C)**.
4. Sew up the shoulder seams, making sure you leave a big enough gap to fit around Penny's neck.
5. Sew sleeves to front and back pieces, lining up center of sleeves to shoulder seams. Matching up the stripes, sew up the sleeve and dress edge seams.

Hat

Sew the edges of the hat together, then sew three tiny buttons to the front to finish **(D)**.

A

B

C

D

Faye

Faye's whole world revolves around bunnies, and she dreams of the day when she might be allowed to have a furry long-eared friend of her own. It's no surprise then that when choosing an outfit for a party she insisted on *that* hat and *that* pink dress. When the cake arrives she'll giggle her way through 'hoppy birthday to you'!

You Will Need

Yarn

- **Yarn A** Beige
- **Yarn B** Cream
- **Yarn C** Charcoal
- **Yarn D** White
- **Yarn E** Pink
- **Yarn F** Black
- **Yarn G** Pale Pink
- Oddments of black and red for eyes and mouth

Finished size

- 11in (28cm) tall

You will also need

- Size 2½ (3mm) knitting needles
- Size 1½ (2.5mm) straight needles
- Size 1½ (2.5mm) double-pointed needles
- Stitch holder
- Tapestry needle
- 3 x ½in (15mm) circles of white felt
- Toy stuffing
- 2 x ¼in (6mm) buttons

Pattern

Cast on using the Long-tail (double cast-on) method (see Techniques, page 102) unless otherwise indicated. Where possible leave long tails when you cast on and bind off and use these for the sewing up.

Head

Using Yarn A and Size 1½ (2.5mm) needles cast on 13 sts.

Starting at neck:

Row 1 (ws): Purl.

Row 2: [K1, M1] 12 times, K1. (25 sts)

Row 3: Purl.

Row 4: K3, [K1, M1] 7 times, K4, [K1, M1] 7 times, K4. (39 sts)

Rows 5–7: St st 3 rows.

Row 8: K3, [K3, M1] 4 times, K6, [K3, M1] 4 times, K6. (47 sts)

Cut yarn.

Rows 9–31: Using intarsia method (see Techniques, page 109) and working in st st, work Hair Chart. Start with a purl row (ws) at the bottom left-hand corner of chart, read purl rows (ws) from left to right and knit rows (rs) from right to left.

For top of head continue in Yarn B.

Row 32: K8, K2tog, K4, SSK, K15, K2tog, K4, SSK, K8. (43 sts)

Row 33: Purl.

Row 34: K8, K2tog, K2, SSK, K15, K2tog, K2, SSK, K8. (39 sts)

Row 35: Purl.

Row 36: K8, K2tog, SSK, K15, K2tog, SSK, K8. (35 sts)

Cut yarn, transfer the stitches onto a stitch holder.

Pigtails

(make 2)

Using Yarn B and Size 2½ (3mm) needles cast on 64 sts.

Row 1: [K1, bind off next 20 sts] rpt to last st, K1. (4 sts)

Cut yarn leaving a long tail, using a tapestry needle thread the tail through the 4 stitches left on the needle and draw up **(A and B)**.

Body

T-SHIRT

Using Yarn D and Size 1½ (2.5mm) needles cast on 9 sts.

Starting at neck:

Row 1 (ws): Purl.

Row 2: K1, [K1, M1] 6 times, K2. (15 sts)

Row 3: Purl.

Row 4: K2, [K1, M1] 3 times, K4, [K1, M1] 3 times, K3. (21 sts)

Row 5: Purl.

Row 6: K3, [K1, M1] 4 times, K6, [K1, M1] 4 times, K4. (29 sts)

Rows 7–9: St st 3 rows.

Row 10: K4, [K1, M1] 6 times, K8, [K1, M1] 6 times, K5. (41 sts)

Rows 11–15: St st 5 rows.

Row 16: K3, [K3, M1] 4 times, K8, [K3, M1] 4 times, K6. (49 sts)

Rows 17–27: St st 11 rows.

TOP OF TIGHTS

Continue working the 49 sts on needle.

Starting with Yarn C, the tights are worked in a stripe pattern of 2 rows each of Yarn C and Yarn D throughout.

Rows 28–29: Knit 2 rows.

Rows 30–43: Starting with a knit row, st st 14 rows.

Bind off.

Arms

(make 2)

Using Yarn A and Size 1½ (2.5mm) needles cast on 12 sts.

Rows 1–3: Starting with a purl row (ws), st st 3 rows.

Row 4: Cast on 3 sts using Knit cast-on method (see Techniques, page 103), knit to end. (15 sts)

Row 5: Cast on 3 sts using Purl cast-on method (see Techniques, page 103), purl to end. (18 sts)

Rows 6–7: St st 2 rows.

Row 8: SSK, K14, K2tog. (16 sts)

Row 9: Purl.

Row 10: SSK, K12, K2tog. (14 sts)

Row 11: Purl.

Row 12: SSK, K10, K2tog. (12 sts)

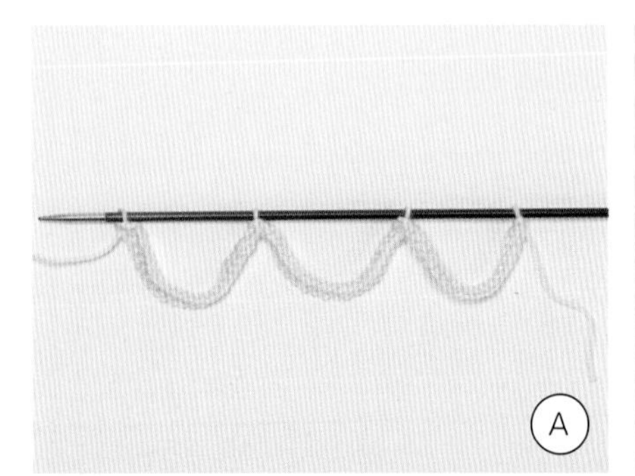

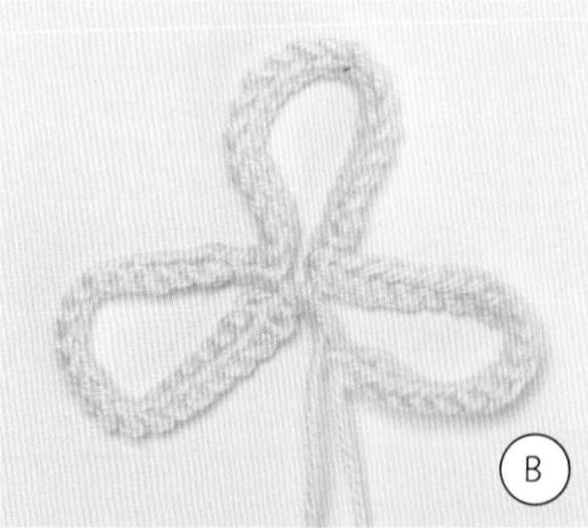

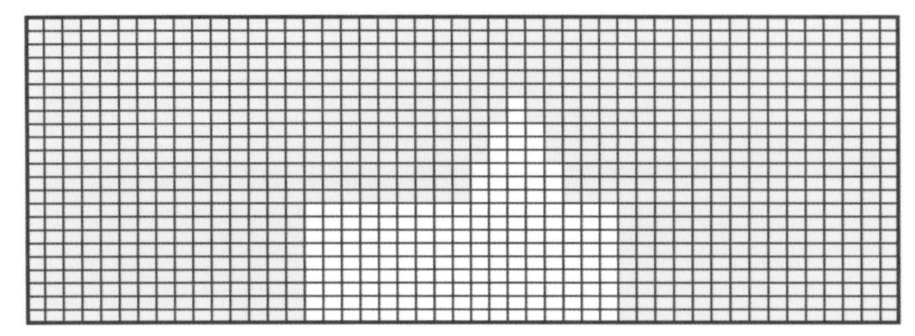

Hair Chart

☐ = Yarn A
☐ = Yarn B

SLEEVES

Continue working the 12 sts on needle.

Change to Yarn D.

Rows 13–14: Purl 2 rows.

Rows 15–47: Starting with a purl row, st st 33 rows.

Row 48: SSK, K8, K2tog. (10 sts)

Row 49: Purl.

Row 50: SSK, K6, K2tog. (8 sts)

Row 51: Purl.

Row 52: SSK, K4, K2tog. (6 sts)

Row 53: Purl.

Row 54: SSK, K2, K2tog. (4 sts)

Row 55: Purl.

Bind off.

Legs and boots

(make 2)

Starting at sole of boot:

Using Yarn F and Size 1½ (2.5mm) needles cast on 12 sts.

Row 1 (ws): Purl.

Row 2: K1, M1, K3, [K1, M1] 3 times, K4, M1, K1. (17 sts)

Row 3: Purl.

Row 4: [K1, M1] 2 times, K3, [K1, M1] 2 times, K2, [K1, M1] 2 times, K3, [K1, M1] 2 times, K1. (25 sts)

Row 5: Purl.

Row 6: [K2, M1] 2 times, K2, [K2, M1] 2 times, K3, [K2, M1] 2 times, K2, [K2, M1] 2 times, K2. (33 sts)

Row 7: Purl.

Row 8: [K3, M1] 2 times, K1, [K3, M1] 2 times, K4, [K3, M1] 2 times, K1, [K3, M1] 2 times, K3. (41 sts)

Row 9: Knit.

Row 10: Purl.

Change to Yarn C.

Rows 11–13: Starting with a purl row, st st 3 rows.

Row 14: K15, SSK, K7, K2tog, K15. (39 sts)

Row 15: Purl.

Row 16: K15, SSK, K5, K2tog, K15. (37 sts)

Row 17: Purl.

Row 18: K15, SSK, K3, K2tog, K15. (35 sts)

Row 19: Purl.

Row 20: K8, [K7, SSK, K1, K2tog, K7] bind off these middle 17 sts as you work them, K to end. (16 sts)

Row 21: P7, P2tog, P7. (15 sts)

BOTTOM OF TIGHTS

Continue working the 15 sts on needle.

Starting with Yarn D, the tights are worked in a stripe pattern of 2 rows each of Yarn D and Yarn C throughout.

Rows 22–77: St st 56 rows.

Bind off using Yarn D.

Boot cuff

(make 2)

Using Yarn C and Size 2½ (3mm) needles cast on 31 sts.

Starting at the top of the cuff:

Row 1 (ws): [P1, K2] to last st, P1.

Row 2: [K1, P2] to last st, K1.

Row 3–18: Rpt last 2 rows, 8 more times.

Row 19: [P1, K2tog] to last st, P1. (21 sts)

Row 20: [K1, P1] to last st, K1.

Row 21: [P1, K1] to last st, P1.

Row 22–27: Rpt last 2 rows, 3 more times.

Row 28: [K1, P1] to last st, K1.

Bind off.

Dress

Front of dress

Using Yarn E and Size 2½ (3mm) needles cast on 49 sts.

Row 1–7: Starting with a purl row (ws), st st 7 rows.

Row 8: K2, [K2tog, K4] 7 times, K2tog, K3. (41 sts)

Row 9: Purl.

Row 10: K1, [K3, K2tog] to end. (33 sts)

Rows 11–12: Purl 2 rows.

Dress chart A is placed in the following rows Using intarsia method (see Techniques, page 109) and worked in st st. Starting at the bottom left-hand corner of chart, read purl rows (ws) from left to right and knit rows (rs) from right to left.

Row 13: P9, work Dress Chart A, P5.

Row 14: K5, work Dress Chart A, K9.

Rows 15–18: Repeat last 2 rows, 2 more times.

Row 19: P9, work Dress Chart A, P5.

Row 20: K2tog, K3, work Dress Chart A, K7, K2tog. (31 sts)

Row 21: P8, work Dress Chart A, P4.

Row 22: K4, work Dress Chart A, K8.

Rows 23–24: Repeat last 2 rows.

Row 25: P8, work Dress Chart A, P4.

Row 26: K2tog, K2, work Dress Chart A, K6, K2tog. (29 sts)

Row 27: P7, work Dress Chart A, P3.

Row 28: K3, work Dress Chart A, K7.

Rows 29–30: Repeat last 2 rows.

Row 31: P7, work Dress Chart A, P3.

Row 32: K2tog, K1, work Dress Chart A, K5, K2tog. (27 sts)

Row 33: P6, work Dress Chart A, P2.

Row 34: K2, work Dress Chart A, K6.

Rows 35–36: Repeat last 2 rows.

Row 37: P6, work Dress Chart A, P2.

Row 38: K2tog, work Dress Chart A, K4, K2tog. (25 sts)

Row 39: P5, work Dress Chart A, P1.

Row 40: K1, work Dress Chart A, K5.

Rows 41–42: Repeat last 2 rows.

Row 43: P5, work Dress Chart A, P1

Row 44: K2tog, Knit to last 2 sts, K2tog. (23 sts)

Row 45: Purl.

Row 46: K2tog, Knit to last 2 sts, K2tog. (21 sts)

Rows 47–57: St st 11 rows.

Bind off.

Back of dress

Using Yarn E and Size 2½ (3mm) needles cast on 49 sts.

Row 1–7: Starting with a purl row (ws), st st 7 rows.

Row 8: K2, [K2tog, K4] 7 times, K2tog, K3. (41 sts)

Row 9: Purl.

Row 10: K1, [K3, K2tog] to end. (33 sts)

Rows 11–12: Purl 2 rows.

Rows 13–19: Starting with a purl row, st st 7 rows.

Row 20: K2tog, knit to last 2 sts, K2tog. (31 sts)

Rows 21–25: St st 5 rows.

Row 26: K2tog, knit to last 2 sts, K2tog. (29 sts)

Rows 27-31: St st 5 rows.

Row 32: K2tog, knit to last 2 sts, K2tog. (27 sts)

Rows 33–37: St st 5 rows.

Row 38: K2tog, knit to last 2 sts, K2tog. (25 sts)

Rows 39–43: St st 5 rows.

RIGHT BUTTON PLACKET

Row 44: K2tog, K12, turn. (13 sts)

Row 45: K3, P10.

Row 46: K2tog, K11, turn. (12 sts)

Row 47: K3, P9.

Row 48: K10, YO, K2tog, turn.

Row 49: K1, Ktbl, K1, P9.

Row 50: K12, turn.

Row 51: K3, P9.

Rows 52–55: Rpt last 2 rows, 2 more times.

Row 56: K10, YO, K2tog, turn.

Row 57: K1, Ktbl, K1, P9.

Bind off 12 sts, cut yarn.

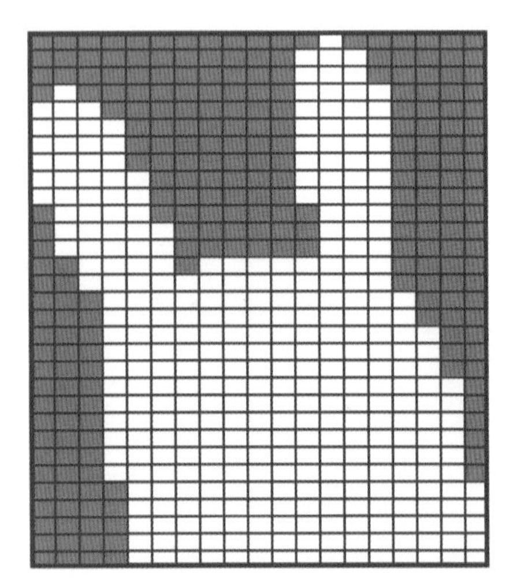

Dress Chart A

■ = Yarn E □ = Yarn D

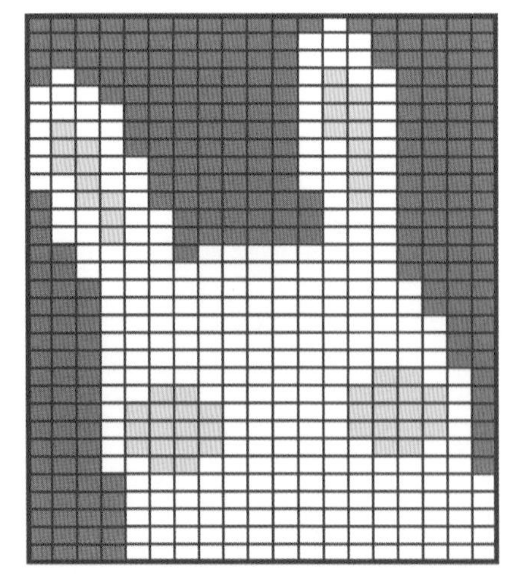

Dress Chart B

■ = Yarn E □ = Yarn D ▨ = Yarn G

LEFT BUTTON PLACKET

Row 1: Returning to stitches still on needle, rejoin Yarn E and pick up and knit 3 sts from behind the first row of right button placket (see Techniques, page 104: Picking Up Stitches), knit across stitches on left-hand needle to last 2 sts, K2tog. (13 sts)

Row 2: P10, K3.

Row 3: Knit to last 2 sts, K2tog. (12 sts)

Row 4: P9, K3.

Row 5: Knit.

Rows 6–13: Rpt last 2 rows, 4 more times.

Row 14: P9, K3.

Bind off.

Sleeves

(make 2)

Using Yarn E and Size 1½ (2.5mm) needles cast on 20 sts.

Row 1 (ws): [P2, K1] to last 2 sts, P2.

Row 2: [K2, P1] to last 2 sts, K2.

Rows 3–6: Rpt last 2 rows, 2 more times.

Change to Size 2½ (3mm) needles.

Rows 7–11: Starting with a purl row, st st 5 rows.

Bind off.

Bunny hat

Hat

Using Yarn C and Size 2½ (3mm) needles cast on 50 sts.

Rows 1 (ws): Knit.

Rows 2–4: Knit 3 rows.

Rows 5–15: Starting with a purl row, st st 11 rows.

Row 16: K4, [K2tog, K8] to last 4 sts, K4. (45 sts)

Row 17: Purl.

Row 18: K3, [K2tog, K7] to last 4 sts, K4. (40 sts)

Row 19: Purl.

Row 20: K2, [K2tog, K6] to last 4 sts, K4. (35 sts)

Row 21: Purl.

Row 22: K1, [K2tog, K5] to last 4 sts, K4. (30 sts)

Row 23: Purl.

Row 24: [K2tog, K4] to end. (25 sts)

Row 25: Purl.

Row 26: K2tog, to last st, K1. (13 sts)

Cut yarn leaving a long tail, using a tapestry needle thread tail through the stitches left on needle and draw up.

Hat ears

(make 2)

Using Yarn C and Size 2½ (3mm) needles cast on 12 sts.

Row 1 (ws): [K1, P1] to end.

Row 2: [P1, K1] to end.

Rows 3–10: Rpt last 2 rows, 4 more times.

Row 11: [K1, P1] to end.

Row 12: [P1, K1] 2 times, P2tog, K2tog, [P1, K1] 2 times. (10 sts)

Row 13: [K1, P1] to end.

Row 14: [P1, K1] to end.

Rows 15–16: Rpt last 2 rows.

Row 17: K1, P1, K1, P2tog, K2tog, P1, K1, P1. (8 sts)

Row 18: [P1, K1] to end.

Row 19: [K1, P1] to end.

Row 20: P1, K1, P2tog, K2tog, P1, K1. (6 sts)

Row 21: K1, P2tog, K2tog, P1. (4 sts)

Row 22: P2tog, K2tog. (2 sts)

Row 23: P2tog. (1 st)

Making Up

Doll

See Making Up Your Doll in Techniques, page 96.

Pigtails

Twist the three loops together so they lie on top of each other, and sew in place on either side of the head **(C)**.

Clothing & Accessories

Dress

1. Using Dress Chart B, work the bunny's ears and cheeks in Duplicate stitch with Yarn G (see Techniques, page 108).
2. Using a length of Yarn C, embroider the bunny's eyes, nose and mouth, using figure **D** as a guide.
3. Block all the pieces of the dress before continuing to make it up.
4. Sew buttons in place, on the left button placket **(E)**.
5. Sew up the shoulder seams leaving a big enough gap to fit around Faye's neck. Sew the sleeves to the front and back pieces, lining up the center of sleeves to shoulder seams.
6. Sew up the sleeve and dress edge seams.

Bunny hat

1. Sew the side edges of the hat together.
2. Weave in the ear cast-off tail down the edge of the ears, on the wrong side of the work **(F)**.
3. With wrong sides facing, fold the ears in half. Thread the cast-on tail through the cast-on stitches and gather up **(G and H)**.
4. Sew the ears to the top of the hat, making sure the seam of the hat is central at the back.
5. Thread any loose ends through to the wrong side of the hat and weave in.

C

D

E

F

G

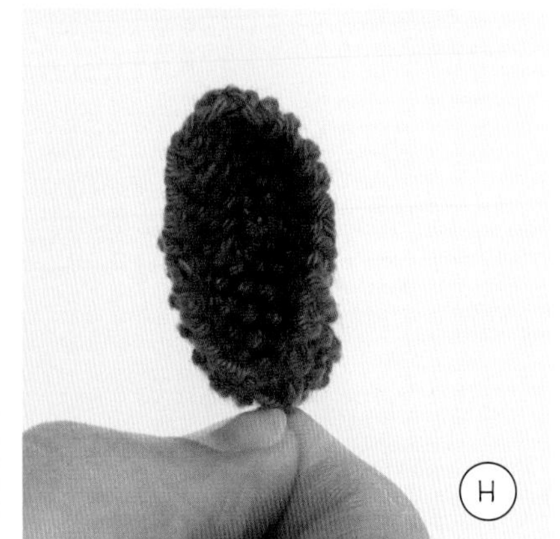
H

Polly has three older brothers so she's learned to stand up for herself. Luckily she's never been very princess-y and would rather sling a few toy cars in her bag and head out for an adventure. If you don't want your pigtails pulled, you have to adapt, and Polly's practical shorts, tights and ankle boots mean she can run like the wind.

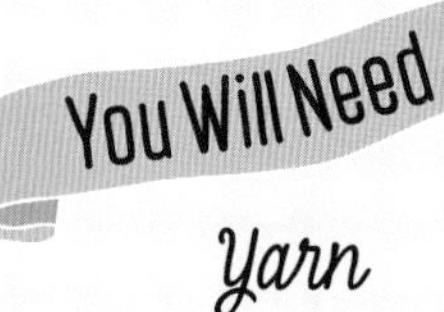

Yarn

- **Yarn A** Beige
- **Yarn B** Camel
- **Yarn C** Cream
- **Yarn D** Orange
- **Yarn E** Sky Blue
- **Yarn F** Petrol Blue
- Oddments of black and red for eyes and mouth

Finished size

- 11in (28cm) tall

You will also need

- Size 2½ (3mm) knitting needles
- Size 1½ (2.5mm) knitting needles
- Size 1½ (2.5mm) double-pointed needles
- Stitch holder
- Stitch markers
- Tapestry needle
- 3 x ½in (15mm) circles of white felt
- Toy stuffing
- 5 x ¼in (6mm) buttons

Pattern

Cast on using the Long-tail (double cast-on) method (see Techniques, page 102) unless otherwise indicated. Where possible leave long tails when you cast on and bind off and use these for the sewing up.

Head

Using Yarn A and Size 1½ (2.5mm) needles cast on 13 sts.

Starting at neck:

Row 1 (ws): Purl.

Row 2: [K1, M1] 12 times, K1. (25 sts)

Row 3: Purl.

Row 4: K3, [K1, M1] 7 times, K4, [K1, M1] 7 times, K4. (39 sts)

Rows 5–7: St st 3 rows.

Row 8: K3, [K3, M1] 4 times, K6, [K3, M1] 4 times, K6. (47 sts)

Cut yarn.

Rows 9–31: Using intarsia method (see Techniques, page 109) and working in st st, work Hair Chart. Start with a purl row (ws) at the bottom left-hand corner of chart, read purl rows (ws) from left to right and knit rows (rs) from right to left.

For top of head continue in Yarn B.

Row 32: K8, K2tog, K4, SSK, K15, K2tog, K4, SSK, K8. (43 sts)

Row 33: Purl.

Row 34: K8, K2tog, K2, SSK, K15, K2tog, K2, SSK, K8. (39 sts)

Row 35: Purl.

Row 36: K8, K2tog, SSK, K15, K2tog, SSK, K8. (35 sts)

Cut yarn, transfer the stitches onto a stitch holder.

Body

T-SHIRT

Using Yarn E and Size 1½ (2.5mm) needles cast on 9 sts.

Starting at neck:

Row 1 (ws): Purl.

Row 2: K1, [K1, M1] 6 times, K2. (15 sts)

Row 3: Purl.

Row 4: K2, [K1, M1] 3 times, K4, [K1, M1] 3 times, K3. (21 sts)

Row 5: Purl.

Row 6: K3, [K1, M1] 4 times, K6, [K1, M1] 4 times, K4. (29 sts)

Rows 7–9: St st 3 rows.

Row 10: K4, [K1, M1] 6 times, K8, [K1, M1] 6 times, K5. (41 sts)

Rows 11–15: St st 5 rows.

Row 16: K3, [K3, M1] 4 times, K8, [K3, M1] 4 times, K6. (49 sts)

Rows 17–27: St st 11 rows.

TOP OF TIGHTS

Continue working the 49 sts on needle.

Starting with Yarn C, the tights are worked in a stripe pattern of 2 rows Yarn C and 2 rows Yarn E throughout.

Rows 28–29: Knit 2 rows.

Rows 30–43: Starting with a knit row, st st 14 rows.

Bind off.

Arms

(make 2)

Using Yarn A and Size 1½ (2.5mm) needles cast on 12 sts.

Rows 1–3: Starting with a purl row (ws), st st 3 rows.

Row 4: Cast on 3 sts using Knit cast-on method (see Techniques, page 103), knit to end. (15 sts)

Row 5: Cast on 3 sts using Purl cast-on method (see Techniques, page 103), purl to end. (18 sts)

Rows 6–7: St st 2 rows.

Row 8: SSK, K14, K2tog. (16 sts)

Row 9: Purl.

Row 10: SSK, K12, K2tog. (14 sts)

Row 11: Purl.

Row 12: SSK, K10, K2tog. (12 sts)

Rows 13–18: St st 6 rows.

SLEEVES

Continue working the 12 sts on needle.

Change to Yarn E.

Rows 19–20: Purl 2 rows.

Rows 21–47: Starting with a purl row, st st 27 rows.

Row 48: SSK, K8, K2tog. (10 sts)

Row 49: Purl.

Row 50: SSK, K6, K2tog. (8 sts)

Row 51: Purl.

Row 52: SSK, K4, K2tog. (6 sts)

Row 53: Purl.

Row 54: SSK, K2, K2tog. (4 sts)

Row 55: Purl.

Bind off.

Legs and boots

(make 2)

Using Yarn B and Size 1½ (2.5mm) needles cast on 12 sts.

Starting at sole of boot:

Row 1 (ws): Purl.

Row 2: K1, M1, K3, [K1, M1] 3 times, K4, M1, K1. (17 sts)

Row 3: Purl.

Row 4: [K1, M1] 2 times, K3, [K1, M1] 2 times, K2, [K1, M1] 2 times, K3, [K1, M1] 2 times, K1. (25 sts)

Row 5: Purl.

Row 6: [K2, M1] 2 times, K2, [K2, M1] 2 times, K3, [K2, M1] 2 times, K2, [K2, M1] 2 times, K2. (33 sts)

Row 7: Purl.

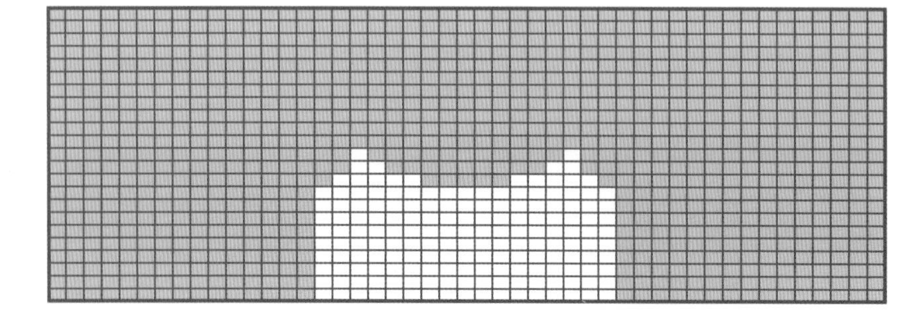

Hair Chart

□ = Yarn A

▩ = Yarn B

Row 8: [K3, M1] 2 times, K1, [K3, M1] 2 times, K4, [K3, M1] 2 times, K1, [K3, M1] 2 times, K3. (41 sts)

Row 9: Knit.

Row 10: Purl.

Rows 11–13: Starting with a purl row, st st 3 rows.

Row 14: K15, SSK, K7, K2tog, K15. (39 sts)

Row 15: Purl.

Row 16: K15, SSK, K5, K2tog, K15. (37 sts)

Row 17: Purl.

Row 18: K15, SSK, K3, K2tog, K15. (35 sts)

Row 19: Purl.

Row 20: K8, [K7, SSK, K1, K2tog, K7] bind off these middle 17 sts as you work them, K to end. (16 sts)

Row 21: P7, P2tog, P7. (15 sts)

BOTTOM OF TIGHTS

Continue working the 15 sts on needle.

Starting with Yarn E, the tights are worked in a stripe pattern of 2 rows each of Yarn E and Yarn C throughout.

Rows 22–77: St st 56 rows.

Bind off using Yarn E.

Boot cuffs

(make 2)

Using Yarn C and Size 2½ (3mm) needles cast on 31 sts.

Start at the top of the cuff:

Row 1 (ws): (P1, K2) to last st, P1.

Row 2: (K1, P2) to last st, K1.

Rows 3–12: Rpt last 2 rows, 5 more times.

Row 13: (P1, K2tog) to last st, P1. (21 sts)

Row 14: (K1, P1) to last st, K1.

Row 15: (P1, K1) to last st, P1.

Rows 16–20: Rpt last 2 rows, 2 more times, then rpt row 14 once more.

Bind off in pattern.

Tunic

The tunic is worked from the top down in one piece and fastened down the back. The button bands (first and last 3 sts on each row) are worked in Yarn C throughout, using Intarsia method (see Techniques, page 109). Color changes along rows are indicated in ().

(C) = Use Yarn C. (D) = Use Yarn D. (E) = Use Yarn E.

Using Yarn C and Size 2½ (3mm) needles cast on 31 sts.

Row 1 (ws): K7, pm, K4, pm, K10, pm, K4, pm, K6.

Row 2: K1, YO, K2tog, [K to marker, m1r, sm, K1, m1l] 4 times, K to end. (39 sts)

Row 3: K3, purl to last 3 sts, K1, Ktbl, K1.

Row 4: [K to marker, m1r, sm, K1, m1l] 4 times, K to end. (47 sts)

Row 5: Rpt row 3.

Row 8: Rpt row 4. (55 sts)

Row 7: Rpt row 3.

Row 8: Rpt row 4. (63 sts)

Row 9: Rpt row 3.

Row 10: Rpt row 2. (71 sts)

Row 11: Rpt row 3.

Row 12: Rpt row 4. (79 sts)

Row 13: Rpt row 3.

Row 14: Rpt row 4. (87 sts)

The stitch markers are no longer needed.

Row 15: K3, P11, K17, P25, K17, P11, K3.

Row 16: K14, bind off 17 sts, K25, bind off 17 sts, K to end. (53 sts)

Row 17: K3, Pfb, [P2, Pfb] 3 times, [Pfb] 2 times, [P2, Pfb] 8 times, [Pfb] 2 times, [P2, Pfb] 3 times, K3. (72 sts)

Row 18: K1, YO, K2tog, knit to end.

Row 19: (C) K3, (D) purl to last 3 sts, (C) K1, Ktbl, K1.

Row 20: (C) K3, (D) K2, *YO, K3, pass first of the 3 knit sts over the 2nd and 3rd sts; rpt from * to last 4 sts, K1, (C) K3.

Rows 21: K3, purl to last 3 sts, K3.

Row 22: K4, *K3, pass first of the 3 knit sts over the 2nd and 3rd sts, YO; rpt from * to last 5 sts, K5.

Row 23: (C) K3, (E) purl to last 3 sts, (C) K3.

Row 24: (C) K3, (E) K2, *YO, K3, pass first of the 3 knit sts over the 2nd and 3rd sts; rpt from * to last 4 sts, K1, (C) K3.

Row 25: (C) K3, (D) purl to last 3 sts, (C) K3.

Row 26: (C) K1, YO, K2tog, (D) K1, *K3, pass first of the 3 knit sts over the 2nd and 3rd sts, YO; rpt from * to last 5 sts, K2, (C) K3.

Row 27: K3, purl to last 3 sts, K1, Ktbl, K1.

Row 28: K5, *YO, K3, pass first of the 3 knit sts over the 2nd and 3rd sts; rpt from * to last 4 sts, K4.

Row 29: (C) K3, (E) purl to last 3 sts, (C) K3.

Row 30: (C) K3, (E) K1, *K3, pass first of the 3 knit sts over the 2nd and 3rd sts, YO; rpt from * to last 5 sts, K2, (C) K3.

Row 31: (C) K3, (D) purl to last 3 sts, (C) K3.

Row 32: (C) K3, (D) K2, *YO, K3, pass first of the 3 knit sts over the 2nd and 3rd sts; rpt from * to last 4 sts, K1, (C) K3.

Row 33: K3, purl to last 3 sts, K3.

Row 34: K1, YO, K2tog, K1, *K3, pass first of the 3 knit sts over the 2nd and 3rd sts, YO; rpt from * to last 5 sts, K5.

Row 35: (C) K3, (E) purl to last 3 sts, (C) K1, Ktbl, K1.

Row 36: (C) K3, (E) K2, *YO, K3, pass first of the 3 knit sts over the 2nd and 3rd sts; rpt from * to last 4 sts, K1, (C) K3.

Row 37: (C) K3, (D) purl to last 3 sts, (C) K3.

Row 38: (C) K3, (D) K1, *K3, pass first of the 3 knit sts over the 2nd and 3rd sts, YO; rpt from * to last 5 sts, K2, (C) K3.

Row 39: K3, purl to last 3 sts, K3.

Rows 40–43: Knit 4 rows.

Bind off.

Shorts

Made in one piece and seamed at the inside leg and back of body.

Left leg

Using Yarn F and Size 2½ (3mm) needles cast on 23 sts.

Starting at the bottom of left leg:

Row 1 (ws): Knit.

Rows 2–3: Knit 2 rows.

Rows 4–17: Starting with a purl row, st st 14 rows.

Row 18: Kfb, K to last st, Kfb. (25 sts)

Slip all stitches onto a stitch holder.

Cut yarn leaving a small tail to weave in later.

Right leg

Work rows 1–18 as left leg.

Row 19: Purl.

Leave these stitches on the right-hand needle and do not cut yarn.

JOIN LEGS

Slip the stitches from stitch holder back onto left-hand knitting needle, purl to end of row. You should now have 50 sts on the needle.

Rows 20–34: St st 15 rows.

Rows 35–37: Knit 3 rows.

.Bind off.

Shopper bag

Bag

Using Yarn D and Size 2½ (3mm) needles cast on 22 sts.

Row 1 (ws): *[Pfb] twice, P7, [Pfb] twice; rpt from * to end. (30 sts)

Row 2: K2, *YO, K3, pass first of the 3 knit sts over the 2nd and 3rd sts; rpt from * to last st, K1.

Row 3: Purl.

Row 4: K1, *K3, pass first of the 3 knit sts over the 2nd and 3rd sts, YO; rpt from * to last 2 sts, K2.

Row 5: Purl.

Rows 6–14: Rpt the last 4 rows, 2 more times, then rpt row 2 once more.

Row 15: Purl.

Row 16: K2, [K2tog, K2] to end. (23 sts]

Rows 17–19: St st 3 rows.

Bind off.

Handle

Using Yarn D and Size 2½ (3mm) needles cast on 70 sts.

Row 1 (ws): Knit and bind off all stitches.

Making Up

Doll

See Making Up Your Doll in Techniques, page 96.

Plaits

(make 2)

1. See Making up plaits in Techniques, page 101.
2. Sew plaits to top of head (see **A** for placement).

Clothing & Accessories

Tunic

1. Block the tunic before making up.
2. Sew the buttons into place on the back of the tunic, matching them up with the button holes **(B).**

Shorts

1. Block the shorts before making up.
2. Sew up the inside leg seams to the crotch, followed by the back seam.

Shopper bag

1. Block the bag pieces before you make up.
2. Start by sewing the side and bottom edges of the bag together.
3. Then attach each end of the bag handle to the top edge of the bag with a couple of stitches **(C).**

A

B

C

Anna

Magpie Anna collects shiny things. Marbles are just about her most favorite treasures. She loves their jewel-like colors. She likes a pop of color in her wardrobe, too, hence the dusky rose ankle boots and bright owl sweater. When you have a pale Scandi complexion, and ice blond hair, a bit of vivid pink lets the world know you're coming.

Yarn

Yarn A Tan

Yarn B Cream

Yarn C Dusky Rose

Yarn D Aqua

Yarn E Teal

Yarn F Deep Fuchsia

Yarn G Orange

Oddments of black and red for eyes and mouth

Finished size

11in (28cm) tall

You will also need

Size 2½ (3mm) knitting needles

Size 1½ (2.5mm) knitting needles

Size 1½ (2.5mm) double-pointed needles

Stitch holder

Tapestry needle

3 x ½in (15mm) circles of white felt

Toy stuffing

4 x ¼in (6mm) buttons

Row 10: K8, work Sweater Chart A, K8.

Row 11: P8, work Sweater Chart A, P8.

Rows 12–26: Rpt the last 2 rows, 7 more times, then rpt row 10 once more.

Rows 27–33: St st 7 rows.

Bind off.

Back of sweater

Using Yarn B and Size 2½ (3mm) needles cast on 27 sts.

Row 1 (ws): Knit.

Rows 2–3: Knit 2 rows.

Rows 4–19: Starting with a knit row, st st 16 rows.

RIGHT BUTTON PLACKET

Row 20: K15, turn. (15 sts)

Row 21: K3, P12.

Rows 22–23: Rpt last 2 rows.

Row 24: K13, YO, K2tog, turn.

Row 25: K1, Ktbl, K1, P12.

Rows 26–31: Rpt rows 20 and 21, 3 more times.

Row 32: Rpt row 24.

Row 33: Rpt row 25.

Bind off 15 sts, cut yarn.

LEFT BUTTON PLACKET

Row 1: Returning to stitches still on needle, rejoin Yarn B and pick up and knit 3 sts from BEHIND the first row of the right button placket (see Techniques, page 104: Picking Up Stitches), knit across stitches on Left-hand needle. (15 sts)

Row 2: P12, K3.

Row 3: Knit.

Rows 4–13: Repeat last 2 rows, 5 more times.

Row 14: P12, K3.

Bind off.

Sleeves

(make 2)

Using Yarn C and Size 2½ (3mm) needles cast on 20 sts.

Row 1 (ws): Knit.

Starting with Yarn B, the sleeves are now worked in a stripe pattern of 2 rows each of Yarn B and Yarn D throughout.

Rows 2–23: Starting with a knit row, st st 22 rows.

Bind off.

Making Up

Doll

See Making Up Your Doll in Techniques, page 96.

Pigtails

1. With wrong sides together, fold the piece in half along the eyelet holes and then sew each side seam together.
2. Stitch in place on either side of Anna's head **(A)**.

Clothing

Sweater

1. Using Sweater Chart B, work the owl's eyes, beak and feet in Duplicate stitch (see Techniques, page 108).
2. Block all the pieces of the sweater before making up.
3. Now sew the buttons into place on the center of each eye **(B)** and on the back of the sweater, matching them up with the button holes **(C)**.
4. Sew up shoulder seams, leaving a big enough gap to fit around Anna's neck. Sew sleeves to front and back pieces, lining up center of sleeves to shoulder seams. Sew up sleeve and sweater edge seams.

Skirt

1. Block skirt before making up.
2. Starting at the hem, sew the edges of the skirt together, creating a side seam.

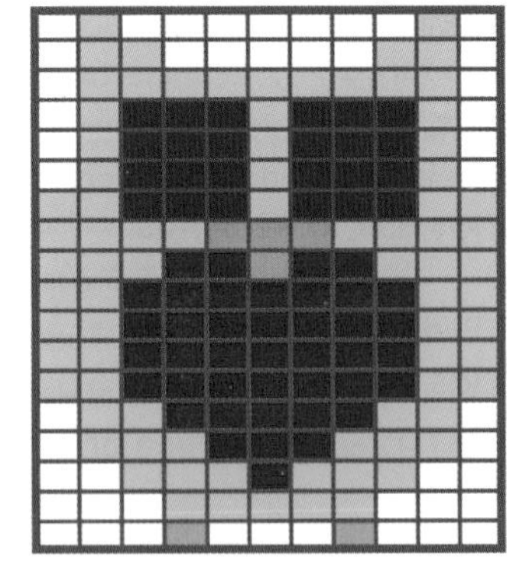

Sweater Chart B

□ = Yarn B ■ = Yarn C
▩ = Yarn D ■ = Yarn E
▩ = Yarn G

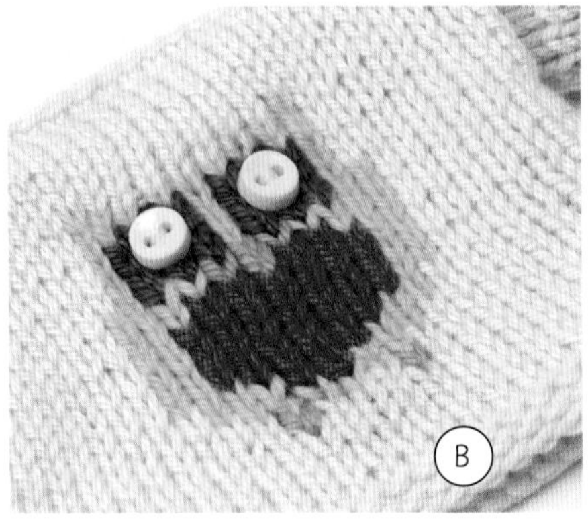

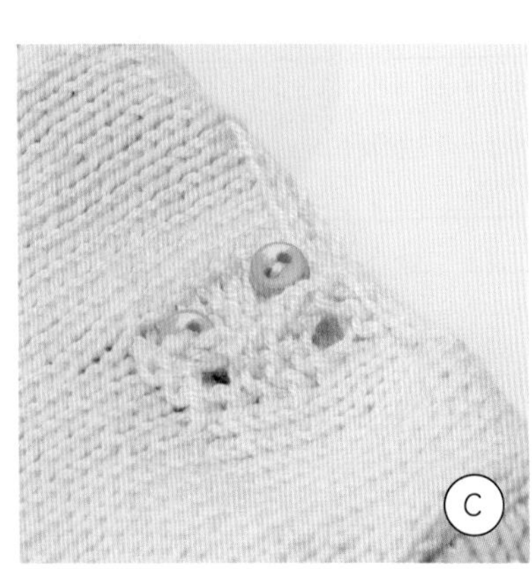

Pippa

A creative little soul, Pippa is never happier than when she's making something lovely. This week it's a beautiful scrapbook using pretty washi tape. Last week she learnt how to knit little flowers. She became an unstoppable flower-knitting machine, and her mummy had to suggest scrapbooking before Pippa's entire wardrobe went 'floral'.

Yarn

- **Yarn A** Cream
- **Yarn B** Camel
- **Yarn C** Nectarine
- **Yarn D** Sage Green
- Oddments of black and red for eyes and mouth

Finished size

- 11in (28cm) tall

You will also need

- Size 2½ (3mm) knitting needles
- Size 1½ (2.5mm) knitting needles
- Size 1½ (2.5mm) double-pointed needles
- Stitch holder
- Tapestry needle
- 3 x ½in (15mm) circles of white felt
- Toy stuffing
- 8 x ¼in (6mm) buttons

Pattern

Cast on using the Long-tail (double cast-on) method (see Techniques, page 102) unless otherwise indicated. Where possible leave long tails when you cast on and bind off and use these for the sewing up.

Head

Using Yarn A and Size 1½ (2.5mm) needles cast on 13 sts.

Starting at neck:

Row 1 (ws): Purl.

Row 2: [K1, M1] 12 times, K1. (25 sts)

Row 3: Purl.

Row 4: K3, [K1, M1] 7 times, K4, [K1, M1] 7 times, K4. (39 sts)

Rows 5–7: St st 3 rows.

Row 8: K3, [K3, M1] 4 times, K6, [K3, M1] 4 times, K6. (47 sts)

Cut yarn.

Rows 9–31: Using intarsia method (see Techniques, page 109) and working in st st, work Hair Chart. Start with a purl row (ws) at the bottom left-hand corner of chart, read purl rows (ws) from left to right and knit rows (rs) from right to left.

For top of head continue in Yarn B.

Row 32: K8, K2tog, K4, SSK, K15, K2tog, K4, SSK, K8. (43 sts)

Row 33: Purl.

Row 34: K8, K2tog, K2, SSK, K15, K2tog, K2, SSK, K8. (39 sts)

Row 35: Purl.

Row 36: K8, K2tog, SSK, K15, K2tog, SSK, K8. (35 sts)

Cut yarn, transfer the stitches onto a stitch holder.

Right pigtail

Using Yarn B and Size 1½ (2.5mm) needles cast on 13 sts.

Row 1 (ws): Purl.

Row 2: K1, *kfb 2 times, K4; rep from * once more. (17 sts)

Rows 3–5: St st 3 rows.

Row 6: K9, K2tog, SSK, K4. (15 sts)

Row 7: Purl.

Row 8: K1, [K2tog, SSK, K3] 2 times. (11 sts)

Row 9: Purl.

Row 10: K5, K2tog, SSK, K2. (9 sts)

Row 11: P1, SSP, P2tog, P4. (7 sts)

Row 12: K2tog, K3tog, SSK. (3 sts)

Row 13: Purl.

Cut yarn leaving a long tail, use a tapestry needle to thread tail through stitches left on needle and draw up.

Left pigtail

Using Yarn B and Size 1½ (2.5mm) needles cast on 13 sts.

Row 1 (ws): Purl.

Row 2: *K4, kfb 2 times; rep from * once more, K1. (17 sts)

Rows 3–5: St st 3 rows.

Row 6: K4, K2tog, SSK, K9. (15 sts)

Row 7: Purl.

Row 8: [K3, K2tog, SSK] 2 times, K1. (11 sts)

Row 9: Purl.

Row 10: K2, K2tog, SSK, K5. (9 sts)

Row 11: P4, SSP, P2tog, P1. (7 sts)

Row 12: K2tog, sl1, SSK, PSSO, SSK. (3 sts)

Row 13: Purl.

Cut yarn leaving a long tail, use a tapestry needle to thread tail through stitches left on needle and draw up.

Head band

Band

Using Yarn D and Size 2½ (3mm) needles cast on 47 sts.

Row 1 (ws): [P1, K1] to last st, P1.

Bind off.

Flowers

(make 3)

Using Yarn A and Size 1½ (2.5mm) needles cast on 12 sts.

Row 1 (ws): Knit.

Row 2: [K2tog] to end.

Cut yarn leaving a long tail, use a tapestry needle to thread tail through stitches left on needle and draw up.

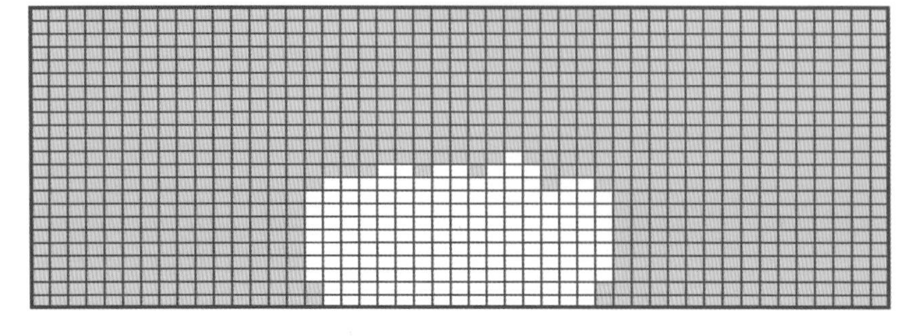

Hair Chart

□ = Yarn A
■ = Yarn B

Body

Using Yarn A and Size 1½ (2.5mm) needles cast on 9 sts.

Starting at neck:

Row 1 (ws): Purl.

Row 2: K1, [K1, M1] 6 times, K2. (15 sts)

Row 3: Purl.

Row 4: K2, [K1, M1] 3 times, K4, [K1, M1] 3 times, K3. (21 sts)

Row 5: Purl.

Row 6: K3, [K1, M1] 4 times, K6, [K1, M1] 4 times, K4. (29 sts)

Rows 7–9: St st 3 rows.

Row 10: K4, [K1, M1] 6 times, K8, [K1, M1] 6 times, K5. (41 sts)

Rows 11–15: St st 5 rows.

Row 16: K3, [K3, M1] 4 times, K8, [K3, M1] 4 times, K6. (49 sts)

Rows 17–27: St st 11 rows.

KNICKERS

Continue working the 49 sts on needle.

Change to Yarn D.

Rows 28–29: Knit 2 rows.

Starting with Yarn C, the knickers are now worked in a stripe pattern of 2 rows Yarn C and 2 rows Yarn A throughout.

Rows 30–43: Starting with a knit row, st st 14 rows.

Bind off using Yarn A.

Arms

(make 2)

Using Yarn A and Size 1½ (2.5mm) needles cast on 12 sts.

Rows 1–3: Starting with a purl row (ws), st st 3 rows.

Row 4: Cast on 3 sts using Knit cast-on method (see Techniques, page 103), knit to end. (15 sts)

Row 5: Cast on 3 sts using Purl cast-on method (see Techniques, page 103), purl to end. (18 sts)

Rows 6–7: St st 2 rows.

Row 8: SSK, K14, K2tog. (16 sts)

Row 9: Purl.

Row 10: SSK, K12, K2tog. (14 sts)

Row 11: Purl.

Row 12: SSK, K10, K2tog. (12 sts)

Rows 13–47: St st 35 rows.

Row 48: SSK, K8, K2tog. (10 sts)

Row 49: Purl.

Row 50: SSK, K6, K2tog. (8 sts)

Row 51: Purl.

Row 52: SSK, K4, K2tog. (6 sts)

Row 53: Purl.

Row 54: SSK, K2, K2tog. (4 sts)

Row 55: Purl.

Bind off.

Legs

(make 2)

Using Yarn A and Size 1½ (2.5mm) needles cast on 16 sts.

Starting at top of leg:

Rows 1–55: Starting with a purl row (ws), st st 55 rows.

TOP OF FOOT

Row 56: Bind off 5 sts, knit to end. (11 sts)

Row 57: Bind off 5 sts pw, purl to end. (6 sts)

Rows 58–75: St st 18 rows.

Bind-off row: SSK, K2, K2tog (bind off all sts as you work them).

T-bar shoes

(make 2)

Using Yarn C and Size 1½ (2.5mm) needles cast on 12 sts.

Row 1 (ws): Purl.

Row 2: K1, M1, K3, [K1, M1] 3 times, K4, M1, K1. (17 sts)

Row 3: Purl.

Row 4: [K1, M1] 2 times, K3, [K1, M1] 2 times, K2, [K1, M1] 2 times, K3, [K1, M1] 2 times, K1. (25 sts)

Row 5: Purl.

Row 6: [K2, M1] 2 times, K2, [K2, M1] 2 times, K3, [K2, M1] 2 times, K2, [K2, M1] 2 times, K2. (33 sts)

Row 7: Purl.

Row 8: [K3, M1] 2 times, K1, [K3, M1] 2 times, K4, [K3, M1] 2 times, K1, [K3, M1] 2 times, K3. (41 sts)

Rows 9–13: St st 5 rows.

Row 14: K15, SSK, K7, K2tog, K15. (39 sts)

Row 15: Purl.

Row 16: K15, SSK, K5, K2tog, K15. (37 sts)

Row 17: Purl.

Row 18: Bind off 15 sts, SSK, K3, K2tog, knit to end. (20 sts)

Row 19: Bind off 15 sts pw, purl to end. (5 sts)

Row 20: SSK, K1, K2tog.

Row 21: K1, P1, K1.

Row 22: Knit.

Rows 23–29: Rpt last 2 rows, 3 more times, then rpt row 21 once more.

Row 30: K1, sl1 pw with yarn at back, K1.

Row 31: K1, sl1 pw with yarn at front, K1.

Bind off.

Shoe straps

(make 2)

Using Yarn C and Size 1½ (2.5mm) needles cast on 10 sts.

Row 1 (ws): K7, P3.

Row 2: K3, turn.

Row 3: P3.

Bind off kw.

Dress

Front of dress

Using Yarn D and Size 2½ (3mm) needles cast on 37 sts.

Row 1 (ws): [K1, P1] to last st, K1.

Rows 2–3: Rpt last row, 2 more times.

Rows 4–37: Starting with a knit row, st st 34 rows.

Row 38: [K1, K2tog] to last st, K1. (25 sts)

Row 39: [K1, P1] to last st, K1.

Row 40: P2tog, [K1, P1] to last 3 sts, K1, SSP. (23 sts)

Row 41: [P1, K1] to last st, P1.

Row 42: SSK, [P1, K1] to last 3 sts, P1, K2tog. (21 sts)

Row 43: [K1, P1] to last st, K1.

Row 44: P2tog, [K1, P1] to last 3 sts, K1, SSP. (19 sts)

Row 45: [P1, K1] to last st, P1.

Rows 46–55: Rpt last row, 10 more times.

Bind off in pattern.

Back of dress

Using Yarn D and Size 2½ (3mm) needles cast on 37 sts.

Row 1 (ws): [K1, P1] to last st, K1.

Rows 2–3: Rpt last row, 2 more times.

Rows 4–37: Starting with a knit row, st st 34 rows.

Row 38: [K1, K2tog] to last st, K1. (25 sts)

Row 39: [K1, P1] to last st, K1.

RIGHT BUTTON PLACKET

Row 40: P2tog, [K1, P1] 6 times, turn. (13 sts)

Row 41: [P1, K1] to last st, P1.

Row 42: SSK, [P1, K1] 5 times, P1, turn. (12 sts)

Row 43: [P1, K1] to end.

Row 44: P2tog, [K1, P1] 5 times, turn. (11 sts)

Row 45: [P1, K1] to last st, P1.

Row 46: [P1, K1] 4 times, P1, YO, P2tog, turn.

Row 47: P1, Ktbl, [P1, K1] to last st, P1.

Row 48: [P1, K1] to last st, P1, turn.

Row 49: [P1, K1] to last st, P1.

Rows 50–53: Rpt last 2 rows, 2 more times.

Row 54: [P1, K1] 4 times, P1, YO, P2tog, turn.

Row 55: P1, Ktbl, [P1, K1] to last st, P1.

Bind off 11 sts in pattern, cut yarn.

LEFT BUTTON PLACKET

Row 1: Returning to stitches still on needle, rejoin Yarn C and pick up and knit 3 sts from BEHIND the first row of right button placket (see Techniques, page 104: Picking Up Stitches), [K1, P1] across stitches on Left-hand needle to last 3 sts, K1, SSP. (13 sts)

Row 2 (ws): [P1, K1] to last st, P1.

Row 3: [P1, K1] to last 3 sts, P1, K2tog. (12 sts)

Row 4: [K1, P1] to end.

Row 5: [P1, K1] to last 2 sts, SSP. (11 sts)

Row 6: [P1, K1] to last st, P1.

Rows 7–16: Rpt last row, 10 more times.

Bind off in pattern.

Flower

Using Yarn A and Size 1½ (2.5mm) needles cast on 31 sts.

FIRST PETAL

Row 1 (ws): Slip 1 pw, P5, turn.

Row 2: K5, turn.

Row 3: P5, turn.

Row 4: K6, turn.

Row 5: [P2tog] 3 times.

REMAINING PETALS

Rpt rows 1–5, 4 more times until 1 st remains, P1.

Row 6: K1, [slip 2 together kw, K1, PSSO] to end.

Cut yarn leaving a long tail, use a tapestry needle to thread the tail through the stitches left on needle and draw up.

Cardigan

Right front of cardigan

Using Yarn C and Size 2½ (3mm) needles cast on 15 sts.

Row 1 (ws): [K1, P1] to last st, K1.

Rows 2–3: Rpt last row, 2 more times.

Row 4: K1, P1, knit to end.

Row 5: Purl to last 3 sts, K1, P1, K1.

Rows 6–21: Rpt last 2 rows, 8 more times.

Row 22: K1, P1, K1, SSSK, knit to end. (13 sts)

Row 23: Rpt row 5.

Row 24: K1, P1, K1, SSSK, knit to end. (11 sts)

Row 25: Rpt row 5.

Row 26: K1, P1, K1, SSSK, knit to end. (9 sts)

Row 27: Rpt row 5.

Row 28: K1, P1, K1, SSSK, knit to end. (7 sts)

Row 29: Rpt row 5.

Bind off.

Left front of cardigan

Using Yarn C and Size 2½ (3mm) needles cast on 15 sts.

Row 1 (ws): [K1, P1] to last st, K1.

Row 2: [K1, P1] to last 3 sts, K1, YO, K2tog.

Row 3: Rpt row 1.

Row 4: Knit to last 2 sts, P1, K1.

Row 5: K1, P1, K1, purl to end.

Rows 6–10: Rpt last 2 rows, 2 more times, then rpt row 4 once more.

Row 11: K1, YO, K2tog, purl to end.

Row 12: Knit to last 2 sts, P1, K1.

Row 13: K1, P1, K1, purl to end.

Rows 14–19: Rpt last 2 rows, 3 more times.

Row 20: Knit to last 2 sts, YO, K2tog.

Row 21: K1, P1, K1, purl to end.

Row 22: K9, K3tog, K1, P1, K1. (13 sts)

Row 23: Rpt row 5.

Row 24: K7, K3tog, K1, P1, K1. (11 sts)

Row 25: Rpt row 5.

Row 26: K5, K3tog, K1, P1, K1. (9 sts)

Row 27: Rpt row 5.

Row 28: K3, K3tog, K1, P1, K1. (7 sts)

Row 29: Rpt row 5.

Bind off.

Back of cardigan

Using Yarn C and Size 2½ (3mm) needles cast on 27 sts.

Row 1 (ws): [K1, P1] to last st, K1.

Rows 2–3: Rpt last row, 2 more times.

Rows 4–26: St st 23 rows.

Row 27: P4, [K1, P1] to last 3 sts, P3.

Row 28: K5, [P1, K1] to last 4 sts, K4.

Row 29: P4, [K1, P1] to last 3 sts, P3.

Bind off.

Sleeves of cardigan

(make 2)

Using Yarn C and Size 2½ (3mm) needles cast on 15 sts.

Row 1 (ws): [K1, P1] to last st, K1.

Rows 2–3: Rpt last row, 2 more times.

Row 4: K1, [K1, Kfb] 6 times, K2. (21 sts)

Rows 5–25: Starting with a purl row, st st 21 rows.

Bind off.

Making Up

Doll

See Making Up Your Doll in Techniques, page 96.

Pigtails

1. Start by folding each side of the pigtail to the back along the middle of both sets of decreases (**A**).
2. Sew the edges together forming a slightly off center back seam **(B)**.
3. Press flat and do not stuff. Sewing through the cast on edges of pigtails, attach them to each side of the head, making sure the back seam is facing towards the back of the completed head, then bury loose ends in head **(C)**.

Clothing

Dress

1. Block all the pieces of the dress before making up.
2. Start by sewing the buttons into place on the back of the dress, matching them up with the button holes **(D)**.
3. Sew up the shoulder seams, make sure you leave a big enough gap to fit around Pippa's neck.
4. Sew up the edge seams, leaving a 1in (2.5cm) gap at the top for the arm holes.
5. Join the first and last petals of the flower together at the 'cast on' edge with a small stitch.
6. Sew onto the front of the dress then add a contrasting button in the center of the flower to finish **(E)**.

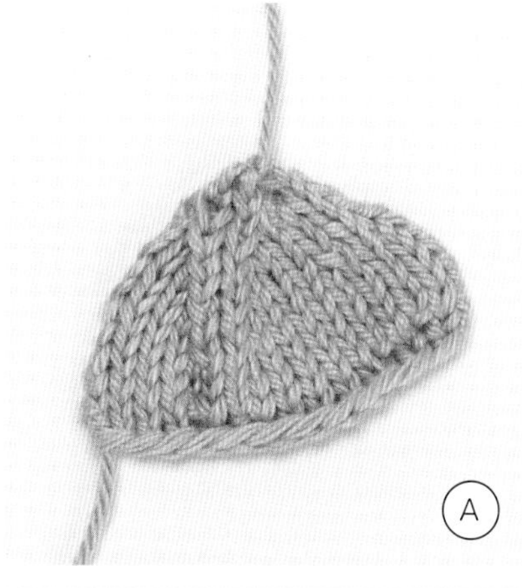
A

B

C

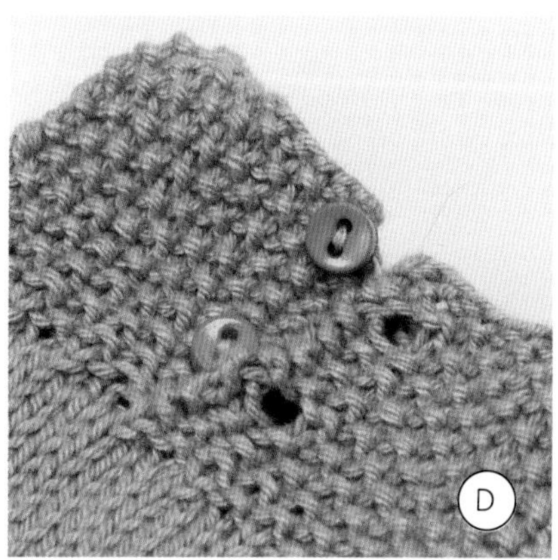
D

E

Cardigan

1. Block all the pieces of the cardigan before making up.
2. Start by sewing up the shoulder seams, then sew the sleeves to the front and back pieces, lining up the center of the sleeves to the shoulder seams.
3. Sew up the sleeve and body edge seams.
4. Sew the buttons into place on the right button band, matching them up with the button holes **(F)**.
5. Finally add the contrast stitching detail using a running stitch. Starting at the right hand side seam, work along the bottom front edge and up towards the neck, continuing all the way around until you reach your starting point **(F)**. Weave ends in along the side seam.

Head band

Sew the ends of the band together. Form the flowers by sewing the first and last cast on stitches together, then knot both tail ends together to secure. Using a sewing needle and thread, attach each flower to the band. To finish, work a French knot (see Techniques, page 107) in contrasting yarn in the center of each flower **(G)**.

F

G

Jane

When it comes to cakes and cafés, Jane is the queen. She's been to all the ones near where she lives because mummy is always 'gasping for a coffee' after a busy morning shopping. In her sophisticated beret, cardi and buttoned skirt, Jane will settle down happily with a babycino and an enormous double-choc muffin.

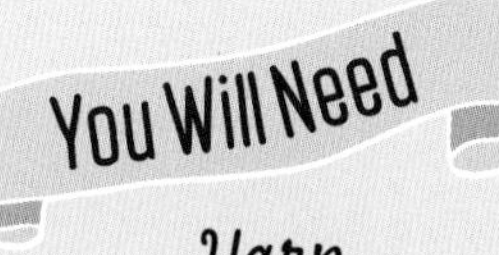

Yarn

- **Yarn A** Beige
- **Yarn B** Chestnut
- **Yarn C** Cream
- **Yarn D** Navy
- **Yarn E** Pale Denim
- **Yarn F** Mustard
- Oddments of black and red for eyes, mouth and details

Finished size

- 11in (28cm) tall

You will also need

- Size 2½ (3mm) knitting needles
- Size 1½ (2.5mm) knitting needles
- Size 1½ (2.5mm) double-pointed needles
- Stitch holder
- Tapestry needle
- 3 x ½in (15mm) circles of white felt
- Toy stuffing
- 6 x ¼in (6mm) buttons
- 2 short lengths of 5mm wide ribbon

Pattern

Cast on using the Long-tail (double cast-on) method (see Techniques, page 102) unless otherwise indicated. Where possible, leave long tails when you cast on and bind off and use these for the sewing up.

Head

Using Yarn A and Size 1½ (2.5mm) needles cast on 13 sts.

Starting at neck:

Row 1 (ws): Purl.

Row 2: [K1, M1] 12 times, K1. (25 sts)

Row 3: Purl.

Row 4: K3, [K1, M1] 7 times, K4, [K1, M1] 7 times, K4. (39 sts)

Rows 5–7: St st 3 rows.

Row 8: K3, [K3, M1] 4 times, K6, [K3, M1] 4 times, K6. (47 sts)

Cut yarn.

Rows 9–31: Using intarsia method (see Techniques, page 109) and working in st st, work Hair Chart. Start with a purl row (ws) at the bottom left-hand corner of chart, read purl rows (ws) from left to right and knit rows (rs) from right to left.

For top of head continue in Yarn B.

Row 32: K8, K2tog, K4, SSK, K15, K2tog, K4, SSK, K8. (43 sts)

Row 33: Purl.

Row 34: K8, K2tog, K2, SSK, K15, K2tog, K2, SSK, K8. (39 sts)

Row 35: Purl.

Row 36: K8, K2tog, SSK, K15, K2tog, SSK, K8. (35 sts)

Cut yarn, transfer the stitches onto a stitch holder.

Pigtails

(make 2)

Using 2.5mm dpns and Yarn B, cast on 5 sts and make an i-cord of 22 rows (see Techniques, page 107).

Body

T-SHIRT

Using Yarn C and Size 1½ (2.5mm) needles cast on 9 sts.

Starting at neck:

Row 1 (ws): Purl.

Row 2: K1, [K1, M1] 6 times, K2. (15 sts)

Row 3: Purl.

The T-shirt is now worked in a stripe pattern of 2 rows Yarn D and 4 rows Yarn C, starting with Yarn D.

Row 4: K2, [K1, M1] 3 times, K4, [K1, M1] 3 times, K3. (21 sts)

Row 5: Purl.

Row 6: K3, [K1, M1] 4 times, K6, [K1, M1] 4 times, K4. (29 sts)

Rows 7–9: St st 3 rows.

Row 10: K4, [K1, M1] 6 times, K8, [K1, M1] 6 times, K5. (41 sts)

Rows 11–15: St st 5 rows.

Row 16: K3, [K3, M1] 4 times, K8, [K3, M1] 4 times, K6. (49 sts)

Rows 17–27: St st 11 rows.

TOP OF LEGGINGS

Continue working the 49 sts on needle.

Change to Yarn E.

Rows 28–29: Knit 2 rows.

Rows 30–43: Starting with a knit row, st st 14 rows.

Bind off.

Arms

(make 2)

Using Yarn A and Size 1½ (2.5mm) needles cast on 12 sts.

Rows 1–3: Starting with a purl row (ws), st st 3 rows.

Row 4: Cast on 3 sts using Knit cast-on method (see Techniques, page 103), knit to end. (15 sts)

Row 5: Cast on 3 sts using Purl cast-on method (see Techniques, page 103), purl to end. (18 sts)

Rows 6–7: St st 2 rows.

Row 8: SSK, K14, K2tog. (16 sts)

Row 9: Purl.

Row 10: SSK, K12, K2tog. (14 sts)

Row 11: Purl.

Row 12: SSK, K10, K2tog. (12 sts)

SLEEVES

Continue working the 12 sts on needle.

The sleeves are worked in a stripe pattern of 2 rows Yarn D and 4 rows Yarn C throughout, starting with Yarn D.

Rows 13–14: Purl 2 rows.

Rows 15–47: Starting with a purl row, st st 33 rows.

Row 48: SSK, K8, K2tog. (10 sts)

Row 49: Purl.

Row 50: SSK, K6, K2tog. (8 sts)

Row 51: Purl.

Row 52: SSK, K4, K2tog. (6 sts)

Row 53: Purl.

Row 54: SSK, K2, K2tog. (4 sts)

Row 55: Purl.

Bind off.

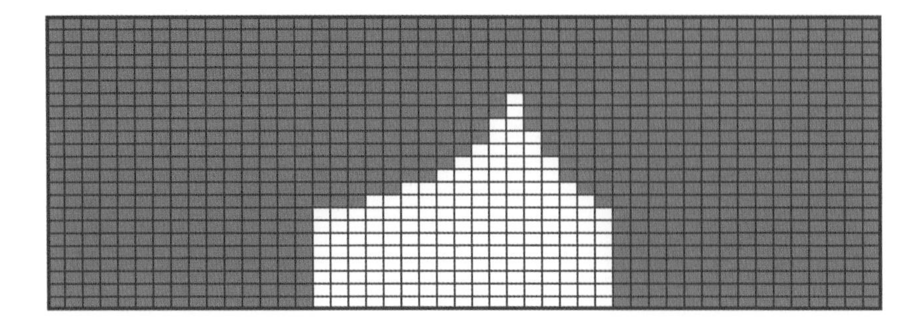

Hair Chart

□ = Yarn A
■ = Yarn B

Legs and sneakers

(make 2)

Using Yarn E and Size 1½ (2.5mm) needles cast on 12 sts.

Starting at base of sneaker:

Row 1 (ws): Purl

Row 2: K1, M1, K3, [K1, M1] 3 times, K4, M1, K1. (17 sts)

Row 3: Purl.

Row 4: [K1, M1] 2 times, K3, [K1, M1] 2 times, K2, [K1, M1] 2 times, K3, [K1, M1] 2 times, K1. (25 sts)

Row 5: Purl.

Row 6: [K2, M1] 2 times, K2, [K2, M1] 2 times, K3, [K2, M1] 2 times, K2, [K2, M1] 2 times, K2. (33 sts)

Row 7: Purl.

Change to Yarn C.

Row 8: [K3, M1] 2 times, K1, [K3, M1] 2 times, K4, [K3, M1] 2 times, K1, [K3, M1] 2 times, K3. (41 sts)

Row 9: Knit.

Row 10: Purl.

The next 8 rows use intarsia method (see Techniques, page 109) for changing yarns:

(D) = Use Yarn D. (C) = Use Yarn C.

Row 11: (D) P14, (C) P13, (D) P14.

Row 12: (D) K14, (C) K13, (D) K14.

Row 13: (D) P14, (C) P13, (D) P14.

Row 14: (D) K14, (C) K1, SSK, K7, K2tog, K1, (D) K14. (39 sts)

Row 15: (D) P14, (C) P11, (D) P14.

Row 16: (D) K14, (C) K1, SSK, K5, K2tog, K1, (D) K14. (37 sts)

Row 17: (D) P14, (C) P9, (D) P14.

Row 18: (D) K7, (C) K8, SSK, K3, K2tog, K8, (D) K7. (35 sts)

Change to Yarn C.

Row 19: Purl.

Row 20: P8, [K7, SSK, K1, K2tog, K7] bind off these middle 17 sts as you work them, P to end. (16 sts)

LEGS AND LEGGINGS

Continue working the 16 sts on needle.

Change to Yarn A.

Row 21: P7, P2tog, P7. (15 sts)

Rows 22–31: St st 10 rows.

Change to Yarn D.

Row 32–33: Knit 2 rows.

Change to Yarn E.

Row 34–35: Starting with a knit row, st st 2 rows.

Change to Yarn D.

Row 36–37: St st 2 rows.

Rows 38–69: Rpt last 4 rows, 8 more times.

Change to Yarn E.

Row 70–77: St st 8 rows.

Bind off.

Skirt

Using Yarn E and Size 2½ (3mm) needles cast on 57 sts.

Row 1 (ws): Knit.

Row 2: Knit.

Row 3: P27, K3, P27.

Row 4: Knit.

Rows 5–14: Rpt last 2 rows, 5 more times.

Row 15: P15, K8, P4, K3, P4, K8, P15.

Row 16: Knit.

Rows 17–22: Rpt last 2 rows, 3 more times.

Row 23: P17, K6, P4, K3, P4, K6, P17.

Row 24: Knit.

Row 25: P18, K5, P4, K3, P4, K5, P18.

Row 26: Knit.

Row 27: P19, K4, P4, K3, P4, K4, P19.

Row 28: Knit.

Row 29: P19, K4, P4, K3, P4, K4, P19.

Row 30: [K2, K2tog] to last st, K1. (43 sts)

Row 31: K3, [P1, K6] 2 times, P1, K7, [P1, K6] 2 times, P1, K3.

Row 32: Knit.

Row 33: K3, [P1, K6] 2 times, P1, K7, [P1, K6] 2 times, P1, K3.

Bind off.

Cardigan

The cardigan is worked in one piece from the top down.

Using Yarn F and Size 2½ (3mm) needles cast on 33 sts.

Row 1 (ws): Knit.

Row 2: K1, YO, K2tog, knit to end.

Row 3: K3, purl to last 3 sts, K3.

Row 4: K3, [Kfb, K1] to last 4 sts, Kfb, K3. (47 sts)

Row 5: K3, purl to last 3 sts, K3.

Rows 6–7: Knit 2 rows.

Row 8: K3, [Kfb, K2] to last 5 sts, Kfb, K4. (61 sts)

Row 9: K3, purl to last 3 sts, K3.

Rows 10–11: Knit 2 rows.

Row 12: K3, [Kfb, K3] to last 2 sts, K2. (75 sts)

Row 13: K3, purl to last 3 sts, K3.

Rows 14–15: Knit 2 rows.

Row 16: K3, [Kfb, K4] to last 2 sts, K2. (89 sts)

Row 17: K3, purl to last 3 sts, K3.

Row 18: K14, bind off 18 sts, K25, bind off 18 sts, K14. (53 sts)

Row 19: K3, P10, P2fb, P23, P2fb, P10, K3. (57 sts)

Row 20: Knit.

Row 21: K3, purl to last 3 sts, K3.

Rows 22–31: Rpt last 2 rows, 5 more times.

Rows 32–35: Knit 4 rows.

Bind off.

Scottie dog bag

Bag

Using Yarn D and Size 1½ (2.5mm) needles cast on 24 sts.

Row 1 (ws): Purl.

Row 2: [K1, M1, K10, M1, K1] 2 times. (28 sts)

Row 3: Purl.

Bag Chart A is placed in the following rows Using intarsia method (see Techniques, page 109) and worked in st st. Starting at the bottom right hand corner, read knit rows (rs) from right to left and purl rows (ws) from left to right.

Row 4: K2, work Bag Chart A, K15.

Row 5: P15, work Bag Chart A, P2.

Rows 6–15: Rpt the last 2 rows, 5 more times.

Rows 16–17: St st 2 rows.

Row 18: K7, YO, K2tog, knit to end.

Row 19: Purl.

Bind off.

Handle

Using Yarn D and Size 2½ (3mm) needles cast on 60 sts.

Row 1 (ws): Knit and bind off all stitches.

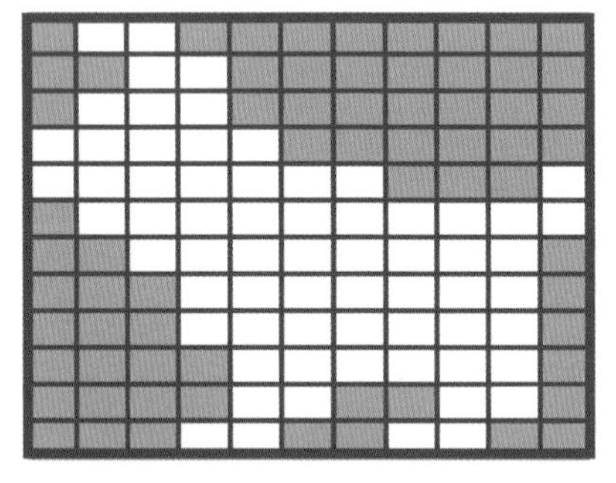

Bag Chart A

□ = Yarn C

▩ = Yarn D

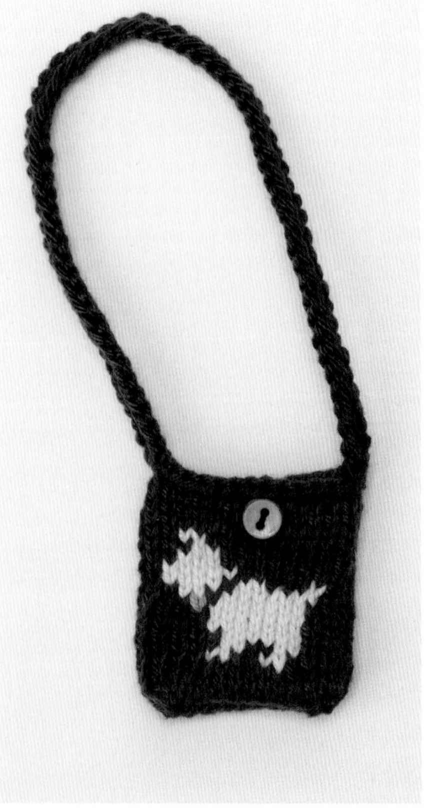

Beret

Using Yarn E and Size 2½ (3mm) needles cast on 36 sts.

Row 1 (ws): Knit.

Rows 2–3: Knit 2 rows.

Row 4: Kfb to end. (72 sts)

Rows 5–13: St st 9 rows.

Row 14: [K5, sl2tog kw, K1, PSSO, K4] to end. (60 sts)

Row 15: Purl.

Row 16: [K4, sl2tog kw, K1, PSSO, K3] to end. (48 sts)

Row 17: Purl.

Row 18: [K3, sl2tog kw, K1, PSSO, K2] to end. (36 sts)

Row 19: Purl.

Row 20: [K2, sl2tog kw, K1, PSSO, K1] to end. (24 sts)

Row 21: Purl.

Row 22: [K1, sl2tog kw, K1, PSSO] to end. (12 sts)

Row 23: Purl.

Row 24: [K2tog] to end. (6 sts)

Row 25: Purl.

Row 26: [K2tog] to end. (3 sts)

Transfer the stitches onto a dpn and work an i-cord of 2 rows (see Techniques, page 107).

Cut yarn leaving a long tail, use a tapestry needle to thread tail through stitches left on needle and draw up.

Making Up

Doll

See Making Up Your Doll in Techniques, page 96.

Pigtails

Bend the i-cord in half forming a loop and tie the cast on and off tail ends together to secure. Sew these ends to the side of the completed head with a few stitches, then finish with a small piece of ribbon tied in a bow **(A)**.

Clothing & Accessories

Skirt

1. Block the skirt piece before making up.
2. Start by sewing the buttons down the center front of the skirt. Sew the back seam together.

Cardigan

1. Block the cardigan bfore making up.
2. Sew the button in place on the front button band, matching it up with the button hole **(B)**.

Bag

1. Using Bag Chart B, work the collar detail in Duplicate stitch (see Techniques, page 108).
2. Block the bag pieces before you make up.
3. Start by sewing the side and bottom edges of the bag together.
4. Then attach each end of the bag handle to the top edge of the bag with a couple of stitches.
5. Finally, sew the button into place on the inside back of bag, matching it up with the button hole **(C)**.

Beret

Sew the side edges of beret together, then block.

Tip

TO BLOCK THE BERET, STRETCH IT OVER A SMALL ROUND DISC OR LID, APPROX 2½IN (6.5CM) IN DIAMETER, THEN SPRAY WITH WATER AND LEAVE TO DRY.

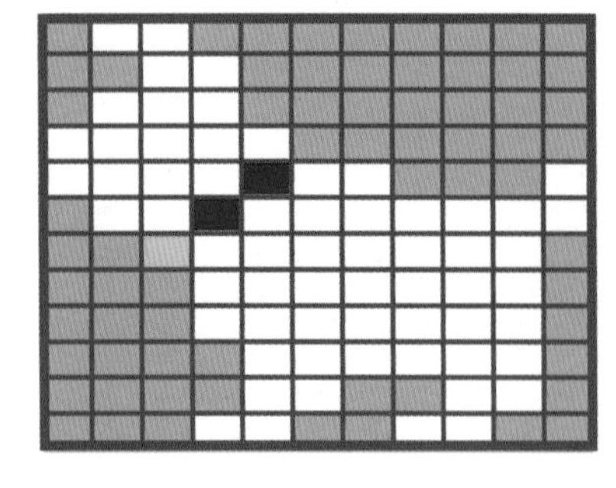

Bag Chart B

□ = Yarn C ▩ = Yarn D
▩ = Yarn F ■ = Oddment of red

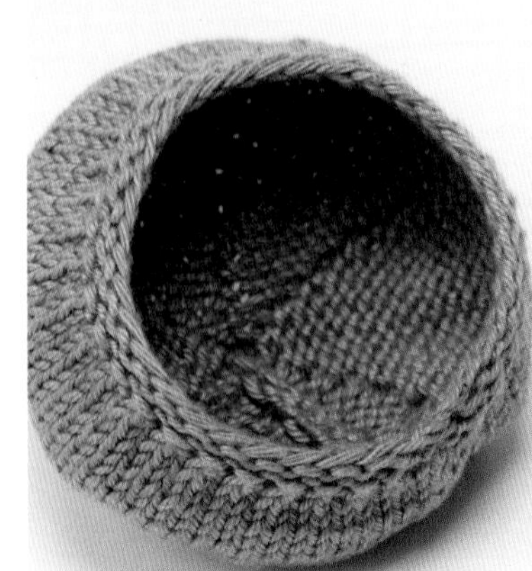

When her friend asked her to help re-pot some plants, Alice put on her favorite striped hoodie and got stuck in. She'd never gardened before and in retrospect the pristine white socks and pale yellow dress might have been a mistake—she hadn't realised there would be quite so much compost involved. Still, socks can always be washed ... by mummy.

Yarn

- **Yarn A** Tan
- **Yarn B** Brown
- **Yarn C** Pale Yellow
- **Yarn D** Pink
- **Yarn E** Red
- **Yarn F** White
- Oddments of black and red for eyes and mouth

Finished size

- 11in (28cm) tall

You will also need

- Size 2½ (3mm) knitting needles
- Size 1½ (2.5mm) knitting needles
- Size 1½ (2.5mm) double-pointed needles
- Stitch holder
- Tapestry needle
- 2 x ½in (15mm) circles of white felt
- Toy stuffing
- 7 x ¼in (6mm) buttons

Pattern

Cast on using the Long-tail (double cast-on) method (see Techniques, page 102) unless otherwise indicated. Where possible leave long tails when you cast on and bind off and use these for the sewing up.

Head

Using Yarn A and Size 1½ (2.5mm) needles cast on 13 sts.

Starting at neck:

Row 1 (ws): Purl.

Row 2: [K1, M1] 12 times, K1. (25 sts)

Row 3: Purl.

Row 4: K3, [K1, M1] 7 times, K4, [K1, M1] 7 times, K4. (39 sts)

Rows 5–7: St st 3 rows.

Row 8: K3, [K3, M1] 4 times, K6, [K3, M1] 4 times, K6. (47 sts)

Cut yarn.

Rows 9–31: Using intarsia method (see Techniques, page 109) and working in st st, work Hair Chart. Start with a purl row (ws) at the bottom left-hand corner of chart, read purl rows (ws) from left to right and knit rows (rs) from right to left.

For top of head continue in Yarn B.

Row 32: K8, K2tog, K4, SSK, K15, K2tog, K4, SSK, K8. (43 sts)

Row 33: Purl.

Row 34: K8, K2tog, K2, SSK, K15, K2tog, K2, SSK, K8. (39 sts)

Row 35: Purl.

Row 36: K8, K2tog, SSK, K15, K2tog, SSK, K8. (35 sts)

Cut yarn, transfer the stitches onto a stitch holder.

Hair bob

Using Yarn B and Size 1½ (2.5mm) needles cast on 29 sts.

Rows 1–3: Starting with a purl row (ws), st st 3 rows.

Cut yarn and transfer the stitches onto a second stitch holder.

Body

T-SHIRT

Using Yarn F and Size 1½ (2.5mm) needles cast on 9 sts.

Starting at neck:

Row 1 (ws): Purl.

Row 2: K1, [K1, M1] 6 times, K2. (15 sts)

Row 3: Purl.

Row 4: K2, [K1, M1] 3 times, K4, [K1, M1] 3 times, K3. (21 sts)

Row 5: Purl.

Row 6: K3, [K1, M1] 4 times, K6, [K1, M1] 4 times, K4. (29 sts)

Rows 7–9: St st 3 rows.

Row 10: K4, [K1, M1] 6 times, K8, [K1, M1] 6 times, K5. (41 sts)

Rows 11–15: St st 5 rows.

Row 16: K3, [K3, M1] 4 times, K8, [K3, M1] 4 times, K6. (49 sts)

Rows 17–26: St st 10 rows.

Rows 27: Knit.

KNICKERS

Continue working the 49 sts on needle.

Change to Yarn D.

Rows 28–43: Starting with a knit row, st st 16 rows.

Bind off.

Arms

(make 2)

Using Yarn A and Size 1½ (2.5mm) needles cast on 12 sts.

Rows 1–3: Starting with a purl row (ws), st st 3 rows.

Row 4: Cast on 3 sts using Knit cast-on method (see Techniques, page 103), knit to end. (15 sts)

Row 5: Cast on 3 sts using Purl cast-on method (see Techniques, page 103), purl to end. (18 sts)

Rows 6–7: St st 2 rows.

Row 8: SSK, K14, K2tog. (16 sts)

Row 9: Purl.

Row 10: SSK, K12, K2tog. (14 sts)

Row 11: Purl.

Row 12: SSK, K10, K2tog. (12 sts)

Rows 13–31: St st 19 rows.

SLEEVES

Continue working the 12 sts on needle.

Change to Yarn F.

Rows 32–33: Knit 2 rows.

Rows 34–47: Starting with a knit row, st st 14 rows.

Row 48: SSK, K8, K2tog. (10 sts)

Row 49: Purl.

Row 50: SSK, K6, K2tog. (8 sts)

Row 51: Purl.

Row 52: SSK, K4, K2tog. (6 sts)

Row 53: Purl.

Row 54: SSK, K2, K2tog. (4 sts)

Row 55: Purl.

Bind off.

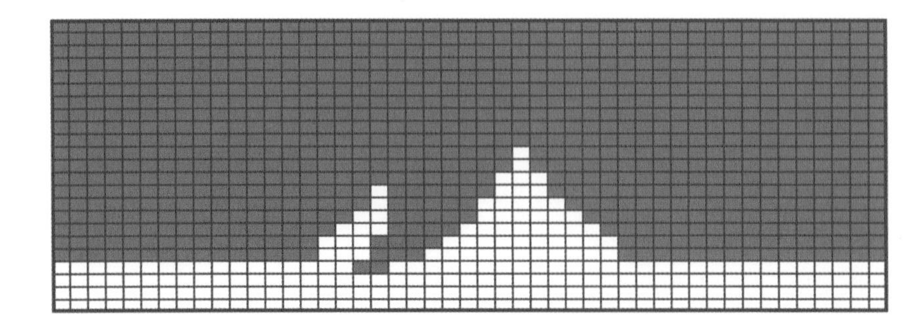

Hair Chart

□ = Yarn A

■ = Yarn B

Legs

(make 2)

Using Yarn A and Size 1½ (2.5mm) needles cast on 16 sts.

Starting at top of leg:

Rows 1–33: Starting with a purl row (ws), st st 33 rows.

SOCKS

Change to Yarn F.

Rows 34–37: Knit 4 rows.

Rows 38–39: Starting with knit row, st st 2 rows.

Change to Yarn C.

Rows 40–41: St st 2 rows.

Change to Yarn F.

Rows 42–55: St st 14 rows.

TOP OF FOOT

Row 56: Bind off 5 sts, knit to end. (11 sts)

Row 57: Bind off 5 sts pw, purl to end. (6 sts)

Rows 58–75: St st 18 rows.

Bind-off row: SSK, K2, K2tog (bind off all sts as you work them).

T-bar shoes

(make 2)

Using Yarn C and Size 1½ (2.5mm) needles cast on 12 sts.

Row 1 (ws): Purl.

Row 2: K1, M1, K3, [K1, M1] 3 times, K4, M1, K1. (17 sts)

Row 3: Purl.

Row 4: [K1, M1] 2 times, K3, [K1, M1] 2 times, K2, [K1, M1] 2 times, K3, [K1, M1] 2 times, K1. (25 sts)

Row 5: Purl.

Row 6: [K2, M1] 2 times, K2, [K2, M1] 2 times, K3, [K2, M1] 2 times, K2, [K2, M1] 2 times, K2. (33 sts)

Row 7: Purl.

Row 8: [K3, M1] 2 times, K1, [K3, M1] 2 times, K4, [K3, M1] 2 times, K1, [K3, M1] 2 times, K3. (41 sts)

Rows 9–13: St st 5 rows.

Row 14: K15, SSK, K7, K2tog, K15. (39 sts)

Row 15: Purl.

Row 16: K15, SSK, K5, K2tog, K15. (37 sts)

Row 17: Purl.

Row 18: Bind off 15 sts, SSK, K3, K2tog, K to end. (20 sts)

Row 19: Bind off 15 sts pw, P to end. (5 sts)

Row 20: SSK, K1, K2tog. (3 sts)

Row 21: K1, P1, K1.

Row 22: Knit.

Rows 23–29: Rpt last 2 rows, 3 more times, then rpt row 21 once more.

Row 30: K1, sl1 pw with yarn at back, K1.

Row 31: K1, sl1 pw with yarn at front, K1.

Bind off.

Shoe straps

(make 2)

Using Yarn C and Size 1½ (2.5mm) needles cast on 10 sts.

Row 1 (ws): K7, P3.

Row 2: K3, turn.

Row 3: P3.

Bind off kw.

Pinafore Dress

Front

Using Yarn C and Size 2½ (3mm) needles cast on 37 sts.

Row 1 (ws): Knit.

Rows 2–3: Starting with a knit row, st st 2 rows.

Row 4: [K4, P2] to last st, K1.

Rows 5–7: St st 3 rows.

Row 8: K1, [P2, K4] to end.

Rows 9–11: St st 3 rows.

Rows 12–27: Rpt rows 4–11, twice more.

Row 28: [K1, K2tog] to last st, K1. (25 sts)

Row 29: [K1, P1] 3 times, K2, P9, K2, [P1, K1] 3 times.

Row 30: [P1, K1] 3 times, K13, [K1, P1] 3 times.

Rows 31–34: Rpt last 2 rows, 2 more times.

Row 35: Bind off 6 sts in pattern, K2, P9, K2, bind off 6 sts in pattern. (13 sts)

Cut yarn, then rejoin to work on remaining 13 sts.

Row 36: Knit.

Row 37: K2, P9, K2.

Rows 38–45: Rpt last 2 rows, 4 more times.

Rows 46–47: Knit 2 rows.

Bind off.

Back

Using Yarn C and Size 2½ (3mm) needles cast on 37 sts.

Row 1 (ws): Knit.

Rows 2–3: Starting with a knit row, st st 2 rows.

Row 4: [K4, P2] to last st, K1.

Rows 5–7: St st 3 rows.

Row 8: K1, [P2, K4] to end.

Rows 9–11: St st 3 rows.

Rows 12–27: Rpt rows 4–11, twice more.

Row 28: [K1, K2tog] to last st, K1. (25 sts)

Row 29: [K1, P1] to last st, K1.

Row 30: [P1, K1] to last st, P1.

Rows 31–34: Rpt last 2 rows, 2 more times.

Bind off in pattern.

Dress straps

(make 2)

Using Yarn C and Size 2½ (3mm) needles cast on 28 sts.

Row 1 (ws): K25, P3.

Row 2: K3, turn.

Row 3: P3.

Bind off kw.

Hoodie

Right front

Using Yarn E and Size 2½ (3mm) needles cast on 16 sts.

Row 1 (ws): Knit.

Rows 2–3: Knit 2 rows.

Use Intarsia method (see Techniques, page 109) for changing yarn across the following rows.

(C) = Use Yarn C. (D) = Use Yarn D. (E) = Use Yarn E.

Row 4: (E) K3, (D) K13.

Row 5: (D) P13, (E) K3.

Row 6: (E) K3, (C) K13.

Row 7: (C) P13, (E) K3.

Rows 8–33: Rpt the last 4 rows, 6 more times, rpt rows 4 and 5 once more.

Bind off.

Left front

Using Yarn E and Size 2½ (3mm) needles cast on 16 sts.

Row 1 (ws): Knit.

Rows 2–3: Knit 2 rows.

Use Intarsia technique (see Techniques) for changing yarn across the following rows.

(C) = Use Yarn C. (D) = Use Yarn D. (E) = Use Yarn E.

Row 4: (D) K13, (E) K3.

Row 5: (E) K3, (D) P13.

Row 6: (C) K13, (E) K3.

Row 7: (E) K3, (C) P13.

Rows 8–19: Rpt the last 4 rows, 3 more times.

Row 20: (D) K13, (E) K1, YO, K2tog.

Row 21: (E) K1, Ktbl, K1, (D) P13.

Rows 22–23: Rpt rows 6 & 7.

Rows 24–25: Rpt rows 4 & 5.

Row 26: (C) K13, (E) K1, YO, K2tog.

Row 27: (E) K1, Ktbl, K1, (C) P13.

Rows 28–29: Rpt rows 4 & 5.

Rows 30–31: Rpt rows 6 & 7.

Rows 32–33: Rpt rows 20 & 21.

Bind off.

Back

Using Yarn E and Size 2½ (3mm) needles cast on 29 sts.

Row 1 (ws): Knit.

Rows 2–3: Knit 2 rows.

Rows 4–33: Starting with a knit row and Yarn D, st st 30 rows working in a stripe pattern repeat of 2 rows Yarn D and 2 rows Yarn C throughout.

Bind off.

Sleeves

(make 2)

Using Yarn E and Size 2½ (3mm) needles cast on 22 sts.

Row 1 (ws): Knit.

Rows 2–3: Knit 2 rows.

Change to Yarn D.

Rows 4–21: Starting with a knit row, st st 20 rows.

Bind off.

Hood

Using Yarn E and Size 2½ (3mm) needles cast on 50 sts.

Row 1 (ws): Knit.

Rows 2–3: Knit 2 rows.

Change to Yarn D.

Rows 4–30: Starting with a knit row and Yarn D, st st 27 rows working in a stripe pattern repeat of 2 rows Yarn D and 2 rows Yarn C throughout, ending with 1 row of Yarn C.

Cut yarn leaving a long tail, transfer the stitches onto a stitch holder.

Making Up

Doll

See Making Up Your Doll in Techniques, page 96. Please note, before joining the top edges of the head together, position a small bow on the front of the hair and sew in place (see **A** for position).

Hair bob

1. Transfer all the stitches of the hair bob onto a dpn. Using Kitchener stitch (see Techniques, page 100) and the bind off tail, attach the hair piece to the bottom of the head working around the first row of hair stitches, from right to left, as follows:
2. Insert the tapestry needle through the back of the hair 'V' stitch on the head and pull the yarn through **(B)**.
3. Next insert the tapestry needle knitwise through the first stitch on the dpn, slipping it off the dpn as you do so **(C)**.
4. Insert the tapestry needle purlwise through the next stitch on the dpn, but do not slip off **(D)**.
5. Repeat steps 2 to 4 until all stitches have been worked.

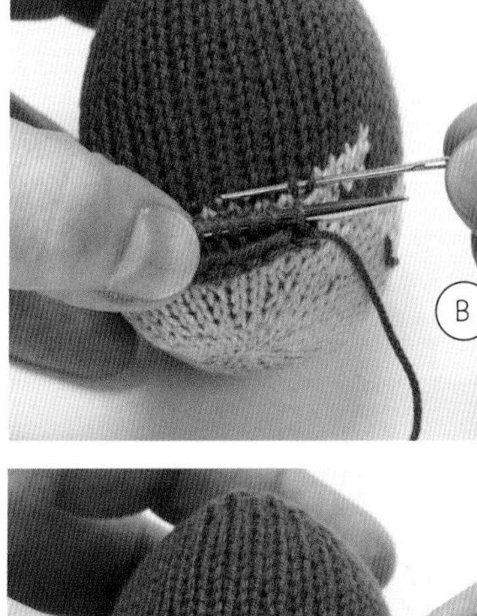

Clothing

Pinafore dress

1. Block all the pieces of the pinafore before making up (see Techniques, page 100).
2. Start by sewing up the edge seams matching the pattern up.
3. Sew the straps onto the back edge of the pinafore, around ¾in (2cm) either side of the center back **(E)**. Crossing the straps over each other first, sew the other end of the straps to the top corners of the bib and then sew on the buttons.

Hoodie

1. Block all the pieces of the Hoodie before making up.
2. Using Mattress stitch (see Techniques, page 105) and starting at the outside edges, sew the front and back pieces together at the shoulders, creating a ¾in (2cm) wide shoulder seam at both sides.
3. Transfer the first 25 stitches of the hood onto a dpn and the next 25 stitches onto a second dpn. Join these stitches together using Kitchener stitch (see tip below) to create an invisible seam for the back of the hood.
4. Next sew the bottom edge of the hood around the neck opening, lining up the invisible back seem of the hood to the center back and the contrast edging of the hood with the button bands at the front.
5. Sew the sleeves to the front and back pieces, lining up the center of the sleeves to the shoulder seams.
6. Sew up the sleeve and body edge seams to finish.
7. Sew the buttons into place on the right button band, matching them up with the button holes.

Tip

IF YOU ARE UNFAMILIAR WITH KITCHENER STITCH, SEE 'JOINING THE TOP EDGES OF THE HEAD USING KITCHENER STITCH' IN TECHNIQUES, PAGE 100.

Florence

Florence is very good at maths. This is important because when she set her heart on a rabbit ornament, she was able to work out exactly how long it would take to save up enough pocket money to buy it. Now she's at the shops in her smartest outfit—a knitted skirt and rosy sweater—and the bunny is hers!

Yarn

- **Yarn A** Cream
- **Yarn B** Auburn
- **Yarn C** Pale Pink
- **Yarn D** Cerise
- **Yarn E** Moss Green
- Oddments of black and red for eyes and mouth

Finished size

- 11in (28cm) tall

You will also need

- Size 2½ (3mm) knitting needles
- Size 1½ (2.5mm) knitting needles
- Size 1½ (2.5mm) double-pointed needles
- Stitch holder
- Tapestry needle
- 3 x ½in (15mm) circles of white felt
- Toy stuffing
- 5 x ¼in (6mm) buttons

Pattern

Cast on using the Long-tail (double cast-on) method (see Techniques, page 102) unless otherwise indicated. Where possible leave long tails when you cast on and bind off and use these for the sewing up.

Head

Using Yarn A and Size 1½ (2.5mm) needles cast on 13 sts.

Starting at neck:

Row 1 (ws): Purl.

Row 2: [K1, M1] 12 times, K1. (25 sts)

Row 3: Purl.

Row 4: K3, [K1, M1] 7 times, K4, [K1, M1] 7 times, K4. (39 sts)

Rows 5–7: St st 3 rows.

Row 8: K3, [K3, M1] 4 times, K6, [K3, M1] 4 times, K6. (47 sts)

Cut yarn.

Rows 9–31: Using intarsia method (see Techniques, page 109) and working in st st, work Hair Chart. Start with a purl row (ws) at the bottom left-hand corner of chart, read purl rows (ws) from left to right and knit rows (rs) from right to left.

For top of head continue in Yarn B.

Row 32: K8, K2tog, K4, SSK, K15, K2tog, K4, SSK, K8. (43 sts)

Row 33: Purl.

Row 34: K8, K2tog, K2, SSK, K15, K2tog, K2, SSK, K8. (39 sts)

Row 35: Purl.

Row 36: K8, K2tog, SSK, K15, K2tog, SSK, K8. (35 sts)

Cut yarn, transfer the stitches onto a stitch holder.

Hair slide

Flower

Using Yarn C and Size 1½ (2.5mm) needles cast on 20 sts.

Row 1 (ws): *P1, sl2 pw, pass 1st slip st over 2nd, transfer remaining slip st back onto Left-hand needle and purl, P1; rpt from * to end. (15 sts)

Change to Yarn D.

Row 2: K1, K2 tog to end. (8 sts)

Bind off pw.

Cut yarn leaving a long tail, use a tapestry needle to thread tail through the bind off stitches and draw up.

Leaf

Using Yarn E and Size 1½ (2.5mm) needles cast on 5 sts.

Row 1 (ws): P3, P1 then slip this stitch back onto Left-hand needle, turn.

Row 2: Pass 1st stitch on right-hand needle over the 2nd, knit and bind off remaining sts.

Body

Using Yarn A and Size 1½ (2.5mm) needles cast on 9 sts.

Starting at neck:

Row 1 (ws): Purl.

Row 2: K1, [K1, M1] 6 times, K2. (15 sts)

Row 3: Purl.

Row 4: K2, [K1, M1] 3 times, K4, [K1, M1] 3 times, K3. (21 sts)

Row 5: Purl.

Row 6: K3, [K1, M1] 4 times, K6, [K1, M1] 4 times, K4. (29 sts)

Rows 7–9: St st 3 rows.

Row 10: K4, [K1, M1] 6 times, K8, [K1, M1] 6 times, K5. (41 sts)

Rows 11–15: St st 5 rows.

Row 16: K3, [K3, M1] 4 times, K8, [K3, M1] 4 times, K6. (49 sts)

Rows 17–27: St st 11 rows.

KNICKERS

Continue working the 49 sts on needle.

Change to Yarn D.

Rows 28–29: Knit 2 rows.

Rows 30–43: Using Fair Isle method (see Techniques, page 108) and working in st st, work Knicker Chart across the stitches, repeating the stitches within the red border 11 times.

Bind off.

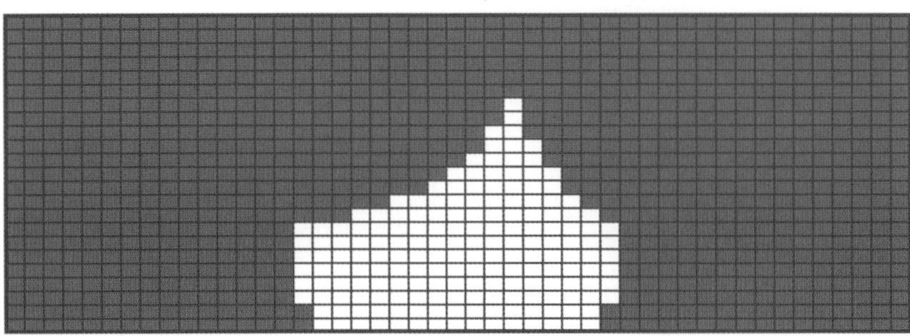

Hair Chart

□ = Yarn A
■ = Yarn B

Arms

(make 2)

Using Yarn A and Size 1½ (2.5mm) needles cast on 12 sts.

Rows 1–3: Starting with a purl row (ws), st st 3 rows.

Row 4: Cast on 3 sts using Knit cast-on method (see Techniques, page 103), knit to end. (15 sts)

Row 5: Cast on 3 sts using Purl cast-on method (see Techniques, page 103), purl to end. (18 sts)

Rows 6–7: St st 2 rows.

Row 8: SSK, K14, K2tog. (16 sts)

Row 9: Purl.

Row 10: SSK, K12, K2tog. (14 sts)

Row 11: Purl.

Row 12: SSK, K10, K2tog. (12 sts)

Rows 13–47: St st 35 rows.

Row 48: SSK, K8, K2tog. (10 sts)

Row 49: Purl.

Row 50: SSK, K6, K2tog. (8 sts)

Row 51: Purl.

Row 52: SSK, K4, K2tog. (6 sts)

Row 53: Purl.

Row 54: SSK, K2, K2tog. (4 sts)

Row 55: Purl.

Bind off.

Legs

(make 2)

Using Yarn A and Size 1½ (2.5mm) needles cast on 16 sts.

Starting at top of leg:

Rows 1–43: Starting with a purl row (ws), st st 43 rows.

SOCKS

Change to Yarn C.

Rows 44–55: St st 12 rows.

TOP OF FOOT

Row 56: Bind off 5 sts, knit to end. (11 sts)

Row 57: Bind off 5 sts pw, purl to end. (6 sts)

Rows 58–75: St st 18 rows.

Bind-off row: SSK, K2, K2tog (bind off all sts as you work them).

Sock frills

(make 2)

Using Yarn C and Size 1½ (2.5mm) needles cast on 17 sts.

Row 1 (ws): [P1, Pfb] to last st, P1. (25 sts)

Row 2: Knit.

Row 3: Purl.

Row 4: Bind off 1 st, *slip remaining stitch back onto Left-hand needle, then cast on 1 st using Knit cast-on method (see Techniques, page 103), bind off 3 sts; rpt from *to end.

Mary Jane shoes

(make 2)

Using Yarn D and Size 1½ (2.5mm) needles cast on 12 sts.

Row 1 (ws): Purl.

Row 2: K1, M1, K3, [K1, M1] 3 times, K4, M1, K1. (17 sts)

Row 3: Purl.

Row 4: [K1, M1] 2 times, K3, [K1, M1] 2 times, K2, [K1, M1] 2 times, K3, [K1, M1] 2 times, K1. (25 sts)

Row 5: Purl.

Row 6: [K2, M1] 2 times, K2, [K2, M1] 2 times, K3, [K2, M1] 2 times, K2, [K2, M1] 2 times, K2. (33 sts)

Row 7: Purl.

Row 8: [K3, M1] 2 times, K1, [K3, M1] 2 times, K4, [K3, M1] 2 times, K1, [K3, M1] 2 times, K3. (41 sts)

Rows 9–13: St st 5 rows.

Row 14: K15, SSK, K7, K2tog, K15. (39 sts)

Row 15: Purl.

Row 16: K15, SSK, K5, K2tog, K15. (37 sts)

Row 17: Purl.

Bind-off row: K15, SSK, K3, K2tog, K15 (bind off all stitches as you work them).

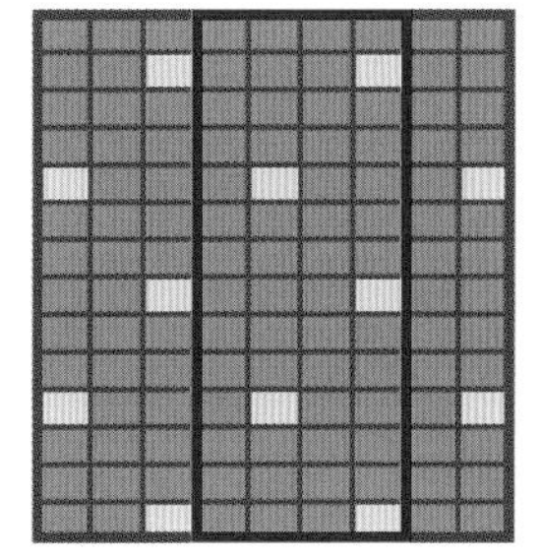

Knicker Chart

■ = Yarn D

□ = Yarn C

□ = Repeat

Shoe straps

(make 2)

Using Yarn D and Size 1½ (2.5mm) needles cast on 10 sts.

Row 1 (ws): K7, P3.

Row 2: K3, turn.

Row 3: P3.

Bind off kw.

Skirt

Using Yarn E and Size 2½ (3mm) needles cast on 66 sts.

Row 1 (ws): Knit.

Row 2: [YO, K2, slip YO over K2] to end.

Row 3: Purl.

Rows 4–21: Rpt last 2 rows, 9 more times.

Row 22: [K2tog, K1] to end. (44 sts)

Rows 23–27: St st 5 rows.

Change to Yarn D.

Row 28: [K5, sl1 pw, K5] to end.

Row 29: [K5, sl1 pw wyif, K5] to end.

Change to Yarn E.

Row 30: Knit.

Row 31: Purl.

Bind off.

Sweater

Front of sweater

Using Yarn C and Size 2½ (3mm) needles cast on 27 sts.

Row 1 (ws): Knit.

Rows 2–3: Knit 2 rows.

Rows 4–11: Starting with a knit row, st st 8 rows.

The Sweater Chart is placed in the following rows using intarsia method (see Techniques, page 109) and worked in st st. Starting at the bottom right hand corner, read knit rows (rs) from right to left and purl rows (ws) from left to right.

Row 12: K6, work Sweater Chart, K5.

Row 13: P5, work Sweater Chart, P6.

Rows 14–26: Rpt the last 2 rows, 6 more times, then rpt row 12 once more.

Rows 27–33: St st 7 rows.

Bind off.

Back of sweater

Using Yarn C and Size 1½ (2.5mm) needles cast on 27 sts.

Row 1 (ws): Knit.

Rows 2–3: Knit 2 rows.

Rows 4–19: Starting with a knit row, st st 16 rows.

RIGHT BUTTON PLACKET

Row 20: K15, turn (15 sts).

Row 21: K3, P12.

Rows 22–23: Rpt last 2 rows.

Row 24: K13, YO, K2tog, turn.

Row 25: K1, Ktbl, K1, P12.

Rows 26–31: Rpt rows 20 and 21, 3 more times.

Row 32: Rpt row 24.

Row 33: Rpt row 25.

Bind off 15 sts, cut yarn.

LEFT BUTTON PLACKET

Row 1: Return to sts still on needle, rejoin Yarn C and pick up and knit 3 sts from BEHIND first row of right button placket (see Techniques, page 104: Picking Up Stitches), knit across stitches on Left-hand needle. (15 sts)

Row 2: P12, K3.

Row 3: Knit.

Rows 4–13: Rpt last 2 rows, 5 more times.

Row 14: P12, K3.

Bind off.

Sleeves of sweater

(make 2)

Using Yarn C and Size 2½ (3mm) needles cast on 20 sts.

Row 1 (ws): Knit.

Rows 2–17: Starting with a knit row, st st 16 rows.

Bind off.

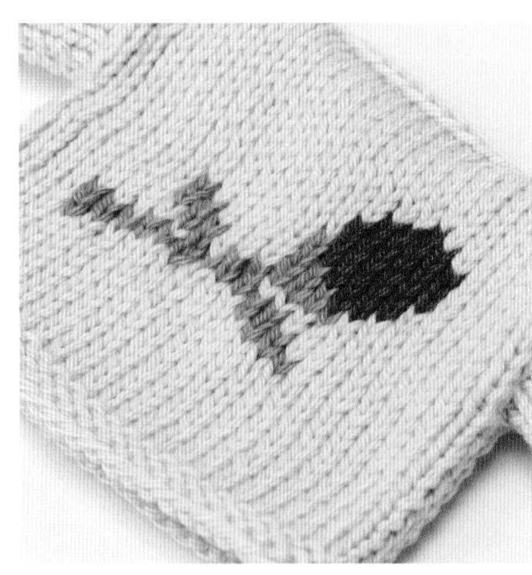

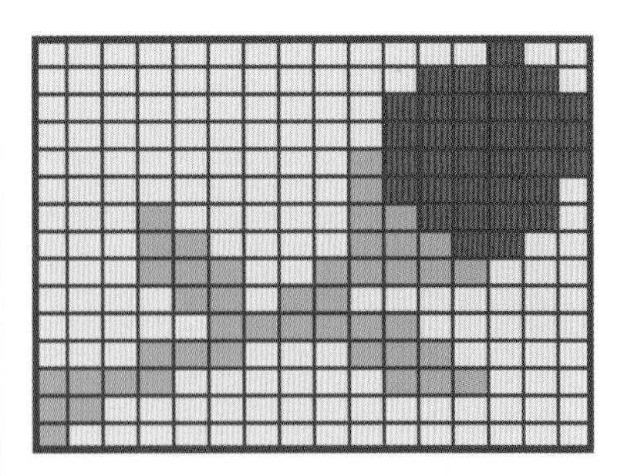

Sweater Chart

□ = Yarn C

■ = Yarn D

▩ = Yarn E

Making up

Doll

See Making Up Your Doll in Techniques, page 96. Please note, attach the sock frills before sewing the legs to the body, and sew hair slide in place before joining the top edges of the head together.

SOCK FRILLS

Sew frill in place on completed leg. Place tapestry needle through the back of the 'V' stitch on the first row of cream **(A)**, then down through the cast-on stitch of the frill **(B)** and back up through the next cast-on stitch **(C)**. Continue in this manner all the way around the sock, making sure both edges of the frill meet at the back. Sew up the back seam of the frill.

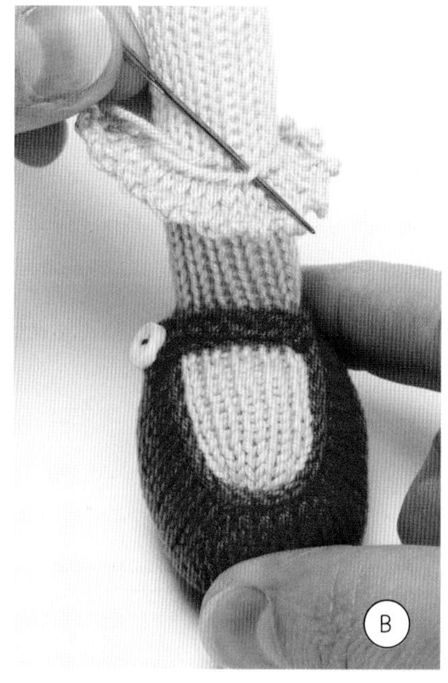

Hair slide

1. Secure the leaf to the back of the flower with a couple of stitches.
2. Do not weave in or tie off any of the loose ends yet. As the flower is quite small, it's best to push any loose ends through to the inside of the head before sewing in place.
3. Position hair slide on Florence's head and sew in place, stitching through the back loops on the first row of Yarn D and then through the back of the hair stitches **(D)**.

Clothing

Sweater

1. Block all the pieces of the sweater before making up.
2. Start by sewing the buttons into place on the back of the sweater, matching them up with the button holes **(E)**.
3. Sew up shoulder seams, leaving a big enough gap to fit around Florence's neck. Sew sleeves to front and back pieces, lining up center of sleeves to shoulder seams. Sew up sleeve and sweater edge seams.

Skirt

1. Block skirt before sewing it up.
2. Starting at the hem, sew the edges of the skirt together, creating a center back seam.
3. Sew button onto the center front of belt **(F)**.

D

E

F

Martha

When she grows up, Martha is going to be a teacher. She's had lots of practice writing on a chalkboard, adding up sums and putting gold stars on her finished work. She reckons jeans and a bright tunic with matching red shoes are the perfect cheerful, but practical outfit for a primary school teacher. She can't wait to get into the classroom!

Yarn

- **Yarn A** Mocha
- **Yarn B** Chocolate
- **Yarn C** Bright Red
- **Yarn D** White
- **Yarn E** Denim Blue
- **Yarn F** Sky Blue
- Oddments of black and red for eyes and mouth

Finished size

- 11in (28cm) tall

You will also need

- Size 2½ (3mm) knitting needles
- Size 1½ (2.5mm) knitting needles
- Size 1½ (2.5mm) double-pointed needles
- Stitch holder
- Stitch markers
- Tapestry needle
- 3 x ½in (15mm) circles of white felt
- Toy stuffing
- 7 x ¼in (6mm) buttons
- 2 short lengths of 5mm wide ribbon

Pattern

Cast on using the Long-tail (double cast-on) method (see Techniques, page 102) unless otherwise indicated. Where possible leave long tails when you cast on and bind off and use these for the sewing up.

Head

Using Yarn A and Size 1½ (2.5mm) needles cast on 13 sts.

Starting at neck:

Row 1 (ws): Purl.

Row 2: [K1, M1] 12 times, K1. (25 sts)

Row 3: Purl.

Row 4: K3, [K1, M1] 7 times, K4, [K1, M1] 7 times, K4. (39 sts)

Rows 5–7: St st 3 rows.

Row 8: K3, [K3, M1] 4 times, K6, [K3, M1] 4 times, K6. (47 sts)

Cut yarn.

Rows 9–31: Using intarsia method (see Techniques, page 109) and working in st st, work Hair Chart. Start with a purl row (ws) at the bottom left-hand corner of chart, read purl rows (ws) from left to right and knit rows (rs) from right to left.

For top of head continue in Yarn B.

Row 32: K8, K2tog, K4, SSK, K15, K2tog, K4, SSK, K8. (43 sts)

Row 33: Purl.

Row 34: K8, K2tog, K2, SSK, K15, K2tog, K2, SSK, K8. (39 sts)

Row 35: Purl.

Row 36: K8, K2tog, SSK, K15, K2tog, SSK, K8. (35 sts)

Cut yarn, transfer the stitches onto a stitch holder.

Buns

(make 2)

Using Yarn B and Size 1½ (2.5mm) needles cast on 4 sts.

Row 1 (ws): Purl.

Row 2: Kfb to end. (8 sts)

Row 3: Purl.

Row 4: kfb 2 times, K4, kfb 2 times. (12 sts)

Row 5: Purl.

Row 6: Kfb, K10, Kfb. (14 sts)

Rows 7–13: St st 7 rows.

Row 14: K2tog, K10, K2tog. (12 sts)

Row 15: Purl.

Row 16: [K2tog] 2 times, K4, [K2tog] 2 times. (8 sts)

Row 17: Purl.

Row 18: [K2tog] to end. (4 sts)

Cut yarn leaving a long tail, thread tail through the stitches left on needle and draw up.

Body

Using Yarn A and Size 1½ (2.5mm) needles cast on 9 sts.

Starting at neck

Row 1 (ws): Purl.

Row 2: K1, [K1, M1] 6 times, K2. (15 sts)

Row 3: Purl.

Row 4: K2, [K1, M1] 3 times, K4, [K1, M1] 3 times, K3. (21 sts)

Row 5: Purl.

Row 6: K3, [K1, M1] 4 times, K6, [K1, M1] 4 times, K4. (29 sts)

Rows 7–9: St st 3 rows.

Row 10: K4, [K1, M1] 6 times, K8, [K1, M1] 6 times, K5. (41 sts)

Rows 11–15: St st 5 rows.

Row 16: K3, [K3, M1] 4 times, K8, [K3, M1] 4 times, K6. (49 sts)

Rows 17–27: St st 11 rows.

KNICKERS

Continue working the 49 sts on needle.

Starting with Yarn D, the knickers are worked in a stripe pattern of 2 rows Yarn D and 2 rows Yarn F throughout.

Rows 28–29: Knit 2 rows.

Rows 30–43: Starting with a knit row, st st 14 rows.

Bind off using Yarn D.

Arms

(make 2)

Using Yarn A and Size 1½ (2.5mm) needles cast on 12 sts.

Rows 1–3: Starting with a purl row (ws), st st 3 rows.

Row 4: Cast on 3 sts using Knit cast-on method (see Techniques, page 103), knit to end. (15 sts)

Row 5: Cast on 3 sts using Purl cast-on method (see Techniques, page 103), purl to end. (18 sts)

Rows 6–7: St st 2 rows.

Row 8: SSK, K14, K2tog. (16 sts)

Row 9: Purl.

Row 10: SSK, K12, K2tog. (14 sts)

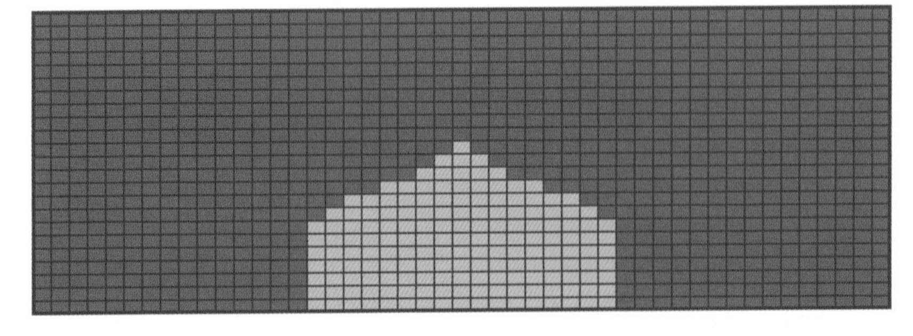

Hair Chart

▫ = Yarn A ▪ = Yarn B

Legs with T-bar shoes

Right Leg and shoe

1. Begin by sewing the top of the shoe to the base of the leg and around the foot in the same way as the Mary Jane shoes, continuing along the same row of back loops as you go around the toe of the shoe (see dotted line in **G** for position).
2. Insert the shoe strap through the loop formed by the slipped stitches at the top of the T-bar, you may need to thread the cast on and off tails onto a tapestry needle first and use these to pull it through **(H and I)**. Sew end of shoe strap onto left edge of shoe, pull ends through to inside and secure.
3. Stitch a button onto the opposite end of the strap, and secure it to the shoe.
4. Sew the bottom edges of the shoe together, starting at the toe working through to the ankle. Then stuff the foot firmly. If necessary, adjust vertical T-bar strap so that it lies in the center of the foot.
5. Sew the leg edges together, making sure any color changes line up, stuffing as you go. Only lightly stuff the top part of the legs to enable them to move into a sitting position.

Left leg and shoe

Make up in the same way as the right leg and shoe, but this time sew the strap onto the right edge of the shoe.

Legs with boots

1. Using whip stitch (see Casting On and Stitches, page 102), sew together the 'bind off' edges at top of foot **(J)**.
2. Sew the bottom edges of the boot together, starting at the toe working through to the ankle.
3. Then stuff the foot firmly.
4. Sew the leg edges together, making sure color changes line up, stuffing as you go. Only lightly stuff the top part of the legs to enable them to move into a sitting position.

Boot cuffs

1. Sew side edges together using mattress stitch.
2. Turn the cuff inside out and slide into position over the leg, lining up the seam on the cuff with the seam on the back of the leg. Stitch it into place by sewing the cast-off edge of the cuff to the leg at the ankle, on the last row of the boot stitches **(K)**.
3. Fold over the top of the cuffs to finish the boots **(L)**.

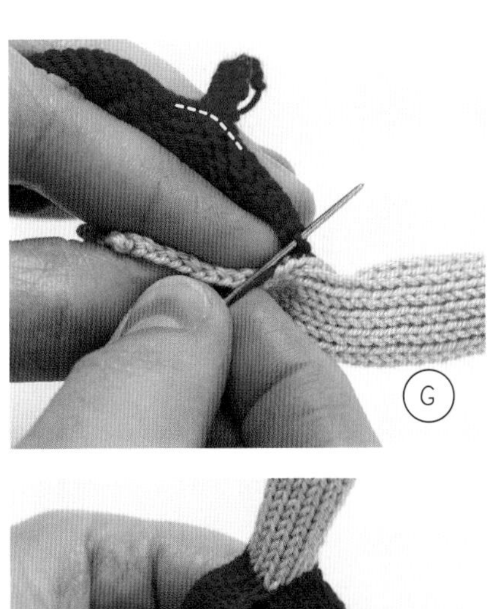

Legs with sneakers

1. Using whip stitch (see Casting On and Stitches, page 102), sew together bind-off edges at the top of the sneakers **(A)**.
2. Embroider shoe laces on top of sneaker **(B)**.
3. Matching up the colors, sew the bottom edges of the sneaker together, starting at the toe working through to the ankle. Then stuff the foot firmly.
4. Sew the leg edges together, making sure any color changes line up, stuffing as you go. Only lightly stuff the top part of the legs to enable them to move into a sitting position.

Sewing the legs to the body

1. Insert the tapestry needle through the back of the 'V' stitch on the first row of the body **(C)**, then down through the cast on stitch of the leg **(D)** and back up through the next cast on stitch **(E)**. Continue in this manner all the way around the leg, but go through the back of two 'V' stitches together at the outer corner of the body seam **(F)**.

ARMS

1. Using a tapestry needle, thread the yarn through the cast on stitches at the start of the hand and draw up **(G and H)**.
2. Sew the side edges together, stuffing the hand and arm firmly as you go, leaving the tapered top of the arm open.
3. Sew the tapered edges of the arm to the body, stuffing lightly as you go (see **I** for position).

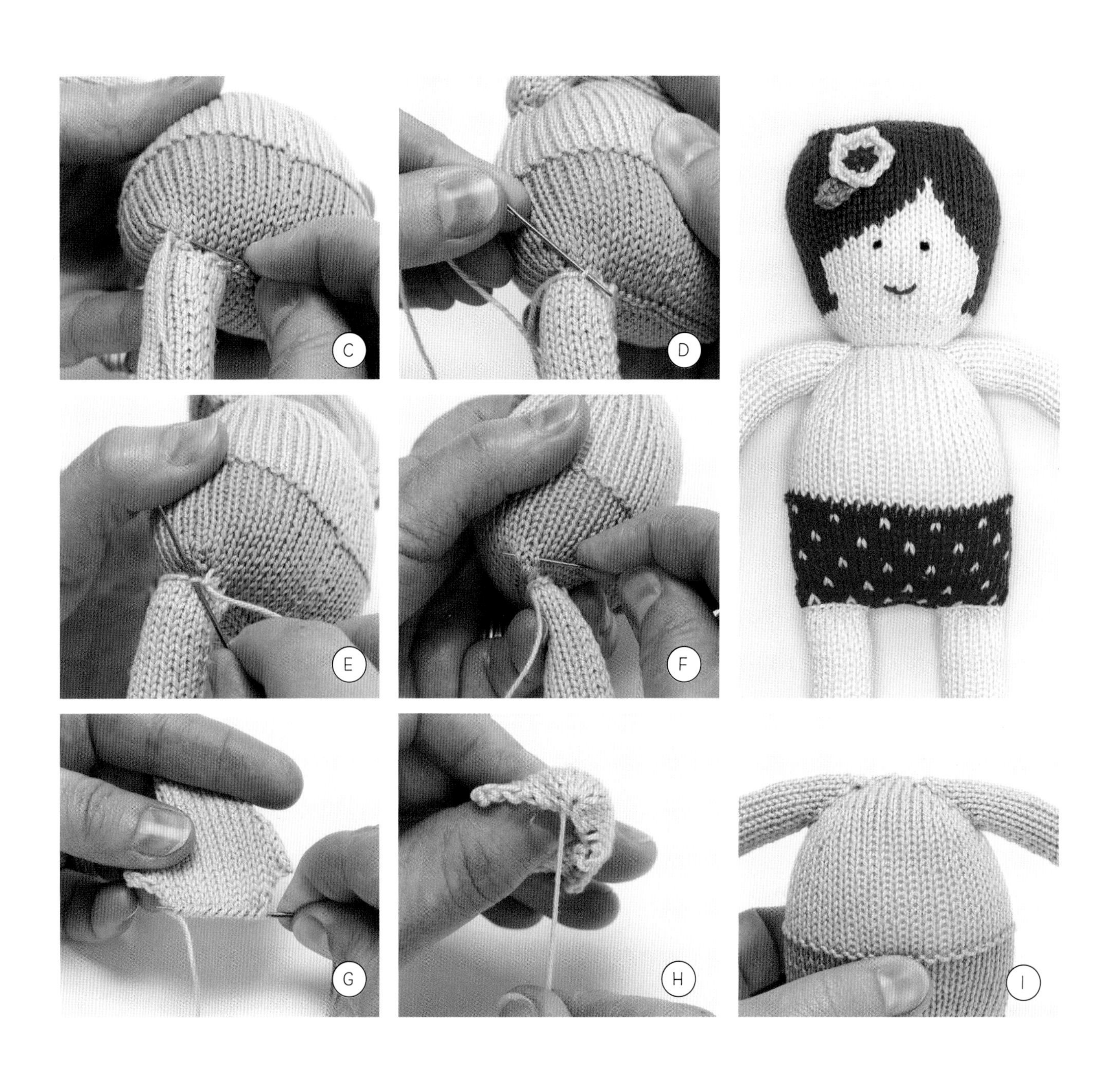

Blocking

Blocking your work will help create a flat, neat finish and help stop edges from curling. Use rust proof pins and leave to dry completely before removing pins. You can use spray blocking or steam blocking with cotton yarn.

Spray blocking

Spray the knitted piece with cold water until it is damp, but not saturated. Pin flat, and leave to dry completely.

Steam blocking

Pin the knitted piece flat and hold a steam iron close to the fabric and steam until it is damp (do not touch the fabric with the iron). Leave to dry.

HEAD

Adding the face detail

Take a small circle of white felt and place at the back of the work, behind where you plan to embroider the first eye. Using the black yarn, place a couple of small stitches to form the eye and knot the black thread securely at the back of the work. Trim off the excess. Repeat for the second eye. Embroider the mouth in the same way as the eyes **(A and B)**.

Joining the top edges of the head using Kitchener stitch

At the making up phase of each doll, the top stitches of the head are joined as follows:

Transfer first 9 stitches onto a double pointed needle, middle 17 stitches onto second double pointed needle and last 9 stitches onto opposite end of first double pointed needle **(C and D)**.

Next, join the top edges using Kitchener stitch (grafting) as follows:

1. Thread a tapestry needle with a length of Yarn E. Hold the work with the stitches parallel in your left hand. Insert the tapestry needle through the first stitch on the front needle as if to PURL **(E)**. Pull the yarn through, leaving a tail that you'll weave in later. Leave the stitch on the front needle.
2. Insert the tapestry needle through the first stitch on the back needle as if to KNIT **(F)**, pull the yarn through, leaving the stitch on the back needle.
3. Insert the tapestry needle through the first stitch on the front needle as if to KNIT, pull the yarn through, removing the stitch from the front needle. Insert the tapestry needle through the next stitch on the front needle as if to PURL, pull the yarn through, leaving the stitch on the front needle.
4. Insert the tapestry needle through the first stitch on the back needle as if to PURL, pull the yarn through, removing the stitch from the back needle. Insert the tapestry needle through the next stitch on the back needle as if to KNIT, pull the yarn through, leaving the stitch on the back needle.

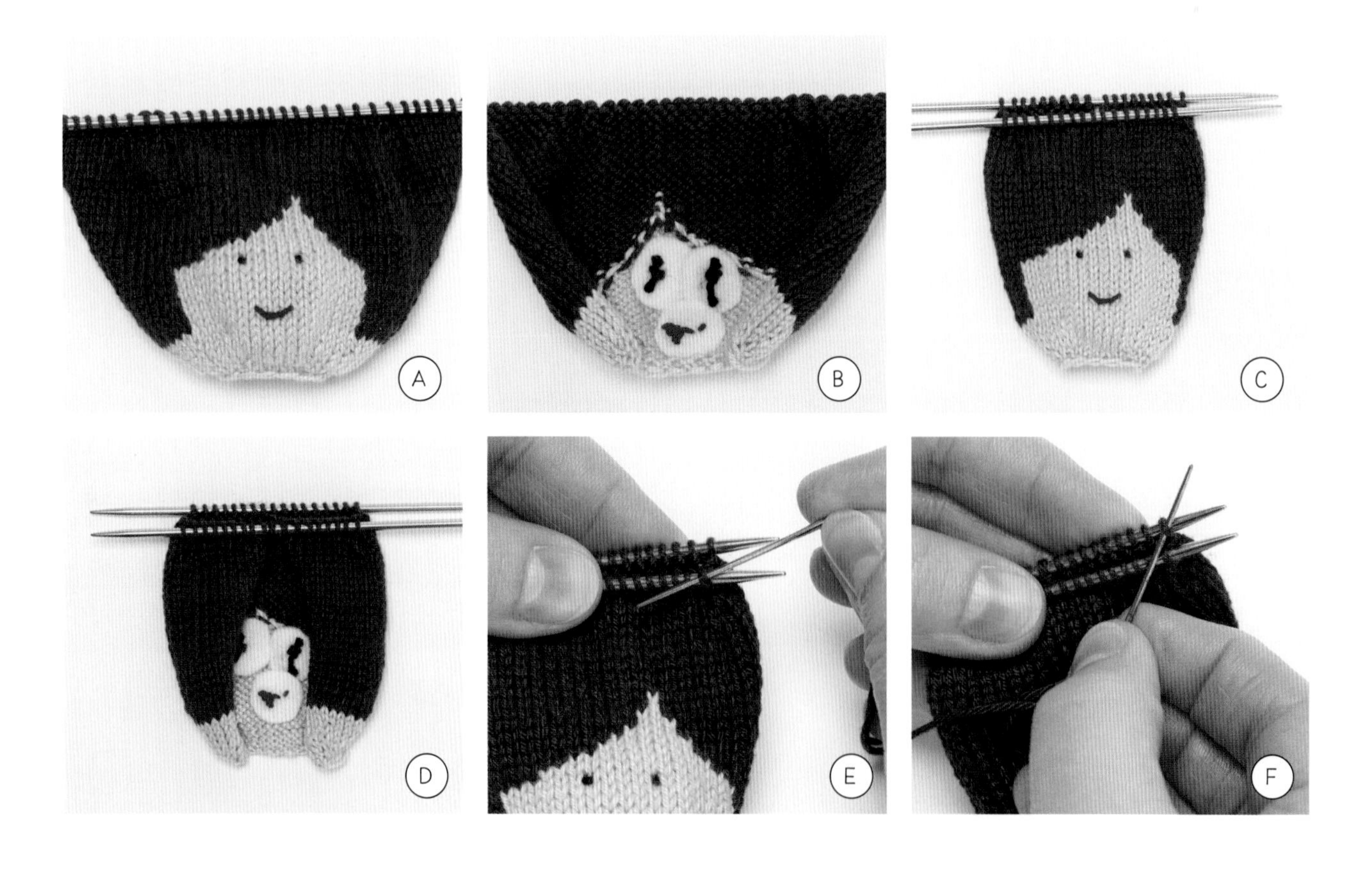

Repeat step 3 and step 4 until you have 11 sts left on the back needle and 9 sts left on the front needle.

5. Insert the tapestry needle through the next stitch on the back needle as if to PURL, pull the yarn through, removing the stitch from the back needle. Insert the tapestry needle through the next two stitches together on the back needle as if to KNIT **(G)**, pull the yarn through, leaving these two stitches on the back needle.

Repeat step 3.

6. Insert the tapestry needle through the first two stitches together on the back needle as if to PURL, pull the yarn through, removing the two stitches from the back needle **(H)**. Insert the tapestry needle through the next stitch on the back needle as if to KNIT, pull the yarn through, leaving the stitch on the back needle.

Repeat step 3 and step 4 until all the stitches have been worked.

Sewing up the head

Starting at the top, join the back edges of the head together, leaving a big enough gap at the neck to push the stuffing through. Stuff, then close up the gap, drawing up the ends.

Once the head is complete, sew to the top of the body (see dotted line in figure **(I)** for position).

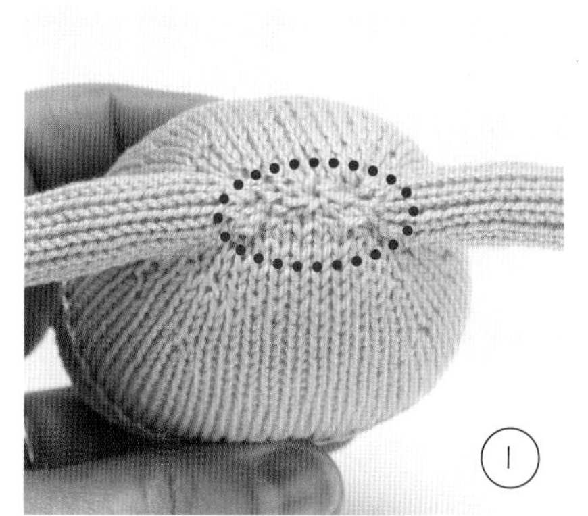

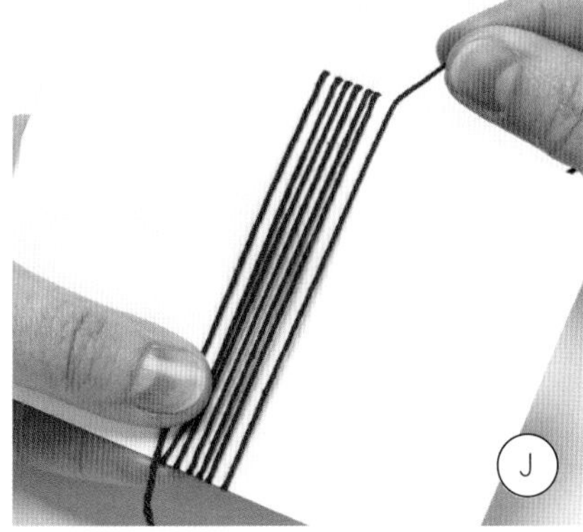

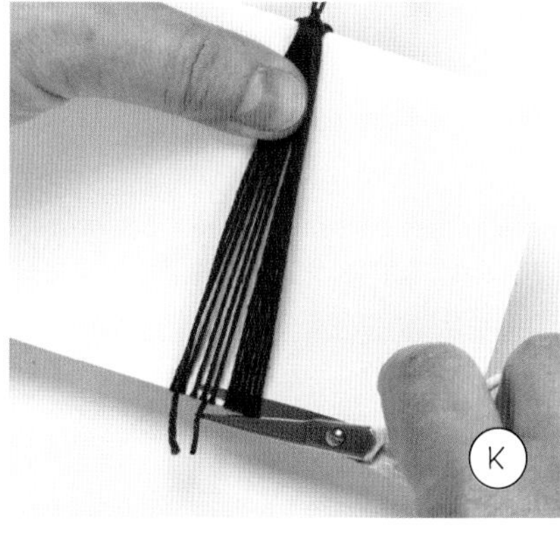

Making up plaits

1. Wrap yarn around a small piece of card (roughly 3½in (9cm) wide for longer plaits and 2½in (6.5cm) wide for shorter plaits) 12 times **(J)**.
2. Thread a short length of yarn through the top of the loops and secure tightly. Cut yarn through the bottom of the loops **(K)**.
3. Divide into three equal sets of strands and plait.
4. Wrap a short length of yarn around the bottom of the plait and secure tightly. Using your tapestry needle, thread the two loose ends back through the middle of the plait **(L)**.
5. Trim uneven ends to neaten up **(M)**.

CASTING ON AND STITCHES

Long-tail cast on

(also known as double cast-on)

To make sure you have a long enough tail to cast on your stitches, wrap the yarn around the needle the same amount of times as the number of stitches you need plus approx 10in (25cm) extra to use for sewing up later if needed.

1. Make a slip knot **(A)**.
2. With needle in your right hand, keeping the ball end closest to you, place your left thumb and forefinger between the two strands of yarn. Grasp the loose ends with your other fingers and hold in palm **(B)**.
3. Spread your thumb and forefinger apart to make yarn taught, then move your thumb up towards the tip of the needle, keeping your palm facing forwards **(C)**.
4. Bring the tip of the needle up through the loop on your thumb **(D)**.
5. Then over the top and around the yarn on your forefinger **(E)**.
6. Take the needle back through the thumb loop (insert from top) **(F)**.
7. Gently pull your thumb out and pull on tail ends to tighten the stitch **(G)**.
8. Repeat steps 3–7 **(H)**.

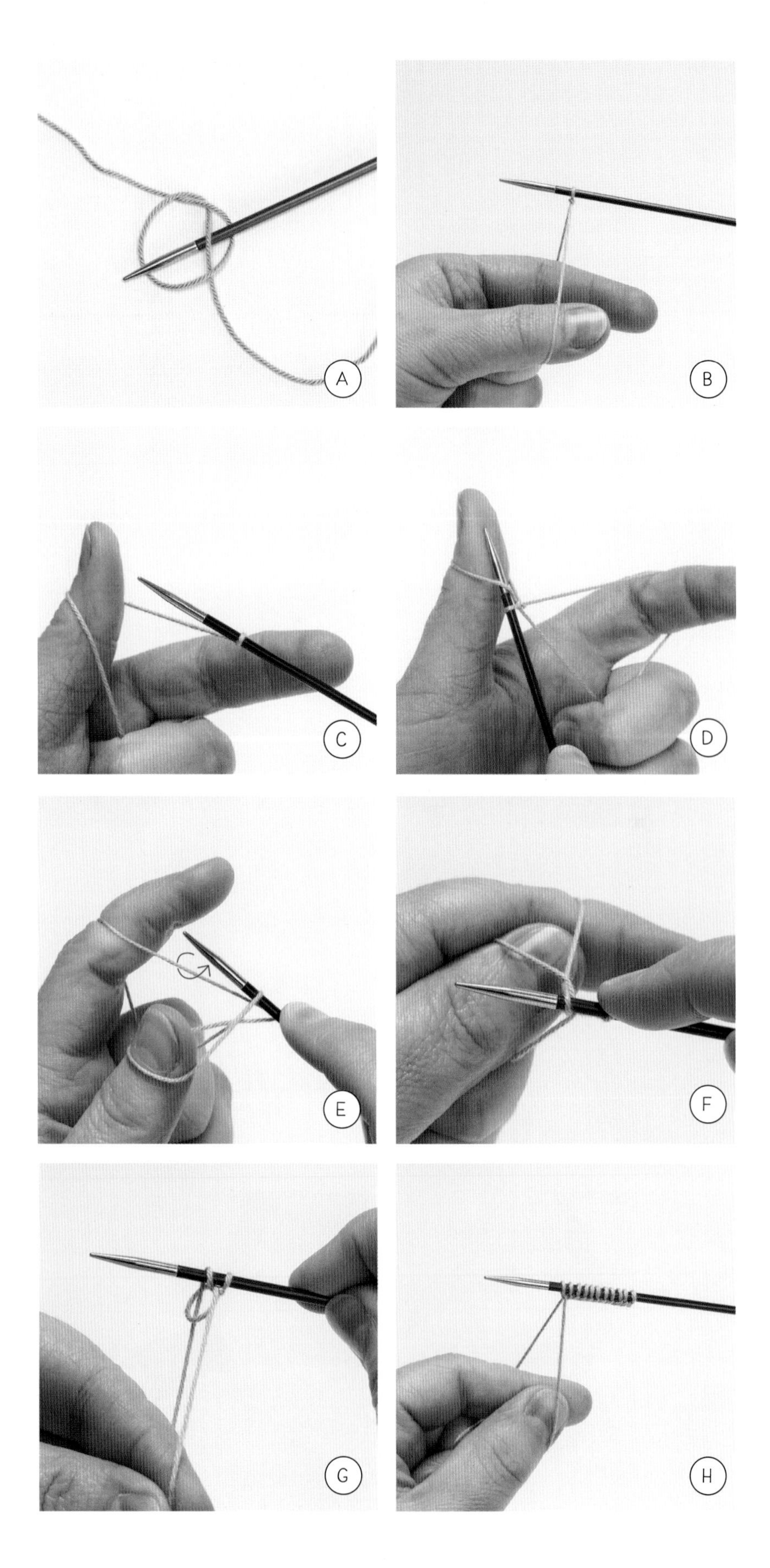

Knit cast on

1. Insert the right needle into the stitch and knit, but do not take the left-hand stitch off the needle **(A)**.
2. Transfer the loop from the right needle to the left needle **(B)**.
3. Repeat steps 1 and 2 **(C)**.

Purl cast on

1. Insert the right needle into the stitch and purl, but do not take the left-hand stitch off the needle **(D)**
2. Transfer the loop on the right needle to the left needle **(E)**.
3. Repeat steps 1 and 2 **(F)**.

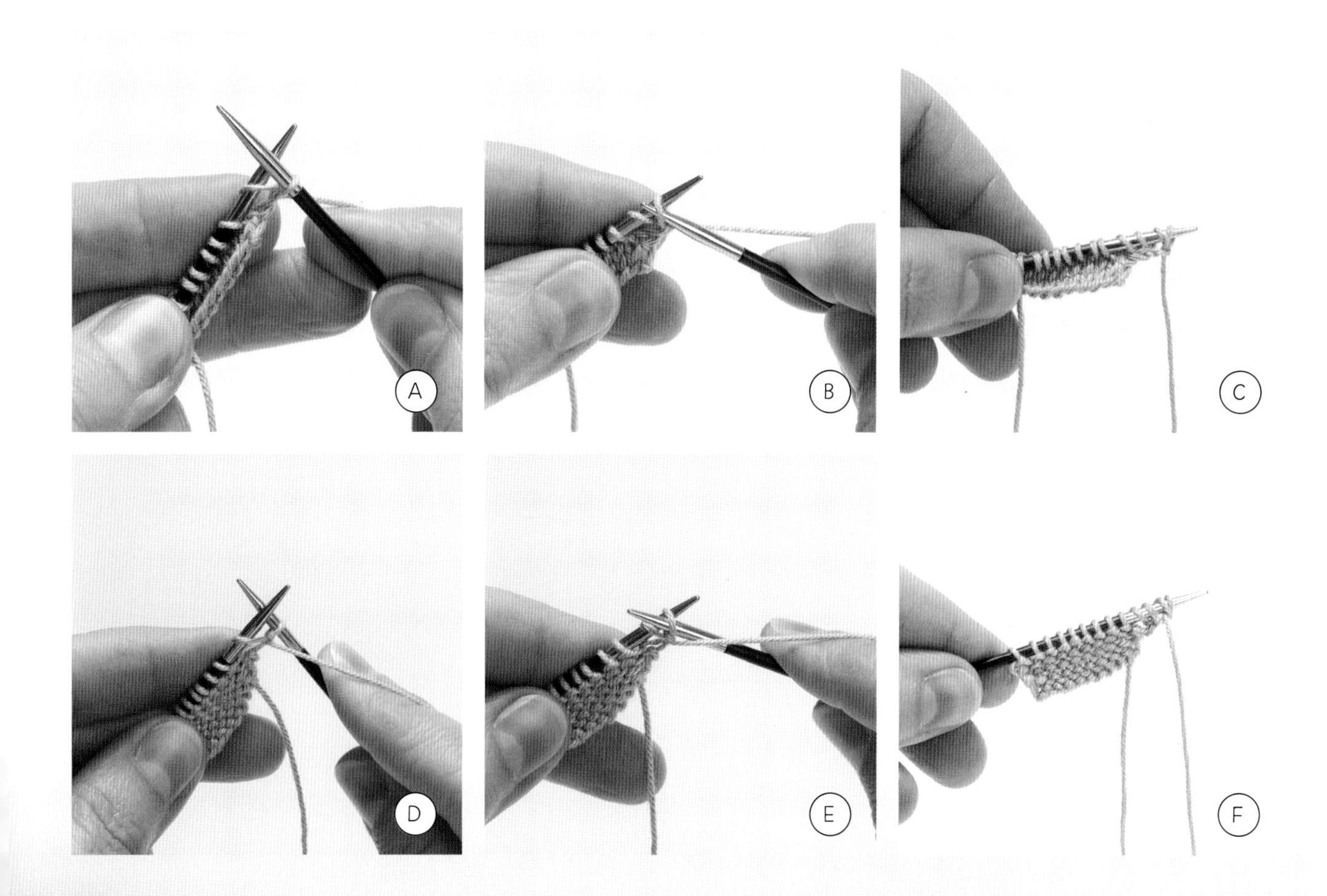

Picking up stitches

(behind button placket)

1. Working from right to left on the first three stitches of the right button placket **(G)**, insert right needle through the back loop of stitch **(H)**.
2. Wrap yarn around needle and pull through as if to knit **(I)**.
3. Repeat steps 1 and 2 for next two stitches **(J)**.

I-cord

(worked on two double-pointed needles)

1. Cast on number of stitches needed using Long-tail cast on **(K)**.
2. Without turning your work, slide stitches to the right-hand end of needle **(L)**.
3. Bringing the working yarn around the back, knit the first stitch, pulling the yarn tight and knit to the end of the row **(M)**.
4. Repeat steps 3 and 4 until the required length is reached, tugging on the cast-on tail after every row to form into a tube **(N)**.

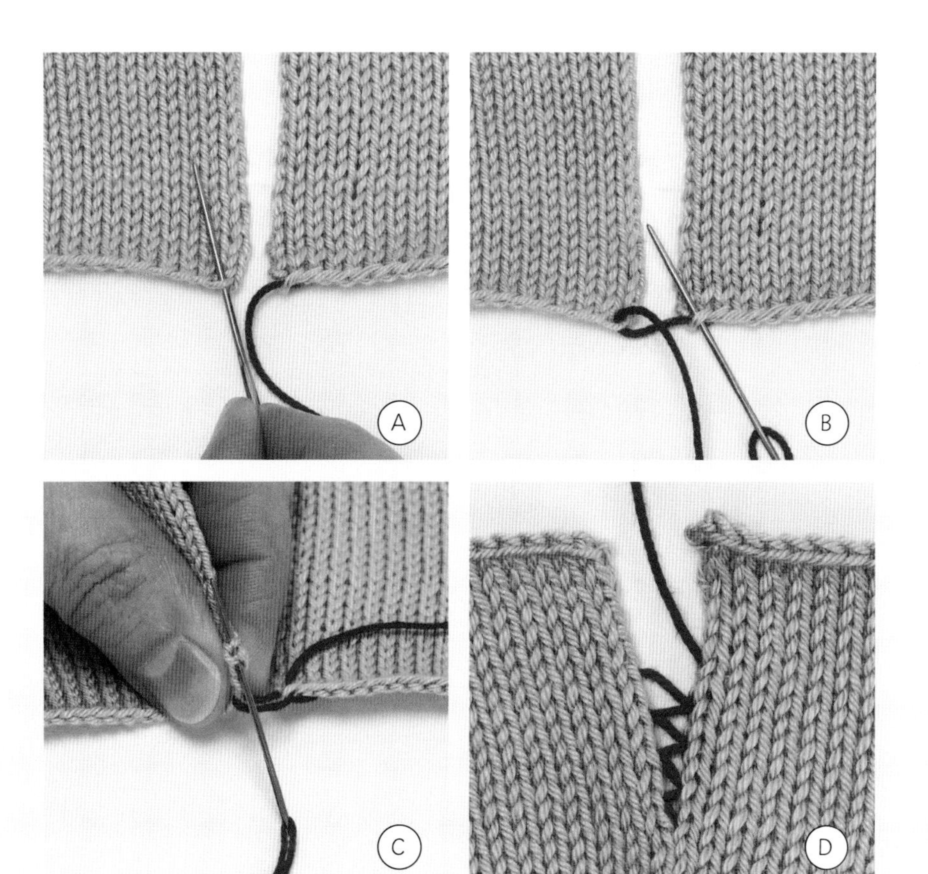

Mattress stitch

Thread the tail (or a length of yarn) onto a tapestry needle. Start with the right sides up and edges side by side.

Vertical mattress stitch

This stitch is used for seaming two selvedge edges together.

1. Insert the needle up through the first cast-on or cast-off loop on the opposite piece, then do the same on the first piece and pull the yarn through **(A and B)**.
2. Take the needle across to the opposite edge again and insert from the front under two horizontal bars in the middle of the outermost stitches **(C)**.
3. Repeat step 2, working back and forth across each side, gently pulling the yarn through to close the seam **(D)**.

Horizontal mattress stitch

This stitch is used for seaming the cast-on or bind-off edges together.

1. Insert needle under the 'V' of the first stitch and pull yarn through **(E)**.
2. Take the needle across to the other edge and do the same with the stitch on that side **(F)**.
3. Repeat steps 1 and 2, working back and forth across each side, gently pulling the yarn through to close the seam **(G)**.

Vertical to horizontal mattress stitch

This stitch is used for seaming the cast-on or cast-off edge to a selvedge edge **(H)**.

1. Insert your needle from the front under two horizontal bars in the middle of the outermost stitches on the selvedge edge and pull the yarn through **(I)**.
2. Take the needle across to the cast-on/off edge and insert under the 'V' of the first stitch **(J)**.
3. Repeat steps 1 and 2, working back and forth across each side, gently pulling the yarn through to close the seam **(K)**.

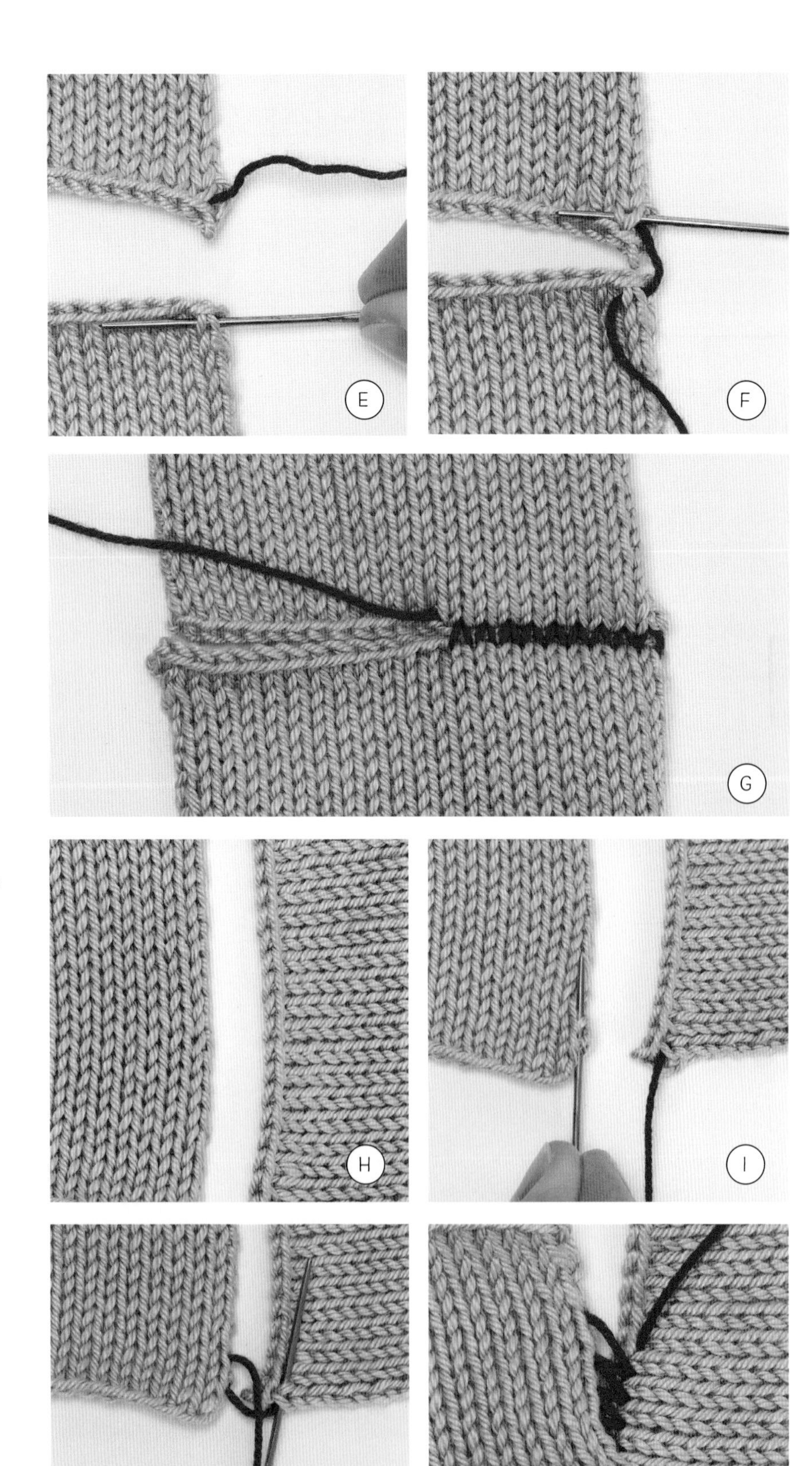

French knot

1. Bring the needle through from the back where you want the French knot to be.
2. Wrap the yarn around the needle twice **(A)**.
3. Holding the yarn taut, insert the needle back through the same place and draw the yarn through **(B)** to create the finished knot **(C)**.

Whip stitch

With edges side by side and working from left to right:

1. Insert a threaded tapestry needle through the outer loops of the first cast-off stitch of both edges, pull yarn through leaving a short tail to weave in **(D)**.
2. Insert needle through outer loop of stitch just worked on right-hand edge and next stitch up on opposite edge, pull yarn through **(E)**.
3. Insert needle through outer loop of next stitch on each edge and pull yarn through **(F)**.
4. Repeat step 3 for each remaining cast-off stitch **(G)**.

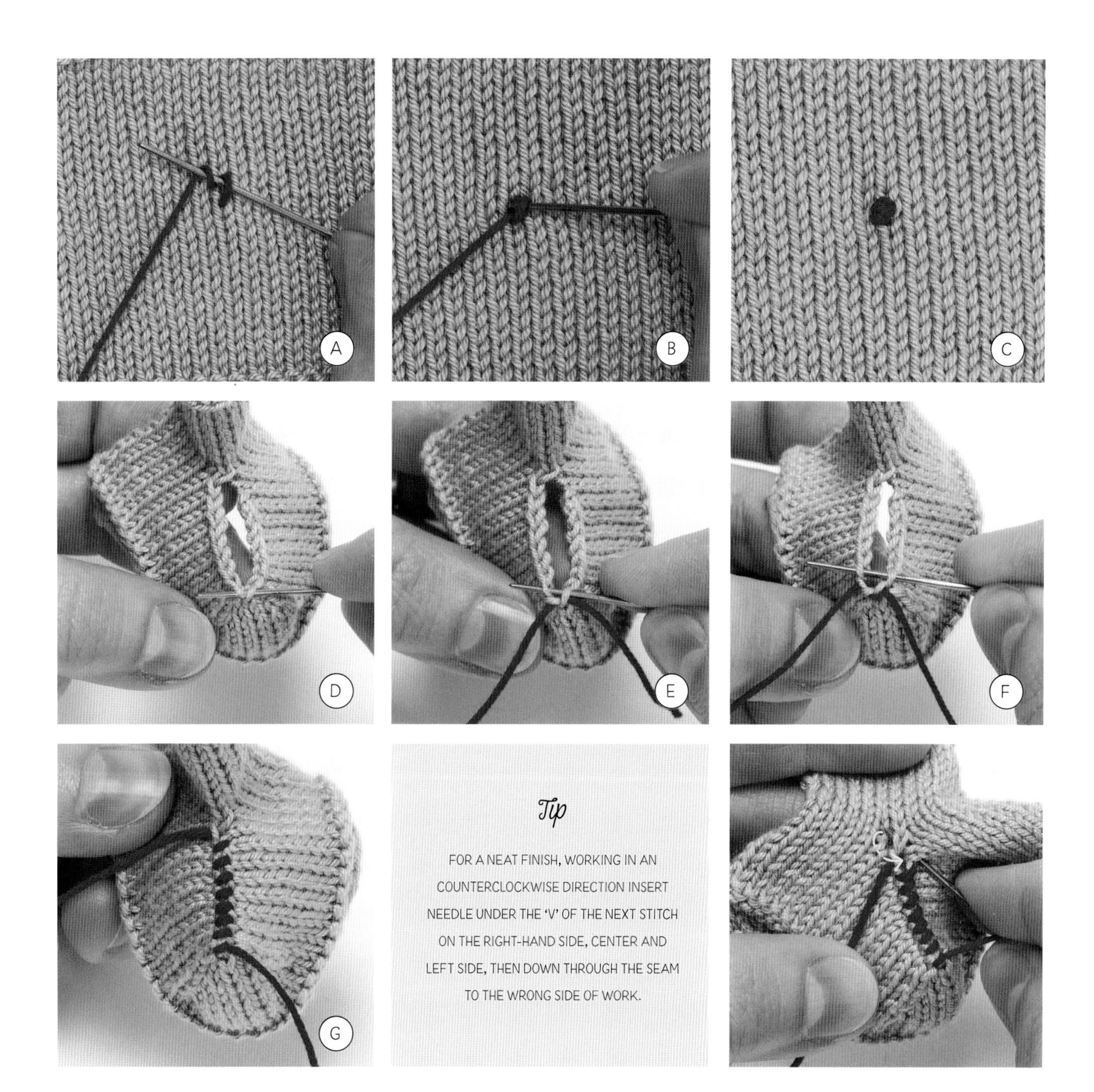

Tip

FOR A NEAT FINISH, WORKING IN AN COUNTERCLOCKWISE DIRECTION INSERT NEEDLE UNDER THE 'V' OF THE NEXT STITCH ON THE RIGHT-HAND SIDE, CENTER AND LEFT SIDE, THEN DOWN THROUGH THE SEAM TO THE WRONG SIDE OF WORK.

COLORWORK

All of the dolls in this section use some sort of color-changing techniques. Many of the girls wear striped tights, so if you knit a few dolls you'll become a master of this simple color-change technique. You'll also find instructions on working Fair Isle, Duplicate stitch and Intarsia, which you'll need in order to create the decorated sweaters and dresses in this section. If any of these techniques are new to you don't be afraid—they are all easier than they look!

Stripes

When working stripes, carry the yarn up the side of the work. Simply drop the old color at the back of the work and pick up the new color to work the first stitch **(A)**.

For thicker stripes (more than four rows) catch the old yarn every couple of rows by twisting it with the working yarn stitch **(B)**.

Fair Isle (stranded)

Fair Isle is a technique for working two (or more) colors of yarn in the same row, carrying the yarn at the back of the work. As you change colors, simply let the old yarn hang down at the back of the work until needed again and pick up the new yarn to work the next stitch. Try not to pull too tightly when changing colors **(C and D)**.

Duplicate stitch

(also known as Swiss darning)

Duplicate stitch is a technique allowing you to add small areas of color to your completed fabric, duplicating the original stitches.

1. Thread your needle with a long piece of the contrast yarn and bring it up through the bottom of the 'V' of the first stitch to duplicate **(E)**.
2. Take the needle under the stitch above **(F)**.
3. Finally go back through the 'V' point of the stitch again **(G)**.
4. Repeat across the row for each area of color **(H)**.

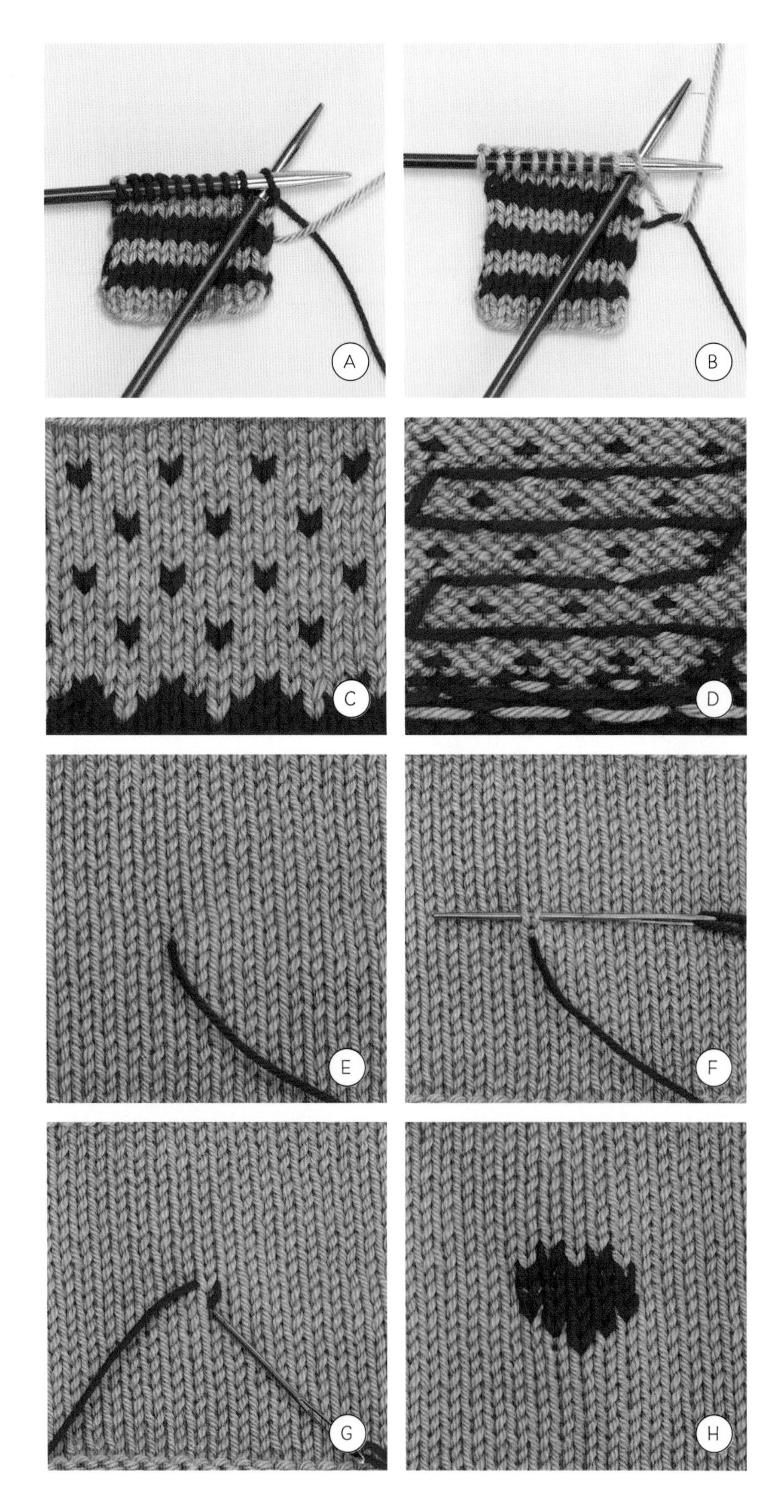

Intarsia

Intarsia uses separate lengths or balls of yarn for each area of color (as opposed to yarns being carried at the back of the work). Although if there is only one stitch between two areas of the same color, the same length of yarn can be used for both and carried across the back of the single stitch.

It is best to work out how many changes of color there are before starting, and wind the longer lengths of yarn onto separate bobbins or clothes pegs.

For example, to work this sample heart chart you would need three lengths of pink yarn and two lengths of red yarn (each separate length of color needed is indicated by a different symbol on the chart).

When following a chart, work from the bottom to the top and read purl rows (ws) from left to right and knit rows (rs) from right to left. This sample chart is worked in stockinette stitch and the first row is a purl row, therefore you would begin reading it in the bottom left-hand corner.

An easy way to estimate how much yarn is needed is to count the number of stitches on the chart for each yarn length. Loosely wrap the yarn around your needle once for each stitch, then add a further 6in (15cm) for each tail.

To avoid holes between two blocks of color, work until you need to change color. Put the needle in the next stitch ready to work it, but pull the old yarn to the left before bringing the new color yarn up and over it to work the stitch **(I)**.

To tighten up any loose stitches once finished, working on the right side of the fabric, insert a tapestry needle into one leg of the loose stitch and pull towards you gently. Repeat on the next few stitches to even out the tension **(J)**.

Intarsia Chart

□ = Pink yarn, length 1
⊡ = Pink yarn, length 2
◙ = Pink yarn, length 3
■ = Red yarn, length 1
■ = Red yarn, length 2

PERSONALISING YOUR DOLL

When it comes to creating a unique personality for your doll, your imagination is the only limitation. Facial expression, hair color and skin tone, clothing and accessories can all be altered to make the perfect doll for you. Here are just a few ideas to fuel your creativity...

Personalising the hair

Consider changing the hair color to match the recipient of your doll. It would be fun to create a red-headed version of Jane to give to the auburn-haired little girl in your life.

Why not change the hair style of your doll? You can mix and match any of the hair graphs, pigtail styles and hair embellishments to create your own style. Make pigtails really long, like Pippi Longstocking from Astrid Lindgren's famous book, or add some ribbon to Polly's plaits.

Personalising the skin and eye color

You may want to consider personalising the skin or eye color of the doll you're making, as well as the hair. There are plenty of different colored yarns available to represent any skin color, I have used a few different ones throughout this section. Although I have used oddments of black for the eyes on my dolls, you could easily substitute oddments of blue, green or brown.

Personalising the outfits

Mix and match any of the clothing and accessories and try out new color combinations to create a whole new wardrobe of outfits for your doll.

SUPPLIERS

Boo-Biloo
www.etsy.com/uk/shop/BooBiloo
www.ravelry.com/designers/boo-biloo

SewandSo
www.sewandso.co.uk

Deramores
www.deramores.com

LoveKnitting
www.loveknitting.com

Wool Warehouse
www.woolwarehouse.co.uk

Purple Linda Crafts
www.purplelindacrafts.co.uk

ABOUT THE AUTHOR

Louise's love of knitting started when her eldest son came home from school one day saying he wanted to learn how to knit... his interest in knitting lasted about a week, but she has been hooked ever since!

Louise, who has a background in textile design, has developed her own successful brand selling knitting patterns for toys and dolls. Her work has been featured in various craft and knitting magazines, as well as this book.

To find out more about Louise's work visit her blog at www.boo-biloo.blogspot.com

THANK YOU

Thanks to all at F+W Media especially Sarah for giving me this opportunity and making the book possible, Anna for her artistic talents, Jane for helping me out when my brain had stopped working and Lynne for her excellent pattern editing.

Thanks also to Petra for patiently answering my 'what do you think?' questions (of which there were many), and to my friends and family for all your enthusiasm and encouragement.

Thanks to my two sons, Jake and Zachary, for not moaning about all the times my mind has been elsewhere in the last few months.

Finally, special thanks go to my husband Kevin, who as always, has been my tower of strength.

Knitted Toy Tales

LAURA LONG

We all have moments that we cherish forever; stories we were told and childhood games that we played. Toys and fairytales were an important part of my childhood and there are certain toys I will never forget. In fact, I still have toys I could never be parted from. This collection of sweet little knitted toys brings out the child in all of us. By creating traditional toys out of yarn, you can make beautiful pieces that can be enjoyed for many years to come.

There are projects in this section for everyone to enjoy knitting, from beginners to more advanced knitters and through to people like my mother, who can knit just about anything! If you are a beginner, I would advise starting with a simple project such as the bunnies (page 114) or the mice (page 160). Once you have mastered simple shaping techniques such as knitting two stitches together (k2tog) to decrease stitches, and knitting into the front and back of a stitch (kfb) to increase stitches, you can knit toys to your heart's content!

Toys are perfect for using up leftover yarns. You can be creative with your yarn and color choice. If you want to knit a purple rabbit, a fluffy orange bear or a pink sparkly snake, go ahead ... in fact, knit two, three or four! Knit a whole family of brightly colored creatures.

Quite a few of the projects combine knitting with fabric detailing. I think this adds a special character to the toys and brings out the nostalgic nature of the work. Over the years, I have collected large amounts of fabrics. Some are truly cherished pieces, and I wait for the perfect project to use them. The toys in the following section provided me with the perfect excuse to use these fabrics, because a special toy deserves a special finishing touch. You could use fabric from an old dress, a childhood blanket, or even an old handkerchief. Make a toy that is truly personal to you; a toy that has some history and a story to tell.

I have thoroughly enjoyed working on this section of your book, and I hope you'll enjoy knitting the characters as much as I have enjoyed creating them.

A cherished toy is remembered forever.

Love, Laura

The Bunny Bunch

Rating

This simple project is just right to get a beginner started on making toys

Two little baby bunnies and their mummy live in Polly Dolly's garden and sleep in a big wooden hutch. They love to jump and play silly games. They like chasing butterflies and eating dandelions and daisies.

The bunnies' heads and bodies are made in one piece from very soft, towelling-type yarn. The boy bunny has a white muzzle, so you'll have to change colors to make him. Fluffy pompoms make the bunnies' tails, and fabric scraps line their ears. They are perfect projects for beginners, as they introduce you to very simple shaping.

yarn

Lightweight (DK) 100% polyester with towelling or chenille texture
Mummy bunny—1 x 1¾oz (50g) ball in white (**A**)
Baby boy bunny—1 x 1¾oz (50g) ball in white (**A**), 1 x 1¾oz (50g) ball in pale blue (**B**)
Baby girl bunny—1 x 1¾oz (50g) ball in pale pink (**C**)

needles

Size 6 (4mm) knitting needles

gauge

16 sts and 31 rows to 4in (10cm)
Don't worry if the gauge is not exact—it doesn't matter if the bunnies are a little bigger or smaller than shown

finished size

Mummy bunny—5½in (14cm) long (not including tail) and 4¼in (11cm) tall
Baby bunnies—3½in (9cm) long (not including tail) and 3½in (9cm) tall

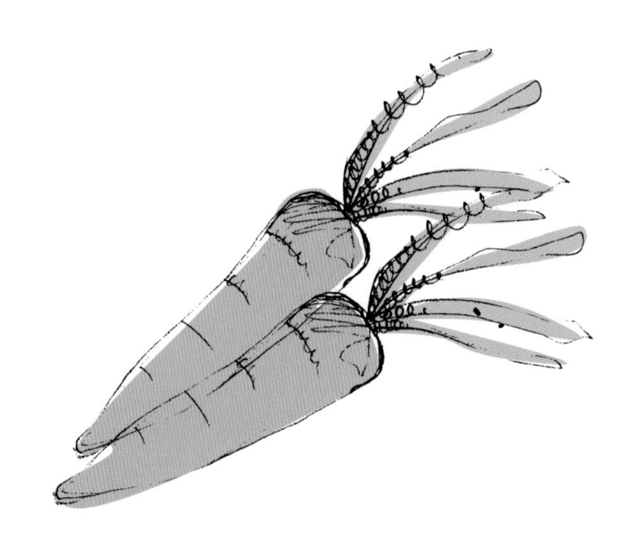

Three little bunnies live in a hutch,
They're cuddly and fluffy and soft to touch.
There's Flopsy, Mopsy and Jemima their mummy.
They hop around the garden when the weather is sunny.

Baby bunnies pattern

HEAD AND BODY

Cast on 5 sts in **yarn A** if you are knitting the boy bunny or **yarn C** if knitting the girl bunny, using size 6 (4mm) knitting needles.

Row 1 Kfb 4 times, k1. 9 sts.
Row 2 P.
Row 3 [kfb, k1] 4 times, k1. 13 sts.
Row 4 P.
Row 5 [kfb, k1, kfb] 4 times, k1. 21 sts.
Row 6 P.
Change to **yarn B** if knitting the boy bunny and continue knitting in **yarn C** if you are knitting the girl bunny.
Row 7 [kfb, k3, kfb] 4 times, k1. 29 sts.
Row 8 P.
Row 9 [kfb, k5, kfb] 4 times, k1. 37 sts.
Row 10 P.
Cont in st st for 4 rows.
Row 15 [kfb, k7, kfb] 4 times, k1. 45 sts.
Row 16 P.
Cont in st st for 8 rows.
Row 25 [k2tog, k7, skpo] 4 times, k1.
Row 26 P.
Row 27 [k2tog, k5, skpo] 4 times, k1.
Row 28 P.
Row 29 [k2tog] rep to last st, k1.
Row 30 P.
Row 31 [k2tog] rep to last st, k1.
Row 32 P.
Thread yarn through rem sts.

EARS (MAKE 2)

Cast on 3 sts in **yarn B** for the boy bunny or **yarn C** for the girl bunny, using size 6 (4mm) knitting needles.

Row 1 Kfb, kfb, k1. 5 sts.
Row 2 P.
Row 3 K1, kfb, kfb, k2. 7 sts.
Row 4 P.
Cont in st st for 12 rows.
Row 17 K2, k3tog, k2. 5 sts.
Row 18 P.
Row 19 K.
Row 20 P.
Thread yarn through rem sts.

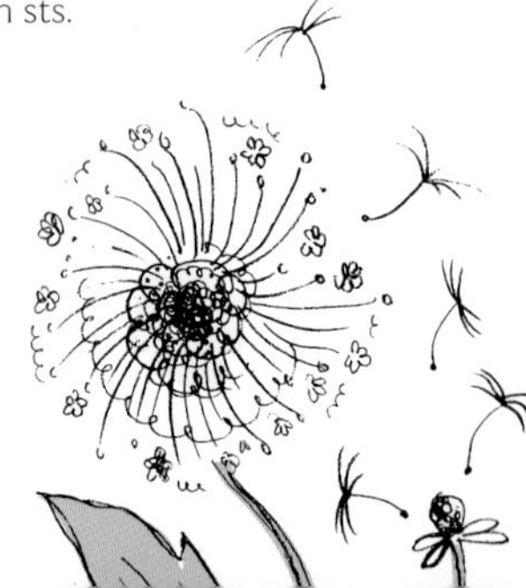

Mummy bunny pattern

HEAD AND BODY

Cast on 9 sts using **yarn A** and size 6 (4mm) knitting needles.

Row 1 [kfb, k1] 4 times, k1 13 sts.
Row 2 P.
Row 3 [kfb, k1, kfb] 4 times, k1. 21 sts.
Row 4 P.
Row 5 [kfb, k3, kfb] 4 times, k1. 29 sts.
Row 6 P.
Row 7 [kfb, k5, kfb] 4 times, k1. 37 sts.
Row 8 P.
Row 9 [kfb, k7, kfb] 4 times, k1. 45 sts.
Row 10 P.
Row 11 [kfb, k9, kfb] 4 times, k1. 53 sts.
Row 12 P.
Cont in st st for 8 rows.
Row 21 [k2tog, k9, skpo] 4 times, k1. 45 sts.
Row 22 P.
Row 23 [k2tog, k7, skpo] 4 times, k1. 37 sts.
Row 24 P.
Row 25 K.
Row 26 P.
Row 27 [kfb, k7, kfb] 4 times, k1. 45 sts.
Row 28 P.
Row 29 [kfb, k9, kfb] 4 times, k1. 53 sts.
Row 30 P.
Row 31 [kfb, k11, kfb] 4 times, k1. 61 sts.
Row 32 P.
Cont in st st for 12 rows.
Row 45 [k2tog, k11, skpo] 4 times, k1.
Row 46 P.
Row 47 [k2tog, k9, skpo] 4 times, k1.
Row 48 P.
Row 49 [k2tog, k7, skpo] 4 times, k1.
Row 50 P.
Row 51 [k2tog] rep to last st, k1.
Row 52 P.
Row 53 [k2tog] rep to last st, k1.
Row 54 P.
Thread yarn through rem sts.

EARS (MAKE 2)

Cast on 5 sts using **yarn A** and size 6 (4mm) knitting needles.

Row 1 K1, kfb, kfb, k2.
Row 2 P.
Row 3 K2, kfb, kfb, k3.
Row 4 P.
Row 5 K3, kfb, kfb, k4.
11 sts.
Row 6 P.
Work in st st for 20 rows.
Row 27 K4, k3tog, k4.
Row 28 P.
Row 29 K.
Row 30 P.
Row 31 K3, k3tog, k3.
Row 32 P.
Bind off.

MAKING UP

Fold the bunny in half with knit sides (right sides) together. Sew up from each end, leaving a gap of approx $\frac{3}{4}$in (2cm) in the middle. Turn the bunny the right way out so the knit sides (right sides) are on the outside. Fill with stuffing. Sew up the gap.

EARS

Cut out two iron-on interfacing-lined fabric ears (see template, page 208). Use two pieces of iron-on interfacing on each ear to make them more rigid. Sew each piece of fabric to the inside of the knitted ear (see page 205). Stitch an ear to each side of the head, using the shaping at the top of the head to position and space them correctly.

FINISHING TOUCHES

Embroider the nose in pink or white yarn and the eyes and mouth in brown or black yarn (as shown in the photograph). Make a pompom tail (see page 207 for instructions and page 208 for template) using white yarn. Attach to the bunny's bottom.

Bertie and Beatrice the Birds

Rating 

The birds are made up of several small, shaped pieces and involve some intarsia colorwork

Bertie and Beatrice love to sing, so they sing all day and night. The problem is they only know one song. Is there anyone who can teach them a new one? Two songs are so much better than one!

These bright little birds are made in pure wool yarn in strong, bold colors with little embroidered details. You can make your birds in one color if you prefer. The birds' legs are made from crocheted chains.

yarn

Lightweight (DK) 100% wool
1 x 1¾oz (50g) ball in pink (**A**)
1 x 1¾oz (50g) ball in yellow (**B**)
1 x 1¾oz (50g) ball in blue (**C**)

needles

Size 6 (4mm) knitting needles
Size E4 (3.5mm) crochet hook

gauge

22 sts and 30 rows to 4in (10cm)
Don't worry if the gauge is not exact—it doesn't matter if the birds are a little bigger or smaller than shown

finished size

Approx 8in (20cm) long and 4in (10cm) tall

Bertie and Beatrice are songbirds,
Who twitter and tweet all day.
They have feathers so bright and beautiful,
You can see them from miles away.

KNITTING NOTES

• The colorwork for this project is done using the intarsia method (see page 200). When knitting using two colors, make sure you wrap the yarns around one another when changing from one color to the next. This prevents holes appearing between colors.

• For this pattern I have written instructions for Beatrice. She has a pink body, a yellow chest and blue wings. To make Bertie, substitute the colors so that:

yarn A = blue

yarn B = yellow

yarn C = green

Bird pattern

HEAD AND BODY

Cast on 9 sts using **yarn A** and size 6 (4mm) knitting needles.

Row 1 [kfb, k1] to last st, k1.

Row 2 P.

Row 3 [kfb, k1, kfb] to last st, k1.

Row 4 P.

Row 5 [kfb, k3, kfb] to last st, k1.

Row 6 P.

Row 7 [kfb, k5, kfb] to last st, k1.

Row 8 P.

Row 9 [kfb, k7, kfb] to last st, k1. 45 sts.

Row 10 P.

Cont in st st for 10 rows.

Beg the color changes:

Row 21 A k16, **B** k13, **A** k16.

Row 22 A p15, **B** p15, **A** p15.

Row 23 A k2tog, k7, skpo, k2tog, k1, **B** k17, **A** k1, skpo, k2tog, k7, skpo. 39 sts.

Row 24 A p10, **B** p19, **A** p10.

Row 25 A k2tog, k5, skpo, k1, **B** k19, **A** k1, k2tog, k5, skpo. 35 sts.

Row 26 A p8, **B** p19, **A** p8.

Row 27 A k8, [**B** k1, kfb] 9 times, k1, **A** k8. 44 sts.

Row 28 A p8, **B** p28, **A** p8.

Row 29 A k8, **B** k28, **A** k8.

Row 30 A p8, **B** p28, **A** p8.

Row 31 A k8, **B** k28, **A** k8.

Row 32 A p8, **B** p28, **A** p8.

Row 33 A k8, **B** k1, kfb, k10, kfb, k1, kfb, k10, kfb, k2, **A** k8. 48 sts.

Row 34 A p8, **B** p32, **A** p8.

Row 35 A k8, **B** k1, kfb, k12, kfb, k1, kfb, k12, kfb, k2, **A** k8. 52 sts.

Row 36 A p8, **B** p36, **A** p8.

Row 37 A k8, **B** k36, **A** k8.

Row 38 A p8, **B** p36, **A** p8.

Row 39 A k1, kfb, k3, kfb, k2, **B** k2, skpo, k11, skpo, k2, k2tog, k11, k2tog, k2, **A** k1, kfb, k3, kfb, k2.

Row 40 A p10, **B** p32, **A** p10.

Row 41 A k1, kfb, k5, kfb, k2, **B** k2, skpo, k9, skpo, k2, k2tog, k9, k2tog, k2 **A** k1, kfb, k5, kfb, k2.

Row 42 A p12, **B** p28, **A** p12.

Row 43 A k1, kfb, k7, kfb, k2, **B** k2, skpo, k7, skpo, k2, k2tog, k7, k2tog, k2, **A** k1, kfb, k7, kfb, k2.

Row 44 A p14, **B** p24, **A** p14.

Row 45 A k1, kfb, k9, kfb, k2, **B** k2, skpo, k5, skpo, k2, k2tog, k5, k2tog, k2, **A** k1, kfb, k9, kfb, k2.

Row 46 A p16, **B** p20, **A** p16.

Row 47 A k1, kfb, k11, kfb, k2, **B** k2, skpo, k1, skpo, skpo, k2, k2tog, k2tog, k1, k2tog, k2, **A** k1, kfb, k11, kfb, k2.

Row 48 A p18, **B** p14, **A** p18.

Row 49 A k1, kfb, k16, [**B** k2tog] 7 times, **A** k16, kfb, k1.

Row 50 A p19, **B** p2tog, p3tog, p2tog, **A** p19.

Row 51 A k1, kfb, k17, k3tog, k17, kfb, k1.

Row 52 P.

Row 53 K1, kfb, k11, [k2tog] 3 times, k3tog, [k2tog] 3 times, k11, kfb, k1.

Row 54 P.

Bind off.

RIGHT WING

Cast on 3 sts using **yarn C** and size 6 (4mm) knitting needles.

Row 1 Kfb, kfb, k1.

Row 2 P.

Row 3 K1, kfb, kfb, k2.

Row 4 P.

Row 5 K2, kfb, kfb, k3.

Row 6 P.

Row 7 K3, kfb, kfb, k4.

Row 8 P.

Cont in st st for 6 rows.

Row 15 K2tog, k to end.

Row 16 P.

Row 17 K2tog, k to end.

Row 18 P.

Bind off.

LEFT WING

Follow instructions for right wing until row 15:

Row 15 K to last 2 sts, k2tog.

Row 16 P.

Row 17 K to last 2 sts, k2tog.

Row 18 P.

Bind off.

BEAK (MAKE 2 PIECES)

Cast on 3 sts using **yarn B** and size 6 (4mm) knitting needles.

Row 1 Kfb, kfb, k1.

Row 2 P.

Row 3 K1, kfb, kfb, k2.

Row 4 P.

Row 5 K2, kfb, kfb, k3.
Row 6 P.
Row 7 K3, kfb, kfb, k4.
Row 8 P.
Bind off.

FEET (MAKE 2)
Cast on 3 sts using **yarn B** and size 6 (4mm) knitting needles, leaving a long piece of yarn to be used to crochet the legs.
Row 1 Kfb, kfb, k1.
Row 2 P.
Row 3 K1, kfb, kfb, k2.
Row 4 P.
Row 5 K2, kfb, kfb, k3.
Row 6 P.
Row 7 K3, kfb, kfb, k4.
Row 8 P.
Row 9 K4, kfb, kfb, k5.
Row 10 P.
Row 11 K4, skpo, k1, k2tog, k4.
Row 12 P.
Row 13 K3, skpo, k1, k2tog, k3.
Row 14 P.
Row 15 K2, skpo, k1, k2tog, k2.
Row 16 P.
Row 17 K1, skpo, k1, k2tog, k1.
Row 18 P5tog.
Cut off yarn, leaving another length of approx 12in (30cm) to crochet the legs (the legs are crocheted with 2 strands of yarn, one length from casting on and the other from the other end of the work).

MAKING UP

BODY
Sew up from the base of the bird to the tip of her tail, leaving the top open.
Fill with stuffing.
Fold the top of the tail over to form a triangle.
The tip of this triangle should touch the top of the sewn-up base to form a V-shape.
Sew along the 'V' to close the gap.

WINGS
Cut out two iron-on interfacing-lined fabric wings (see page 211 for template).
Sew each piece of fabric to the inside of the knitted wing (see page 205).
Stitch the wings to each side of the bird's body using the shaping at the top of the breast to position them correctly. The fabric enables the wing to bend as though the bird is flying.

BEAK
Sew both pieces together.
Fill with a small amount of stuffing.
Stitch the beak to the bird's head using the shaping at the front of the head to position it correctly.

LEGS AND FEET
Fold the feet in half and make a crochet stitch through both sides using the leftover yarn.
Crochet a chain (see page 206) of 10 rows with the 2 strands of leftover yarn attached to the feet. (Using a double thickness of yarn creates a thicker leg.)
Sew around the edges of the feet.
Thread the crochet chain with foot through the base of the body.

FINISHING TOUCHES
Embroider eyes on each side of the head using brown or black yarn (as shown in the photograph).
Using a contrast-color yarn, embroider details onto the wings.

Frederick the Frog Prince

Rating 

Frederick is made from two types of green yarn, and you'll need to use intarsia to work the color changes

Frederick Frog has a dream, a dream that he hopes will come true. Many years ago a wicked witch cast a spell on Prince Frederick and he has been a frog ever since. This spell can be broken only by a kiss from a beautiful girl. Every day Frederick Frog sits and dreams that a beautiful girl will come his way.

Have fun making Frederick's crown fit for a prince and decorate it with little beads to resemble jewels.

yarn

Lightweight (DK) 100% wool
1 x 1¾oz (50g) ball in variegated dark greens (**A**)
1 x 1¾oz (50g) ball in light green (**B**)
Oddment of yarn in white (**C**)
Oddment of yarn in black (**D**)

needles

Size 6 (4mm) knitting needles
You'll need three needles this size

gauge

22 sts and 28 rows to 4in (10cm)
Don't worry if the gauge is not exact—it doesn't matter if Frederick is a little bigger or smaller than shown

finished size

Approx 5in (13cm) wide and 8¼in (21cm) tall

Frederick Frog looks all around,
There's no-one about, not even a sound.
But Frederick Frog is not what he seems,
He may turn into the prince of your dreams.

KNITTING NOTES

• The colorwork for this project is done using the intarsia method (see page 200). When knitting using two colors, make sure you wrap the yarns around one another when changing from one color to the next. This prevents holes appearing between colors.

• Frederick is knitted from the head down to the legs in one piece. The arms and hands are also knitted in one piece and then attached to the body.

Frederick the Frog pattern

HEAD AND BODY

Cast on 9 sts using **yarn A** and size 6 (4mm) knitting needles.

Row 1 [kfb, k1] 4 times, k1. 13 sts.
Row 2 P.
Row 3 [kfb, k1, kfb] 4 times, k1. 21 sts.
Row 4 P.
Row 5 [kfb, k3, kfb] 4 times, k1. 29 sts.
Row 6 P.
Row 7 [kfb, k5, kfb] 4 times, k1. 37 sts.
Row 8 P.
Row 9 [kfb, k7, kfb] 4 times, k1. 45 sts.
Row 10 P.
Row 11 [kfb, k9, kfb] 4 times, k1. 53 sts.
Row 12 P.
Cont in st st for 8 rows.
Row 21 [k2tog, k9, skpo] 4 times, k1.
Row 22 P.
Row 23 [k2tog, k7, skpo] 4 times, k1.
Row 24 P.
Row 25 K.
Row 26 P.
Row 27 [kfb, k7, kfb] 4 times, k1.
Row 28 P.
Row 29 [kfb, k9, kfb] 4 times, k1.
Row 30 P.
Row 31 [kfb, k11, kfb] 4 times, k1. 61 sts.
Row 32 P.
Beg the color changes.
Row 33 K23 in **A**, k15 in **B**, k23 in **A**.
Row 34 P22 in **A**, p17 in **B**, p22 in **A**.
Row 35 K21 in **A**, k19 in **B**, k21 in **A**.
Row 36 P20 in **A**, p21 in **B**, p20 in **A**.
Row 37 K19 in **A**, k23 in **B**, k19 in **A**.
Row 38 P19 in **A**, p23 in **B**, p19 in **A**.
Rep rows 37 and 38, 2 more times.
Row 43 K20 in **A**, k21 in **B**, k20 in **A**.
Row 44 P21 in **A**, p19 in **B**, p21 in **A**.
Row 45 K22 in **A**, k17 in **B**, k22 in **A**.
Row 46 P23 in **A**, p15 in **B**, p23 in **A**.
Row 47 K in **A**.
Row 48 P.
Row 49 [k2tog, k11, skpo] 4 times, k1.
Row 50 P.
Row 51 [k2tog, k9, skpo] 4 times, k1.
Row 52 P.
Row 53 [k2tog, k7, skpo] 4 times, k1.
Row 54 P.
Row 55 [k1, k2tog] rep to last st, k1. 25 sts.
Row 56 P.

RIGHT LEG

Cont on rem 25 sts as follows:

Row 57 K 12 sts and turn; cont on these sts to make right leg.
Row 58 P.
Row 59 K.
Row 60 P.
Row 61 K in **yarn B**.
Row 62 P.
Row 63 K.
Row 64 P.
Rep last 8 rows, 5 more times.

RIGHT FOOT

Cont on sts for leg as follows:

Row 105 K 6 sts in **yarn A**. Fold sts in half so 1st 6 sts are facing 2nd 6 sts.
Row 106 Using a 3rd needle, knit together the 1st pair of sts, then the 2nd, and cont in this way to the end of the row. 6 sts.
Row 107 K2tog, k4.
Row 108 P.
Row 109 K1, kfb, kfb, k2.
Row 110 P.
Row 111 K2, kfb, kfb, k3.
Row 112 P.
Row 113 K3, kfb, kfb, k4.
Row 114 P.
Row 115 K4, kfb, kfb, k5.
Row 116 P.
Row 117 K5, kfb, kfb, k6. 15 sts.
Row 118 P.
Row 119 K5, skpo, k1, k2tog, k5.
Row 120 P.
Row 121 K4, skpo, k1, k2tog, k4.
Row 122 P.
Row 123 K3, skpo, k1, k2tog, k3.
Row 124 P.
Row 125 K2, skpo, k1, k2tog, k2.
Row 126 P.
Row 127 K1, skpo, k1, k2tog, k1.
Row 128 P5tog.
Tie off yarn.

LEFT LEG AND FOOT

Return to the 13 sts rem on the left side.

Row 57 K2tog, k. 12 sts.

Cont, repeating patt instructions for right leg and foot.

RIGHT ARM

Cast on 12 sts using **yarn A** and size 6 (4mm) knitting needles.

Row 1 K.
Row 2 P.
Row 3 K.
Row 4 P.
Row 5 K in **yarn B**.
Row 6 P.
Row 7 K.
Row 8 P.

Rep last 8 rows, 2 more times.

RIGHT HAND

Cont on sts for arm as follows:

Row 25 K 6 sts in **yarn A**. Fold sts in half so 1st 6 sts are facing 2nd 6 sts.

Row 26 Using a 3rd needle, knit together the 1st pair of sts, then the 2nd. Cont in this way to the end of the row. 6 sts.

Row 27 K2 tog, k4.
Row 28 P.
Row 29 K1, kfb, kfb, k2.
Row 30 P.
Row 31 K2, kfb, kfb, k3.
Row 32 P.
Row 33 K3, kfb, kfb, k4.
Row 34 P.
Row 35 K4, kfb, kfb, k5.
Row 36 P.
Row 37 K4, skpo, k1, k2tog, k4.

Row 38 P.
Row 39 K3, skpo, k1, k2tog, k3.
Row 40 P.
Row 41 K2, skpo, k1, k2tog, k2.
Row 42 P.
Row 43 K1, skpo, k1, k2tog, k1.
Row 44 P5tog.
Tie off yarn.

LEFT ARM AND HAND
Follow instructions for right arm and hand.

EYES (MAKE 2)
Cast on 4 sts using **yarn B** and size 6 (4mm) knitting needles.
Row 1 Kfb in each st.
Row 2 P.
Row 3 Kfb in each st.
Row 4 P.
Cont in st st for 4 rows.
Row 9 Using **yarn C**, k.
Row 10 P.
Row 11 [K2tog] to end of row.
Row 12 Using **yarn D**, p.
Row 13 [K2tog] to end of row.
Thread yarn through rem sts, pull together to close the gap, and cut yarn.

MAKING UP

Fold the body of the frog in half with knit sides (right sides) together.
Sew up from the top of the head to the legs.
Turn frog the right way out so the knit sides (right sides) are on the outside.
Fill with stuffing.

LEGS
Sew from each end leaving a gap of approx 1 1/8in (3cm) in the middle. Fill with stuffing.
With a few stitches, join the third and fourth dark-green stripe at the seam to bend the frog's legs at the knees.

FEET
Fold the feet in half and sew around the edges.
With a few stitches, sew the frog's feet at the ankle end to his legs so they are bent at the ankle.

ARMS
Sew from each end leaving a gap of approx 1 1/8in (3cm) in the middle.
Fill with stuffing.
Sew onto the body using shaping to position correctly.

HANDS
Fold the hands in half and sew around the edges.
Sew up gap.

EYES
Sew up eyes and fill with stuffing. Sew onto top of the head using shaping to position correctly.

FINISHING TOUCHES
Embroider the mouth in black yarn.
Make the crown out of yellow felt (see page 209 for template). Use gold thread to embroider details or add small beads for the jewels if desired.

Babushkas

Rating 

The colorwork on the babushkas is done using intarsia, which you might need to practise

The babushkas are three very pretty Russian dolls. They are good friends with Polly Dolly, but sometimes they play tricks on her by jumping and hiding one inside the other.

The babushkas are fully lined on the inside to give them some stability and to allow you to stack them inside each other, just like real Russian dolls. Each doll is decorated with different styles of flower; you can cut out pieces of felt for the flowers or embroider them.

yarn

Lightweight (DK) acrylic and wool mix yarn
1 x 3½oz (100g) ball in yellow (**A**)
1 x 3½oz (100g) ball in pink (**B**)
1 x 3½oz (100g) ball in white (**C**)
1 x 3½oz (100g) ball in red (**D**)

needles

Size 6 (4mm) knitting needles

gauge

22 sts and 30 rows to 4in (10cm)
Don't worry if the gauge is not exact—it doesn't matter if the babushkas are a little bigger or smaller than shown

finished size

Large babushka—9in (23cm) tall
Medium babushka—6¾in (17cm) tall
Small babushka—4in (10cm) tall

There's Olga who's tall, and Tanya who's small,
And Nadia who fits in between.
They are three Russian dollies, who like to be jolly,
Their smiles are the best ever seen.

KNITTING NOTES

- The colorwork for this project is done using the intarsia method (see page 200). When knitting using two colors, make sure you wrap the yarns around one another when changing from one color to the next. This prevents holes appearing between colors.
- The babushkas are knitted from the head down.

Large babushka pattern

Cast on 9 sts using **yarn A** and size 6 (4mm) knitting needles.

Row 1 [kfb, k1] 4 times, k1.
Row 2 P.
Row 3 [kfb, k1, kfb] 4 times, k1.
Row 4 P.
Row 5 [kfb, k3, kfb] 4 times, k1.
Row 6 P.
Row 7 [kfb, k5, kfb] 4 times, k1.
Row 8 P.
Row 9 [kfb, k7, kfb] 4 times, k1. 45 sts.
Row 10 P.
Beg the color changes.
Row 11 A k16, **B** k13, **A** k16.
Row 12 A p15, **B** p15, **A** p15.
Row 13 A k14, **B** k17, **A** k14.
Row 14 A p13, **B** p19, **A** p13.
Row 15 A k13, **B** k19, **A** k13.
Rep rows 14 and 15, 3 more times.
Row 22 A p13, **B** p19, **A** p13.
Row 23 A k14, **B** k17, **A** k14.
Row 24 A p15, **B** p15, **A** p15.
Row 25 A k16, **B** k13, **A** k16.
Row 26 A p17, **B** p11, **A** p17.
Row 27 A k.
Row 28 P.
Row 29 C [skpo, k7, k2tog] 4 times, k1.
Row 30 P.
Row 31 [skpo, k5, k2tog] 4 times, k1.
Row 32 P.
Row 33 [kfb, k1] rep to last st, kfb. 44 sts.
Row 34 P.
Row 35 K.
Row 36 P.
Row 37 D k18, **C** k8, **D** k18.
Row 38 D p17, **C** p10, **D** p17.
Row 39 D k16, **C** k12, **D** k16.
Row 40 D p15, **C** p14, **D** p15.
Row 41 D kfb, k13, **C** k7, kfb, kfb, k7, **D** k13, kfb.
Row 42 D p14, **C** p20, **D** p14.
Row 43 D k13, **C** k22, **D** k13.
Row 44 D p12, **C** p24, **D** p12.
Row 45 D kfb, k10, **C** k12, kfb, kfb, k12, **D** k10, kfb.
Row 46 D p12, **C** p28, **D** p12.
Row 47 D k12, **C** k28, **D** k12.
Rep rows 46 and 47, 5 more times.
Row 58 D p12, **C** p28, **D** p12.
Row 59 D k13, **C** k26, **D** k13.
Row 60 D p14, **C** p24, **D** p14.
Row 61 D k15, **C** k22, **D** k15.
Row 62 D p16, **C** p20, **D** p16.
Row 63 D k17, **C** k18, **D** k17.
Row 64 D p18, **C** p16, **D** p18.
Row 65 D k19, **C** k14, **D** k19.
Row 66 D p20, **C** p12, **D** p20.
Row 67 D k21, **C** k10, **D** k21.
Row 68 D p22, **C** p8, **D** p22.
Row 69 D k.
Row 70 P.
Row 71 K.
Row 72 K.
Row 73 K.
Row 74 K.
Bind off.

Medium babushka pattern

Cast on 5 sts using **yarn A** and size 6 (4mm) knitting needles.

Row 1 Kfb 4 times, k1.
Row 2 P.
Row 3 [kfb, k1] 4 times, k1.
Row 4 P.
Row 5 [kfb, k1, kfb] 4 times, k1.
Row 6 P.
Row 7 [kfb, k3, kfb] 4 times, k1. 29 sts.
Row 8 P.
Beg the color changes.
Row 9 A k10, **B** k9, **A** k10.
Row 10 A p9, **B** p11, **A** p9.
Row 11 A k8, **B** k13, **A** k8.
Row 12 A p8, **B** p13, **A** p8.
Rep rows 11 and 12, 3 more times.
Row 19 A k9, **B** k11, **A** k9.
Row 20 A p10, **B** p9, **A** p10.
Row 21 A k11, **B** k7, **A** k11.
Row 22 A p.
Row 23 [skpo, k3, k2tog] 4 times, k1.
Row 24 P.
Row 25 C [k1, kfb] rep to last st, k1. 31 sts.
Row 26 P.
Row 27 K.
Row 28 P.
Row 29 D k13, **C** k5, **D** k13.
Row 30 D p12, **C** p7, **D** p12.
Row 31 D kfb, k10, **C** k3, kfb, kfb, k4, **D** k10, kfb.
Row 32 D p11, **C** p13, **D** p11.
Row 33 D k10, **C** k15, **D** k10.
Row 34 D p9, **C** p17, **D** p9.
Row 35 D kfb, k8, **C** k7, kfb, kfb, k8, **D** k8, kfb.
Row 36 D p10, **C** p19, **D** p10.
Row 37 D k10, **C** k19, **D** k10.
Rep row 36 and 37, 3 more times.
Row 44 D p10, **C** p19, **D** p10.
Row 45 D k11, **C** k17, **D** k11.
Row 46 D p12, **C** p15, **D** p12.
Row 47 D k13, **C** k13, **D** k13.
Row 48 D p14, **C** p11, **D** p14.
Row 49 D k15, **C** k9, **D** k15.

Olga and Nadia are happy little dolls...

Row 50 D p16, **C** p7, **D** p16.
Row 51 D k.
Row 52 P.
Row 53 K.
Row 54 K.
Row 55 K.
Row 56 K.
Bind off.

Small babushka pattern

Cast on 5 sts using **yarn A** and size 6 (4mm) knitting needles.
Row 1 Kfb 4 times, k1. 9 sts.
Row 2 P.
Row 3 [kfb, k1, kfb] 3 times. 15 sts.
Row 4 P.
Beg the color changes.
Row 5 A k6, **B** k3, **A** k6.
Row 6 A p5, **B** p5, **A** p5.
Row 7 A k4, **B** k7, **A** k4.
Row 8 A p4, **B** p7, **A** p4.
Row 9 A k4, **B** k7, **A** k4.
Row 10 A p5, **B** p5, **A** p5.
Row 11 A k6, **B** k3, **A** k6.
Row 12 A p.
Row 13 C k1, [kfb, k2] 4 times, kfb, k1.
Row 14 P.
Row 15 D k8, **C** k4, **D** k8.
Row 16 D p7, **C** p6, **D** p7.
Row 17 D k6, **C** k8, **D** k6.
Row 18 D p5, **C** p10, **D** p5.
Row 19 D kfb, k4, **C** k4, kfb, k5, **D** k4, kfb.
Row 20 D p6, **C** p11, **D** p6.
Row 21 D k6, **C** k11, **D** k6.
Row 22 D p6, **C** p11, **D** p6.
Row 23 D k6, **C** k11, **D** k6.
Row 24 D p6, **C** p11, **D** p6.
Row 25 D k7, **C** k9, **D** k7.
Row 26 D p8, **C** p7, **D** p8.
Row 27 D k9, **C** k5, **D** k9.
Row 28 D p10, **C** p3, **D** p10.
Row 29 D k.
Row 30 P.
Row 31 P.
Row 32 P.
Bind off.

MAKING UP

It's easier to embroider all the details before sewing up the back of the body.

FACE

Using brown yarn, embroider around the edge of the babushka's pink face.
Embroider hair, eyes and nose onto the face using the same brown yarn.
Embroider a few little stitches using red yarn for the mouth and add a few more around the top of the babushka's neck.

BODY

For the large and medium babushkas, cut out the petals, leaves and flowers from red and green felt (see page 211 for templates).
Sew these in place (see pages 204–205).
Add yarn details if desired.
Sew the babushkas down the back of their bodies.
Leave the bottom open.
Cut a strip of red felt and tie it in a neat bow at the front of each babushka's neck.
Neatly sew the bow to the neck.

LINING

Place each babushka onto double-thickness lining material. It is best to use T-shirt-type material as it has a bit of stretch.
Draw around the edge of each babushka, 3/16in (5mm) bigger than the doll.
Sew around the sides of this fabric, leaving the bottom open. Slip the fabric inside the babushka and neatly sew to the base of the doll. This lining enables you to fit one babushka inside the other, just like real Russian dolls.

Three Hungry Bears

Rating 

A touch of shaping makes the bears easier to sew up

Teddy bears love having breakfast parties, and the more bears you knit, the bigger the party will be! They like to have lots of different food at breakfast time, but don't forget to make plenty of porridge just in case Goldilocks comes to visit.

Knit these bears in the softest alpaca yarn you can find. Whether you're making the bears for small or big children, the luxurious feel of the yarn will offer warmth and comfort with every cuddle.

yarn

Lightweight (DK) 100% alpaca
Mummy bear—1 x 1¾oz (50g) ball in light brown (**A**)
Daddy bear—2 x 1¾oz (50g) balls in cream (**B**)
Baby bear—1 x 1¾oz (50g) ball in grey-blue (**C**)

needles

Size 6 (4mm) knitting needles

gauge

22 sts and 30 rows to 4in (10cm)
Don't worry if the tension is not exact—it doesn't matter if the bears are a little bigger or smaller than shown

finished sizes

Mummy bear—approx 12in (30cm) tall
Daddy bear—approx 14in (35cm) tall
Baby bear—approx 9in (23cm) tall

Mummy bear likes porridge,
Daddy bear likes honey,
Baby bear loves eggs with jelly,
which must taste rather funny.

KNITTING NOTES

Each component of the teddies is knitted separately and assembled at the end.

Mummy bear pattern

HEAD

Cast on 7 sts using **yarn A** and size 6 (4mm) knitting needles.

Row 1 P.
Row 2 Kfb to end of row. 14 sts.
Row 3 P.
Row 4 Kfb to end of row. 28 sts.
Row 5 P.
Row 6 Kfb to end of row. 56 sts.
Row 7 P.
Work 16 rows in st st.
Row 24 [k2tog, k10, skpo] 4 times.
Row 25 P.
Row 26 [k2tog, k8, skpo] 4 times.
Row 27 P.
Row 28 [k2tog, k6, skpo] 4 times.
Row 29 P.
Row 30 [k2tog, k4, skpo] 4 times.
Row 31 P.
Row 32 [k2tog, k2, skpo] 4 times.
Row 33 P.
Row 34 [k2tog, skpo] 4 times.
Thread yarn through rem sts and pull together.

NOSE

Cast on 30 sts using **yarn A** and size 6 (4mm) knitting needles.
Work 6 rows in st st.
Row 7 [k1, k2tog] rep to end of row.
Row 8 P.
Row 9 [k2tog] rep to end of row.
Thread yarn through rem sts and pull together.

BODY

Cast on 8 sts using **yarn A** and size 6 (4mm) knitting needles.

Row 1 P.
Row 2 Kfb to end of row. 16 sts.
Row 3 P.
Row 4 Kfb to end of row. 32 sts.
Row 5 P.
Row 6 Kfb to end of row. 64 sts.
Row 7 P.
Work 20 rows in st st.
Row 28 [k2tog, k12, skpo] 4 times.
Row 29 P.
Row 30 [k2tog, k10, skpo] 4 times.
Row 31 P.
Row 32 [k2tog, k8, skpo] 4 times.
Row 33 P.
Row 34 [k2tog, k6, skpo] 4 times.
Row 35 P.
Row 36 [k2tog, k4, skpo] 4 times.
Row 37 P.
Row 38 [k2tog, k2, skpo] 4 times.
Row 39 P.
Row 40 [k2tog, skpo] 4 times.
Thread yarn through rem sts and pull together.

LEGS (MAKE 2)

Cast on 25 sts using **yarn A** and size 6 (4mm) knitting needles.
Work 20 rows in st st.
Row 21 K11, kfb, kfb, k12.
Row 22 P.
Row 23 K12, kfb, kfb, k13.
Row 24 P.
Row 25 K13, kfb, kfb, k14.
Row 26 P.
Row 27 K14, kfb, kfb, k15.
Row 28 P.
Row 29 K15, kfb, kfb, k16.
Row 30 P.
Row 31 K2tog, k31, k2tog.
Row 32 P.
Row 33 [k2tog, k1] rep to end.
Row 34 P.
Row 35 [k2tog] rep to end. 11 sts.
Thread yarn through rem sts and pull together.

ARMS (MAKE 2)

Cast on 10 sts using **yarn A** and size 6 (4mm) knitting needles.
Row 1 Kfb, k8, kfb.
Row 2 P.
Row 3 Kfb, k10, kfb.
Row 4 P.
Cont in this way until 24 sts on needle.
Row 15 K.
Row 16 P.
Work 18 rows in st st.
Row 35 [k2tog, k1] rep to end.
Row 36 P.
Row 37 K2tog, rep to end.
Row 38 P.
Thread yarn through rem sts and pull together.

EARS (MAKE 2)

Cast on 26 sts using **yarn A** and size 6 (4mm) knitting needles.
Work 5 rows in st st.
Row 6 [p2 tog, p1] rep to last 2 sts, p2tog.
Row 7 K.
Row 8 [p2tog] rep to last st. P1.
Thread yarn through rem sts.

Mummy bear likes porridge ...

mmmm ...

Daddy bear pattern

HEAD

Refer to the pattern for Mummy bear's body (see page 138), but use **yarn B**.

NOSE

Cast on 36 sts using **yarn B** and size 6 (4mm) knitting needles.
Work 6 rows in st st.
Row 7 [k1, k2tog] rep to end of row.
Row 8 P.
Row 9 [k2tog] rep to end of row.
Row 10 P.
Thread yarn through rem sts and pull together.

BODY

Cast on 9 sts using **yarn B** and size 6 (4mm) knitting needles.
Row 1 P.
Row 2 Kfb to end of row. 18 sts.
Row 3 P.
Row 4 Kfb to end of row. 36 sts.
Row 5 P.
Row 6 Kfb to end of row. 72 sts.
Row 7 P.
Work 20 rows in st st.
Row 28 [k2tog, k14, skpo] 4 times.
Row 29 P.
Row 30 [k2tog, k12, skpo] 4 times.
Row 31 P.
Row 32 [k2tog, k10, skpo] 4 times.
Row 33 P.
Row 34 [k2tog, k8, skpo] 4 times.
Row 35 P.
Row 36 [k2tog, k6, skpo] 4 times.
Row 37 P.
Row 38 [k2tog, k4, skpo] 4 times.
Row 39 P.
Row 40 [k2tog, k2, skpo] 4 times.
Thread yarn through rem sts and pull together.

LEGS (MAKE 2)

Cast on 29 sts using **yarn B** and size 6 (4mm) knitting needles.
Work 24 rows in st st.
Row 25 K13, kfb, kfb, k14.
Row 26 P.
Row 27 K14, kfb, kfb, k15.
Row 28 P.
Row 29 K15, kfb, kfb, k16.
Row 30 P.
Row 31 K16, kfb, kfb, k17.
Row 32 P.
Row 33 K17, kfb, kfb, k18.
Row 34 P2 tog, p35, p2tog.
Row 35 [k1, k2tog] rep to last st, k1.
Row 36 P.

Row 37 [k2tog] rep to last st, k1.
Thread yarn through rem sts and pull together.

ARMS (MAKE 2)
Cast on 12 sts using **yarn B** and size 6 (4mm) knitting needles.
Row 1 Kfb, k10, kfb. 14 sts.
Row 2 P.
Row 3 Kfb, k12, kfb. 16 sts.
Row 4 P.
Cont in this way until 26 sts on needle.
Work 24 rows in st st.
Row 39 [k2tog, k1] rep to last 2 sts, k2tog.
Row 40 P.
Row 41 [k2tog] rep to last st, k1.
Thread yarn through rem sts and pull together.

EARS (MAKE 2)
Cast on 28 sts using **yarn B** and size 6 (4mm) knitting needles.
Work 5 rows in st st.
Row 6 [p2tog, p1] rep to last st, p1.
Row 7 K.
Row 8 [p2tog] rep to last st, p1.
Thread yarn through rem sts.

Baby bear pattern

HEAD
Cast on 6 sts using **yarn C** and size 6 (4mm) knitting needles.
Row 1 P.
Row 2 Kfb to end of row. 12 sts.
Row 3 P.
Row 4 Kfb to end of row. 24 sts.
Row 5 P.
Row 6 Kfb to end of row. 48 sts.
Row 7 P.
Work 12 rows in st st.
Row 20 [k2tog, k8, skpo] 4 times.
Row 21 P.
Row 22 [k2tog, k6, skpo] 4 times.
Row 23 P.
Row 24 [k2tog, k4, skpo] 4 times.
Row 25 P.
Row 26 [k2tog, k2, skpo] 4 times.
Row 27 P.
Row 28 [k2tog, skpo] 4 times.
Thread yarn through rem sts and pull together.

NOSE
Cast on 24 sts using **yarn C** and size 6 (4mm) knitting needles.
Work 4 rows in st st.
Row 5 [k1, k2tog] rep to end of row.
Row 6 P.
Row 7 [k2tog] rep to end of row.
Thread yarn through sts and pull together.

BODY
Refer to the pattern for Mummy bear's head (see page 138), but using **yarn C**.

LEGS (MAKE 2)
Cast on 19 sts using **yarn C** and size 6 (4mm) knitting needles.
Work 14 rows in st st.
Row 15 K8, kfb, kfb, k9.
Row 16 P.
Row 17 K9, kfb, kfb, k10.
Row 18 P.
Row 19 K10, kfb, kfb, k11.
Row 20 P.
Row 21 K2tog, k21, k2tog.
Row 22 P.
Row 23 [k2tog, k1] rep to last 2 sts, k2tog.
Row 24 P.
Row 25 [k2tog] rep to last st, k1.
Thread yarn through rem sts and pull together.

ARMS (MAKE 2)
Cast on 8 sts using **yarn C** and size 6 (4mm) knitting needles.
Row 1 Kfb, k6, kfb.

Row 2 P.
Row 3 Kfb, k8, kfb.
Row 4 P.
Cont in this way until 18 sts on needle.
Row 11 K.
Row 12 P.
Work 14 rows in st st.
Row 27 [k2tog, k1] rep to end.
Row 28 P.
Row 29 [k2tog] rep to end.
Thread yarn through rem sts and pull together.

EARS (MAKE 2)
Cast on 20 sts using **yarn C** and size 6 (4mm) knitting needles.
Work 4 rows in st st.
Row 5 [k2tog, k1] rep to last 2 sts, k2tog.
Row 6 P.
Row 7 [k2tog] rep to last st, k1.
Thread yarn through rem sts.

i love honey in my tummy ...

MAKING UP

HEAD
Fold the head in half with the knit sides together. Sew from each end of the head, leaving a gap of approx 1½in (4cm) in the middle. Turn the right way so that the knit sides are now on the outside. Fill with stuffing and sew up the 1½in (4cm) gap.

NOSE
Fold the nose in half with the knit sides together. Sew up the seam starting from the tip of the nose. Turn the right way so that the knit sides are now on the outside. Loosely fill with stuffing (be careful not to overfill or the nose could look too large). Stitch the nose onto the front of the head.

EARS
Fold the ears in half with the knit sides together. Stitch around the sides from the center of the ear. Turn the right way so that the knit sides are now on the outside. Sew along the bottom straight edge to form a double-sided ear. Stitch the ears to each side of the head using the shaping at the top of the head to position them evenly apart.

BODY
Fold the body in half with the knit sides together. Sew from each end of the body leaving a gap of approximately 1½in (4cm) in the middle. Turn the right way so that the knit sides are now on the outside. Fill with stuffing and sew up the 1½in (4cm) gap.

ARMS
Fold the arms in half with the knit sides together. Sew from the hand to under the arm. Turn the right way so that the knit sides are on the outside and fill with stuffing. Position the arms to each side of the body and sew, leaving a small gap to insert stuffing for the top of the arm. Sew up the gap.

LEGS
Fold the legs in half with the knit sides together. Sew from the heel to the top of the leg. Turn the right way so that the knit sides are on the outside and fill with stuffing. Position the legs to the base of the body and sew them on tightly.

FINISHING TOUCHES
Embroider the nose, mouth, and eyes using brown yarn. Using the correct size teddy bear templates for the bear you are making (see page 209), cut out two iron-on interfacing-lined fabric feet pads, two paw pads and two ear linings. Position them correctly and sew on (see page 205).

Polly Dolly's Dress-up Day

Rating from ✿ to ✿✿✿

See individual project patterns for more detail

Polly Dolly loves dressing up. She is really quite vain and spends a lot of time looking at herself in the mirror. She likes to wear a different dress every day of the week. On Monday she wears a green dress, on Tuesday she wears a blue dress, on Wednesday she wears a purple dress, on Thursday she wears a pink dress, on Friday she wears a yellow dress, and at the weekend she wears her favorite dresses—the red dress on Saturday and the white dress with its little flower on Sunday.

There are various elements to this project. First come the instructions on how to make Polly Dolly herself (pages 144-147), including her hair. Then there are patterns for her outfits. On pages 150-151 are the patterns for her red dress with blue stripes, and for her blue shoes. On page 150-151 are the instructions to make her white dress. Finally, there are instructions for Polly's underwear (page 151), which is sewn rather than knitted.

Polly the dolly has plaits in her hair,
She has beautiful dresses she loves to wear,
A red dress, a white dress all patterned with flowers,
She looks in the mirror for hours and hours.

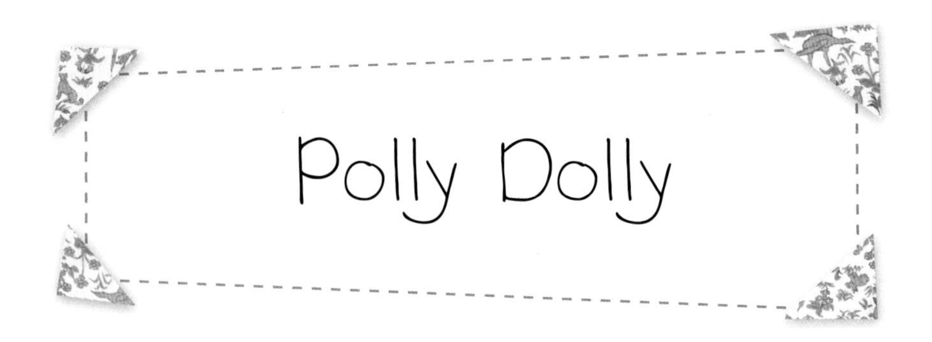

Polly Dolly

Rating

This is quite an advanced project because of the different components involved and the importance of getting Polly's face and hair to look right

You start knitting from the top of the doll's head. The head, shoulders, and body are knitted in one piece. The arms are picked up from stitches set aside while making the body. The legs are knitted separately. Take care when adding Polly's finishing touches, particularly her hair and facial features. Try to make her face look as realistic as you can, and arrange her hair into a pretty style.

yarn

Lightweight (DK) merino wool, microfibre and cashmere mix
1 x 1¾oz (50g) ball in pale pink

needles

Size 6 (4mm) knitting needles
2 stitch holders

gauge

22 sts and 30 rows to 4in (10cm)

finished size

18½in (47cm) from head to toe

Polly Dolly pattern

HEAD

Cast on 8 sts using size 6 (4mm) knitting needles.

Row 1 Kfb 7 times, k1.

Row 2 P.

Row 3 [k1, kfb] 7 times, k1. 22 sts.

Row 4 P.

Row 5 [k2, kfb] 3 times, k3 [kfb, k2] 2 times, kfb, k3.

Row 6 P.

Row 7 K2, kfb, k3, kfb, k3, kfb, k5, kfb, k3, kfb, k3, kfb, k3.

Row 8 P.

Row 9 K2, kfb, k4, kfb, k4, kfb, k7, kfb, k4, kfb, k4, kfb, k3. 40 sts.

Row 10 P.

Cont in st st for 18 rows.

Row 29 K2, skpo, k4, skpo, k4, skpo, k7, k2tog, k4, k2tog, k4, k2tog, k3.

Row 30 P.

Row 31 K2, skpo, k3, skpo, k3, skpo, k5, k2tog, k3, k2tog, k3, k2tog, k3.

Row 32 P.

Row 33 K2, skpo, k6, skpo, k3, k2tog, k6, k2tog, k3. 24 sts.

Row 34 P.

Row 35 K.

Row 36 P.

Row 37 [kfb, k1] 5 times, kfb 3 times, [k1, kfb] 5 times, k1. 37 sts.

Row 38 P.

SHOULDER AND ARMHOLE SHAPING

Row 39 K7, kfb, k1, kfb, k1, kfb, k13, kfb, k1, kfb, k1, kfb, k7.

Row 40 P.

Row 41 K7, [kfb, k1] 4 times, k13, [kfb, k1] 4 times, k7. 51 sts.

Row 42 P.

Row 43 K.

Row 44 P.

BODY

Row 45 K7, put next 12 sts (for 1st arm) on a stitch holder, cast 8 sts onto 1st 7 sts, k13, put next 12 sts (for 2nd arm) on a stitch holder, cast on 8 sts to the middle 13 sts, k7.

Row 46 P across 43 sts, leaving arm sts on the stitch holders to be picked up later.

Row 47 K10, kfb, k20, kfb, k11. 45 sts.

Row 48 P.

Cont in st st for 28 rows.

Row 77 [k2tog, k7, skpo] 4 times, k1. 37 sts.

Row 78 P.

Row 79 [k2, k2tog] rep to last st, k1.

Row 80 P.

Bind off loosely.

ARMS (MAKE 2)

Pick up 12 sts from 1st stitch holder.

Row 1 K.

Row 2 P.

Row 3 Kfb, k to last st, kfb.

Row 4 P.

Cont in st st for 36 rows.

Row 41 [k2, k2tog,] 3 times, k2.

Row 42 P.

Row 43 [k1, k2tog] 3 times, k2.

Row 44 P.

Row 45 [k2tog] 4 times.

Row 46 P.

Thread yarn through rem sts.

LEGS (MAKE 2)

Cast on 17 sts using size 6 (4mm) knitting needles.

Work in st st for 50 rows.

Row 51 K7, kfb, kfb, k8.

Row 52 P.

Row 53 K8, kfb, kfb, k9.

Row 54 P.

Row 55 K9, kfb, kfb, k10.

Row 56 P.

Row 57 K10, kfb, kfb, k11.
Row 58 P.
Row 59 K11, kfb, kfb, k12.
Row 60 P.
Row 61 K2tog, k23, k2tog.
Row 62 P.
Row 63 K2tog, k9, k3tog, k9, k2tog. 21 sts.
Row 64 P.
Bind off.

MAKING UP

BODY
The head, body, and arms are knitted all in one piece. Because the arms and legs are thin it is easier not to have to turn the pieces inside out to sew.
Sew along the arms and fill with stuffing.
Sew down the back of the body and head and fill with stuffing, leaving the bottom seam open for the legs.

LEGS
Sew down the back of the legs to the tips of the toes.
Fill with stuffing.
Sew the legs into the gap left at the bottom of the body, with the leg seam at the back.

KNEES
Halfway down the leg, pull up two or three stitches using the pink yarn. Sew the yarn neatly inside the leg so that no yarn is visible.

HAIR
Use two shades of brown yarn for the hair. Wrap the yarn around a large book (the book I used was approx 10½in/27cm tall). The bigger the book, the longer the hair. Continue wrapping the yarn around the book until it is approx 2⅜in (6cm) wide and 3/16–⅜in (5mm–1cm) thick. The more yarn you wrap, the thicker the hair.
Carefully stitch over and under one side of the hair, then back again so that every strand of hair is captured in the stitches.
Cut the hair on the other side of the book so that there is an even amount of hair on each side of the stitches.
Position the hair at the top of the head with the stitches in the center. Spread the hair so that it runs down the side and back of Polly's head.
Sew the hair tightly along the top of her head and around the bottom, back, and sides of the head.
Every strand of hair needs to be sewn down.
Divide the hair in two and plait each side. Tie the bottom of the plaits with more brown yarn to hold them in place.

FACIAL FEATURES
Embroider the eyes using brown or black yarn (as shown in the photograph).
Using the pink yarn, pull up two stitches just below the center of the eyes and pull tightly (just like the knees, but much smaller). This creates the nose.
Thread the pink yarn neatly inside the body so that no thread is visible on the outside.
Using bright pink yarn, make two or three stitches just below the nose. This creates the mouth.

Polly Dolly's red dress and blue shoes

Rating

Polly Dolly's red dress and blue shoes are fairly simple to make

The red dress is mostly knitted in stockinette stitch, with a few contrast bands in blue and a few textured bands in reverse stockinette stitch to form a waistband and a hem. The blue shoes are worked in garter stitch. You can make any color dress you like just by altering the yarn from the ones I have suggested. Make lots of different dresses in all shades of colors so Polly Dolly has a new dress to wear every day of the week!

yarn
Lightweight (DK) wool and cotton mix yarn
1 x 1¾oz (50g) ball in red (**A**)
1 x 1¾oz (50g) ball in blue (**B**)

needles
Size 6 (4mm) knitting needles

gauge
20 sts and 30 rows to 4in (10cm)

finished size
8in (20cm) long (not including straps)

Red dress and blue shoes pattern

DRESS
Cast on 90 sts using **yarn A** and size 6 (4mm) knitting needles.
Row 1 K.
Row 2 P.
Row 3 K.
Row 4 K.
Row 5 B k.
Row 6 P.
Row 7 K.
Row 8 P.
Row 9 K.
Row 10 A k.
Cont in st st for 24 rows.
Row 35 [k2tog] rep to end of row. 45 sts.
Row 36 K.
Row 37 P.
Row 38 K.
Row 39 P.
Row 40 K.
Row 41 K.
Row 42 P.
Cont in st st for 6 rows.
Row 49 B k
Row 50 P.
Row 51 A k
Row 52 P.
Row 53 Bind off 15 sts, k15 (work only on these middle 15 sts).
Row 54 P.
Row 55 K.
Row 56 P.
Bind off middle 15 sts.
Bind off rem 15 sts.

DRESS STRAPS (MAKE 2)
Cast on 4 sts using **yarn B** and size 6 (4mm) knitting needles.
Work in st st for 22 rows.
Bind off.

SHOES (MAKE 2)
Cast on 26 sts using **yarn B** and size 6 (4mm) knitting needles.
K 6 rows.
Row 7 K11, skpo, k2tog, k11.
Row 8 K10, skpo, k2tog, k10.
Row 9 K9, skpo, k2tog, k9.
Bind off.

SHOE STRAPS (MAKE 2)
Cast on 3 sts using **yarn B** and size 6 (4mm) knitting needles.
Work in st st for 22 rows.
Bind off.

MAKING UP

DRESS
Sew down the back of the dress.
Sew each strap to the front and back of the dress.

SHOES
Sew up the back and bottom of the shoes, attaching both ends of the straps at the top.

Polly Dolly's white dress

Rating

This dress has more detail than the red dress, so you may find it more challenging

The white dress features a lacy panel around the bottom edge. It is also decorated with a pretty appliquéd flower motif. Polly Dolly's underwear is sewn rather than knitted; use the templates on pages 212–213 and follow the instructions on page 151 to make the vest and knickers. We've given you a template for the flower (see page 212), but you could add an appliqué of another pretty design if you like; maybe your Polly would prefer a butterfly or a star shape?

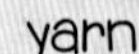

yarn

Lightweight (DK) merino wool, microfibre and cashmere mix
1 x 1¾oz (50g) ball in cream

needles

Size 6 (4mm) knitting needles

gauge

24 sts and 34 rows to 4in (10cm)

finished size

7in (18cm) long (not including straps)

White dress pattern

DRESS
Cast on 93 sts using size 6 (4mm) knitting needles.
Row 1 K1 [yon, sl1 pw, k2tog, psso, yon, k5] rep to last 4 sts, yon, sl1, k2tog, psso, yon, k1.
Row 2 P.
Row 3 K1 [yon, sl1 pw, k2tog, psso, yon, k5] rep to last 4 sts, yon, sl1, k2tog, psso, yon, k1.
Row 4 P.
Row 5 K1 [k3, yon, skpo, k1, k2tog, yon] rep to last 4 sts, k4.
Row 6 P.
Row 7 K1 [yon, sl1, k2tog, psso, yon, k1] rep to last 4 sts, yon, sl1, k2tog, psso, yon, k1.
Row 8 P.
Row 9 K.
Row 10 K.
Row 11 K.
Row 12 P.
Cont in st st for 24 rows, or 34 rows to make a slightly longer dress, adjusting the following row numbers by 10.
Row 37 k3tog [k2tog] rep to end of row. 46 sts.
Row 38 K.
Row 39 P.
Row 40 K.
Row 41 P.
Row 42 K.
Cont in st st for 12 rows.
Row 55 Bind off 15 sts, k16 (work only on these middle 16 sts).
Row 56 P.
Row 57 K.
Row 58 K.
Row 59 K.
Row 60 P.
Bind off 16 sts.
Bind off rem 15 sts.

STRAPS
Cast on 3 sts using size 6 (4mm) knitting needles.
Work in st st for 24 rows.
Bind off.

MAKING UP

Sew down the back of the dress.
Sew the straps to the front and back of the dress.
Cut out iron-on interfacing-lined fabric petals (see page 212 for template).
Sew each petal to the dress (see page 205). You could add more flowers if you want the dress to be more decorated.

Dolly's underwear

The templates for the vest and knickers are on pages 212–213.

KNICKERS
Using the template, cut out the knickers using T-shirt material. This stretchy type of fabric is perfect because it doesn't fray and has the added stretch that real knickers have.
Sew each side of the knickers together.
Turn the right way and sew a neat running stitch around the top for extra detail.

VEST
Using the same fabric as the knickers, cut out the vest using the template.
Sew a lace trim around the top of the vest.
Sew along the back of the vest.
Cut out two pieces of ribbon approx 3 1/8in (8cm) long.
Sew the ribbon to the top of the vest to form straps.

lovely lace

Simon Snake

Rating 

Simon's colorful patterns are made using the Fair Isle technique, which you might need to practise

Simon Snake is a very inquisitive snake. He loves to explore everything around him. He might seem scary, but he is actually a bit clumsy and not good at climbing, which is why he falls out of trees.

Simon's long, narrow body is knitted in the round using a circular needle, with double-pointed needles for the tip of the tail. You could knit his whole body in stripes if you prefer; use up the oddments in your stash.

yarn

Lightweight (DK) 100% merino wool
3 x 1¾oz (50g) balls in dark green **(A)**
1 x 1¾oz (50g) ball in blue **(B)**
1 x 1¾oz (50g) ball in pink **(C)**
1 x 1¾oz (50g) ball in red **(D)**
1 x 1¾oz (50g) ball in light green **(E)**
Oddment of white yarn **(F)**
Oddment of black yarn **(G)**

needles

Size 6 (4mm) knitting needles
Size 10 (6mm) circular needle
3 x size 10 (6mm) double-pointed needles

gauge

16 sts and 21 rows to 4in (10cm)
Don't worry if the gauge is not exact—it doesn't matter if Simon is a little bigger or smaller than shown

finished size

35¼in (90cm) long

Simon Snake lives in the trees,
He slithers along the bright green leaves.
You'd better watch out if you're below,
He'll drop on your head and land on your toe.

KNITTING NOTES

- You'll be knitting with 2 strands of yarn throughout for the head and body of the snake.
- You start the snake from the straight part of the tail end, but not from the very end. This is finished later.
- Stuff the snake's head and body while you knit; the longer the tube of the body is, the harder it is to stuff.
- See page 208 for the chart for the Fair Isle pattern on the snake's body.

Simon Snake pattern

BODY

Using waste yarn, cast on 32 sts on a size 10 (6mm) circular needle.
K 4 rows.
(This provisional cast on will be removed later.)

Change to **yarn A** using 2 strands. Cont using 2 strands for the entire snake in all colors.
Row 1 K.
Row 2 K.
Row 3 K.
Row 4 Start pattern in **yarn B** using the chart on page 208 (this is an 8-row pattern).
Rep these 8 pattern rows 13 times (14 color bands in all).
The color order is **B, C, D, C, B, E,** repeating until you get to the head.

HEAD (CONT FROM BODY)

Row 1 Using **yarn A** k7, kfb, kfb, k14, kfb, kfb, k7.
Row 2 K.
Row 3 K8, kfb, kfb, k16, kfb, kfb, k8.
Row 4 K.
Row 5 K9, kfb, kfb, k18, kfb, kfb, k9.
K 11 rows.

Row 17 K8, skpo, k2, k2tog, k16, skpo, k2, k2tog, k8.
Row 18 K.
Row 19 K7, skpo, k2, k2tog, k14, skpo, k2, k2tog, k7.
Row 20 K.
Row 21 K6, skpo, k2, k2tog, k12, skpo, k2, k2tog, k6.
Row 22 K.
Row 23 K5, skpo, k2, k2tog, k10, skpo, k2, k2tog, k5.
Row 24 K.
Row 25 K4, skpo, k2, k2tog, k8, skpo, k2, k2tog, k4.
Row 26 K.
Row 27 K3, skpo, k2, k2tog, k6, skpo, k2, k2tog, k3.
Row 28 K.
Row 29 K2, skpo, k2, k2tog, k4, skpo, k2, k2tog, k2. 16 sts.
Row 30 K.
Bind off.

TAIL

Unravel the waste yarn from the start of the snake and slip the **yarn A** stitches back onto the circular needles. Make sure you start on the 1st stitch.
Keep stuffing the snake as you go along; as you knit, the hole becomes smaller and you won't be able to stuff it at the end.

Row 1 Using **yarn E**, k. 32 sts.
Row 2 K.
Row 3 Using **yarn A**, k.
Row 4 [k6, k2tog] 4 times. 28 sts.
Row 5 Using **yarn B**, k.
Row 6 K.
Row 7 Using **yarn A**, k.
Row 8 [k5, k2tog] 4 times. 24 sts.
Row 9 Using **yarn C** k.
Row 10 K.
Row 11 Using **yarn A**, k.
Row 12 [k4, k2tog] 4 times. 20 sts.
Row 13 K.
Row 14 K.
Row 15 Using **yarn D**, k.
Row 16 [k3, k2tog] 4 times. 16 sts.
Row 17 K.
Row 18 K.

Because you have only a few stitches now, I would advise changing to 3 double-pointed needles instead of the circular needle as the work will be easier to manage.

Row 19 [k2, k2tog] 4 times. 12 sts.
Row 20 K.
Row 21 K.

Row 22 [k1, k2tog] to end of row. 8 sts.
Row 23 K.
Row 24 K.
Row 25 K.
Row 26 K.
Row 27 K.
Pull yarn through rem sts.

EYES (MAKE 2)
Cast on 4 sts with a single strand of **yarn A** using size 6 (4mm) knitting needles.
Row 1 Kfb in each st. 8 sts.
Row 2 P.
Row 3 Kfb in each st. 16 sts.
Row 4 P.
Cont in st st for 4 rows.
Row 9 Using **yarn F**, k.
Row 10 P.
Row 11 [K2tog] to end of row.
Row 12 Using **yarn G**, p.
Row 13 [K2tog] to end of row.
Thread yarn through needle to close.

FINISHING TOUCHES
Using the template (see page 208), cut out the snake's tongue in red felt and stitch it into the gap at the front of the head.
Close the gap with the tongue included.
Sew eyes onto the head (as shown in the photograph).
Embroider little nose details.

Rating 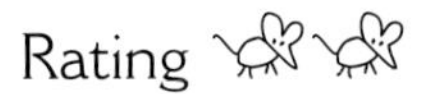

Easy to knit and assemble with minimal sewing

Percy, Penny, and Pickle are very happy pigs. Percy likes going to the market and Penny likes making cakes for her friends, the three bears. But watch out for naughty little Pickle; he loves Penny's cakes and when no one is looking, he will quickly gobble them all up!

Whether you make one or all three of the little pigs, choose a dusky pink yarn for adorable results. Their cute curly tails can be crocheted or simply plaited from the same yarn.

yarn

Lightweight (DK) merino wool, microfibre and cashmere mix
1 x 1¾oz (50g) ball per pig in pale pink

needles

Size 6 (4mm) knitting needles
Size E4 (3.5mm) crochet hook (optional)

gauge

22 sts and 30 rows to 4in (10cm)
Don't worry if the tension is not exact—it doesn't matter if the piggies are a little bigger or smaller than shown

finished size

Approx 7in (18cm) long and 5in (13cm) tall

percy Pig loves shopping, while penny loves to bake,
pickle Pig likes playing games and eating lots of cake.

KNITTING NOTES

You start knitting the piggies from the nose, then the rest of the head, and then the rest of the body, all in one piece. The piggies' ears and legs are knitted in separate pieces and attached to the body later.

Piggy pattern

HEAD

Cast on 4 sts using size 6 (4mm) knitting needles.

Row 1 Kfb 3 times, k1.
Row 2 P.
Row 3 Kfb 6 times, k1.
Row 4 K.
Row 5 K3, kfb, k4, kfb, k4.
Row 6 P.
Row 7 K4, kfb, k4, kfb, k5.
Row 8 P.
Row 9 K5, kfb, k4, kfb, k6.
Row 10 P.
Row 11 K6, kfb, k4, kfb, k7.
Row 12 P.
Row 13 K2 [kfb, k4] 3 times, kfb, k3.
Row 14 P.
Row 15 K2, kfb, k6, kfb, k4, kfb, k6, kfb, k3.
Row 16 P.
Row 17 K2, kfb, k8, kfb, k4, kfb, k8, kfb, k3.
Row 18 P.
Row 19 K2, kfb, k10, kfb, k4, kfb, k10, kfb, k3.
Row 20 P.
Row 21 K2, kfb, k12, kfb, k4, kfb, k12, kfb, k3. 41 sts.
Row 22 P.
Row 23 K.
Row 24 P.
Row 25 K2, skpo, k12, skpo, k5, k2tog, k12, k2tog, k2.
Row 26 P.
Row 27 K2, skpo, k10, skpo, k5, k2tog, k10, k2tog, k2.

Row 28 P.
Row 29 K2, skpo, k8, skpo, k5, k2tog, k8, k2tog, k2. 29 sts.
Row 30 P.
Row 31 K.
Row 32 P.

BODY
Row 33 K1 [kfb, k1] rep to end of row. 43 sts.
Row 34 P.
Work 26 rows in st st.
Row 61 K1 [k2tog, k1] rep to end of row.
Row 62 P.
Row 63 K1 [k2tog] rep to end of row. 15 sts.
Row 64 P.
Thread yarn through rem 15 sts and pull together to form the pig's bottom.
Leave a length of thread to sew the pig up.

EARS (MAKE 2)
Cast on 3 sts using size 6 (4mm) knitting needles.
Row 1 Kfb, k2.
Row 2 Kfb, p3.
Row 3 Kfb, k4.
Cont in this way until there are 9 sts.
Work 4 rows in st st.
Run thread through rem sts and pull up to form the base of the pig's ears.

LEGS (MAKE 4)
Cast on 16 sts using size 6 (4mm) knitting needles.
Work 14 rows in st st.
Row 15 [k2tog] rep to end of row.
Row 16 P.
Thread yarn through rem sts to close up feet.

TAIL
Use size E4 (3.5mm) crochet hook to make a chain, leaving approx 4in (10cm) of yarn before 1st chain stitch. Work 18 chains.
Thread yarn through last sts and sew through all the chain sts until you join the initial 3in (7.5cm) of yarn at beg of pig's tail. These 2 yarns are used to sew the tail onto the pig.

Alternatively, plait 3 ends of yarn together for approx 4in (10cm) and use this as the tail. Remember to leave some yarn at the end to sew the tail onto the pig.

MAKING UP

BODY
Fold the piggy in half with both knit sides (right sides) together. Sew from each end of the pig (his nose and bottom), leaving a gap of approx 1½in (4cm) in the middle. Turn the pig the right way out so that the knit sides (right sides) are on the outside. Fill with stuffing and sew up the gap.

LEGS
Fold the legs in half with the knit sides together. Sew up from the feet using the saved yarn. Turn the legs the right way out so that the knit sides are on the outside. Fill with stuffing and sew evenly and tightly to the underside of the body.

EARS
Sew the ears onto the top of the head using the shaping as a guide to position them evenly apart.

TAIL
Sew the tail onto the center of the pig's bottom. Twist the tail to make it curly and stitch into place.

FINISHING TOUCHES
Embroider the eyes and nose using little stitches. Using the templates on page 208, cut out four iron-on interfacing-lined fabric feet pads and two ear pads. Position as shown in the photograph and sew on (see page 205).

Mischievous Mice

Rating

Quick and simple to knit

These little mice are very naughty; they love to nibble on your favorite treats. They will happily eat your last cookie or slice of cake, and will even munch on the mouldy bits of cheese found down the side of your favorite armchair—yuck!

Mice are the perfect stash busters. You can enjoy creating lots of lovely mice, each using a mixture of different yarns left over from other knitted toys—this is a great chance to experiment.

yarn

Any small amounts of lightweight (DK) yarn from your stash

needles

Size 6 (4mm) knitting needles
Size 4 (3.5mm) knitting needles
Size E4 (3.5mm) crochet hook (optional)

gauge

22 sts and 30 rows to 4in (10cm)

finished size

Those shown are approx 4in (10cm) from nose to tail
The size of your mice and the gauge will vary depending on the type of yarn used

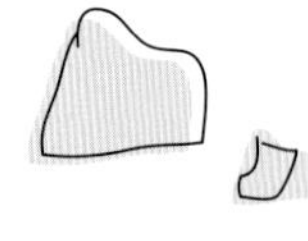

Little mice cause mischief,
running round and round,
They search for cheese and nibbles,
then hide them underground.

KNITTING NOTES

- You start knitting the mice from the nose all the way along to the bottom.
- To make the stripy mouse, work 2 rows in stockinette stitch in one color and the next 2 rows in another color. Continue this 4-row pattern throughout the mouse body. Carry the yarn not in use up the side of the work rather than cutting and rejoining yarn for each color change.

Mouse pattern

BODY

Using size 6 (4mm) knitting needles, cast on 7 sts, leaving approx 4in (10cm) of yarn before the 1st cast-on st. This is used for sewing up the mouse.

Row 1 K.

Row 2 P.

Row 3 K2, kfb, kfb, k3. 9 sts.

Row 4 P.

Row 5 K3, kfb, kfb, k4. 11 sts.

Row 6 P.

Row 7 K4, kfb, kfb, k5. 13 sts.

Cont in this way until there are 31 sts.

Row 26 P.

Row 27 K.

Row 28 P.

Row 29 K1 [skpo] 7 times, k1 [k2tog] 7 times, k1. 17 sts.

Row 30 P.

Row 31 K1 [skpo] 3 times, k3 [k2tog] 3 times, k1. 11 sts.

Row 32 P.

Slip thread through all 11 sts to close and pull to form the mouse's bottom.

EARS (MAKE 2)

Cast on 3 sts using size 4 (3.5mm) knitting needles.

Row 1 Kfb, k2. 4 sts.

Row 2 Kfb, p3. 5 sts.

Row 3 Kfb, k4. 6 sts.

Row 4 Kfb, p5. 7 sts.

Row 5 K.

Slip thread through all 7 sts to close and pull in to form the base of the ear.

Save approx 4in (10cm) of yarn to sew the ear onto the body.

TAIL

Use size E4 (3.5mm) crochet hook to make a chain, leaving approx 4in (10cm) of yarn before the 1st chain stitch.

Work 24 chains.

Thread yarn through the last sts and sew through all the chain sts until you join the initial 4in (10cm) of yarn at the beginning of the tail. These 2 yarns are used to sew the tail onto the mouse.

Alternatively, plait 3 ends of yarn together for approx 4in (10cm) to use as the tail. Remember to leave some yarn at the end to sew the tail onto the mouse.

MAKING UP

BODY

Fold the mouse in half with both knit sides (right sides) together. Sew up from each end, leaving a gap of approx 1in (2.5cm) in the middle. Turn the mouse the right way out so that the knit sides (right sides) are on the outside. Fill with stuffing and sew up the 1in (2.5cm) gap. Sew on the ears and the tail.

FEATURES

Wrap a different colored yarn several times around the nose of the mouse until it is completely covered. Knot a small piece of yarn above the nose and unravel to create whiskers. Embroider small stitches for the eyes.

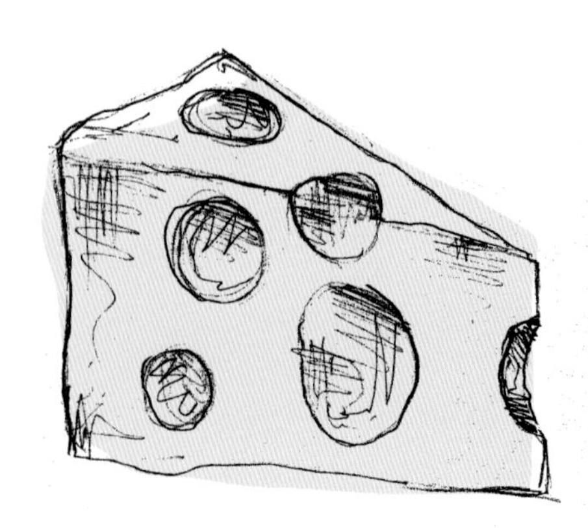

little mice running round and round ...

Eddie the Friendly Elephant

Rating

Eddie's head, body, and legs feature simple shaping, but you may find his trunk and tusks a little fiddly

Eddie Elephant is a gentle giant. He has big flapping ears to hear even the tiniest of sounds, but that doesn't stop him from getting scared. The naughty little mice always try to make him jump, and when an elephant jumps, everyone knows!

Eddie's ears and feet are lined with pretty scraps of fabric, and his tail is made from a crocheted chain. Purl ridges make the wrinkles in his trunk.

yarn

Medium-weight (aran) cotton and acrylic mix yarn
1 x 1¾oz (50g) ball in grey (**MC**)
Oddment of white yarn (**CC**)

needles

Size 8 (5mm) knitting needles
Size H8 (5mm) crochet hook

gauge

17 sts and 24 rows to 4in (10cm)
Don't worry if the gauge is not exact—it doesn't matter if Eddie is a little bigger or smaller than shown

finished size

Approx 5¾in (15cm) tall, 9in (23cm) long and 4in (10cm) wide

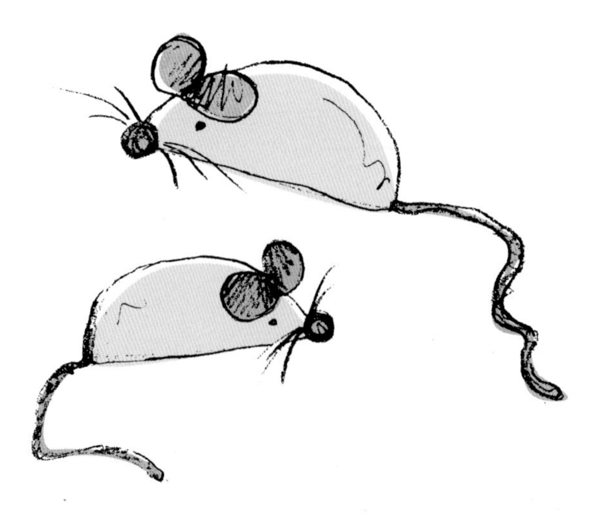

Eddie the elephant is grey and big.
He is very friendly with Percy Pig.
But Eddie Elephant is scared of mice.
They hide and jump, which is not very nice.

KNITTING NOTES

You start knitting from Eddie's trunk, then shape his head, then the main part of his body. His ears, legs, and tusks are all made separately and attached later.

Eddie Elephant pattern

BODY

Cast on 3 sts in **MC yarn** using size 8 (5mm) knitting needles.

Row 1 K1, kfb, k1.
Row 2 Kfb, kfb, kfb, k1.
Row 3 K.
Row 4 K.
Row 5 P.
Row 6 K.
Row 7 Kfb, k5, kfb.
Row 8 K.
Row 9 P.
Row 10 K.
Row 11 Kfb, k7, kfb.
Row 12 K.
Row 13 P.
Row 14 K.
Row 15 Kfb, k9, kfb.
Row 16 K.
Row 17 P.
Row 18 K.
Row 19 Kfb, k11, kfb.
Row 20 K.
Row 21 P.
Row 22 K.
Row 23 K.
Row 24 K4, kfb, k4, kfb, k5.
Row 25 P.
Row 26 K.
Row 27 K.
Row 28 K5, kfb, k4, kfb, k6.
Row 29 P.
Row 30 K.
Row 31 K.
Row 32 K6, kfb, k4, kfb, k7.
Row 33 P.
Row 34 K.
Row 35 K.
Row 36 K7, kfb, k4, kfb, k8. 23 sts.
Row 37 P.
Row 38 K.
Row 39 K3, [kfb, k4] 4 times.
Row 40 K.
Row 41 P.
Row 42 K5, [kfb, k4] 3 times, kfb, k6.
Row 43 P.
Row 44 K7, [kfb, k4] 3 times, kfb, k8.
Row 45 P.
Row 46 K9, [kfb, k4] 3 times, kfb, k10.
Row 47 P.
Row 48 K11, [kfb, k4] 3 times, kfb, k12.
Row 49 P.
Row 50 K13, [kfb, k4] 3 times, kfb, k14.
Row 51 K.
Row 52 k15, [kfb, k4] 3 times, kfb, k16.
Row 53 P.
Row 54 K17, [kfb, k4] 3 times, kfb, k18. 55 sts.
Row 55 P.
Row 56 K.
Row 57 P.
Row 58 K17, k2tog, k4, k2tog, k5, skpo, k4, skpo, k17.
Row 59 P.
Row 60 K15, k2tog, k4, k2tog, k5, skpo, k4, skpo, k15.
Row 61 P.
Row 62 K13, k2tog, k4, k2tog, k5, skpo, k4, skpo, k13.
Row 63 P.
Row 64 K11, k2tog, k4, k2tog, k5, skpo, k4, skpo, k11.
Row 65 P.
Row 66 K9, k2tog, k4, k2tog, k5, skpo, k4, skpo, k9. 35 sts.
Row 67 P.
Row 68 [kfb, k1] rep to last stitch, kfb. 53 sts.
Row 69 P.
Row 70 Kfb, k51, kfb. 55 sts.
Row 71 P.
Cont in st st for 30 rows.
Row 102 [k1, k2tog] rep to last st, k1.
Row 103 P.
Row 104 [k2tog] rep to last st. 19 sts.
Row 105 P.
Thread yarn through rem sts.

EARS (MAKE 2)

Cast on 12 sts in **MC yarn** using size 8 (5mm) knitting needles.

Row 1 K.
Row 2 P.
Row 3 Kfb at beg and end of row.
Row 4 P.
Rep rows 3 and 4 until there are 20 sts.
Cont in st st for 4 rows.
K2tog at beg and end of row. 18 sts.
Bind off.

LEGS (MAKE 4)

Cast on 5 sts in **MC yarn** using size 8 (5mm) knitting needles.

Row 1 Kfb in all sts. 10 sts.
Row 2 P.
Row 3 Kfb in all sts. 20 sts.
Row 4 K.
Row 5 K.
Row 6 P.
Cont in st st for 16 rows.
Bind off.

TUSKS (MAKE 2)

Cast on 5 sts in **CC yarn** using size 8 (5mm) knitting needles.
Work in st st for 4 rows.
Row 5 K1, kfb, kfb, k2.

ssshhhh ... don't scare Eddie ...

... he can hear everything with his big ears!

Row 6 P.
Row 7 K.
Row 8 P.
Row 9 K2, kfb, kfb, k3.
Row 10 P.
Row 11 K.
Row 12 P.
Row 13 K3, kfb, kfb, k4.
Row 14 P.
Row 15 K2tog, k7, k2tog.
Row 16 P.
Row 17 K2tog, k5, k2tog.
Row 18 P.
Bind off.

TAIL
Use size H8 (5mm) crochet hook to make a chain, leaving approx 4in (10cm) of yarn before 1st chain stitch. Work 18 chains. Thread yarn through last sts and sew through all the chain sts until you join the initial 3in (7.5cm) of yarn at beg of Eddie's tail. These 2 yarns are used to sew the tail onto the elephant.

Alternatively, plait 3 ends of yarn together for approx 4in (10cm) and use this as the tail. Remember to leave some yarn at the end to sew the tail onto Eddie.

MAKING UP

BODY
Fold the body in half with knit sides (right sides) together.
Sew from each end, leaving a gap of approx 1 1/8in (3cm) in the middle.
Turn the right way out so the knit sides (right sides) are on the outside.
Fill with stuffing.
Sew up the 1 1/8in (3cm) gap.
Attach the trunk to the body with a few stitches.

LEGS
Fold the legs in half with knit sides (right sides) together.
Sew from the heel to top of the leg.
Turn the right way out so the knit sides (right sides) are on the outside.
Fill with stuffing.
Position the legs to the base of the body and sew them on tightly.

EARS
Cut out two iron-on interfacing-lined fabric ears (see page 211 for template).
Sew each piece of fabric to the inside of the knitted ear (see page 205).
Stitch an ear to each side of the elephant's head using the shaping at the top of the head to position them correctly and evenly apart.

TUSKS
Fold the tusk in half and sew along the edge.
Fill with stuffing.
Position tusks to the sides of the trunk and attach securely.

FINISHING TOUCHES
Embroider eyes above the trunk using brown or black yarn (as shown in the photograph).
Using the template on page 211, cut out four iron-on interfacing-lined fabric feet pads.
Position correctly and sew on.

Three Little Fish

Rating 

The fish are a simple shape, but feature some Fair Isle and intarsia colorwork

The three little fish love to dart about in the waves. They dive deep down to the bottom of the seabed. But they had better watch out, because Peter Penguin loves eating fish for his tea!

These fish make the ideal project for using up colorful little scraps of yarn; I used yarn left over from Bertie and Beatrice the Birds (page 118). I've included some Fair Isle patterning, but you could make these fish in stripes or in plain, bright colors.

yarn

Lightweight (DK) 100% wool

I have given instructions for the fish with the blue tail. You need only small amounts of yarn in:

blue (**A**)
pink (**B**)
yellow (**C**)
green (**D**)

needles

Size 6 (4mm) knitting needles

gauge

22 sts and 30 rows to 4in (10cm)

Don't worry if the gauge is not exact—it doesn't matter if the fish are a little bigger or smaller than shown

finished size

7in (18cm) long and 2¾in (7cm) across the widest part of the body

Three little stripy fish, yellow, pink and blue,
One got caught by peter penguin, then there were two.
Two little stripy fish, having lots of fun,
One swam to deeper water, then there was one.
One little stripy fish, swimming all alone,
Was missing all his friends so he went back home.

KNITTING NOTES

• For this pattern I have written instructions for the fish with the **blue** tail. He has a **pink** nose, **pink** fins, and **green** and **yellow** details. Change the colors as you desire.

• This pattern features both intarsia and Fair Isle colorwork. The tail is worked in intarsia (see page 200), and the pattern around the fish's middle is worked in Fair Isle (see page 201). I have written out the pattern in full, but there are also templates and a Fair Isle chart on page 210 if you find that easier to follow.

• The fish is knitted from the tail to the head.

Fish pattern

BODY

Cast on 32 sts using **yarn A** and size 6 (4mm) knitting needles.

Work in st st for 4 rows.

Beg intarsia color changes.

Row 5 [**A** k2, **B** k5, **A** k2, **B** k5, **A** k2] rep to end of row.

Row 6 [**A** p2, **B** p5, **A** p2, **B** p5, **A** p2] rep to end of row.

Row 7 [**A** k2, **B** k5, **A** k2, **B** k5, **A** k2] rep to end of row.

Row 8 [**A** p2, **B** p5, **A** p2, **B** p5, **A** p2] rep to end of row.

Row 9 [**A** k2, **B** skpo, k1, k2tog, k2, **A** skpo, k1, k2tog, k2] rep to end of row.

Row 10 [**A** p2, **B** p3, **A** p2, **B** p3, **A** p2] rep to end of row.

Row 11 [**A** k2, **B** k3, **A** k2, **B** k3, **A** k2] rep to end of row.

Row 12 [**A** p2, **B** p3, **A** p2, **B** p3, **A** p2] rep to end of row.

Row 13 [**A** k2, **B** k3tog, **A** k2, **B** k3tog, **A** k2] rep to end of row.

Row 14 [**A** p2, **B** p1, **A** p2, **B** p1, **A** p2] rep to end of row.

Row 15 A k.

Row 16 P.

Row 17 [kfb, k5, kfb, k1] rep to end of row.

Row 18 P.

Row 19 [kfb, k7, kfb, k1] rep to end of row.

Row 20 C p.

Row 21 [kfb, k9, kfb, k1] rep to end of row.

Row 22 P.

Row 23 [kfb, k11, kfb, k1] rep to end of row.

Row 24 A p.

Row 25 [kfb, k13, kfb, k1] rep to end of row.

Row 26 D p.

Row 27 [kfb, k15, kfb, k1] rep to end of row. 40 sts.

Row 28 P.

Beg Fair Isle pattern.

Row 29 [**B** k2, **D** k2, **B** k2, **D** k2, **B** k2] 4 times.

Row 30 [**B** p1, **D** p2, **B** p4, **D** p2, **B** p1] 4 times.

Row 31 [**D** k2, **B** k2, **D** k2, **B** k2, **D** k2] 4 times.

Row 32 [**D** p1, **B** p2, **D** p4, **B** p2, **D** p1] 4 times.

Row 33 [**B** k2, **D** k2, **B** k2, **D** k2, **B** k2] 4 times.

Row 34 [**B** p1, **D** p2, **B** p4, **D** p2, **B** p1] 4 times.

Row 35 D k.

Row 36 P.

Row 37 [**A** skpo, k16, k2tog] rep to end of row.

Row 38 P.

Row 39 [skpo, k14, k2tog] rep to end of row.

Row 40 P.

Row 41 [**C** skpo, k12, k2tog] rep to end of row.

Row 42 P.

Row 43 [**B** skpo, k10, k2tog] rep to end of row.

Row 44 P.

Row 45 [skpo, k8, k2tog] rep to end of row.

Row 46 P.

Row 47 [skpo, k6, k2tog] rep to end of row.

Row 48 P. 16 sts.

Thread yarn through rem sts.

FINS (MAKE 2)
Cast on 7 sts using **yarn B** and size 6 (4mm) knitting needles.
Row 1 K2, kfb, kfb, k3.
Row 2 P.
Row 3 K3, kfb, kfb, k4.
Row 4 P.
Row 5 K4, kfb, kfb, k5. 13 sts.
Row 6 P.
Bind off.

MAKING UP

BODY
Sew the loose ends in to stop holes forming.
Fold the body in half with knit sides (right sides) together.
Sew from each end, leaving a gap of approx 1 1/8in (3cm) in the middle.
Turn the right way out so the knit sides (right sides) are on the outside.
Fill with stuffing.
Sew up the 1in (3cm) gap.

FINS
Cut out two iron-on interfacing-lined fabric fins (see page 210 for template).
Sew each piece of fabric to the inside of the knitted fin (see page 205).
Stitch the fins to each side of the fish body using the patterning to position them correctly.

FINISHING TOUCHES
Embroider eyes to each side of the head using brown or black yarn in the center. Edge the eyes with white or cream yarn (as shown in the photograph opposite).

Peter Penguin's Fishing Trip

Rating 

Peter is made up of simple shapes, but his coloring is worked in intarsia

Peter Penguin is very good at fishing. He can catch fish of all different sizes. Big fish, little fish, enormous fish, and tiny baby fish ... it all depends on how hungry he is and how many friends he has around for dinner.

This is quite a simple project, although you'll need to practise your intarsia technique, particularly wrapping the colors around each other where they change. Use plenty of stuffing so the penguin looks nice and plump.

yarn

Lightweight (DK) 100% wool
1 x 1¾oz (50g) ball in black (**A**)
1 x 1¾oz (50g) ball in white (**B**)
Small amount of yarn in yellow (**C**)

needles

Size 6 (4mm) knitting needles

gauge

22 sts and 30 rows to 4in (10cm)
Don't worry if the gauge is not exact—it doesn't matter if Peter is a little bigger or smaller than shown

finished size

Approx 7in (18cm) tall

Peter Penguin lives by the sea,
He dives in the water to catch fish for his tea.

KNITTING NOTES

• The colorwork for this project is done using the intarsia method (see page 200). When changing between the black and the white yarns, make sure you wrap the yarns around one another. This prevents holes appearing between colors.

• Peter is knitted from the head down.

Peter Penguin pattern

HEAD AND BODY

Cast on 9 sts using **yarn A** and size 6 (4mm) knitting needles.

Row 1 [kfb, k1] 4 times, k1.
Row 2 P.
Row 3 [kfb, k1, kfb] 4 times, k1.
Row 4 P.
Row 5 [kfb, k3, kfb] 4 times, k1.
Row 6 P.
Row 7 [kfb, k5, kfb] 4 times, k1.
Row 8 P.
Row 9 [kfb, k7, kfb] 4 times, k1. 45 sts.
Row 10 P.
Beg color changes.
Row 11 A k16, **B** k13, **A** k16.
Row 12 A p15, **B** p15, **A** p15.
Row 13 A k14, **B** k17, **A** k14.
Row 14 A p13, **B** p19, **A** p13.
Row 15 A k12, **B** k21, **A** k12.
Row 16 A p11, **B** p23, **A** p11.
Row 17 A k11, **B** k23, **A** k11.
Row 18 A p12, **B** p21, **A** p12.
Row 19 A k13, **B** k19, **A** k13.
Row 20 A p14, **B** p17, **A** p14.
Row 21 A k15, **B** k15, **A** k15.
Row 22 A p16, **B** p13, **A** p16.
Row 23 A k.
Row 24 P.
Row 25 [k2tog, k7, k2tog] 4 times, k1.
Row 26 P.
Row 27 [k2tog, k5, k2tog] 4 times, k1. 29 sts.
Row 28 P.
Row 29 [kfb, k1] rep to last st, kfb. 44 sts.
Row 30 P.
Row 31 A k18, **B** k8, **A** k18.
Row 32 A p17, **B** p10, **A** p17.
Row 33 A k16, **B** k12, **A** k16.
Row 34 A p15, **B** p14, **A** p15.
Row 35 A kfb, k13, **B** k7, kfb, kfb, k7, **A** k13, kfb.
Row 36 A p14, **B** p20, **A** p14.
Row 37 A k13, **B** k22, **A** k13.
Row 38 A p12, **B** p24, **A** p12.
Row 39 A kfb, k10, **B** k12, kfb, kfb, k12, **A** k10, kfb. 52 sts.
Row 40 A p11, **B** p30, **A** p11.
Row 41 A k10, **B** k32, **A** k10.
Row 42 A p9, **B** p34, **A** p9.
Row 43 A k8, **B** k36, **A** k8.
Row 44 A p7, **B** p38, **A** p7.
Row 45 A k6, **B** k40, **A** k6.
Row 46 A p5, **B** p42, **A** p5.
Row 47 A k4, **B** k44, **A** k4.
Row 48 A p3, **B** p46, **A** p3.
Row 49 A k2, **B** k48, **A** k2.
Row 50 B p.
Row 51 K.
Row 52 P.
Row 53 [k2tog, k9, skpo] 4 times.
Row 54 P.
Row 55 [k2tog, k7, skpo] 4 times.
Row 56 P.
Row 57 [k2tog, k5, skpo] 4 times.
Row 58 P.
Row 59 [k2tog, k3, skpo] 4 times.
Row 60 P.
Row 61 [k2tog, k1, skpo] 4 times. 12 sts.
Row 62 P.
Thread yarn through rem sts.

BEAK (MAKE 2 PIECES)

Cast on 3 sts using **yarn C** and size 6 (4mm) knitting needles.

Row 1 K1, kfb, kfb.
Row 2 P.
Row 3 K2, kfb, kfb, k1.
Row 4 P.
Row 5 K3, kfb, kfb, k2.
Row 6 P.
Row 7 K4, kfb, kfb, k3. 11 sts.
Row 8 P.
Bind off.

WINGS (MAKE 2)

Cast on 3 sts using **yarn A** and size 6 (4mm) knitting needles.

Row 1 K1, kfb, kfb.
Row 2 P.
Row 3 K2, kfb, kfb, k1.
Row 4 P.
Cont until there are 17 sts.
Row 14 P.
Cont in st st for 8 rows.
Row 23 K2tog each end of row.
Row 24 P2tog each end of row.
Rep these 2 rows until there are 3 sts.
P3tog.
Tie off yarn.

peter penguin is very hungry ...

... what size fish will he choose for his tea?

FEET (MAKE 2)

Cast on 3 sts using **yarn C** and size 6 (4mm) knitting needles.

Row 1 Kfb, kfb, k1.
Row 2 P.
Row 3 K1, kfb, kfb, k2.
Row 4 P.
Row 5 K2, kfb, kfb, k3.
Row 6 P.
Row 7 K3, kfb, kfb, k4.
Row 8 P.
Row 9 K4, kfb, kfb, k5.
Row 10 P.
Row 11 K5, kfb, kfb, k6. 15 sts.
Row 12 P.
Row 13 K5, skpo, k1, k2tog, k5.
Row 14 P.
Row 15 K4, skpo, k1, k2tog, k4.
Row 16 P.
Row 17 K3, skpo, k1, k2tog, k3.
Row 18 P.
Row 19 K2, skpo, k1, k2tog, k2.
Row 20 P.
Row 21 K1, skpo, k1, k2tog, k1.
Row 22 P5tog.
Tie off yarn.

MAKING UP

BODY

Fold the body in half with knit sides (right sides) together. Sew up from each end leaving a gap of approx $1^{1}/_{8}$in (3cm) in the middle.
Turn the right way out so the knit sides (right sides) are on the outside.
Fill with stuffing.
Sew up the $1^{1}/_{8}$in (3cm) gap.

FEET

Fold the feet in half and sew around the edges.
Position feet to the base of the body and sew them on tightly.

WINGS

Fold the wings in half and sew around the edges.
Position the wings to each side of the body just below the neck, with the pointed part of the wings facing downwards.

BEAK

Sew the two sides together and fill with stuffing.
Position the beak correctly at the bottom of the white part of the penguin's face.
Sew on tightly.

FINISHING TOUCHES

Embroider eyes using brown or black yarn (as shown in the photograph).

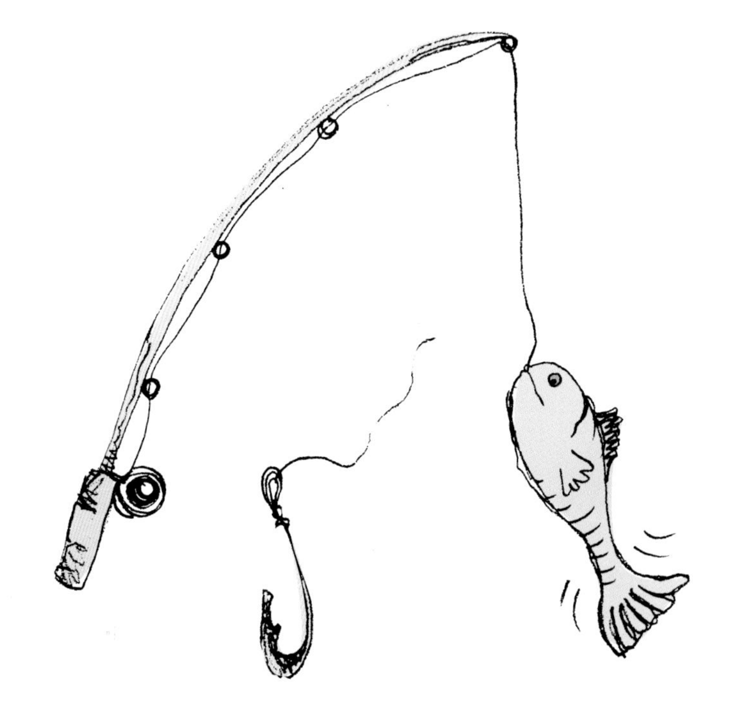

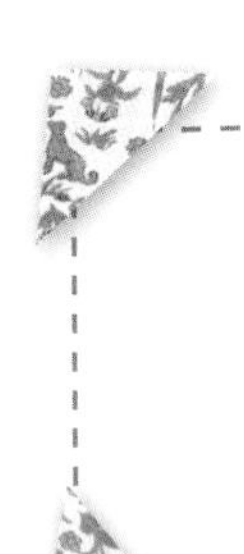

The Owl and the Pussycat

Rating from [icon] to [icon][icon]

See individual project patterns for more detail

The owl and the pussycat set out on their adventures to explore the secret islands. In their boat they packed lots of lovely food and treats made by all their friends. There was a delicious cake made by the three little pigs, carrot sandwiches from the bunnies, biscuit crumbs from all the naughty little mice, and a big pot of tea from the three bears. By the light of the moon they sailed away as they waved goodbye to the animals on the sand.

There are various pieces involved in making this project. There are the owl and the pussycat, of course, and then there is their boat (pages 188–189), complete with an anchor embroidered with their initials. The inside of the boat is reinforced with lining material to give it some structure and help support the knitted characters.

The owl and the pussycat went to sea
In a beautiful pea-green boat.
They took some cake and lots of sweets
Wrapped up in the owl's winter coat.
They waved goodbye to their friends on the sand
And sailed towards a faraway land.

The Owl

Rating

The owl is fairly easy, although you'll need to use intarsia to give him his snowy-white front

I used two shades of variegated yarn to give the owl a look of tawny feathers contrasting with his white chest. His round eyes are made out of felt and stitched on—see page 209 for the template. Take care with the owl's finishing touches and give him beautiful big eyes. Fill him with plenty of stuffing to make his ears pointed and his belly nice and round.

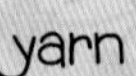

yarn

Lightweight (DK) wool or wool mix yarn
1 x 1¾oz (50g) ball in variegated deep reds (**A**)
1 x 1¾oz (50g) ball in cream (**B**)
1 x 1¾oz (50g) ball in variegated bright reds (**C**)
Small amount of yellow (**D**)

needles

Size 6 (4mm) knitting needles

gauge

22 sts and 28 rows to 4in (10cm)
Don't worry if the gauge is not exact—it doesn't matter if the owl is a little bigger or smaller than shown

finished size

Approx 8¼in (21cm) tall and 5in (13cm) wide (not including wings)

Owl pattern

EARS

Cast on 5 sts using **yarn A** and size 6 (4mm) knitting needles.

Working in st st, inc 1 st at end of every row until there are 27 sts. Slip onto a spare needle.

Rep for 2nd ear.

Slip the sts of both ears onto 1 needle.

P across all 54 sts.

BODY

Cont with the 54 sts from the ears.

Row 1 K.

Row 2 P.

Rep these 2 rows, 3 more times.

Row 9 K13, skpo, k24, k2tog, k13.

Row 10 P.

Row 11 K13, skpo, k22, k2tog, k13. 50 sts.

Row 12 P.

Row 13 K13, kfb, k21, kfb, k14.

Row 14 P.

Row 15 K13, kfb, k23, kfb, k14.

Row 16 P.

Row 17 K13, kfb, k25, kfb, k14. 56 sts.

Row 18 P.

Row 19 [kfb, k12, kfb] rep 4 times.

Row 20 P.

Row 21 [kfb, k14, kfb] rep 4 times. 72 sts.

Row 22 P.

Beg the color changes.

Row 23 K30 in **A,** k12 in **B,** k30 in **A.**

Row 24 K29 in **C,** p14 in **B,** k29 in **C.**

Row 25 K28 in **C,** k16 in **B,** k28 in **C.**

Row 26 P27 in **C,** p18 in **B,** p27 in **C.**

Row 27 K26 in **C,** k20 in **B,** k26 in **C.**

Row 28 K25 in **A,** p22 in **B,** k25 in **A.**

Row 29 K24 in **A,** k24 in **B,** k24 in **A.**

Row 30 P23 in **A,** p26 in **B,** p23 in **A.**

Row 31 K22 in **A,** k28 in **B,** k22 in **A.**

Row 32 K21 in **C,** p30 in **B,** k21 in **C.**

Row 33 K20 in **C,** k32 in **B,** k20 in **C.**

Row 34 P20 in **C,** p32 in **B,** p20 in **C.**

Row 35 K20 in **C,** k32 in **B,** k20 in **C.**

Row 36 K20 in **A,** p32 in **B,** k20 in **A.**

Row 37 K20 in **A,** k32 in **B,** k20 in **A.**

Row 38 P20 in **A,** p32 in **B,** p20 in **A.**

Row 39 K20 in **A,** k32 in **B,** k20 in **A.**

Row 40 K20 in **C,** p32 in **B,** k20 in **C.**

Row 41 K20 in **C,** k32 in **B,** k20 in **C.**

Row 42 P20 in **C,** p32 in **B,** p20 in **C.**

Row 43 K20 in **C,** k32 in **B,** k20 in **C.**

Row 44 K21 in **A,** p30 in **B,** k21 in **A.**

Row 45 K22 in **A,** k28 in **B,** k22 in **A.**

Row 46 P23 in **A,** p26 in **B,** p23 in **A.**

Row 47 K24 in **A,** k24 in **B,** k24 in **A.**

Row 48 K25 in **C,** p22 in **B,** k25 in **C.**

Row 49 K26 in **C,** k20 in **B,** k26 in **C.**

Row 50 P27 in **C,** p18 in **B,** p27 in **C.**

Row 51 K28 in **C,** k16 in **B,** k28 in **C.**

Row 52 K29 in **A,** p14 in **B,** k29 in **A.**

Row 53 K30 in **A,** k12 in **B,** k30 in **A.**

Row 54 Cont in **A,** p.

Row 55 [k2tog, k14, skpo] rep 4 times.

Row 56 Change to **C,** k.

Row 57 [k2tog, k12, skpo] rep 4 times.

Row 58 P.

Row 59 [k2tog] rep to end of row.

Row 60 P.

Row 61 [k2tog] rep to end of row.

Row 62 P.

Thread yarn through rem sts.

WINGS (MAKE 2)

Cast on 12 sts using **yarn A** and size 6 (4mm) knitting needles.

Row 1 K.

Row 2 Kfb, p11.

Row 3 K12, kfb.

Row 4 Kfb, k13.

Row 5 K13, k2tog.

Row 6 P2tog, p12.

Row 7 K11, k2tog.

Row 8 Kfb, k11.

KNITTING NOTES

- You start knitting the owl from his ears and work down towards his feet.
- The colorwork for this project is done using the intarsia method (see page 200). When knitting using two colors, make sure you wrap the yarns around one another when changing from one color to the next. This prevents holes appearing between colors.

Row 9 K12, kfb.
Row 10 Kfb, p13.
Row 11 K14, kfb.
Row 12 K2tog, k14.
Row 13 K13, k2tog.
Row 14 P2tog, p12.
Row 15 K11, k2tog.
Row 16 Kfb, k11.
Row 17 K12, kfb.
Row 18 Kfb, p13.
Row 19 K14, kfb.
Row 20 K2tog, k14.
Row 21 K13, k2tog.
Row 22 P2tog, p12.
Row 23 K11, k2tog.
Rep from row 8 to row 23.
Bind off.

FEET (MAKE 2)
Cast on 3 sts using **yarn D** and size 6 (4mm) knitting needles.
Row 1 Kfb, kfb, k1.
Row 2 P.
Row 3 K1, kfb, kfb, k2.
Row 4 P.
Row 5 K2, kfb, kfb, k3.
Row 6 P.
Row 7 K3, kfb, kfb, k4.
Row 8 P.
Row 9 K4, kfb, kfb, k5.
Row 10 P.
Row 11 K5, kfb, kfb, k6. 15 sts.
Row 12 P.
Row 13 K5, skpo, k1, k2tog, k5.
Row 14 P.
Row 15 K4, skpo, k1, k2tog, k4.
Row 16 P.
Row 17 K3, skpo, k1, k2tog, k3.
Row 18 P.
Row 19 K2, skpo, k1, k2tog, k2.
Row 20 P.
Row 21 K1, skpo, k1, k2tog, k1.
Row 22 P5tog.
Tie off yarn.

BEAK (MAKE 2 PIECES)
Cast on 3 sts in **yarn D**.
Row 1 Kfb, kfb, k1.
Row 2 P.
Row 3 K1, kfb, kfb, k2.
Row 4 P.
Row 5 K2, kfb, kfb, k3.
Row 6 P.
Row 7 K3, kfb, kfb, k4.
Row 8 P.
Bind off.

MAKING UP

BODY
Fold both sides of the body together with the seam at the back and the cream tummy at the front.
Starting from the top of each ear, sew to the top of the back seam, then sew from the top and bottom of each end, leaving a gap of approx 1 1/8in (3cm) in the middle.
Turn the right way out so the knit sides (right sides) are on the outside.
Fill with stuffing.
Sew up the 1 1/8in (3cm) gap.

FEET
Fold the feet in half and sew around the edges.
Position feet to the base of the body and sew them on tightly.

WINGS
Fold the wings in half and sew around the edges.
Pull up at the top of each wing to slightly gather.
Stitch the wings to each side of the owl's body using the white breast to help position them correctly.

BEAK
Sew both pieces together and fill with stuffing.
Stitch the beak to the owl's head using the shaping at the front of the head to position it correctly.

FINISHING TOUCHES
Cut out two felt eyes using the template provided (see page 209).
Position the eyes correctly on the owl's face using the beak and ears to help space them evenly apart.
Stitch around the edge of the eyes using brown thread.
In the center of the eye, embroider pupils using brown or black yarn (as shown in the photograph).
Use brown or black yarn to add a few stitches to the beak to make nostrils.

Southampton to Cape Town 5947
St Helena
(Br)

The Pussycat

Rating

The pussycat is quite easy to make, but take care over embroidering her features

I made the pussycat in two shades of variegated yarn to give her the look of tabby-striped fur. Use whatever color you like—maybe a pure black cat with green eyes, or a stripy orange one to look like a favorite ginger puss.

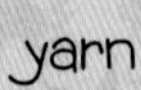

yarn

Lightweight (DK) 100% wool
1 x 1¾oz (50g) ball in variegated browns (**A**)
1 x 1¾oz (50g) ball in variegated bright reds (**B**)

needles

Size 6 (4mm) knitting needles

gauge

22 sts and 28 rows to 4in (10cm)
Don't worry if the gauge is not exact—it doesn't matter if the pussycat is a little bigger or smaller than shown

finished size

7in (18cm) tall and 4¾in (12cm) wide (not including tail)

Pussycat pattern

HEAD AND BODY

Cast on 9 sts using **yarn A** and size 6 (4mm) knitting needles.

Row 1 [kfb, k1] rep 4 times, k1.
Row 2 P.
Row 3 [kfb, k1, kfb] rep 4 times, k1. 21 sts.
Row 4 P.
Row 5 [kfb, k3, kfb] rep 4 times, k1. 29 sts.
Row 6 P.
Row 7 [kfb, k5, kfb] rep 4 times, k1. 31 sts.
Row 8 P.
Row 9 [kfb, k7, kfb] rep 4 times, k1. 45 sts.
Row 10 P.
Row 11 [kfb, k9, kfb] rep 4 times, k1. 53 sts.
Row 12 P.
Cont in st st for 8 rows.
Row 21 [kfb, k11, kfb] rep 4 times, k1. 61 sts.
Row 22 P.
Row 23 K.
Row 24 P.
Row 25 Change to **yarn B,** k.
Row 26 P.
Row 27 [kfb, k13, kfb] rep 4 times, k1. 69 sts.
Row 28 P.
Row 29 A, k.
Row 30 P.
Row 31 B, k.
Row 32 P.
Row 33 A, k.
Row 34 P.
Row 35 K.
Row 36 P.

Row 37 B, k.
Row 38 P.
Row 39 A, k.
Row 40 P.
Row 41 B, k.
Row 42 P.
Row 43 K.
Row 44 P.
Rep from row 29 to row 41.
Row 57 B, [k2tog, k13, skpo] rep 4 times, k1.
Row 58 P.
Row 59 [k2tog, k11, skpo] rep 4 times, k1.
Row 60 P.
Row 61 A, [k2tog] rep to last st, k1.
Row 62 P.
Row 63 B, [k2tog] rep to last st, k1.
Row 64 P. 14 sts.
Pull thread through rem sts.

EARS (MAKE 2)

Cast on 5 sts using **yarn A** and size 6 (4mm) knitting needles.
Row 1 K1, kfb, kfb, k2.
Row 2 P.
Row 3 K2, kfb, kfb, k3.
Row 4 P.
Row 5 K3, kfb, kfb, k4.
Row 6 P.
Row 7 K4, kfb, kfb, k3.
Row 8 P.
Bind off.

TAIL

Cast on 20 sts using **yarn A** and size 6 (4mm) knitting needles.
Row 1 K.
Row 2 P.
Row 3 K.
Row 4 P.
Row 5 Change to **yarn B,** k.
Row 6 P.
Row 7 K.
Row 8 P.
Rep rows 1 to 8, 4 more times.
Row 41 Change to **yarn A**, k.
Row 42 P.
Row 43 [k2tog] rep to end of row.
Row 44 [p2tog] rep to end of row.
Thread yarn through rem sts.

MAKING UP

BODY

Fold the pussycat in half with knit sides (right sides) together.
Making sure the stripes match up correctly, sew from each end of the cat, leaving a gap of approx 1 1/8in (3cm) in the middle.
Turn the right way out so the knit sides (right sides) are on the outside. Fill with stuffing.
Sew up the 1 1/8in (3cm) gap.

EARS

Cut out two iron-on interfacing-lined ear pads (see page 209 for template) and sew onto the purl side of the ear (see page 205).
Stitch an ear to each side of the cat's head using the shaping at the top to position them evenly apart.

TAIL

Fold the tail in half with knit sides (right sides) together.
Making sure the stripes match up correctly, sew up the tail to make a tube with the shaped end closed.
Turn the right way out so the knit sides (right sides) are on the outside. Fill with stuffing.
Position the tail to the back of the cat using the seam as a center guide.
Make a small stitch to attach the tail to the side of the cat.

FINISHING TOUCHES

Embroider the nose using pink yarn and the mouth, eyes, and whiskers using brown or black yarn (as shown in the photograph). Unravel the yarn if you want to create curly whiskers.

KNITTING NOTES

- You start knitting the pussycat from her head downwards.
- The pussycat's body is worked in stripes. It's best to work these by carrying the yarn currently not being worked up the side. Avoid breaking the yarn at the end of each stripe; carrying the yarns up the side instead ensures an even, straight edge. Keep your gauge consistent and don't pull the edge too tight.

The Owl and the Pussycat's Boat

Rating

The shapes of the boat are easy to make, although you may find the anchor a little fiddly

The boat features some garter-stitch ridges to look like the planks of a rowing boat. I used variegated greens for a pea-green boat, but you could use brown yarn to make it look more like a traditional wooden sailing boat.

yarn

Lightweight (DK) 100% wool
Boat—2 x 1¾oz (50g) balls in variegated greens (**A**)
Anchor—small amount of grey (**B**)

needles

Size 10½ (7mm) knitting needles
3 size 8 (5mm) double-pointed needles
Size E4 (3.5mm) crochet hook

gauge

14 sts and 22 rows to 4in (10cm)
Don't worry if the gauge is not exact—it doesn't matter if the boat is a little bigger or smaller than shown

finished size

Approx 12½in (32cm) long

Boat pattern

Note that the sides and ends of the boat are knitted using 2 strands of yarn together. This creates a more sturdy boat.

BOAT SIDES (MAKE 2)
Cast on 40 sts using **yarn A** and size 10½ (7mm) knitting needles.
K 4 rows.
Row 5 P.
Row 6 K2tog, k to last 2 sts, k2tog. 38 sts.
Row 7 P.
Row 8 K.
Row 9 K.
Row 10 K2tog, k to last 2 sts, k2tog. 36 sts.
Row 11 P.
Row 12 K.
Row 13 P.
Row 14 K.
Row 15 K.
Row 16 K2tog, k to last 2 sts, k2tog. 34 sts.
Row 17 P.
Row 18 K.
Row 19 P.
Row 20 K.
Row 21 K.
Row 22 K2tog, k to last 2 sts, k2tog. 32 sts.
Row 23 P.
Row 24 K.
Row 25 P.
Row 26 K.
Bind off.

BOAT ENDS (MAKE 2)
Cast on 8 sts using **yarn A** and size 10½ (7mm) knitting needles.
K 4 rows.
Row 5 P.
Row 6 K.
Row 7 P.
Row 8 K.
Row 9 K.
Row 10 K.
Rep rows 5 to 10.
Row 17 P.
Row 18 K.
Row 19 P.
Row 20 K.
Bind off.

ANCHOR BOTTOM
Cast on 4 sts using **yarn B** and size 8 (5mm) double-pointed needles.
Transfer 2 sts onto the 2nd needle.
Knit in the round for 4 rows.
Row 5 [k1, kfb] twice. 6 sts.
Introduce the 3rd double-pointed needle and put 2 sts on each needle.
Row 6 K.
Row 7 K.
Row 8 K.
Row 9 [k1, kfb] 3 times. 9 sts.
Row 10 K.
Row 11 K.
Row 12 [k2, kfb] 3 times. 12 sts.
Knit 4 rows.
Row 17 [k2, k2tog] 3 times. 9 sts.
Row 18 K.
Row 19 K.
Row 20 [k1, k2tog] 3 times. 6 sts.
Row 21 K.
Row 22 K.
Row 23 K.
Row 24 [k1, k2tog] 2 times. 4 sts.
Put aside the 3rd needle and put 2 sts on the rem 2 needles.
Knit in the round for 4 rows.
Bind off.

ANCHOR TOP
Pick up 4 sts from the top of the anchor bottom (2 sts on each needle).
Knit in the round for 10 rows.
Transfer 2 sts onto a holding needle. Save these for later.
Row 11 P2
Row 12 K2.
Rep rows 11 and 12, 10 more times.
Join the 2 sts left on the holding needle to those on the knitting needle to create a ring.
Bind off all sts, leaving length of yarn to crochet the anchor chain.

ANCHOR CHAIN
Using 1 end of yarn and a size E4 (3.5mm) crochet hook, make a crochet chain approx 4in (10cm) long.
Loop through the anchor top ring.
Tie off yarn.

MAKING UP

Sew together the bottom of both boat sides.
Sew a boat end to each end.
Cut out a 1 1/8in (3cm) wide strip of iron-on interfacing-lined fabric to reinforce the inside of the boat. Measure around the inside of the boat and cut a piece of fabric the same length. (A thick ribbon instead of a strip of fabric would work too.)
Sew neatly around the inside top for an extra detail. This also adds support to the boat sides.
Attach the anchor chain to the end of the boat.
Embroider 'O&P' on the anchor using yellow yarn.

KNITTING NOTES

You'll be knitting with 2 strands of yarn throughout for the 2 sides and ends of the boat.

Techniques

Abbreviations

All knitting patterns use abbreviations to save time and space when writing out the instructions. These may seem a bit daunting if you are not familiar with the terms, but you'll quickly pick up the language. Below is a list of all the abbreviations used in the patterns for this section.

approx approximately
beg beginning
CC contrast color
cm(s) centimetre(s)
cont continue
dec decrease
DK double knitting
g gram(s)
in(s) inch(es)
inc increase
k knit
k2tog knit the next two stitches together (decrease by one stitch)
k3tog knit the next three stitches together (decrease by two stitches)
kfb knit forward and back into the same stitch (increase by one stitch)
m metre(s)
MC main color
mm millimetre(s)
oz ounce(s)
p purl
p2tog purl the next two stitches together (decrease by one stitch)
p3tog purl the next three stitches together (decrease by two stitches)
p5tog purl the next five stitches together (decrease by four stitches)
patt pattern
psso pass the slipped stitch over (decrease by one stitch)
rem remaining
rep repeat
skpo slip one, knit one, pass the slipped stitch over (decrease by one stitch)
sl slip
sl1 slip one stitch
st(s) stitch(es)
st st stockinette stitch (stocking stitch)
tog together
yd yard(s)
yon yarn over/yarn over needle (increase by one stitch in lace pattern)

Casting on

I wanted to make my patterns appealing to beginner knitters as well as to those with more experience. If you are new to knitting, or could do with a reminder of some of the main techniques, I have included instructions for some of the basics you'll need to make the toys. Any project starts with casting on the stitches—this means getting the initial stitches onto the knitting needles.

There are quite a few different ways of casting on, and you may have your own favorite method. However, the knitting-on method is a simple and versatile technique.

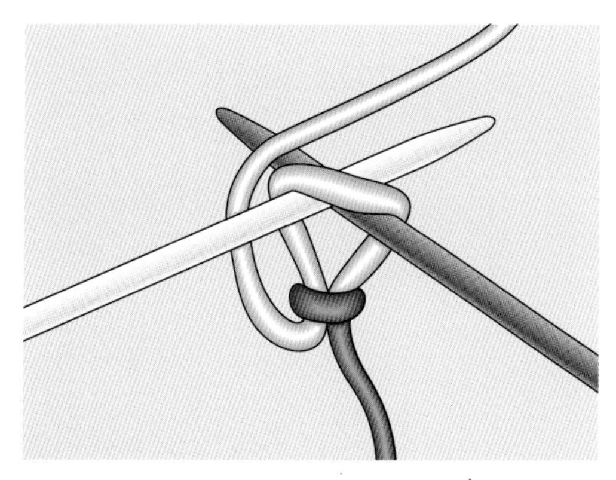

1 Make a slipknot in the working end of your yarn and place it on the left-hand needle. Insert your right needle into the loop of the slipknot and wrap the yarn around the tip of the needle, from back to front.

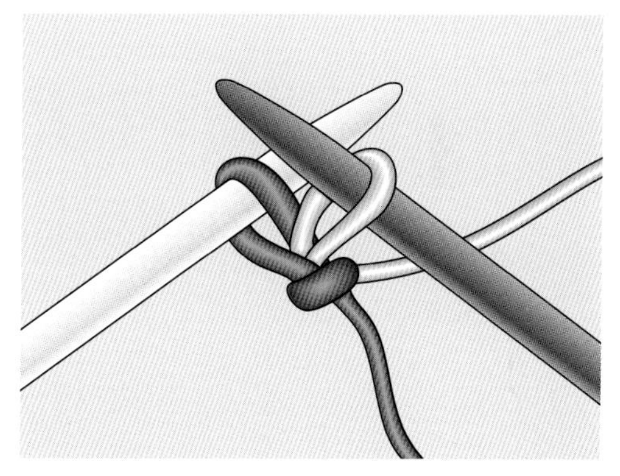

2 Slide the tip of the right-hand needle down to catch this new loop of yarn.

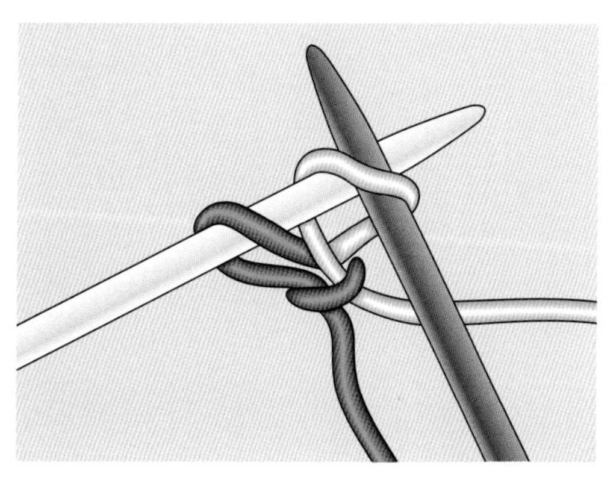

3 Place the new loop on the left-hand needle.

4 Repeat this process until you have cast on as many stitches as the project requires.

The knit and purl stitches

The knit stitch and the purl stitch are the two most basic stitches in knitting, but you'll get a long way just knowing these two. The toys are mostly knitted in stockinette stitch (sometimes called stocking stitch by European knitters), which involves knitting one row and purling the next row.

The knit stitch

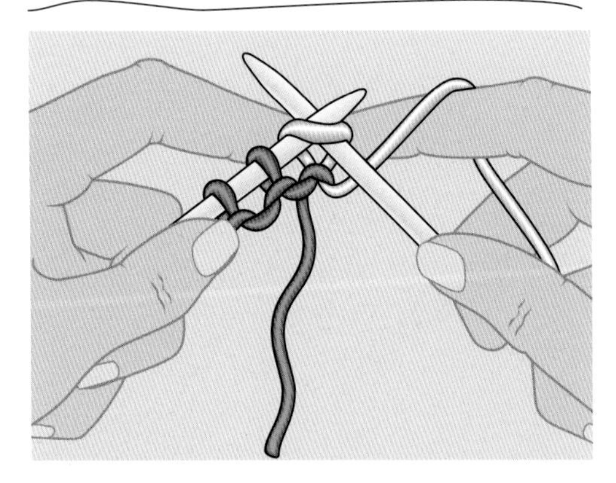

1 The working stitches will be on the left-hand needle. Take the right-hand needle and insert the tip from right to left into the first loop on the left-hand needle.

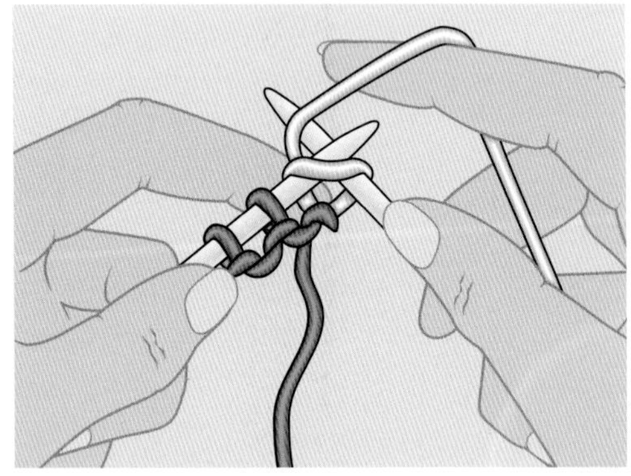

2 Wrap the yarn from back to front around the tip of the right-hand needle.

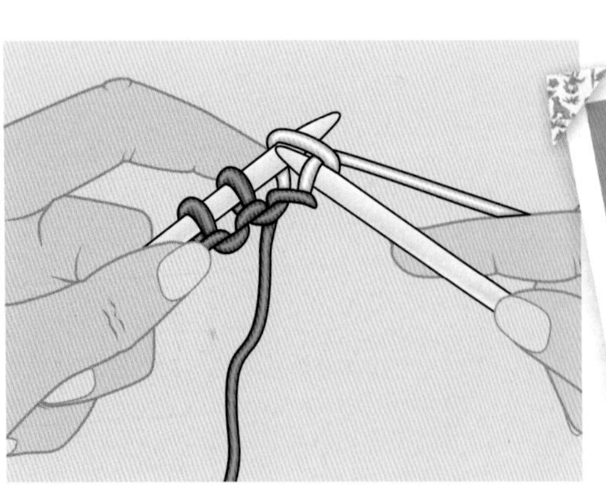

3 Slide the needle down to catch this new loop of yarn. Slip the loop off the left-hand needle and onto the right-hand needle. This is your first stitch. Repeat the process until all the stitches have been knitted off the left-hand needle onto the right-hand one.

The purl stitch

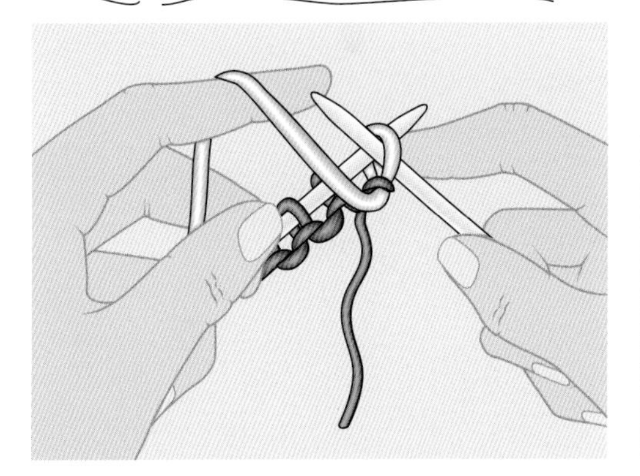

1 The working stitches will be on your left-hand needle.

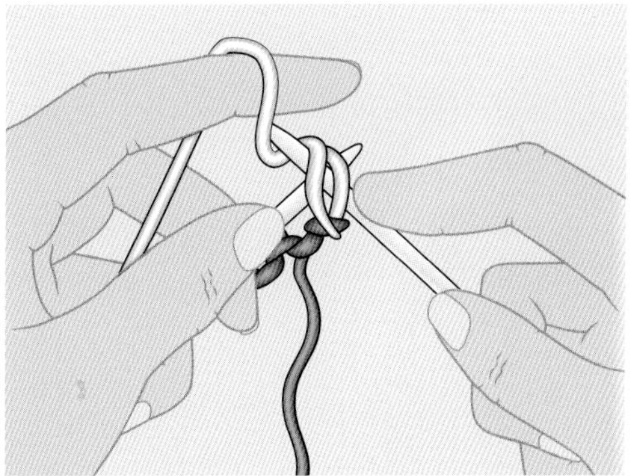

2 Wrap the yarn counterclockwise around the tip of the right-hand needle.

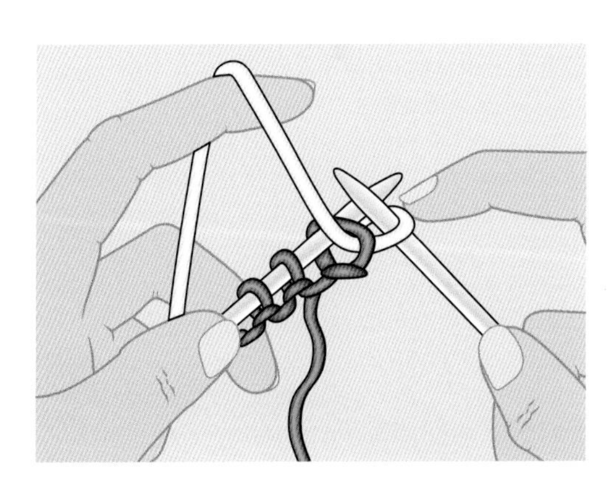

3 Use the tip of this needle to pick up the new loop of yarn. Slide the loop off the left-hand needle and onto the right-hand needle. This is your first stitch. Repeat the process until all the stitches have been knitted off the left-hand needle onto the right-hand one.

Basic stitch patterns

I have used basic stitch patterns to make the knitted toys in this section; they are mostly knitted in stockinette stitch, with a few details knitted in reverse stockinette stitch and garter stitch.

Stockinette stitch

Stockinette stitch (also referred to as stocking stitch by Europeans) is the main knitted fabric and the one that features most often in knitted designs. It is created by knitting one row and purling the next row. The knitted side forms the 'right side' or the outer side; the purl side forms the 'wrong side', or the inside.

Reverse stockinette stitch

Reverse stockinette stitch is made in the same way as stockinette stitch, but this time the purl side forms the right side. I have used reverse stockinette stitch to add a few details to some of the toys.

Garter stitch

Garter stitch is created by knitting every row. This creates quite a dense fabric that looks the same on both sides. Polly Dolly's shoes are knitted in garter stitch. The bottom edges of the babushkas are also knitted in garter stitch to give the dolls a firm edge around their bases.

Gauge

On the band or sleeve of every ball of yarn there is information on the gauge (what European knitters call 'tension') of the yarn. This tells you how many stitches and rows you should aim to achieve over 4in (10cm) square. The gauge will differ depending on the size of the needles you use and the thickness of the yarn. However, we all knit differently. Some people are naturally loose knitters and others knit more tightly. The beauty about toys is that the gauge doesn't really matter in most cases. If your toy is a little bit bigger or smaller than mine, who's to know! Knitting is fun and should be for everyone. The only exception in this section is with Polly Dolly (pages 142–151); you should try to achieve the suggested gauge for both the doll and her clothes, or you may find that the clothes don't fit her properly.

Binding off

The last stage of knitting the toys will be binding off. Then you can move onto the making up!

Standard bind-off

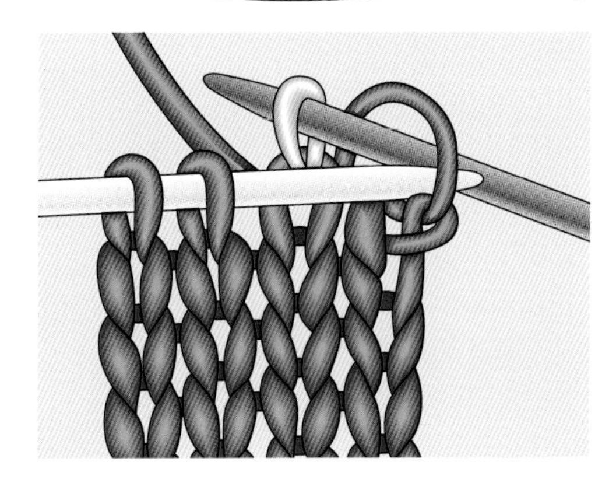

1 Work the first stitch on the left-hand needle as if making a usual knit stitch. Then knit the second stitch. Insert the left-hand needle into the first stitch on the right-hand needle.

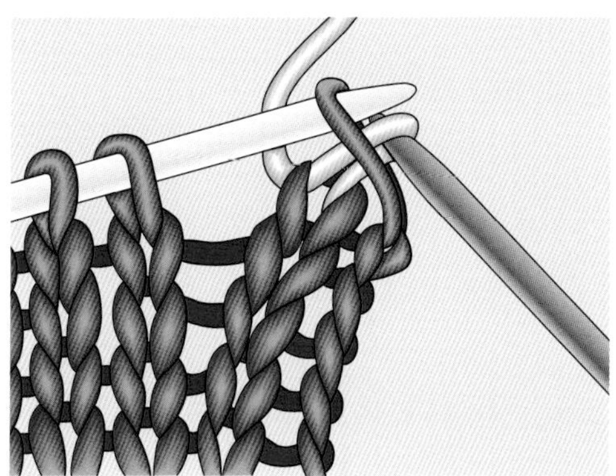

2 Pass this over the second loop on the right-hand needle and drop it off the needle. This makes the first bind-off stitch. To continue, knit the next stitch. Use your left-hand needle to pass the first stitch over the second stitch and drop it off the needle. Carry on until all the stitches in the row have been bound off.

Shaping

I am not a fan of knitting lots of components for each toy and then having to sew them up at the end. I like to see the toy develop as it is being knitted. Therefore, my patterns have been created with shaping (increasing and decreasing stitches). This gives you a three-dimensional effect without all the sewing. I have used several shaping techniques, which are explained below.

Decreasing stitches

Decreasing stitches is where you lose a stitch. This can be achieved in several ways.

SKPO (SLIP ONE, KNIT ONE, PASS THE SLIPPED STITCH OVER)

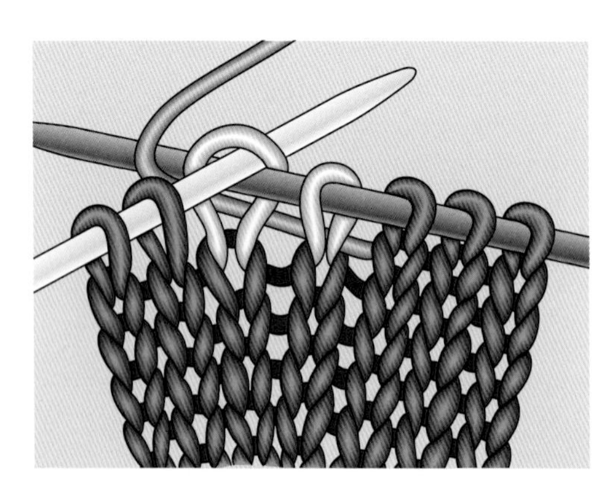

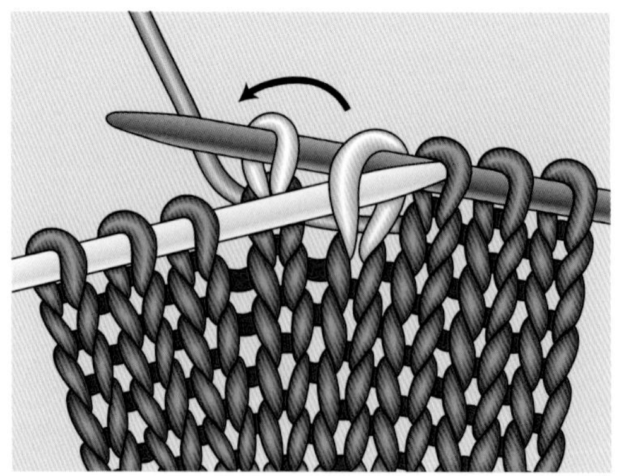

1 Knit along the row until you reach the area you want to decrease. Slip the stitch (unknitted) onto the right-hand needle. Knit the next stitch.

2 Lift the slipped stitch over the knitted stitch and off the needle. This decreases by one stitch.

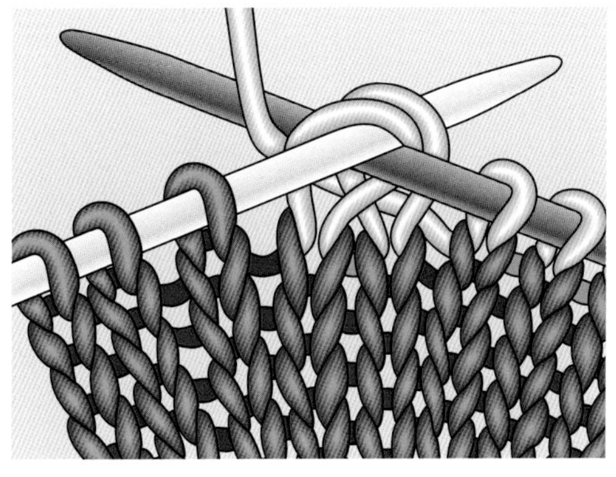

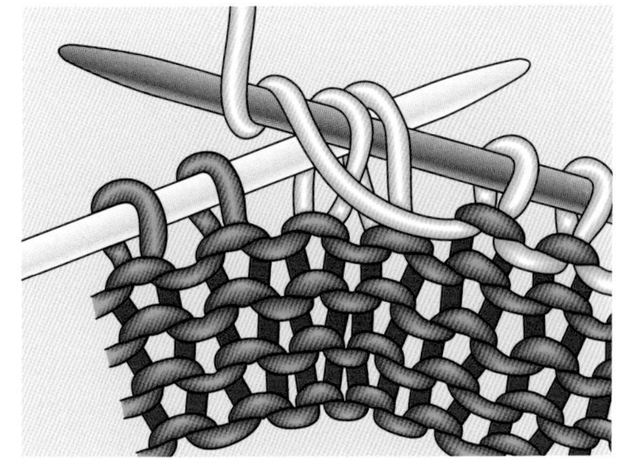

K2TOG (KNIT TWO STITCHES TOGETHER)
Knit along the row until you reach the area you want to decrease. Knit through the next two stitches as though they were one stitch. This decreases by one stitch.

P2TOG (PURL TWO STITCHES TOGETHER)
Purl along the row until you reach the area you want to decrease. Purl through the next two stitches as though they were one stitch. This decreases by one stitch.

MULTIPLE DECREASES
You can decrease by more than one stitch at a time. Some of the pattern instructions ask you to k3tog, p3tog and even p5tog. Work these decreases as explained above; you'll just need to insert your working needle through three (or five) stitches and knit or purl them together as though they were one stitch. K3tog and p3tog decrease by two stitches; p5tog decreases by four stitches.

Increasing stitches

Increasing stitches is where you make a stitch.

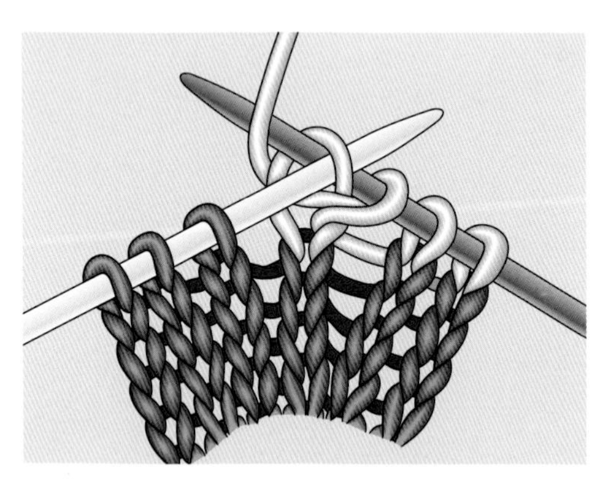

KFB (KNIT INTO THE FRONT AND BACK)
Knit along the row until you reach the area you want to increase. Knit into the front of the stitch on the left-hand needle. Instead of removing it from the needle (as with a normal knitted stitch), knit into it again through the back loop. Then slip the original stitch off the left-hand needle.

YON (YARN OVER/YARN OVER NEEDLE)
The lace panel for Polly Dolly's white dress (pages 150–151) features another way of shaping. To make the lacy pattern you'll need to pair yarnovers (a way of adding a stitch) with 'psso', or pass the slipped stitch over (a way of losing a stitch).

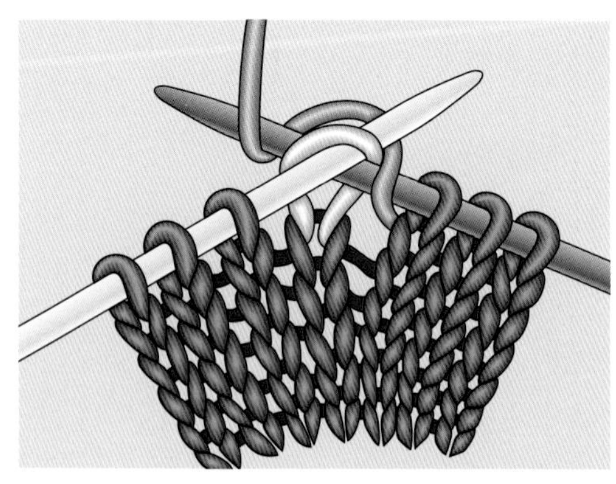

Bring the yarn over between the two needles. Knit the next stitch, taking the yarn over the right needle. This creates an extra stitch and also creates a hole in the knitted fabric.

Knitting in the round

Most of the toys in this section are knitted using two straight knitting needles, so you need to sew a seam up the back afterwards to make up the toy. However, some of the projects suggest that you knit in the round, using either a circular needle or double-pointed needles.

Knitting on a circular needle

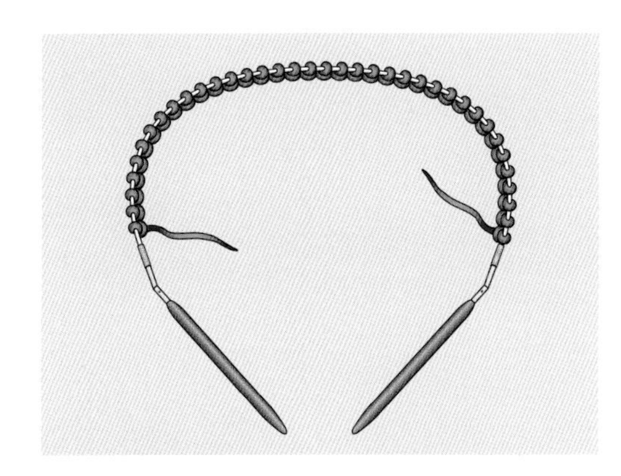

A circular needle consists of two pointed ends joined together by a flexible cord. This type of needle enables you to knit a tube of material seamlessly. Circular needles are great for knitting tubular pieces as you need to for Simon Snake (pages 152–155). It saves you having to sew up a very long and fiddly seam afterwards. Circular needles are available in different lengths. As the snake is a narrow tube, use the shortest circular needle you can find.

Cast on as you would normally and spread the stitches along the entire length of the needle, including the flexible cord. Sometimes there are not enough stitches to reach each end, but the beauty of the flexible cord is that you can bend it through some of the stitches so that they meet. You may want to place a marker (a piece of scrap yarn will be fine) to mark the start of the round.

If you knit every round you make a tube of stockinette stitch; there's no need to turn the work or to work any purl rounds. Try to ensure that the first round is not twisted.

Knitting on double-pointed needles

I've suggested working on double-pointed needles to work the tip of Simon Snake's tail and also to work the anchor on The Owl and the Pussycat's boat (pages 188–189).

Double-pointed needles are shorter than standard needles and are easier to handle than a circular needle when you have only a few stitches to work in the round.

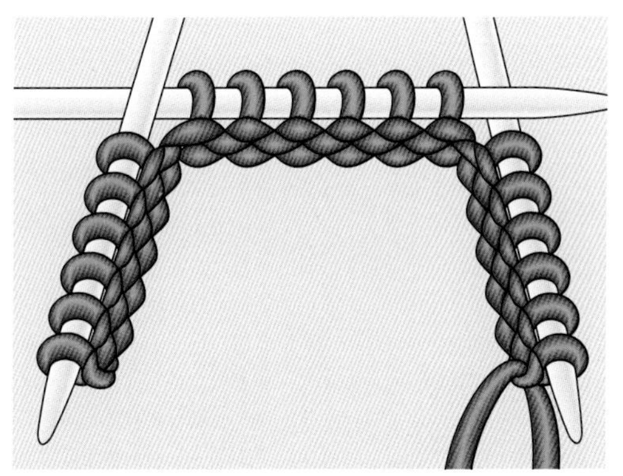

1 Cast on as you would normally and distribute the stitches equally over three double-pointed needles.

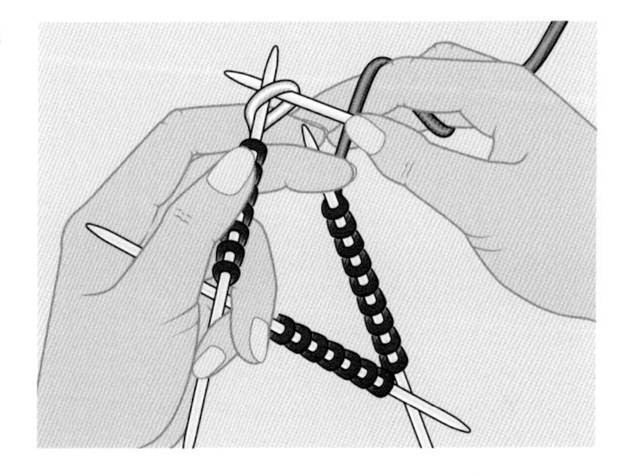

2 Continue knitting round, transferring the stitches along each needle so that you have an equal number of stitches on each needle. Again, you may want to place a marker at the beginning of the round.

Colorwork

There are two main ways to knit designs using two or more colors: Fair Isle and intarsia. Fair Isle is used to produce small-scale, intricate color patterns, often using repeated motifs. You usually use two colors of yarn in a single row of knitting, and these yarns are stranded (carried) across the row at the back of the work. Consequently, Fair Isle fabric is double-layered. Intarsia is used to create larger chunks or blocks of color. You'll need a separate ball of yarn for each color, and you'll often have to change colors in the middle of a row. The yarns are not stranded at the back of the work, so intarsia fabric is single-layered.

Intarsia

Intarsia is used for designs with big blocks of color. Separate balls of wool are used for each block. Unlike with Fair Isle, no floats (or strands) of yarn are created at the back of the work. Intarsia colorwork is used in a few of the designs: Bertie and Beatrice the Birds (pages 118–123), Frederick the Frog Prince (pages 124–129), the Babushkas (pages 130–135), the tails of the Three Little Fish (pages 170–173), Peter Penguin (pages 174–179) and the Owl (pages 180–189).

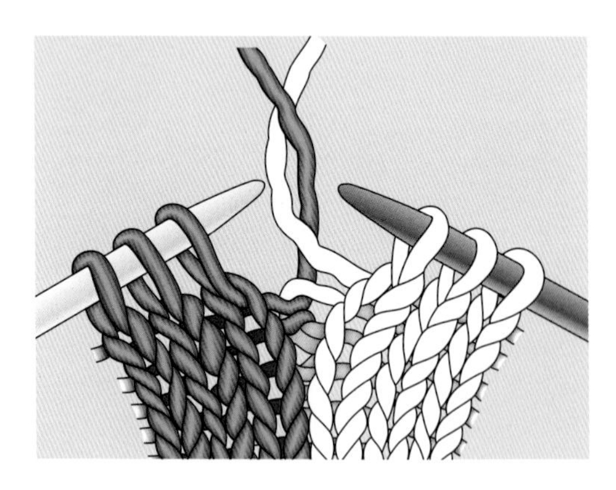

Knit along the row until the new color is needed. Drop the first color and pick up the second color underneath the first color, crossing the two colors over before knitting the next stitch in the second color. The crossing of the stitches ensures that no holes are created between colors.

Fair Isle

Fair Isle knitting is used on more complicated colored patterns with small, repeated motifs. I have used a Fair Isle pattern on Simon Snake's body (pages 152–155). There is also Fair Isle patterning around the middle of the Three Little Fish body (pages 170–173).

In Fair Isle knitting, each ball of wool is kept in action; you never cut the wool between stitches. Floats or strands are created as you work; these are horizontal strands of yarn that lie on the reverse side of the knitted fabric.

Knit along the row in your first color until you come to the stitch where you need to change. To knit a stitch in your second color, put the right-hand needle through the next stitch, pulling the new colored yarn through as the stitch. This will create a float. It is important not to pull the stitches too tightly when working on the next stitch or the knitted fabric will be distorted.

The best way to work Fair Isle is to hold one color yarn in your right hand (usually the background color) and the other color yarn in your left hand.

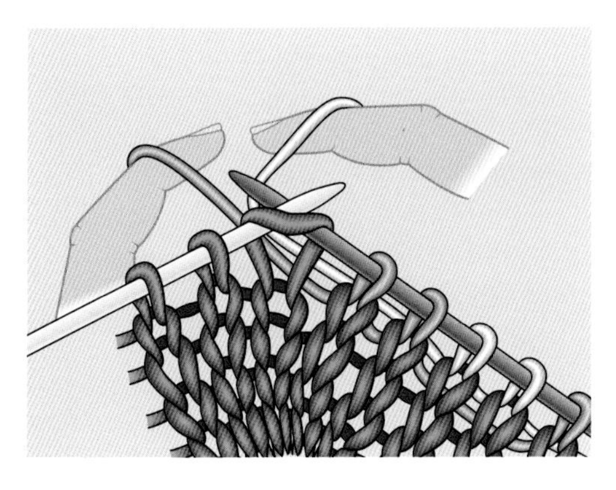

1 When knitting with the right-hand color, keep the left-hand color below the needle and out of the way of the working yarn.

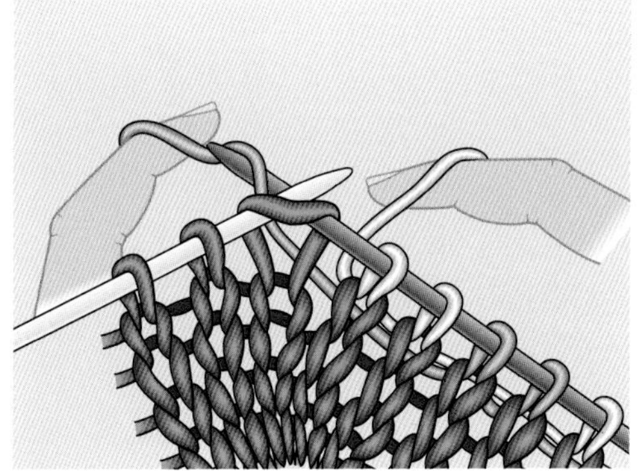

2 When knitting with the left-hand color, keep the right-hand color above the needle.

FAIR ISLE CHARTS

Fair Isle patterns are usually shown on a chart because it makes it easier to see how the pattern should look. You start at the bottom of the chart and work up. Each line represents a new row of knitting. Every time a colored-in square is shown, you change color.

The chart for Simon Snake is on page 208; the chart for the pattern on the Three Little Fish is on page 210.

Making up

All the patterns have been designed with the minimum amount of sewing, but there is always some sewing to be done! There are several ways to sew up knitting, so use whichever method you find easiest. Always use the same yarn you knitted with so the stitches are less visible. Tapestry or darning needles with a large eye and blunt end are best so that you don't split the yarn.

Weaving in ends

You'll have some loose yarn ends from casting on and binding off, so weave these in first. One of the best ways to weave in the loose ends so they will be invisible is to thread the yarn end through a tapestry needle and sew it into the seam by passing the needle through the 'bumps' of the stitches on the wrong side of the work. Sew them in for approx 1–2in (2.5–5cm) and then snip off any excess yarn.

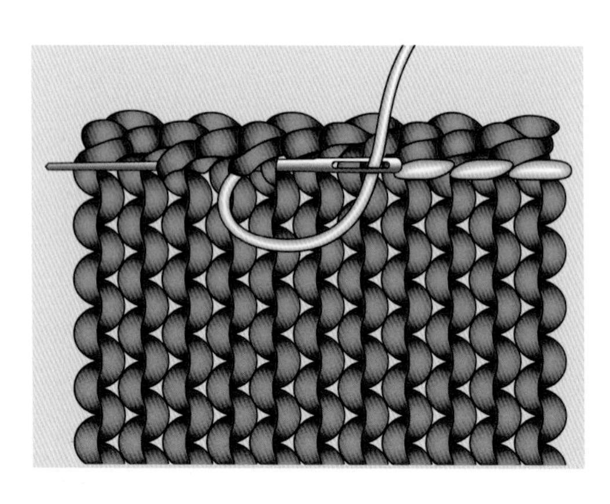

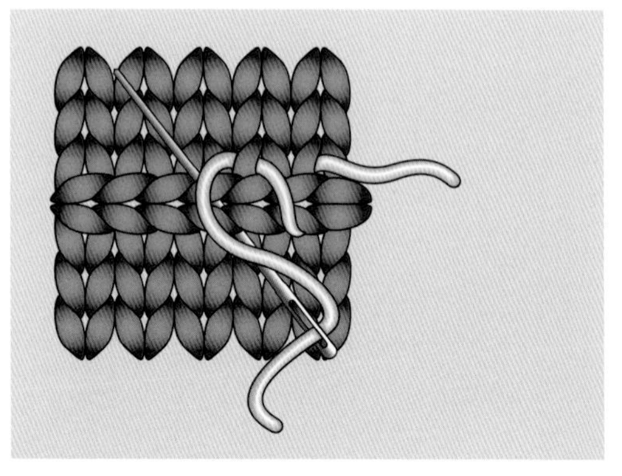

Backstitch (reverse sides out)

Put both knit sides (right sides) together so the wrong sides are facing you. Carefully make small running stitches along the edge, one stitch at a time. Make sure you are sewing in a straight line as close to the edge as possible. It might sound obvious, but it is very easy to pick up stitches that are further away from the edge than you thought. You want the sewing to be as invisible as possible.

Slip stitch (knit sides out)

Put the two pieces of knitting one above the other, knit sides out. Run the thread through the center of the first stitch on the top piece of knitting, then down through the center of the first stitch on the bottom piece of knitting. Next go through the second stitch on the top piece of knitting and down through the center of the bottom second stitch. Continue in this way along the row.

Stuffing the toys

Toy stuffing is an essential component for toys. Don't stuff the toys too fully or they will become solid and have no movement. You want the toys to be cuddly. Some of the projects require you to stuff the toys as you go along. This is generally when the toy is long and narrow, such as Simon Snake (pages 152–155). This ensures you distribute an even amount of stuffing throughout the toy.

The stuffing I use is Minicraft Supersoft Toy Stuffing. It comes in bags of 9oz (250g) and is made of 100% polyester. If you can't find this particular brand, other suitable brands should be available at haberdashery and craft stores. It is best to use stuffing designed especially for toys so that you can be sure that it is safe for children. Check for the safety logo before you buy it.

I always use my hands to put the stuffing in the toys. You can use your fingers to push the stuffing into small or fiddly pieces.

Sewing in final ends

Once you have stuffed the toy, you'll need to close the small gap in the middle of the seam. I knot together the two ends of the yarn used for sewing the seams, then thread the ends through the toy so that the knot is hidden and the ends are kept long. You don't want to cut the ends too short because it makes the knot more likely to come undone.

Finishing touches

One of the best parts about making toys is adding the finishing touches and really bringing the toys to life. It is amazing what adding a pair of beady eyes or a little pink nose can do. Here I've outlined a few techniques for sewing facial features. I also look at adding the little fabric appliqués that some of the toys have, and other little details like crocheted tails and pompoms.

Embroidering details

Spend time making the facial features perfect. It is really effective at making the toys characterful. Use leftover bits of yarn from previous projects. You can use any sewing stitches to create these features; there really is no rule. You need the stitches to be as firm as possible so that they don't undo and look neat as well. You could use backstitch for the mouth of the pussycat (page 187) or Frederick the Frog Prince (page 128), or a single running stitch sewn over and over itself to create the shape of a large eye. You could use a French knot to make the eyes on the smaller toys if you find this easier. Choose what works best for you.

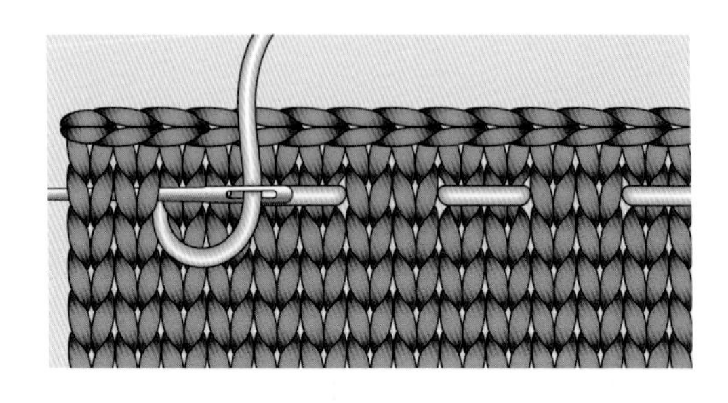

RUNNING STITCH

This is a very simple stitch. Thread a tapestry or darning needle with the yarn you want to use and insert it from the back of the work through to the front where you want the stitch to start. Insert it back through your knitting where you want your stitch to end. This creates an effect like a line of dashes.

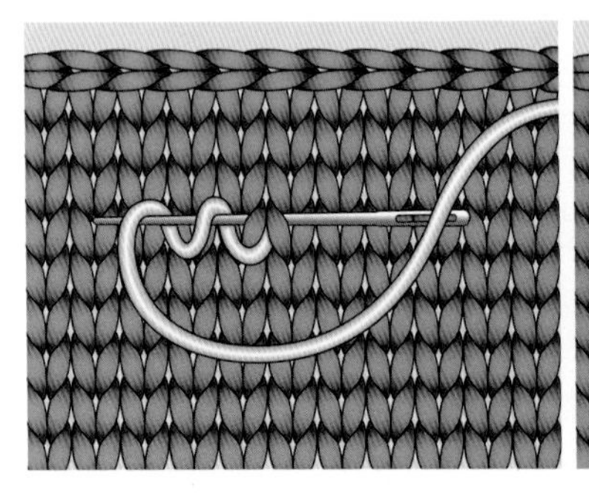

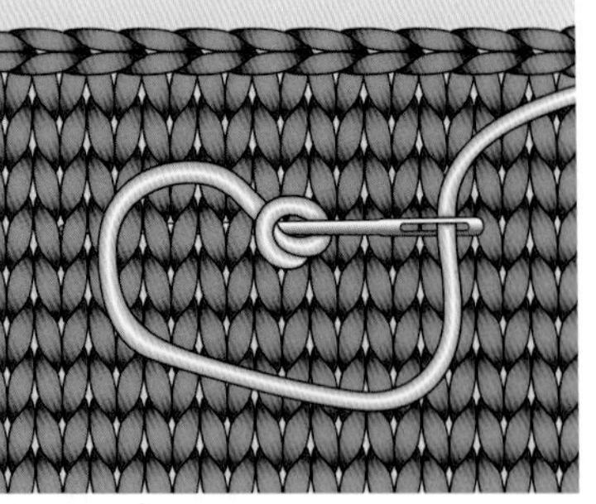

FRENCH KNOT

Bring the needle from the back to the front of the work and wind the yarn twice around the needle. Pull the needle through the twists bringing the yarn through too. This creates the knot. You can twist the yarn around the needle more times if you want a bigger knot and once only for a smaller knot.

BACKSTITCH

Sew a running stitch to create the pattern you want. Once you have reached the end of your pattern go back on yourself, filling in the gaps between the stitches. This should create one single line.

Appliqués

A large number of the projects combine knitting with fabric appliqués; for example, the fabric patches sewn under the birds' wings or in the teddies' ears. I think this adds a special character to the toys and brings out the nostalgic, personalized nature of the work. You can use cherished pieces of fabric set aside for a special project. Toys provide you with the perfect reason to use such fabrics.

IRON-ON INTERFACING

Iron-on interfacing is perfect for lining your fabric. It stops the edges from fraying and makes the fabric more solid, thereby enabling you to cut out small shapes like the foot pads, ear pads or flower shapes. You can buy iron-on interfacing from most haberdashery stores; Vilene is a popular brand.

When using the iron-on interfacing, I cut out a piece that is bigger than the template. I then iron this piece onto the fabric and peel off the paper. The interfacing makes the fabric stiffer so it is easier to cut out the shape.

Hold the cut-out piece onto the toy and sew around the edges. If you find it easier, you could pin the cut-out piece to the toy before sewing it on.

SEWING THE FABRIC ON

There are several ways you can sew the fabric details onto the knitting. Try to get your stitching as neat as possible and be creative with the color of thread you use. The most important thing to ensure is that the fabric is sewn securely to the knitting. Use normal sewing thread rather than yarn.

Crochet chains

Some of the toys feature crocheted chains; Eddie Elephant, the piggies and the mice have crochet-chain tails, while the birds have crochet-chain legs. Crocheting a chain is quite simple.

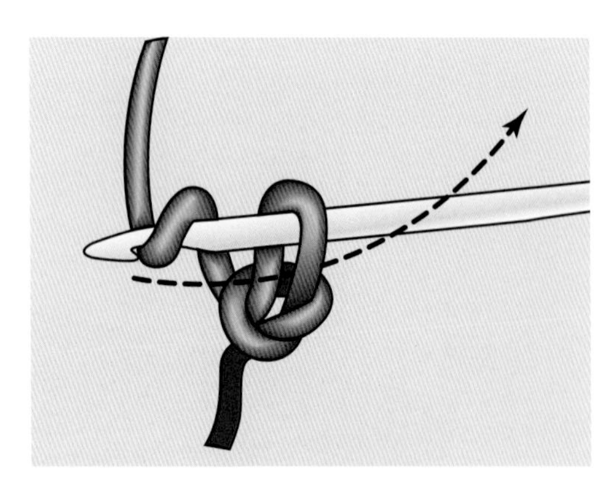

1 Tie a slipknot in the working end of the yarn and place the loop on your crochet hook. Wrap the yarn clockwise over the hook.

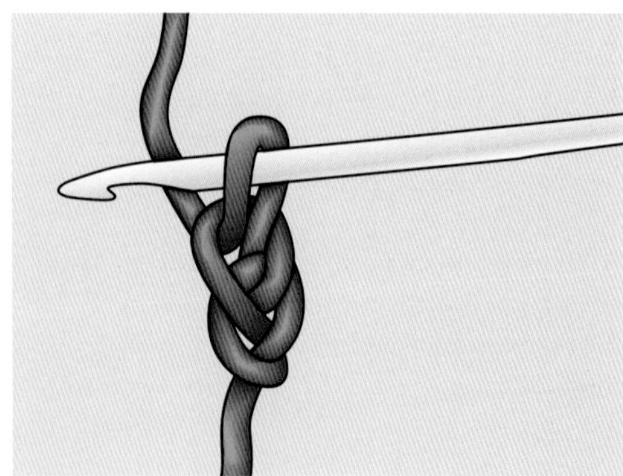

2 Pull the yarn through the loop on the hook to form a fresh loop. This is the first chain. Repeat the process until the chain is as long as you want it.

Pompoms

Pompoms are used for the tails of the bunnies. They are very simple to make. You can buy pompom kits that make the process quicker, but here are instructions for the old-fashioned way.

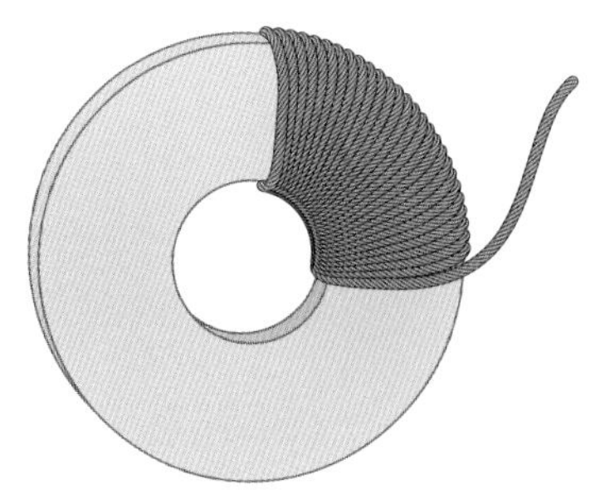

1 Using the template on page 208, cut out two pieces of card. Remember to cut out the center hole too. Wrap the wool in and out of the center hole, working your way around the pompom ring.

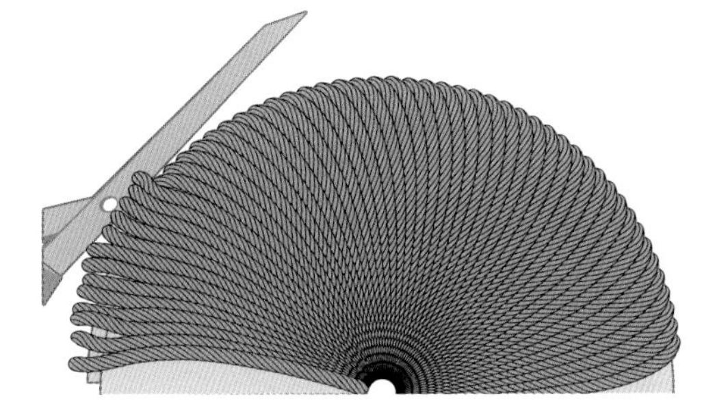

2 Continue wrapping the wool around the ring until it completely covers all the card. Carefully cut around the edge of the pompom. The two rings of card mean you can slip your scissors between the rings to make cutting easier.

3 Pull the two pieces of card slightly apart and slip a piece of string around the pompom center. Wrap the string around a few times and knot tightly. It is important to wrap tightly to ensure that the pompom doesn't fall apart. Slip out the pieces of card (cut them if you need to).

Your pompom is complete. Trim around the edge to create a perfectly round ball with no longer tufty bits of yarn.

Templates

THE BUNNY BUNCH
(PAGES 114–117)

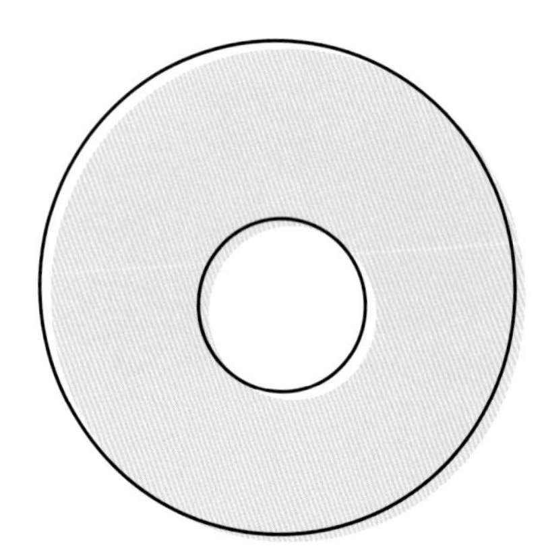

Pompom template for bunnies' tails

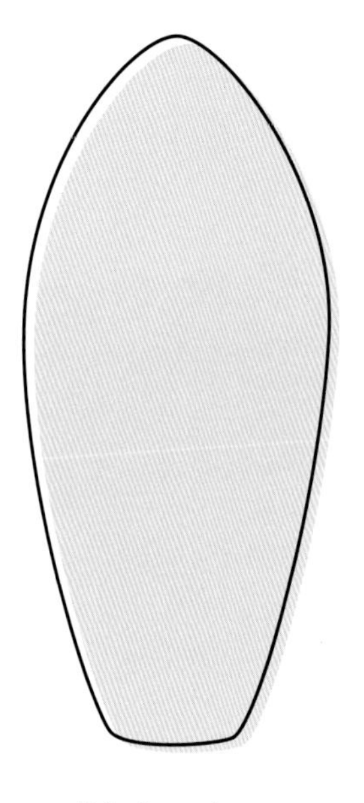

Baby bunny's ear

Mummy bunny's ear

SIMON SNAKE (PAGES 152–155)

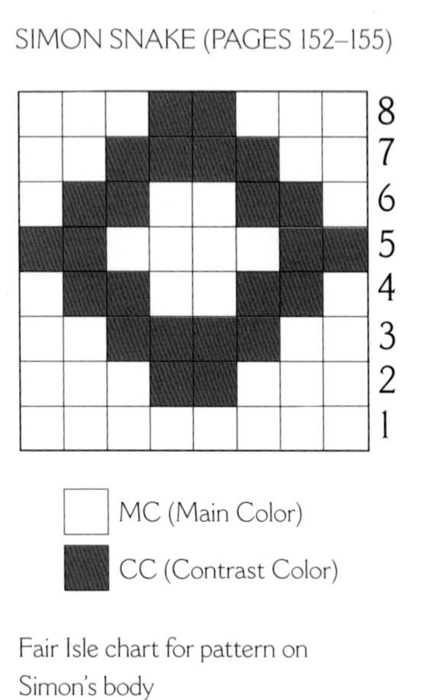

Fair Isle chart for pattern on
Simon's body

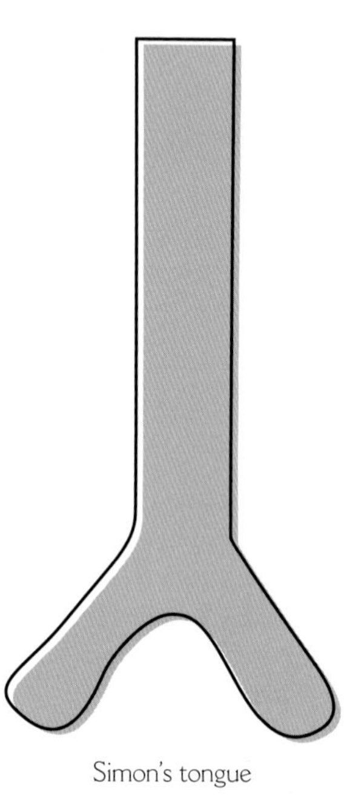

Simon's tongue

PIGGIES AT PLAY (PAGE 156–159)

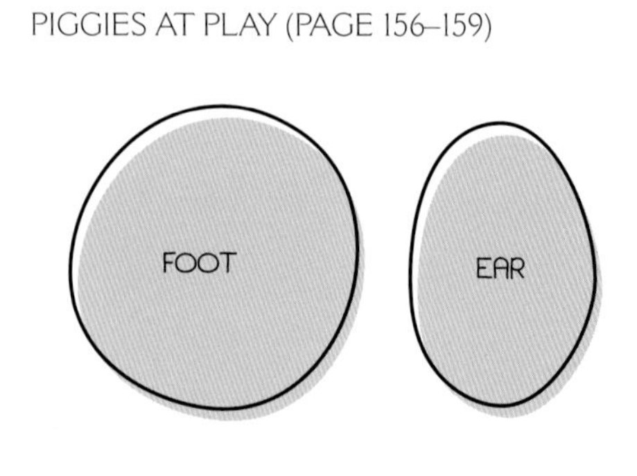

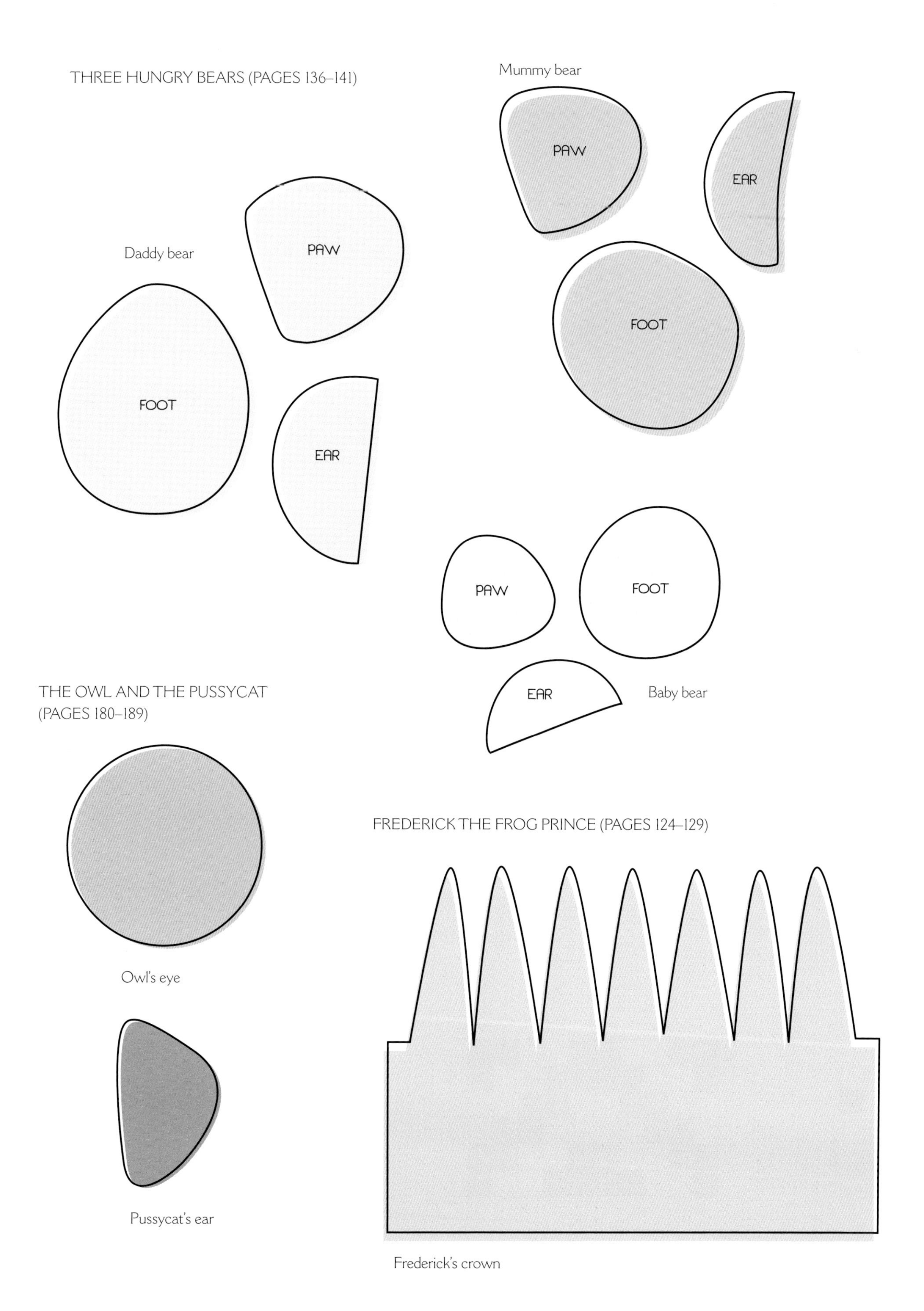
THREE HUNGRY BEARS (PAGES 136–141)
Mummy bear
PAW
EAR
FOOT
Daddy bear
PAW
FOOT
EAR
PAW
FOOT
EAR
Baby bear
THE OWL AND THE PUSSYCAT
(PAGES 180–189)
Owl's eye
Pussycat's ear
FREDERICK THE FROG PRINCE (PAGES 124–129)
Frederick's crown

THREE LITTLE FISH (PAGE 170–173)

Three colorways for the fish

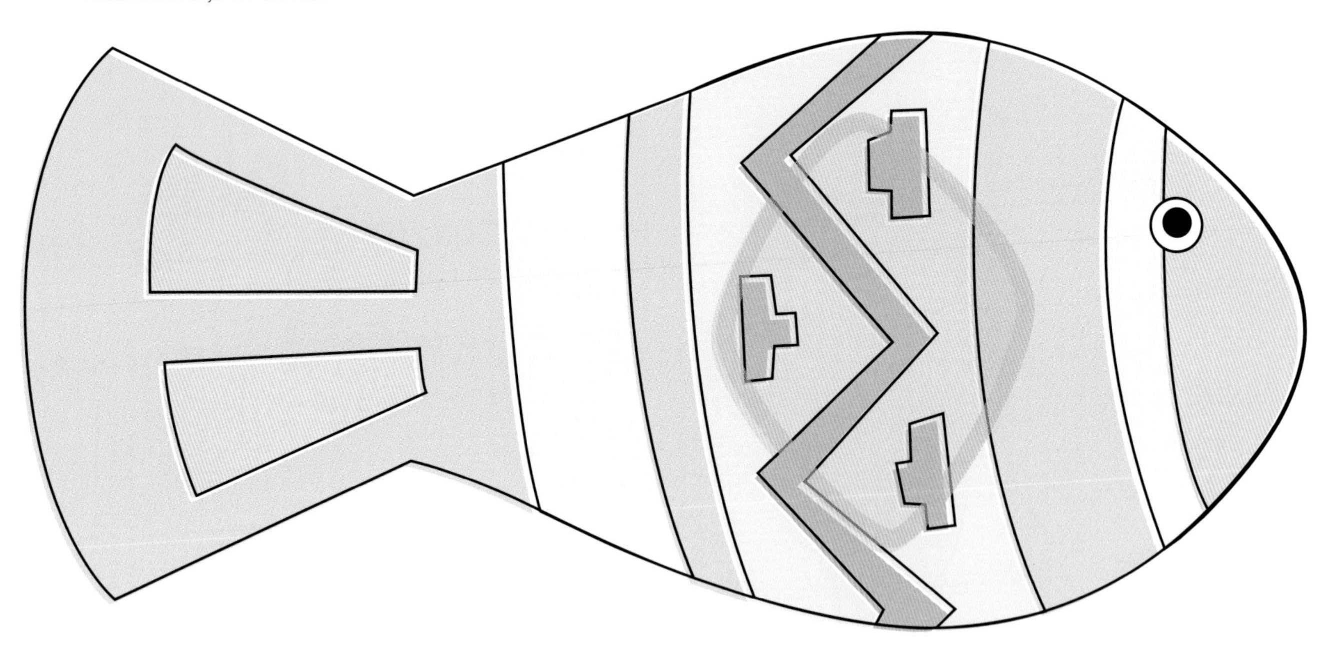

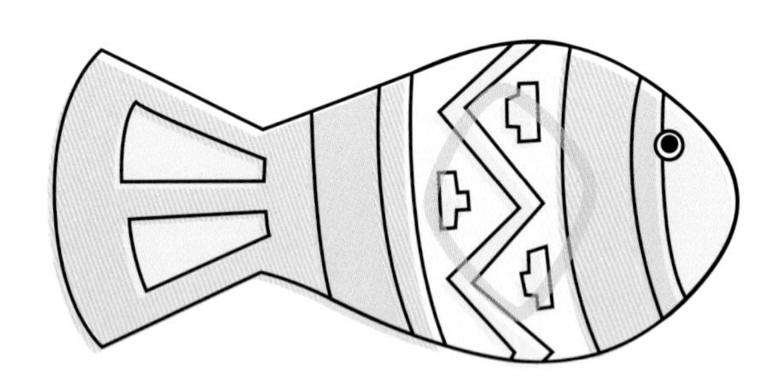

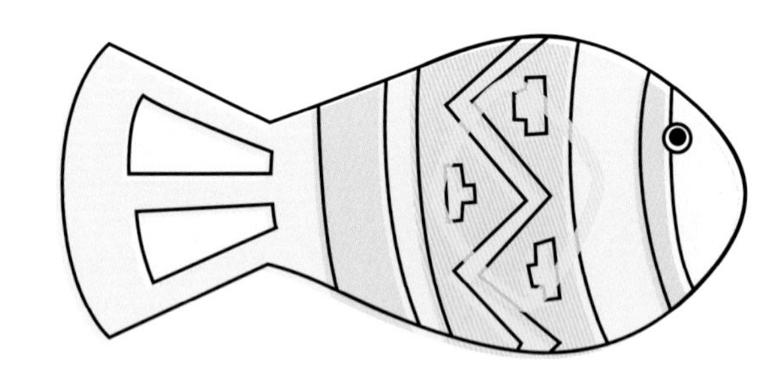

Fair Isle chart for pattern on the blue tailed fish's body

KEY

yarn B

yarn D

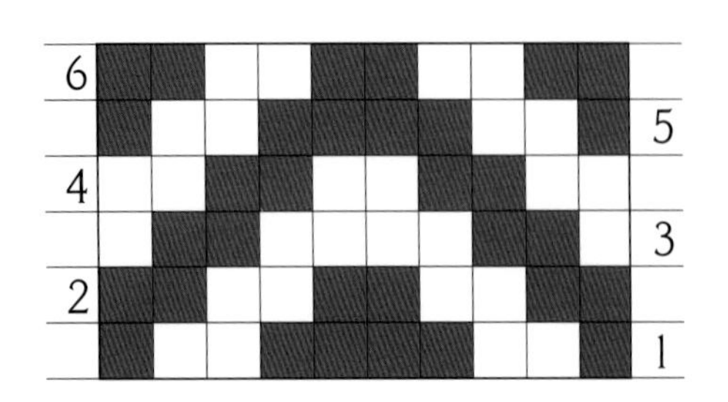

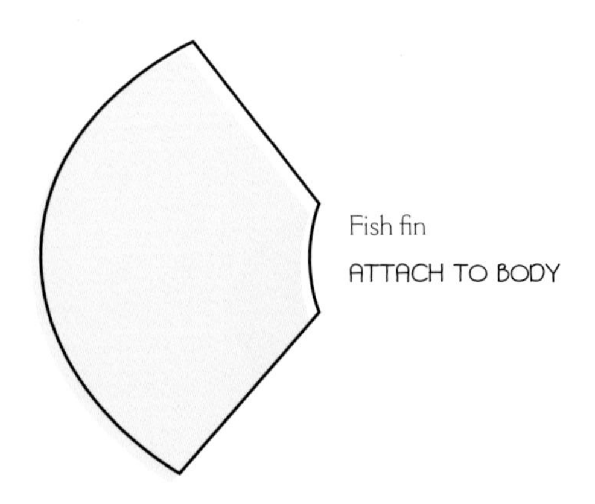

BERTIE AND BEATRICE THE BIRDS (PAGE 118–121)

EDDIE THE FRIENDLY ELEPHANT (PAGE 164–169)

BABUSHKAS (PAGE 130–135)

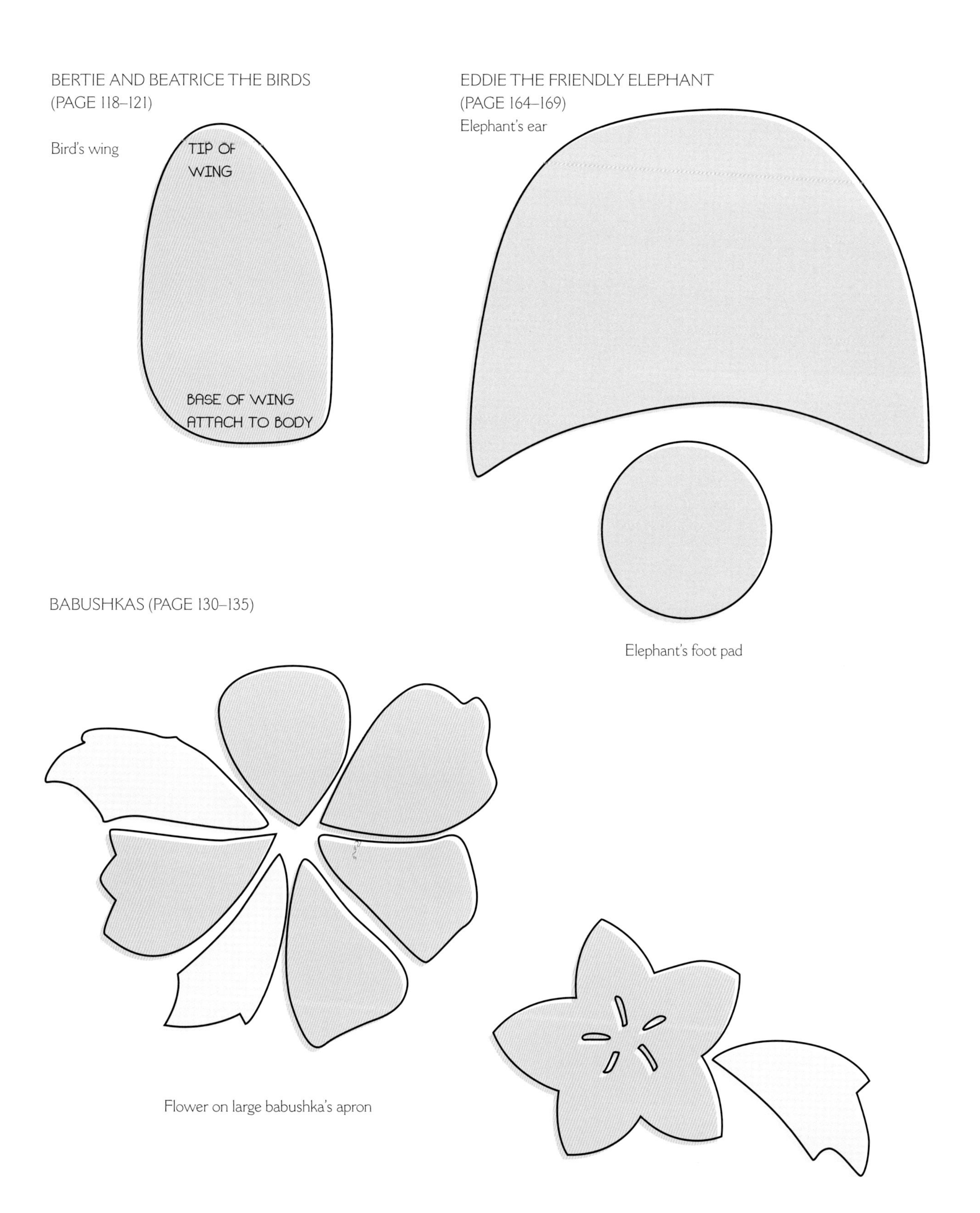

Elephant's foot pad

Flower on large babushka's apron

Flower on medium babushka's apron

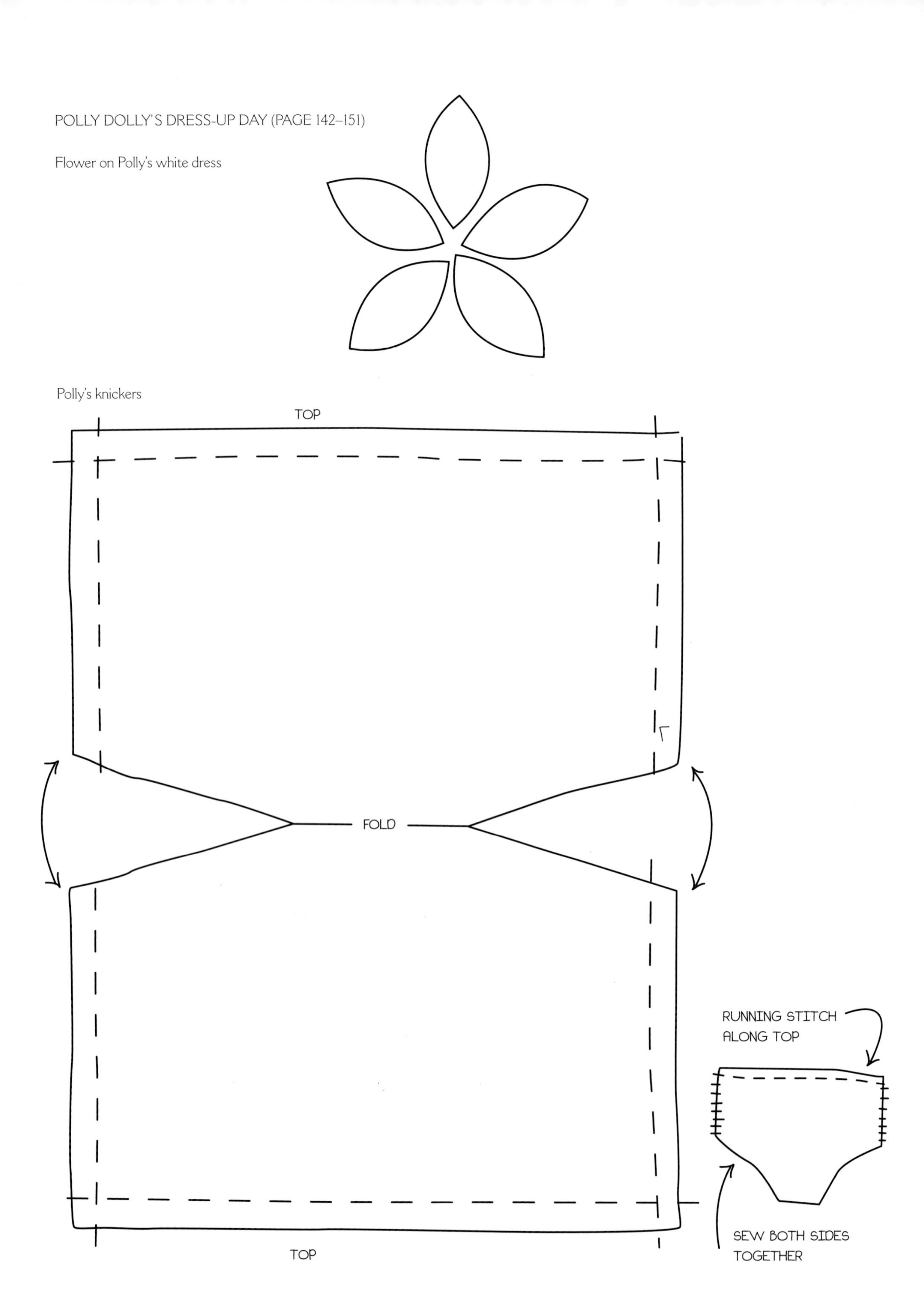
POLLY DOLLY'S DRESS-UP DAY (PAGE 142–151)
Flower on Polly's white dress
Polly's knickers
TOP
FOLD
TOP
RUNNING STITCH ALONG TOP
SEW BOTH SIDES TOGETHER

Polly's vest

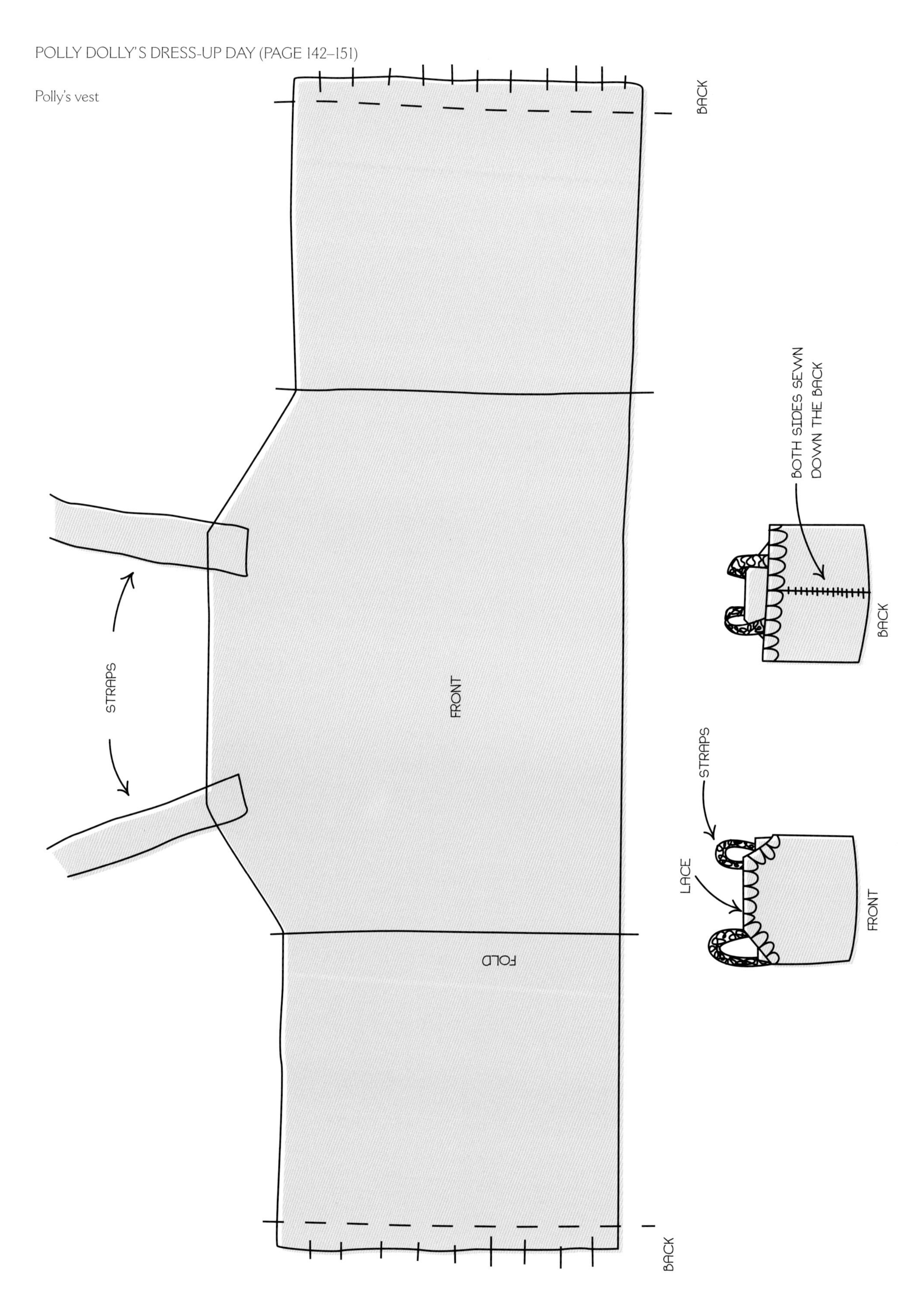
BACK
STRAPS
FRONT
FOLD
BACK
BOTH SIDES SEWN
DOWN THE BACK
BACK
STRAPS
LACE
FRONT

Yarns used

In the project instructions I have given a generic description of the yarn used for the project so you can easily source a yarn to use or pick something suitable out of your stash. However, if you want to recreate the project exactly, I have specified the yarns used below.

Be warned that yarn companies frequently update their lines, so they may discontinue a certain type of yarn or a certain color. If the yarns specified below become unavailable, or if you want to use a substitute yarn, you'll need to work out how much replacement yarn you need—the meterage or yardage of a ball of yarn can vary considerably between lines and between brands. Make this calculation:

- **The number of balls of the recommended yarn x the number of yards/metres per ball = A.**
- **The number of yards/metres per ball of the substitute yarn = B.**
- **Divide A by B to calculate the number of balls of substitute yarn required.**

Many of the projects use only small amounts of yarn, so you may only need one or two balls of yarn anyway.

PAGE 114 THE BUNNY BUNCH

Peter Pan Darling DK (100% polyester; 122yd/112m per 1¾oz/50g ball)

MUMMY BUNNY
1 ball in color 360 (**A**)

BABY BOY BUNNY
1 ball in each of colors 360 (**A**) and 365 (**B**)

BABY GIRL BUNNY
1 ball in color 363 (**C**)

(NB: 1 ball of **A** is enough to make both the mummy bunny and the face of the baby boy bunny)

PAGE 118 BERTIE AND BEATRICE THE BIRDS

Patons Fairytale Color 4 Me DK (100% wool; 95yd/90m per 1¾oz/50g ball)

BERTIE BIRD
1 ball in each of colors 4955 (**A**), 4960 (**B**) and 4952 (**C**)

BEATRICE BIRD
1 ball in each of colors 4958 (**A**), 4960 (**B**) and 4955 (**C**)

PAGE 124 FREDERICK THE FROG PRINCE

(**A**) Twilleys of Stamford Freedom Spirit (100% wool; 131yd/120m per 1¾oz/50g ball)
1 ball in color 514
(**B**) Patons Fairytale Color 4 Me DK (100% wool; 95yd/90m per 1¾oz/50g ball)
1 ball in color 4952
(**C**) Oddment of yarn in white
(**D**) Oddment of yarn in black

PAGE 130 BABUSHKAS

Sirdar Country Style DK (45% acrylic, 40% nylon, 15% wool; 348yd/318m per 3½oz/100g ball)
1 ball in each of colors 593 (**A**), 584 (**B**), 412 (**C**) and 402 (**D**)

PAGE 136 THREE HUNGRY BEARS

Rowan RYC Baby Alpaca DK (100% baby alpaca; 109yd/100m per 1¾oz/50g ball)

MUMMY BEAR
1 ball in color 206

DADDY BEAR
2 balls in color 205

BABY BEAR
1 ball in color 202

PAGE 142 POLLY DOLLY'S DRESS-UP DAY

POLLY DOLLY
Rowan RYC Cashsoft Baby DK (57% extra-fine merino, 33% microfibre, 10% cashmere; 142yd/130m per 1¾oz/50g ball)
1 ball in color 807

POLLY DOLLY'S RED DRESS AND BLUE SHOES
Rowan Wool Cotton (50% merino wool, 50% cotton; 122yd/113m per 1¾oz/50g ball)
(**A**) 1 ball in color 911
(**B**) 1 ball in color 909

POLLY DOLLY'S WHITE DRESS
Rowan RYC Cashsoft DK (57% extra-fine merino, 33% microfibre, 10% cashmere; 142yd/130m per 1¾oz/50g ball)
1 ball in color 500

PAGE 152 SIMON SNAKE

Cygnet Pure Merino DK (100% merino wool; 110yd/101m per 1¾oz/50g ball)
(**A**) 3 balls in color 2150
(**B**) 1 ball in color 2837
(**C**) 1 ball in color 2151
(**D**) 1 ball in color 0298
(**E**) 1 ball in color 2817
(**F**) Oddment of yarn in white
(**G**) Oddment of yarn in black

PAGE 156 PIGGIES AT PLAY

Rowan RYC Cashsoft Baby DK (57% extra-fine merino, 33% microfibre, 10% cashmere; 142yd/130m per 1¾oz/50g ball)
1 ball in color 807

(NB: one ball makes one pig, so you'll need more yarn to make all three pigs)

PAGE 160 MISCHIEVOUS MICE

You can use any lightweight (DK) yarn from your stash; only small amounts are needed so you can use up scraps and oddments of leftover yarn as well as single balls.

PAGE 164 EDDIE THE FRIENDLY ELEPHANT

Rowan All Seasons Cotton (60% cotton, 40% acylic/microfibre; 97yd/90m per 1¾oz/50g ball)
1 ball in color 234

PAGE 170 THREE LITTLE FISH

Patons Fairytale Color 4 Me DK (100% wool; 95yd/90m per 1¾oz/50g ball)
Small amounts in colors 4960, 4955, 4952 and 4958

PAGE 174 PETER PENGUIN'S FISHING TRIP

Rowan Pure Wool DK (100% superwash wool; 137yd/125m per 1¾oz/50g ball)
1 ball in each of colors 004 (**A**) and 013 (**B**)
Small amount in color 032 (**C**)

PAGE 180 THE OWL AND THE PUSSYCAT

THE OWL
Twilleys of Stamford Freedom Spirit (100% wool; 131yd/120m per 1¾oz/50g ball)
1 ball in each of colors 518 (**A**) and 502 (**C**)

Rowan RYC Cashsoft DK (57% extra-fine merino, 33% microfibre, 10% cashmere; 142yd/130m per 1¾oz/50g ball)
1 ball in color 500 (**B**)

Rowan Pure Wool DK (100% superwash wool; 137yd/125m per 1¾oz/50g ball)
Small amount in color 032 (**D**)

THE PUSSYCAT
Twilleys of Stamford Freedom Spirit (100% wool; 131yd/120m per 1¾oz/50g ball)
1 ball in each of colors 503 (**A**) and 502 (**B**)

THE OWL AND THE PUSSYCAT'S BOAT
Boat—Twilleys of Stamford Freedom Spirit (100% wool; 131yd/120m per 1¾oz/50g ball)
2 x balls in color 514

Anchor—Small amount of yarn in grey

Suppliers

Below are some contact details for the suppliers of yarns that I used for making the toys.

SIRDAR

www.sirdar.co.uk
(USA) Knitting Fever Inc.
315 Bayview Avenue
Amityville, NY 11701
Tel: +1 516 546 3600
www.knittingfever.com
(UK) Sirdar Spinning Ltd
Flanshaw Lane, Alvethorpe
Wakefield WF2 9ND
Tel: +44 (0)1924 371501
email: enquiries@sirdar.co.uk
(AUS) Creative Images
PO Box 106
Hastings, Victoria 3915
Tel: +61 (0)3 5979 1555
email: creative@peninsula.starway.net.au

CYGNET

www.cygnetyarns.com
Cygnet Yarns Ltd
12-14 Adelaide Street
Bradford
West Yorkshire
BD5 0EF
Tel: +44 (0)1274 743374
www.cygnetyarns.co.uk

TWILLEYS

www.twilleys.co.uk
(UK) Twilleys of Stamford
For craft/haberdashery:
Roman Mill, Stamford PE9 1BG
Tel: +44 (0)1780 752661
email: twilleys@tbramsden.co.uk
For head office, administration, handknitting, industrial yarns and shade fringes:
Thomas B. Ramsden (Bradford) Ltd,
Netherfield Road, Guiseley, Leeds LS20 9PD
Tel: +44 (0)1943 872264
email: sales@tbramsden.co.uk

(note: **also suppliers of Peter Pan Darling DK**)

ROWAN

www.knitrowan.com
(USA) Westminster Fibers Inc
165 Ledge Street, Nashua
New Hampshire 03060
Tel: +1 603 886 5041/5043
www.westminsterfibers.com
email: info@westminsterfibers.com
(UK) Rowan
Green Lane Mill, Holmfirth HD9 2DX
Tel: +44 (0)1484 681881
email: info@knitrowan.com
(AUS) Australian Country Spinners Pty Ltd
Level 7, 409 St Kilda Road
Melbourne, Victoria 3004
Tel: +61 (0)3 9380 3888
email: tkohut@auspinners.com.au

PATONS

www.makeitcoats.com
(USA/CAN) 320 Livingstone Avenue South
Listowel, ON, N4W 3H3
Canada
Tel: +1 888 368 8401
email: inquire@patonsyarns.com
(UK) Coats Crafts UK
PO Box 22, Lingfield House
Lingfield Point, McMullen Road
Darlington DL1 1YJ
Tel: +44 (0)1325 394237
knitpatons.com/en
email: knitpatons@me3crafts.com
(AUS) Patons
PO Box 7276, Melbourne Victoria 3004
Tel: +61 (0)3 9380 3888
email: enquiries@auspinners.com.au

About the author

Laura Long graduated in 2003 with a First Class knitted textiles degree from Central St. Martins College of Art and Design. Since then she has been working out of her central London studio designing, making, and selling her knitted creations to boutiques and galleries all over the world. Teaching and freelance work has played an important part in her business. She designs, makes and creates patterns and pieces for designers, knitting magazines and pattern books, and her clients have included John Rocha, Rowan yarns, *Simply Knitting,* and *Knit Today* magazines, and publications such as *Collective Knitting* and *Holiday Knits.*
She has taught both machine and hand knitting to people of all ages at Greenwich Community College, Loop, and the Cockpit Arts.

Dolls, fairytales, and fantasy played an important part in Laura's childhood, a childhood full of happy, everlasting memories.
It's for this reason that she's developed a collection of cute characters, knitted creatures, and dolls, each with a personality all of their own.

Acknowledgments

Thank you to everyone at David and Charles, particularly Jennifer Fox-Proverbs, Prudence Rogers, Sabine Eulau, Sarah Underhill, Bethany Dymond and Kate Nicholson for all their amazing work and support. Thank you Sian Irvine for bringing my characters to life—your photography is fantastic! I would also like to thank all the yarn companies for the fantastic yarns they have supplied.

Knit & Purl Pets

CLAIRE GARLAND

For a child, the idea of having your very own pet to love and care for rarely becomes a reality, forever to stay a pipedream. However, children constantly continue to cry, 'I need my own pet!' If only I had a coin for every time my children—ages seven, nine, and twelve—have uttered those words ...

Well, entre nous, here is my very effective answer—knit and purl them one, two, or more pets. And in answer to the type of pets that have been yearned for, and these have been numerous and change like the weather, I've designed patterns for a variety of familiar and unusual pets. They need only a little basic knitting knowledge and can be knocked-out to meet demands in very little time at all. And what's more, you don't have any vets bills or mess to contend with, or need to be constantly nagging—'can you clean out your pet's hutch/cage/basket—now!' A knitted pet for child or grown-up is the perfect solution!

In this section there is an array—a veritable (knitted) pets shop—of creatures to knit, some with their own accessories, from a lolloping Labrador puppy to an inquisitive kitten and a docile ginger tom with his favorite knitted basket, the cutest of bunnies and the tiniest ponies to a multi-colored chameleon and a ... stegosaurus! There are also design hints on how to go about personalizing your own special pet.

All the pets are knitted with as few components as possible, many in one piece, and because many of them are so small only small amounts of yarn are needed—a great excuse for using up your stash! There are projects for beginners through to more challenging pieces for more advanced knitters. Each piece is patterned like a three-dimensional sculpture—a slightly different method to the usual knitting of separate parts before sewing everything together.

These patterns were a joy to create. The pets are enormously satisfying for the knitter and the pet-loving/wanting child or adult. So now over to you. Which one first?

Enjoy!

Claire

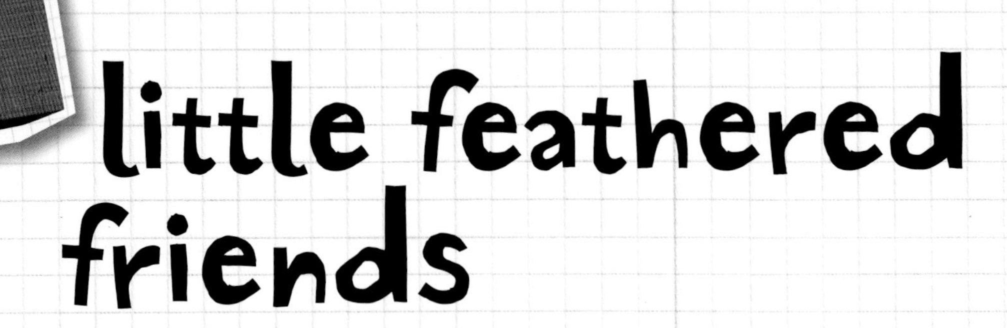

little feathered friends

This project is just right for a beginner to get started on knitting pets.

Rosey, Bluey, and Sunny are sitting pretty in their spring colors. Watch them flip and flap, but whatever you do don't tempt them with an open window—they might find their wings and fly away!

You can really let your imagination soar when choosing colors for your pretty little birds. Bluebirds, chaffinches, or robins—the sky's the limit!

RATING *

yarn

For each bird

Fingering-weight (4-ply) yarn

- ½ x 1¾oz (50g) ball for body (**MC**)
- oddment for beak (**A**)
- oddment for wings (**C**) (optional)

needles

- 4 x size 0 (2mm) double-pointed needles

notions

For each bird

- 2 x ¼in- (6mm-) diameter toy safety eyes (or black yarn)
- Oddments of brown yarn for legs
- 50:50 sugar (or PVA adhesive) and water solution
- Scraps of fabric (optional)

gauge

17½ sts and 25 rows to 2in (5cm) of st st, using **MC** and size 0 (2mm) needles

Don't worry if the gauge is not exact—it doesn't matter if the birds are a little bigger or smaller than shown.

finished size

Approx 5 1/8in (13cm) long x 2in (5cm) tall (although you can vary the length of the tail)

One day I'll fly away . . .

knitting notes

- The main part of the bird is worked in one piece from the beak to the tail.
- The birds are worked on double-pointed needles working in the round (see page 327).
- Do not use even safety eyes on toys for an infant, as they can be a potential choking hazard. Instead, embroider the eyes in place with yarn.

BIRD PATTERN

BEAK, HEAD, BODY, WINGS AND TAIL

Cast on 3 sts, using **A** and size 0 (2mm) needles.

Row 1 (RS) K1, kfb, k1. 4 sts.

Row 2 P.

Row 3 K1, kfb twice, k1. 6 sts.

Row 4 P.

Row 5 K1, kfb, k2, kfb, k1. 8 sts.

Row 6 P.

Cut yarn. Change to **MC** and cont as follows:

Row 7 K.

Shape head

Row 8 Pfkb, k to last st, pkfb. 10 sts.

Row 9 Kfb, k4, M1, k4, kfb. 13 sts.

Row 10 P.

Row 11 Kfb, k2, kfb 7 times, k2, kfb. 22 sts.

Row 12 P.

Shape throat

Cast on 3 sts at beg of next 2 rows, so ending with a WS row. 28 sts.

Row 15 Divide sts: k8 onto n1, k12 onto n2, k8 onto n3. With RS facing, keeping gauge fairly tight on rnd 1, work in the rnd (see page 327) as follows:

Rnd 16 K28.

Rnd 17 [M1, k1] 6 times, k16, [M1, k1] 6 times. 40 sts.

Rnd 18 K40.

Rnd 19 K40.

Shape breast

Rnd 20 [M1, k1] 4 times, k32, [M1, k1] 4 times. 48 sts.

Rnd 21 K48.

Rnd 22 K48.

Shape back of head

Rnd 23 K22, k2tog, skpo, k22. 46 sts.

Rnd 24 K21, k2tog, skpo, k21. 44 sts.

Rnd 25 K44.

Rnd 26 K44.

Rnd 27 K2tog, k40, skpo. 42 sts.

Rnd 28 K42.

Rnd 29 K42.

Divide for wings

Rnd 30 K12, sl next st onto a safety pin, k16, sl next st onto a safety pin, k12. 40 sts.

Rnd 31 K13, sl next st onto same safety pin as previous rnd, k12, sl next st onto same safety pin as previous rnd, k13. 38 sts.

Rnd 32 K14, sl next st onto same safety pin as before, k8, sl next st onto same safety pin as before, k14. 36 sts.

Rnd 33 K15, sl next st onto same safety pin as before, k4, sl next st onto same safety pin as before, k15. 34 sts.

Two little dickie birds sitting on a branch ...

I wonder if they'll lay any eggs!

Each bird has its own pretty, distinctive markings.

Rnd 34 K34.
Rnd 35 K2tog, k30, skpo. 32 sts.
Rnd 36 K32.
Place marker.
Rnd 37 K, dec 1 st at beg and end of rnd. 30sts.
Rnd 38 K.
Rep last 2 rnds 3 times. 24 sts.
Shape tail
Rnd 45 K9, [k2tog] 3 times, k9. 21 sts.
Rnd 46 K21.
Rnd 47 K9, k3tog, k9. 19 sts.
Rnd 48 K19.
Rnd 49 Divide sts: k4 onto n1, k11 onto n2, k4 onto n3.
Rnd 50 K8, k3tog, k8. 17 sts.
Rnd 51 K17.
Rnd 52 K8, skpo, k7. 16 sts.
Work tail
K4 so that last 8 sts are on one needle. Sl rem 8 sts onto another needle. Kitchener stitch (see page 323) the two sets of sts tog. 8 sts.
Next row P.
Work 8 rows in st st (or more for a longer tail).
Bind off. Weave in end.

LEFT WING
*Rejoin yarn **MC** or **C** to 4 sts on one of the safety pins.
Row 1 (WS) P.
Work 2 rows in st st.
Row 4 (RS) Kfb, k2, kfb. 6 sts.
Row 5 P.
Row 6 Kfb, k to last st, kfb. 8 sts.
Row 7 P.
Rep last 2 rows once more. 10 sts.
Work 4 rows in st st. **
Row 14 (RS) K2tog, k to end. 9 sts.
Row 15 P.
Rep last 2 rows 6 more times. 3 sts.
Row 28 (RS) K3tog.
Fasten off. Weave in the end or use it to sew the wing against the tail.

RIGHT WING
Work as left wing from * to **. 10 sts.
Row 14 (RS) K to last 2 sts, k2tog. 9 sts.
Row 15 P.
Rep last 2 rows 6 more times. 3 sts.
Row 28 (RS) K3tog.
Fasten off. Weave in the end or use it to sew the wing against the tail.

MAKING UP

EYES
Following the manufacturer's instructions, snap the eyes in place on each side of the nose. Alternatively embroider the eyes with yarn.

They obvious;y love their home sweet home.

BODY AND HEAD
Stuff the body, breast, and head. Mattress stitch (see page 329) the beak and throat to close the seam.

LEGS [MAKE 2]
Cut a 9¾in (25cm) length of brown yarn. Thread a 3in (8cm) length of brown yarn through a tapestry needle. Thread the short yarn through the longer one, splitting it 1½in (4cm) from one end. Pull the short length through, stopping when there is 1½in (4cm) of end and then take another st through the split yarn to secure. Trim all three ends (claws) to the same length.
Use the same method to make a back claw, trimming one end close to the 'knot' at the join.
To stiffen the legs, make up a solution of equal quantities of sugar (or PVA adhesive, which will make the legs stiffer) and water. Paint or dip the solution onto the legs. Leave them to dry.
Sew the top end of each leg to the bottom of the bird, overstitching a few times to secure it. Bend the legs as required.

DIFFERENT OPTIONS
Cut an oval shape from fabric for the cap, wing or breast marking. Appliqué it in place (see page 332), over-sewing with a matching thread.
Give your bird a different colored face and/or work the tail as k1, p1 rib.

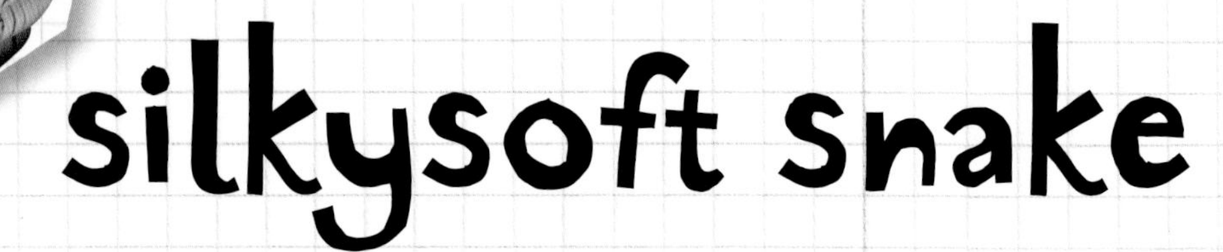

This snake is super simple for you to start knitting i-cord.

Silkysoft is a small snake, who will slither smoothly into your affections. She might be small, but she has a huge, colorful personality. Watch her slipping in and out of sleeves and fingerless gloves as if they were a super-soft jungle gym. This little charmer only eats sssweetsss (because I can't bear to keep frozen mice in my freezer!).

Make Silkysoft as long as you like and choose a piece of red ribbon or fabric to make her slippery tongue look life-like.

RATING *

yarn

Fingering-weight (4-ply) yarn

- ½ x 1¾oz (50g) ball in blue/green (**MC**)

needles

- 4 x size 2 (2.5mm) double-pointed needles

notions

- 2 x ¼in- (6mm-) diameter toy safety eyes (or black yarn)
- Scrap of red fabric or ribbon

gauge

15 sts and 19 rows to 2in (5cm) in st st, using **MC** and size 2 (2.5mm) needles

Don't worry if the gauge is not exact—it doesn't matter if the snake is a little bigger or smaller than shown.

finished size

Work to the desired length

... ssslithering iss sso sssatisssfying!

Knitting notes

- The snake is worked in one piece.
- She is worked on double-pointed needles using the i-cord technique (see page 328).
- If you are knitting for a very young child, embroider the eyes with yarn instead of using toy eyes. Even safety eyes can be a choking hazard.

SNAKE PATTERN

HEAD, BODY AND TAIL

Cast on 2 sts using **MC** and size 2 (2.5mm) needles.

Row 1 K2.

Work as i-cord (see page 328) as follows:

Slide sts to other end of needle without turning.

Keeping gauge tight, pull working yarn across the back of the i-cord.

Row 2 K1, M1, k1. 3 sts.

Row 3 K1, kfb, k1. 4 sts.

Row 4 K1, kfb twice, k1. 6 sts.

Row 5 K1, kfb, k2, kfb, k1. 8 sts.

Work as i-cord until the snake measures the desired length.

Shape head

With WS facing, cast on 4 sts.

Row 1 (WS) P.

Row 2 Cast on 4 sts, k to end. 16 sts.

Row 3 P.

Row 4 K3, k2tog, k6, skpo, k3. 14 sts.

Row 5 P2tog, p to last 2 sts, p2tog. 12 sts.

Row 6 K2, k2tog, k4, skpo, k2. 10 sts.

Row 7 P.

Row 8 K2, k2tog, k2, skpo, k2. 8 sts.

Row 9 P.

Row 10 K2, k2tog, skpo, k2. 6 sts.

Row 11 P.

Cut yarn and thread end through sts. Pull up tight and secure.

MAKING UP

Following the manufacturer's instructions, snap the eyes in place on each side of the nose. Alternatively, embroider the eyes with yarn.

Mattress stitch (see page 329) around the nose and the head.

Cut a V shape into the end of a strip of fabric or length of ribbon. Cut this tongue to the desired length and sew it to the end of the nose.

Have you been hiding behind the sofa?

Butter wouldn't melt in her mouth!

haughty hen trio

The hens' feet, wattles, and feathery finery are a little bit fiddly, but otherwise the hens are easy to knit.

You can call your hens Clucky, Plucky, and Lucky if you wish, but these laying ladies very decidedly prefer Charlotte, Penelope (never Penny), and Lavinia! Quite. They do have a certain sophisticated air about them—proud of their eggs (see page 236–237) and delighted by their fancy feathers.

The hens are knitted in pure wool and the tweedy look of the brown and grey yarns particularly recreates the colors of real feathers. Choose any yarn that will give the hens a similar rustic quality.

RATING *

yarn

For each hen

Lightweight (DK) yarn

- ½ x 1¾oz (50g) ball in ecru, grey or brown (**MC**)
- Oddment in grey marl (**A**)

Fingering-weight (4-ply) yarn

- Oddment in red (**B**)
- Oddment in yellow (**C**)

needles

- 4 x size 6 (4mm) double-pointed needles
- 4 x size 3 (3mm) double-pointed needles

notions

- 2 x ¼in- (6mm-) diameter toy safety eyes (or black yarn)

gauge

11 sts and 14 rows to 2in (5cm) of st st, using **MC** and size 6 (4mm) needles

Don't worry if the gauge is not exact—it doesn't matter if the hens are a little bigger or smaller than shown.

finished size

Approx 11in (28cm) long x 6 in (15.5cm) tall (not including the legs)

Cluck cluck cluck . . .
aren't we so fine!

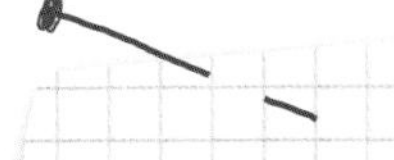

Knitting notes

- The main pattern is for the white hen. The grey hen is worked with just bottom tail feathers, the brown hen with just top tail feathers.
- The main part of the hen is worked in one piece from the tail to the head.
- The hens are worked on double-pointed needles using the techniques i-cord (see page 328) and working in the round (see page 327).
- Even safety eyes can present a choking hazard for a very young child. So, instead of using toy eyes, embroider the eyes with yarn.
- Once you've mastered the techniques, try knitting with one size smaller needles to give a tighter fabric that gives stuffing no chance to show through.

WHITE HEN PATTERN

TAIL, BODY, NECK AND HEAD
Cast on 3 sts using **MC** and size 6 (4mm) needles.
Row 1 K3 and work as i-cord (see page 328):
Slide sts to other end of needle without turning.
Keeping gauge tight, pull working yarn across the back of the i-cord.
Row 2 Kfb, k1, kfb. 5 sts.
Row 3 K.
Row 4 Kfb, k3, kfb. 7 sts.
Row 5 K.
Row 6 Kft, k5, kfb. 9 sts.
Turn, so WS facing.
Sl 9 sts p-wise, dividing them equally onto 3 needles.
Turn, so RS facing.
Place a marker at beg of row 1.
With RS facing, keeping gauge fairly tight on first rnd, work in the rnd (see page 327) as follows:
Rnd 7 (RS) [Kfb, k2] 3 times. 12 sts.
Rnd 8 K.
Shape tail
Rnd 9 [Kfb, k3] 3 times. 15 sts.
Rnd 10 K.
Rnd 11 [Kfb, k4] 3 times. 18 sts.
Rnd 12 K.
Rnd 13 [Kfb, k5] 3 times. 21 sts.
Rnd 14 K.
Rnd 15 [Kfb, k6] 3 times. 24 sts.
Rnd 16 K.
Rnd 17 [Kfb, k7] 3 times. 27 sts.
Rnd 18 K.
Rnd 19 [Kfb, k8] 3 times. 30 sts.
Work 5 rows in garter st.
Shape body
Rnd 25 [K4, M1] 3 times, k1, skpo, k2tog, k1, [M1, k4] 3 times. 34 sts.
Rnd 26 Kfb, k14, [k2tog] twice, k14, kfb.
Rnd 27 [K4, M1] 3 times, k3, skpo, k2tog, k3, [M1, k4] 3 times. 38 sts.
Rnd 28 Kfb, k16, [k2tog] twice, k16, kfb.
Rnd 29 [K4, M1] 3 times, k5, skpo, k2tog, k5, [M1, k4] 3 times. 42 sts.
Divide sts: 11 sts onto n1, 20 sts onto n2, 11 sts onto n3.
Rnd 30 Kfb, k18, [k2tog] twice, k18, kfb.
Rnd 31 [K4, M1] 3 times, k7, skpo, k2tog, k7, [M1, k4] 3 times. 46 sts.
Work feathers
Place a marker at beg of next rnd.
Rnd 32 K2, *p2, k2, rep from *.
Rnd 33 P2, *k2, p2, rep from *.
Rnd 34 P2, *k2, p2, rep from *.
Rnd 35 K2, *p2, k2, rep from *.
Rep rnds 26–29, 3 more times.
Shape neck
Rnd 48 Skpo, k2tog, k38, k2tog, skpo. 42 sts.
Rnd 49 Skpo, k2tog, k16, [M1, k1] twice, M1, k16, k2tog, skpo. 41 sts.
Rnd 50 Skpo, k2tog, k16, M1, k1, M1, k16, k2tog, skpo. 39 sts.
Rearrange work so 16 sts on n1, 7 sts on n2, 16 sts on n3.
Rnd 51 Skpo, k2tog, k15, M1, k1, M1, k15, k2tog, skpo. 37 sts.
Rnd 52 Skpo, k2tog, k14, M1, k1, M1, k14, k2tog, skpo. 35 sts.
Rnd 53 Skpo, k2tog, k13, M1, k1, M1, k13, k2tog, skpo. 33 sts.
Rnd 54 Skpo, k2tog, k12, M1, k1, M1, k12, k2tog, skpo. 31 sts.
Rnd 55 Skpo, k2tog, k11, M1, k1, M1, k11, k2tog, skpo. 29 sts.
Rnd 56 Skpo, k2tog, k10, M1, k1, M1, k10, k2tog, skpo. 27 sts.
Rnd 57 Skpo, k2tog, k9, M1, k1, M1, k9, k2tog, skpo. 25 sts.
Turn, so WS facing.
Cont in st st as follows:
Divide for wattle
Row 58 (WS) P25 onto 1 needle (this pulls gauge at the neck a little).
Cont with 2 needles.
Row 59 (RS) skpo, k2tog, k to last 4 sts, k2tog, skpo. 21 sts.
Row 60 P.
Rep last 2 rows once more. 17 sts.
Row 63 (RS) K8, skpo, k to end. 16 sts.
Row 64 P.
Row 65 Skpo, k5, k2tog, k to last 2 sts, k2tog. 13 sts.
Row 66 P.
Row 67 Skpo, k3, k3tog, k3, k2tog. 9 st.
Row 68 P.
Row 69 Skpo, k1, k3tog, k1, k2tog. 5 sts.
Row 70 P2tog, p1, p2tog. 3 sts.
Cut **MC** and join yarn **C**.
Cont to work as i-cord (see page 328).
Row 71 (RS) K.
Row 72 K.
Row 73 K3tog.
Fasten off.

COMB
Cast on 10 sts using **B** and size 3 (3mm) needles.
Row 1 (RS) K.
Row 2 P.
Make picot edge
Row 3 Picot 5, k1, picot 4, k1, picot 3, k1, picot 2, k1, picot 1, k1.
Make sure all picots are on RS.
Row 4 P.
Row 5 K.
Bind off k-wise.

WATTLE
Cast on 4 sts using **B** and size 3 (3mm) needles.
Row 1 (RS) Kfb, k2, kfb. 6 sts.
Row 2 P.
Row 3 Kfb, k to last st, kfb. 8 sts.
Rep last 2 rows 4, more times. 16 sts.
Row 12 (WS) P.
Row 13 Kfb, k3, [M1, k4] 3 times. 20 sts.
Row 14 P.
Row 15 Kfb, k4, [M1, k5] 3 times. 24 sts.
Row 16 P.
Row 17 K8, turn.
Row 18 Sl 1, p6, turn.
Row 19 Sl 1, k5, turn.
Row 20 Sl 1, p4, turn.
Row 21 Sl 1, k20 to end.
Row 22 Sl 1, p6, turn.
Row 23 Sl 1, k5, turn.
Row 24 Sl 1, P4, turn.
Row 25 Sl 1, k6 to end.
Bind off k-wise.

Lavinia can't help showing off her speckled plumage.

LEGS (MAKE 2)
Cast on 5 sts using **C** and size 3 (3mm) needles.
Row 1 K.
Work as i-cord until work measures 2in (5cm).
Divide for claws
Claw 1 Kfb in 1st st, using a 3rd needle. *Work on these 2 kfb sts as i-cord until claw measures 7/8in (2cm). K2tog.
Bind off. Weave in end**.
Claw 2 RS facing, rejoin **C** to rem 4 sts. Kfb into next st. Rep from * to **.
Claw 3 Rep as for claw 2.
Back claw RS facing, rejoin **C** to rem 2 sts. Kfb twice. Work on these 4 sts as i-cord until claw measures 7/8in (2cm). [k2tog] twice, k2tog.
Bind off.

TOP TAIL FEATHERS
Cast on 10 sts using **MC** and size 6 (4mm) needles.
Row 1 (RS) K.
Row 2 Sl 1, [k1, yfd, k2tog] twice, k1, yon twice, k1, yon twice, k1.
Row 3 [K2, p1] twice, k2, [yfd, k2tog, k1] twice.
Row 4 Sl 1, [k1, yfd, k2tog] twice, k7.
Row 5 Bind off 4 sts, k3, [yfd, k2tog, k1] twice.
Rows 2–5 form the feathered edge. Rep them 12 more times.
Bind off k-wise.
With RS facing, pick up and k27 across straight edge.
Row 67 (WS) P12, p3tog, p to end. 25 sts.
Row 68 Kfb, k10, k3tog, k10, kfb.
Row 69 P11, p3tog, p to end. 23 sts.
Row 70 Kfb, k9, k3tog, k9, kfb.
Row 71 P10, p3tog, p to end. 21 sts.
Row 72 Kfb, k8, k3tog, k8, kfb.
Bind off k-wise.

BOTTOM TAIL FEATHERS
Cast on 5 sts using **A** and size 6 (4mm) needles.
Row 1 (RS) K.
Row 2 K2, M1, k3.
Row 3 K4, M1, k2.
Row 4 K3, M1, k4.
Row 5 K5, M1, k3.
Row 6 Bind off 4 sts, k to end.
Rows 1–6 form the feathered edge. Rep them 9 more times.
Bind off k-wise.
With RS facing, pick up and k33 across straight edge.
Row 62 (WS) P15, p3tog, p to end. 31 sts.
Row 63 Kfb, k13, k3tog, k13, kfb.
Row 64 P14, p3tog, p to end. 29 sts.
Row 65 Kfb, k12, k3tog, k12, kfb.
Row 66 P13, p3tog, p to end. 27 sts.
Row 67 Kfb, k11, k3tog, k11, kfb.
Row 68 P12, p3tog, p to end. 25 sts.
Row 69 Kfb, k10, k3tog, k10, kfb.
Row 70 P11, p3tog, p to end. 23 sts.
Row 71 Kfb, k9, k3tog, k9, kfb.
Row 72 P10, p3tog, p to end. 21 sts.
Row 73 Kfb, k8, k3tog, k8, kfb.
Bind off k-wise.

MAKING UP

FACE
Weave in the yarn end at the tip of the beak.
Thread a tapestry needle with yarn **C** and work straight stitches to make a star shape for the eye on each side of the head. Using yarn **C**, make a few straight stitches at the top of the beak.
Following the manufacturer's instructions, snap the eyes in the center of the eye markings. Alternatively, embroider the eyes with yarn.

Charlotte isn't jealous of Lavinia— she's got her own fine plumage!

HEAD AND BODY
Stuff the head and body through the opening at the front of the neck.
Using yarn **MC**, close the opening with mattress stitch (see page 329).

COMB AND WATTLE
Join the row ends of the comb.
Sew the comb to the top of the head with the largest picot towards the back.
Sew on the wattle, with the bind-off end under the beak. Run a couple of gathering stitches from the bind-off end and draw up to give shape to the wattle.

FEATHERS
Whip stitch the edging of the top tail feathers halfway between the top of the tail shaping and the moss stitch pattern on the body.
Sew the bottom tail feathers beneath.

LEGS
Sew the legs to the underside of the hen.

egg-stra good layers

These eggs are knitted in the round and need stuffing carefully to keep their egg shape.

The haughty hens think their eggs are the most beautiful ever laid and you can have fun knitting a whole clutch. Make as many as you like—perfect for Easter!

Choose a variety of subtle eggy colors to make your hens really proud of their eggs.

RATING *

yarn
- Oddments of 4-ply yarn in egg colors

needles
- 4 x size 1 (2.25mm) double-pointed needles

gauge
You don't really need to worry about the gauge—it doesn't matter if the eggs are a little bigger or smaller than shown.

finished size
Approx 5½in (14cm) long

EGG PATTERN

Cast on 6 sts using size 1 (2.25mm) needles.
Divide 6 sts equally onto 3 needles.
With WS facing, keeping gauge fairly tight on first rnd, work in the rnd (see page 327) as follows:
Rnd 1 (WS) [Kfb, k1] 3 times. 9 sts.
Rnd 2 [Kfb, k2] 3 times. 12 sts.
Rnds 3–7 Inc 1 st in 1st st on each needle. 27 sts.
Place marker at beg of next rnd.
Rnds 8–10 K.
Rnd 11 [Skpo, k7] 3 times. 24 sts.
Rnd 12 K.
Rnd 13 [Skpo, k6] 3 times. 21 sts.
Rnd 14 K.
Rnd 15 [Skpo, k5] 3 times. 18 sts.
Rnds 16–19 Dec 1 st in 1st st on each needle. 6 sts.
Cut yarn and thread end through rem sts. Pull up tight and secure.

MAKING UP

Carefully turn the work to the wrong side and stuff the egg.
Pull up the stitches at the top and secure the thread to the inside. Weave in the yarn end at the bottom of the egg, securing the stitches inside.
Gently manipulate the work into an egg shape.

itty bitty guinea pigs

The guinea pigs are knitted mainly in the round, but their legs are knitted as i-cord to make them more spindly.

Itty and Bitty! A third guinea pig would, of course, be called Boo but, alas, there are only two—and two is plenty of these little rascals! Cute, but mischievous, they nibble everything and are very squeaky in a knitted squeak kind of way.

You can use a fancy yarn to give your guinea pigs a long beatnik hairdo or plain yarn for a short-haired look.

RATING *

yarn

For each guinea pig

Lightweight (DK) yarn

- ½ x 1¾oz (50g) ball in body color (**MC**)
- Oddment in contrasting color (**C**)

For the long-haired guinea pig

- Oddment in brown for legs (**A**)

needles

- 4 x size 3 (3mm) double-pointed needles
- 2 x size 0 (2mm) double-pointed needles

gauge

13 sts and 16 rows to 2in (5cm) in st st, using **MC** and size 3 (3mm) needles

Don't worry if the gauge is not exact—it doesn't matter if the guinea pigs are a little bigger or smaller than shown

finished size

Approx 5½in (14cm) long x 2in (5cm) tall (not including the legs)

Knitting notes

- Both the long and the short-haired guinea pigs are worked in the same way, except for the color changes on the short-haired one. For the long-haired guinea pig, work all the instructions for yarn **MC** and **C** as **MC** only.
- The main part of the guinea pig is worked in one piece from the head through the body.
- Even safety eyes can present a choking hazard for a very young child. So, instead of using toy eyes, embroider the eyes with yarn.

Where did we put that ball of wool?

knitting notes

- The guinea pigs are worked on double-pointed needles using the techniques i-cord (see page 328) and working in the round (see page 327).
- You can knit any yarn with needles one size smaller than the size recommended on the ball band to give a tight fabric that doesn't allow the stuffing to show through.

GUINEA PIG PATTERN

HEAD, LEGS AND BODY

Cast on 4 sts using **MC** and size 3 (3mm) needles.

Row 1 (WS) P.

For short-haired guinea-pig only: join **C**, working intarsia (see page 324). For long-haired guinea pig, work all sts (**MC** and **C**) in **MC** here and throughout. Cont as follows:

Row 2 (RS) **MC** kfb, **C** k2, **MC** kfb. 6 sts.

Row 3 MC p2, **C** p2, **MC** p2.

Row 4 MC kfb twice, **C** kfb twice, **MC** kfb twice. 12 sts.

Row 5 MC p4, **C** p4, **MC** p4.

Row 6 MC kfb twice, k2, **C** k4, **MC** k2, kfb twice. 16 sts.

Row 7 MC p6, **C** p4, **MC** p6.

Row 8 Divide sts: **MC** k5 onto n1, **MC** k1, **C** k4, **MC** k1 onto n2, **MC** k5 onto n3.

With RS facing, keeping gauge fairly tight on first rnd, work in the rnd (see page 327) as follows:

Rnd 9 (RS) **MC** kfb, k5, **C** k4, **MC** k5, kfb. 18 sts.

Rnd 10 MC kfb, k6, **C** k4, **MC** k6, kfb. 20 sts.

Rnd 11 MC k2, kfb twice, k4, **C** k4, **MC** k4, kfb twice, k2. 24 sts.

Rnd 12 MC k10, **C** k4, **MC** M10.

Rnd 13 MC k3, kfb 3 times, k5, **C** k2, **MC** k5, kfb 3 times, k3. 30 sts.

Can you see anything under all that hair?

Rnd 14 MC k14, **C** k2, **MC** M14.

For short-haired guinea-pig only: cut **C**. Cont with **MC** as follows:

Rnd 15 Kfb, k28, kfb. 32 sts.

Rnd 16 K32.

Rep last rnd twice more.

Shape head back

Rnd 19 K13, k2tog, k2, skpo, k13. 30 sts.

For short-haired guinea-pig only: join **C** and work with **MC** (as 2 strands) as follows:

Rnd 20 K30.

For short haired guinea pig only: cut **MC** and cont with **C** as follows:

Rnd 21 K30.

Rnd 22 K2tog, skpo, k22, k2tog, skpo. 26 sts.

Rnd 23 K26.

Rep last rnd 6 more times.

Make eyes

Following the manufacturer's instructions, snap the eyes in place on each side of the nose. Alternatively, embroider eyes with yarn.

Divide for front legs

Rnd 30 Kfb 3 times, sl next 6 sts onto a safety pin, kfb 8 times, sl next 6 sts onto a safety pin, kfb 3 times. 28 sts. (Keep gauge tight to avoid gaps as you knit under the sts on safety pins.)

Rnd 31 K28.

Rep last rnd twice more.

For short-haired guinea pig only: join **MC** and work with **C** (as 2 strands) as follows:

Rnd 34 K28.

For short-haired guinea pig only: cut **C** and cont with **MC** as follows:

Shape back

Rnd 35 K14, M1, k14. 29 sts.

Rnd 36 K29.

Rnd 37 K14, M1, k1, M1, k14. 31 sts.

Rnd 38 K31.

Rnd 39 K15, M1, k1, M1, k15. 33 sts.

Rnd 40 K33.

Rnd 41 K16, M1, k1, M1, k16. 35 sts.

Rnd 42 K35.

Rnd 43 K17, M1, k1, M1, k17. 37 sts.

Rnd 44 K37.

Rnd 45 K18, M1, k1, M1, k18. 39 sts.

Rnd 46 K39.

Rnd 47 K19, M1, k1, M1, k19. 41 sts.

Rnd 48 K41.

Rnd 49 K20, M1, k1, M1, k20. 43 sts.

Rnd 50 K43.

Begin to stuff the head and body.

Place marker and work 5 rnds without shaping.

For short-haired guinea-pig only: join **C** and work with **MC** (as 2 strands) as follows:

Rnd 56 k43.

You look bright and beady eyed.

I think they've confused their basket with the ball of yarn!

For short-haired guinea pig only: cut **MC** and cont with **C** as follows:
Rnd 57 K43.
Rnd 58 K20, k3tog, k20. 41 sts.
Rnd 59 K41.
Rnd 60 K19, k3tog, k19. 39 sts.
Rnd 61 K39.
Rnd 62 K18, k3tog, k18. 37 sts.
Rnd 63 K37.
Divide for back legs
Rnd 64 (RS) K4, sl next 8 sts onto a safety pin, k5, k3tog, k5, sl next 8 sts onto a safety pin, k4. 18 sts. (Keep gauge tight to avoid gaps as you purl above the sts on safety pins.)
Rnd 65 *K2tog, rep from * to end. 9 sts.
Cut yarn and thread end through rem sts. Stuff the rest of the body. Pull yarn up tight to close the opening and secure. Weave in end.
Shape front legs (make 2)
Sl 6 sts held on the safety pin for the front leg onto size 3 (3mm) needle.
With RS facing, rejoin **C** (**A** for long-haired guinea pig).
Rnd 66 (RS) K6. *Work as i-cord (see page 328) for 12 more rows or until the leg measures 1½in (4cm).
Rnd 67 K3, turn, bind off 3 sts p-wise. 3 sts.
Rejoin **C** (**A**) to rem 3 sts, k3, turn, bind off 3 sts p-wise.
Weave in ends.**
Shape back legs (make 2)
Sl 8 sts held on one safety pin for a back leg onto size 3 (3mm) needle.
Rnd 68 (RS) **C** (**A**) K8.
Work as i-cord as follows:
Rnd 69 K8.
Rnd 70 K2tog, k4, k2tog. 6 sts.
Work as front legs from * to **.

EARS (MAKE 2)
Cast on 5 sts using **MC** (or **A** for long-haried guinea pig) and size 0 (2mm) needles.
Row 1 (RS) Kfb, k3, kfb. 7 sts.
Row 2 P.
Row 3 K2, k3tog, k2. 5 sts.
Row 4 P.
Row 5 K1, k3tog, k1. 3 sts.
Cut yarn and thread end through sts. Pull up tight and secure.

MAKING UP

NOSE
Working mattress stitch (see page 329), join the seam under the nose. Using black yarn, embroider a couple of straight sts at the tip of the nose for nostrils.

LEGS
Weave in the ends at the legs and feet. Sew a couple of stitches to join the front legs to the side of the body to give a slightly bent leg effect and to conceal any gap left under the legs.
Pinch and then stitch the back legs approx 1in (2.5cm) up from the toes to make ankle joints. Work mattress stitch (see page 329) to close the opening where the back legs divide.

EARS
Sew the cast-on edge of an ear to one side of the head where the shaping decreases. Repeat for the other ear.

mittens & socks, lop-eared rabbits

Knitted in the round, these rabbits grow like topsy.

How to fall in love with a soft toy! Mittens and Socks are so doe-eyed, they're simply adorable—and, of course, cuddly. Make them a blanket for their own cardboard box hutch and they'll snuggle in—if you can bear to put them down.

Tweedy wool gives these bunnies a rustic charm, but experiment with chenille or angora if you want silky soft house rabbits.

RATING *

yarn

For each rabbit

Lightweight (DK) yarn

- 2 x 1¾oz (50g) balls in brown speckles or white (**MC**)
- Oddment for feet in brown speckles (**A**)
- Oddment for feet and tail in grey (**B**)

needles

- 4 x size 3 (3mm) double-pointed needles

notions

- 2 x ½in- (12mm-) diameter toy safety eyes (or black yarn)
- Oddment of pink yarn for nostrils and toenails
- Beige machine sewing thread for whiskers (optional)

gauge

13 sts and 16 rows to 2in (5cm) in st st, using **MC** and size 3 (3mm) needles

Don't worry if the gauge is not exact—it doesn't matter if the rabbits are a little bigger or smaller than shown.

finished size

Approx 10in (25cm) long x 7in (18cm) tall

This one's yummy, but I wonder if the others are sweeter ...

knitting notes

- The main part of the rabbit is worked in one piece from the head through the body.
- The rabbits are worked on double-pointed needles working in the round (see page 327).
- Do not use even safety eyes on toys for an infant, as they can be a potential choking hazard. Instead, embroider the eyes with yarn.
- You can knit any yarn with needles one size smaller than the size recommended on the ball band to give a tight fabric that doesn't allow the stuffing to show through.

RABBIT PATTERN

HEAD, LEGS AND BODY
Cast on 6 sts using **MC** and size 3 (3mm) needles.
Row 1 (WS) P.
Row 2 Cast on 4 sts, k4, k2tog, k to end. 9 sts.
Row 3 Cast on 4 sts, p4, p2tog, p to end. 12 sts.
Shape cheeks
Row 4 (RS) K1, kfb 3 times, k4, kfb 3 times, k1. 18 sts.
Row 5 P.
Row 6 K1, kfb 6 times, k4, kfb 6 times, k1. 30 sts.
Row 7 P.
Row 8 K1, [M1, k1] 8 times, k12, [M1, k1] 8 times, k1. 46 sts.
Work 3 rows in st st.
Row 12 (RS) K19, k2tog, k4, skpo, k to end. 44 sts.
Shape right side of face
Row 13 (WS) P18, turn.
Row 14 Sl 1, k15, turn.
Row 15 Sl 1, p13, turn.
Row 16 Sl 1, k11, turn.
Row 17 Sl 1, p to last 2 sts at other side of head, turn.
Shape left side of face
Row 18 (RS) Sl 1, k15, turn.
Row 19 Sl 1, p13, turn.
Row 20 Sl 1, k11, turn.
Row 21 Sl 1, p9, turn.
Row 22 Sl 1, k to end.
Row 23 P.
Row 24 Divide sts: k15 onto n1, k14 onto n2, k15 onto n3.
With RS facing, keeping gauge fairly tight in first rnd, work in the rnd (see page 327) as follows:
Rnd 25 K44.
Rep last rnd twice more.
Shape front of head and create ear holes
Rnd 28 K29, turn. Work back and forth across last 14 sts at the head front as follows:
Row 29 (WS) P14, turn.
Row 30 Sl 1, k10, skpo, k1, turn.
Row 31 Sl 1, p9, p2tog, p1, turn.
Row 32 Sl 1, k8, skpo, k1, turn.
Row 33 Sl 1, p7, p2tog, p1, turn.
Row 34 Sl 1, k6, skpo, k1, turn.
Row 35 Sl 1, p5, p2tog, p1, turn.
Row 36 Sl 1, k4, skpo, k1, turn.
Row 37 Sl 1, p3, p2tog, p1, turn.
Row 38 Sl 1, k2, skpo, k1. Do not turn.
K50 to join into rnd and beg at start of rnd (at rabbit's chin) once more. (Keep gauge tight across the ear hole gaps left at the head front shaping.)
Cont to work on last 35 sts as follows:
Rnd 39 K35.
Rep last rnd 3 more times.
Shape neck
Rnd 43 K2tog, skpo, k27, k2tog, skpo. 31 sts.
Rnd 44 K31.
Rnd 45 K2tog, skpo, k23, k2tog, skpo. 27 sts.
Rnd 46 K27.
Divide for front
Rnd 47 K4, sl last 8 sts onto a safety pin, k19. 19 sts.
With WS facing, work back and forth as follows:
Shape front legs
Speckled rabbit only:
Row 48 (WS) Cast on 22 sts, p to end.
Row 49 Cast on 22 sts, k to end.
White rabbit only:
Join **A**, stranding yarn (see intarsia, page 324) at back of work as follows:
Row 48 (WS) **MC** cast on 17 sts, **A** cast on 5 sts , **A** p5, **MC** p to end.
Row 49 MC cast on 17 sts, **A** cast on 5 sts, **A** k5, **MC** k to last 5 sts, **A** k5.
Now work first 5 sts at beg and end of next 17 rows in **A**.
Shape feet (*both rabbits*)
Row 50 (WS) P5, turn.
Row 51 Sl 1, k3, turn.
Row 52 Sl 1, p2, turn.
Row 53 Sl 1, k1, turn.
Row 54 Sl 1, p to end.
Row 55 K5, turn.
Row 56 Sl 1, p3, turn.
Row 57 Sl 1, k2, turn.
Row 58 Sl 1, p1, turn.
Row 59 Sl 1, k to end.
Work 7 rows in st st.
Work inside front left leg
*Cont as follows, using **MC** for brown rabbit and **A** for white rabbit:*
Work first 5 sts at beg and end of next 13 rows.
Row 67 (RS) K22, turn.
Work 7 rows in st st on these 22 sts for the inside left leg.
Shape inside left foot
Row 75 (RS) K5, turn.
Row 76 Sl 1, p3, turn.
Row 77 Sl 1, k2, turn.
Row 78 Sl 1, p1, turn.
Row 79 Sl 1, k19 to end of the inside leg, turn.
Bind off 22 sts.
With WS facing, rejoin yarn to the foot end of the right leg.
*Cont as follows, using **MC** for brown rabbit and **A** for white rabbit:*
Work first 5 sts at beg and end of next 11 rows in **A**.
Work inside front right leg
Row 80 (WS) P22, turn.
Work 5 rows in st st.

Mittens wants to see in the dark

Only organic veggies are good enough!

The rabbits love the garden—playing there encourages them to eat their greens.

Shape inside right foot
Row 86 (WS) P5, turn.
Row 87 Sl 1, k3, turn.
Row 88 Sl 1, p2, turn.
Row 89 Sl 1, k1, turn.
Row 90 Sl 1, p19 to the end of the inside leg, turn.
Bind off 22 sts.
Leave rem 19 sts from the back on their needles.
Work front
Sl 8 sts at the neck off the safety pin onto size 3 (3mm) needle. With RS facing, rejoin **MC**.
Row 91 (RS) K.
Work 9 rows in st st.
Join front to back
Row 101(RS) K8, k12 sts from the back onto n2, k7 sts from the back onto n3. 27 sts.
With RS facing, keeping gauge tight across junctions, work in the rnd as follows:
Rnd 102 K27.
Shape tummy
Rnd 103 (RS) K8, M1, k1, M1, k17, M1, k1, M1. 31 sts.
Rnd 104 K31.
Rnd 105 K8, M1, k23, M1. 33 sts.
Rnd 106 K33.
Rnd 107 K8, M1, k25, M1. 35 sts.
Rnd 108 K35.
Rnd 109 K8, M1, k27, M1. 37 sts.
Rnd 110 K37.
Shape back
Rnd 111 K22, M1, k1, M1, k14. 39 sts.
Rnd 112 K39.
Rnd 113 K23, M1, k1, M1, k15. 41 sts.
Rnd 114 K41.
Rnd 115 K24, M1, k1, M1, k16. 43 sts.
Rnd 116 K43.
Rep last rnd 4 more times.
Divide for back legs
K8, sl last 8 sts onto a safety pin. 35 sts.
With RS facing, work back and forth as follows:
Shape upper back legs
Cast on 10 sts at beg of next 2 rows. 55 sts.
Shape back
Row 119 (RS) K26, k3tog, k to end. 53 sts.
Work 3 rows in st st.
Row 123 (RS) K25, k3tog, k to end. 51 sts.
Work 3 rows in st st.
Row 127 (RS) K24, k3tog, k to end. 49 sts.
Work 2 rows in st st.
Work inside back right leg
Row 130 (WS) P10, turn.
Work 10 rows in st st on these 10 sts for the inside right leg.
Bind off 10 sts.
With RS facing, return to rem 39 sts.

Work inside back left leg
Row 141 (RS) Rejoin **MC**, k10, turn.
Work 10 rows in st st on these 10 sts for the inside right leg.
Bind off 10 sts.
With RS facing, rejoin **MC** to rem 29 sts.
Divide for tail
Row 152 Bind off 8 sts, k5, k2tog, k5, bind off last 8 sts. 12 sts.
Work tail
With RS facing, rejoin yarn.
Row 153 (RS) *K2tog, rep from * to end. 6 sts. Leave sts on needle.
Work underside of tail
Row 154 With WS facing, sl first loop from the back of 6 sts for the tail onto a needle. Knit into this loop with **B** (brown rabbit) or **MC** (white rabbit). Pick up the next loop and knit into that, cont working along the row, ending with 6 loops and 2 rows on knitting adjacent to each other. Turn. With WS of the 'new' row facing, cont as follows:
Row 155 (WS) P6.
Work 8 rows in st st.
Row 164 (RS) [k2tog] 3 times. 3 sts.
Cut yarn and thread end through sts. Pull up tight and secure.
Shape top of tail
Row 165 Return to 6 sts from the top of the tail, k6 in **MC**.
Work 8 rows in st st to mirror the under tail, so ending with a WS row.
Row 174 (RS) [k2tog] 3 times. 3 sts.
Using a tapestry needle, join along the row ends to join the top and bottom tails, and stuff to puff out the tail slightly.
Shape gusset between back legs
With RS facing, rejoin **MC** to 8 sts on the safety pin before the back legs.
Row 175 (RS) K.
Work 5 rows in st st.
Row 181 (RS) K2tog, k to last 2 sts, k2tog. 6 sts.
Row 182 P.
Rep last 2 rows once more. 4 sts.
Row 185 [K2tog] twice. 2 sts.
Row 186 P.
Bind off.

BACK FEET (MAKE 2)
Cast on 22 sts using **MC** (white rabbit) or **B** (brown rabbit) and size 3 (3mm) needles.
Row 1 (WS) P.
Row 2 *Kfb, rep from * to end. 44 sts.
Row 3 P.
Row 4 [K1, M1] twice, k18, [M1, k1] 5 times, k17, [M1, k1] twice. 53 sts.

Work 5 rows in st st.
Row 10 (RS) K24, k2tog, k1, skpo, k to end. 51 sts.
Row 11 P.
Row 12 K23, k2tog, k1, skpo, k to end. 49 sts.
Row 13 P.
Row 14 K22, k2tog, k1, skpo, k to end. 47 sts.
Row 15 P.
Row 16 K13, bind off next 21 sts, k to end. 26 sts.
Row 17 P26.
Work 2 rows in st st.
Bind off.

EARS (MAKE 2)
Cast on 9 sts using **MC** and size 3 (3mm) needles.
Row 1 (WS) P.
Row 2 Kfb, k3, M1, k1, M1, k3, kfb. 13 sts.
Row 3 P.
Row 4 Kfb, k5, M1, k1, M1, k5, kfb. 17 sts.
Row 5 P.
Row 6 Kfb, k7, M1, k1, M1, k7, kfb. 21 sts.
Row 7 P.
Row 8 Kfb, k9, M1, k1, M1, k9, kfb. 25 sts.
Work 3 rows in st st.
Row 12 (RS) K2tog, k to last 2 sts, k2tog. 23 sts.
Row 13 P.
Rep last 2 rows twice more. 19 sts.
Row 18 (RS) K2tog, k7, skpo, k6, k2tog. 16 sts.
Row 19 P.
Row 20 K2tog, k4, skpo, k2tog, k4, k2tog. 12 sts.
Row 21 K2tog, p to last 2 sts, p2tog. 10 sts.
Row 22 K2tog, k2, skpo, k2, k2tog. 7 sts.
Row 23 P2tog, p to last 2 sts, p2tog. 5 sts.
Work 2 rows in st st.
Bind off.

MAKING UP

HEAD
Working mattress stitch (see page 329), join the seam under the nose and chin.
Embroider a couple of straight sts in pink yarn at the tip of the nose for nostrils.
Secure **MC** at one end of the nose bridge and push the needle through the head to the other side of the nose bridge. Pull the yarn to draw the sides slightly together and create an indentation for eye sockets. Secure the yarn.

EYES
Following the manufacturer's instructions, snap the eyes in place in the eye sockets. Alternatively, embroider the eyes with yarn.

EARS
Sew an ear onto each side of the rabbit's head, with the cast-on edge in the opening and the back seam facing backwards.

HEAD
Stuff the head and neck fairly firmly, manipulating the stuffing to shape cheeks, nose bridge, and forehead.

FRONT LEGS
With wrong side facing, fold the front leg in half, joining the row ends and matching the foot shaping. Leaving the tops (bind-off edges) of the legs unsewn, mattress stitch the row ends to join the inside leg to the outer leg. Work a running stitch around the bind-off end at the foot, pull it up tight to gather and secure, stuffing the foot as you go. Weave the end in.

BACK LEGS
Join the back legs along the row ends, leaving the cast-on and bind-off edges unsewn.
Join the instep, sole, and back feet seams. Stuff the feet. Attach the feet to the back legs with mattress stitch, matching the front of the foot with the seam.

TOES
Create toes on all the feet with pink yarn, sewing three straight stitches and pulling the yarn tight to create an indent.

BODY
Join the rows ends at the back of the rabbit under the tail.
Mattress stitch the short seams at the front legs along the sides of the body and around the tops of the front legs, easing in the fullness to fit the shapings.
Mattress stitch the gusset at the back legs along the sides of the body, around the tops of the front legs, and up to the back, leaving an opening for stuffing.
Lightly stuff the body.

WHISKERS
If you wish to make whiskers, cut short lengths of thread. Thread one length into a tapestry needle and pass it through a knitted stitch in the nose, so both ends are the same length. Make another stitch to secure. Work other strands into other knitted stitches to create more whiskers. Trim.

PATCH
Work a patch onto the front of the white rabbit's nose using Duplicate stitch (see page 331) and contrasting yarn.

Are you on a diet, Socks?!

speckle the kitten

This kitten combines simple shaping with knitting in the round to create a truly lovable pet.

Speckle is simply adorable with her little pink nose, bright attentive eyes, and white socks. Her cat's curiosity makes her eager to leap about as she plays with her favorite toy—a yellow mouse on wheels (see pages 260–261)!

Once you get used to knitting in the round, you'll find Speckle easy to make.

RATING *

yarn
Lightweight (DK) yarn
- 1 x 1¾oz (50g) ball in grey/white tweed (**MC**)
- Oddment in ecru (**A**)
- Oddment in pink for nose

needles
- 4 x size 3 (3mm) double-pointed needles
- 2 x size 3 (3mm) knitting needles (optional)

notions
- 2 x 5⁄16in- (8mm-) diameter toy safety eyes (or black yarn)

gauge
13 sts and 16 rows to 2in (5cm) of st st, using **MC** and size 3 (3mm) needles
Don't worry if the gauge is not exact—it doesn't matter if the kitten is a little bigger or smaller than shown.

finished size
Approx 9½in (21cm) long (including the tail) x 6in (12cm) tall

I love having friends for dinner ...

knitting notes

- The main part of the body is worked in one piece from the nose to the tail.
- The kitten is worked on double-pointed needles, sometimes working in the round (see page 327). Kitchener stitch (see page 323) is used to make a 'seamless' join.
- If you are knitting for a very young child, embroider the eyes with yarn instead of using toy eyes. Even safety eyes can be a choking hazard.
- If you want a tighter fabric, simply knit using needles that are one size smaller than specified.

KITTEN PATTERN

HEAD, EARS, BODY, LEGS AND TAIL
Cast on 3 sts using **A** and size 3 (3mm) needles.
Row 1 (RS) *Kfb, rep from * to end. 6 sts.
Row 2 P.
Rows 3–6 Rep rows 1–2 twice more. 24 sts.
Row 7 (RS) Divide sts: k8 sts onto n1, 8 sts onto n2, 8 sts onto n3. 24 sts.
With RS facing, keeping gauge fairly tight on first rnd, work in the rnd (see page 327) as follows:
Rnd 8 (RS) [K8, M1] 3 times, sl last st back onto n3. 27 sts. Cut yarn. Join **MC**. Without turning work, cont as follows:
Rnd 9 (RS) K13, kfb, k13. 28 sts.
Rnd 10 (Kfb, k3) 7 times. 35 sts.
Rnd 11 K.
Rnd 12 (Kfb, k4) 7 times. 42 sts.
Rnd 13 K.
Shape top of head
Rnd 14 K18, kfb 6 times, k18. 48 sts.
Rnd 15 K.
Rnd 16 K20, [kfb, k1] 4 times, k20. 52 sts.
Place marker at beg of next rnd and k 4 rnds.
Divide for neck and back of head
Rnd 21 K5, bind off 13, place marker, k15, place marker, bind off 13 sts, K4.
K across next 5 sts so all 10 sts from under the chin are on one needle.
Cut yarn, leaving sts on needle.
With RS facing, rejoin **MC** to 16 sts from the back of the head (also on one needle).
Row 22 (RS) K, turn.
Row 23 P.
Row 24 Skpo, k to last 2 sts, k2tog. 14 sts.
Rep last 2 rows, 3 more times. 8 sts.
Place marker at each end of next row for the back of the ear position.
Row 31 (WS) P.
Row 32 K1, M1, k to last st, M1, k1. 10 sts.
Row 33 P.
Row 34 K1, M1, k to last st, M1, k1. 12 sts.
Work 5 rows in st st, beg with p row.
Cut yarn, leaving sts on the needle.
Shape ears
*With RS facing, pick up and k 11 sts between markers on the right side of the head.
Work 3 rows in st st, beg with p row.
Row 44 (RS) K10, turn.
Row 45 Sl 1, p8, turn.
Row 46 Sl 1, k7, turn.
Row 47 Sl 1, p6, turn.
Row 48 Sl 1, k5, turn.
Row 49 Sl 1, p4, turn.
Row 50 Sl 1, k3, turn.
Row 51 Sl 1, p2, turn.
Row 52 Sl 1, k1, turn.
Row 53 Sl 1, p5 to end.
Row 54 (RS) K2tog, k to last 2 sts, k2tog. 9 sts.
Row 55 P2 tog, p to last 2 sts, p2tog. 7 sts.
Rep last 2 rows once more. 3 sts.
Row 58 (RS) ***K2tog, k1. 2 sts.
Row 59 P2tog. 1 st.
Fasten off.**
Rep from * to ** for other ear, reversing shaping at ***.
Weave in ends.
Shape neck
Row 60 (RS) **MC** Divide sts: K10 sts from the neck onto n1, k6 (joining neck to back of head) onto n2, k6 onto n3. 22 sts.
With RS facing, work in the rnd. K5 to center of neck and place marker for beg of rnds from now on.
K 2 rnds.
Rnd 63 (K1, M1) 21 times, k1 43 sts.
K 3 rows.
Divide for front
Rnd 67 K5 sts, sl last 10 sts onto a safety pin, K4, sl 4 sts onto working needle, k 12 sts (18 sts on needle), K 17 sts onto n2. 33 sts.
Shape front legs
With WS facing, work st st over 2 needles (working all sts onto one needle if you prefer) as follows:
Cast on 15 sts at beg of next 2 rows. 63 sts.
Shape feet
Row 70 (WS) p5, turn.
Row 71 Sl 1, k3, turn.
Row 72 Sl 1, p2, turn.
Row 73 Sl 1, k1, turn.
Row 74 Sl 1, p to end.
Row 75 K5, turn.
Row 76 Sl 1, p3, turn.
Row 77 Sl 1, k2, turn.
Row 78 Sl 1, p1, turn.
Row 79 Sl 1, k to end.
Work 5 rows in st st.
Work inside front left leg
Row 85 (RS) K15, turn.
Work 5 rows in st st.
Shape inside left left
Row 91 (RS) K5, turn.
Row 92 Sl 1, p3, turn.
Row 93 Sl 1, k2, turn.
Row 94 Sl 1, p1, turn.
Row 95 Sl 1, k12 to end, turn.
Bind off 15 sts.
With RS facing, rejoin **MC** to rem 48 sts.
Row 96 K.
Work inside front right leg
Row 97 (WS) p15, turn.
Work 5 rows in st st.

Speckle loves to 'help' me knit!

gone fishing

Shape inside right foot

Row 103 (WS) p5, turn.

Row 104 Sl 1, k3, turn.

Row 105 Sl 1, p2, turn.

Row 106 Sl 1, k1, turn.

Row 107 Sl 1, p12 to end, turn.

Bind off 15 sts.

Shape back

With WS facing, rejoin **MC** to rem 33 sts.

Row 108 (WS) P.

Work 2 rows in st st.

Row 111 (RS) K16, M1, k1, M1, k to end. 35 sts.

Row 112 P.

Row 113 K17, M1, k1, M1, k to end. 37 sts.

Row 114 P.

Row 115 K18, M1, k1, M1, k to end. 39 sts.

Row 116 P.

Shape back legs

Row 117 (RS) Cast on 7 sts, k26, M1, k1, M1, k to end. 48 sts.

Row 118 Cast on 7 sts, p to end. 55 sts.
Work st st for 2 rows.
Row 121 (RS) K26, k3tog, k to end. 53 sts.
Row 122 P.
Row 123 K25, k3tog, k to end. 51 sts.
Row 124 P.
Row 125 K24, k3tog, k to end. 49 sts.
Row 126 P.
Divide for tail
Row 127 (RS) K19, sl next 11 sts onto a safety pin, k19 under the tail to end of row. 38 sts. (Keep gauge tight as you knit under the sts held on safety pin.)
Row 128 P18, p2tog, p to end. 37 sts.
Shape inside back left leg
Row 129 (RS) K7, turn.
With WS facing, work 9 rows in st st.
Bind off 7 sts.
With RS facing, rejoin **MC** to rem 30 sts.
Row 139 K2tog 5 times, k3tog, k2tog 5 times, k7. 18 sts.
Shape inside back right leg
Row 140 (WS) P7, turn.
With RS facing, work 9 rows in st st.
Bind off.
Work underbody
With WS facing, rejoin **MC** to rem 11 sts.
Row 150 P.
Work 8 rows in st st.
Cut yarn, leave sts on needle.
Work neck
With RS facing, sl 10 sts at neck off the safety pin, p-wise, onto size 2 (2.5mm) needle.
Row 159 (WS) **MC** P.
Work 22 rows in st st.
Cut yarn, leaving sts on needle.
Weave in ends.
Join seam under back legs
With WS tog, hold needles parallel. Work Kitchener st (see page 323) to close the seam, taking off last st k-wise. Weave in end.
Work tail
Sl 11 sts at the tail off the safety pin onto size 2 (2.5mm) needle.
Divide sts over two more needles.
Join for working in the rnd and place marker at beg of rnd.
Rnd 182 K.
Rep last rnd 4 more times.
Rnd 187 [K3, kfb] twice, k3. 13 sts.
Place marker at beg of rnd. Work 5 rnds.
Fasten off.
Weave in loose end at the tip of the tail.
Use loose end at the body end of the tail to close any opening under the tail.

BACK FEET (MAKE 2)
Cast on 12 sts, using **A** and size 3 (3mm) needles.
Row 1 (WS) P.
Row 2 K1, *M1, k1, rep from * to end. 23 sts.
Row 3 P.
Row 4 K1, M1, k8, [M1, k1] 6 times, k7, M1, k1. 31 sts.
Rows 5–7 St st.
Row 8 K13, k2tog, k1, skpo, k13. 29 sts.
Row 9 P.
Row 10 K12, k2tog, k1, skpo, k12. 27 sts.
Row 11 P.
Row 12 K8, bind off next 11 sts, k7. 16 sts.
Row 13 P.
Rows 14–16 St st.
Bind off.

INNER EAR (MAKE 2)
Cast on 11 sts using **A** and size 3 (3mm) needles.
Row 1 (RS) P.
Row 2 K10, turn.
Row 3 Sl1, p8, turn.

Row 4 Sl1, k7, turn.
Row 5 Sl1, p6, turn.
Row 6 Sl1, k5, turn.
Row 7 Sl1, p4, turn.
Row 8 Sl1, k3, turn.
Row 9 Sl1, p2, turn.
Row 10 Sl1, k1, turn.
Row 11 Sl1, p5 to end.
Row 12 K2tog, k to last 2 sts, k2tog. 9 sts.
Row 13 P2tog, p to last 2 sts, p2tog. 7 sts.
Rep last 2 rows once more. 3 sts.
Row 16 (RS) K3tog.
Fasten off.
Weave all ends into WS.

I keep finding her favorite toy under the fridge!

MAKING UP

EARS
Using yarn **MC**, oversew the inner ear to the inside of the outer ear, matching shaping and closing the opening. Use your thumbs to push in a 'hollow' shaping at the inside ear against the outer ear. Join the seams at each side of the head.

EYES AND NOSE
Following the manufacturer's instructions, snap the eyes in place on each side of the nose. Alternatively, embroider the eyes with yarn. Embroider a nose using yarn **B** and straight stitches.

FRONT LEGS
With wrong side facing, fold the front leg in half, joining the row ends and matching the foot shaping. Leaving the tops (bind-off edges) of the legs unsewn, mattress stitch (see page 329) the row ends to join the inside leg to the outer leg. Work a running stitch around the bind-off edge at the foot, pull the yarn up tight to gather, and secure. Stuff the leg fairly firmly, shaping the foot as you do so. Weave the yarn end through the stuffing back inside the foot. Repeat for the other leg.

BACK LEGS
Join the back seam on the back leg. Join the instep, sole and back feet seams. Stuff the foot. Attach the feet to the back leg using mattress seam. Stuff fairly firmly, shaping the foot as you do so. Weave the yarn end back through the stuffing inside the foot. With yarn **B**, sew four straight stitches at the tips of the feet to create toe pads. Repeat for the other leg.

BODY
Join the row ends at the back of the kitten. Beginning at the tail end, join the seam along the sides of the body and around the tops of the legs, leaving an opening for stuffing. Stuff the kitten fairly firmly into the head, but less so into the body to allow it to be a bit floppy. Sew the opening closed. Manipulate the stuffing at the legs and feet, and along the neck and body, to really give a kitten shape, while keeping it soft and cuddly.

Oh no! I don't like getting my paws wet.

toy mouse

Have fun choosing the color for your toy mouse from your stash.

Speckle the kitten loves playing with her toy mouse, so thank goodness it's easy to knit.

RATING ✱

knitting notes

- Even safety eyes can present a choking hazard for a very young child. So, instead of using toy eyes, embroider the eyes with yarn.
- The main body is worked in one piece.
- The mouse is worked on double-pointed needles, sometimes in the round (see page 327).

yarn

Lightweight (DK) yarn

- Oddment in yellow (**MC**)
- Oddment in shale grey (**A**)

needles

- 4 x size 2 (2.5mm) double-pointed needles

notions

- 4 x ¼in- (6mm-) diameter toy safety eyes in plain black (or black yarn)

gauge

15 sts and 19 rows to 2in (5cm) of st st, using **MC** and size 1 (2.25mm) needles

Don't worry if the gauge is not exact—it doesn't matter if the mouse is a little bigger or smaller than shown.

finished size

Approx 3in (7.6cm) long

MOUSE PATTERN

Cast on 3sts using **MC** and size 2 (2.5mm) needles.

Row 1 (RS) *Kfb, rep from * to end. 6 sts.

Row 2 Divide sts: k2 sts onto n1, 2 sts onto n2, 2 sts onto n3.

With RS facing, keeping gauge fairly tight on first rnd, work in the rnd (see page 327) as follows:

Rnd 3 K.

Rnd 4 *Kfb, rep from * to end. 12 sts.

Rnd 5 K.

Rnd 6 *K1, kfb, rep from * to end. 18 sts.

Rnd 7 K.

Rnd 8 *K2, kfb, rep from * to end. 24 sts.

Rnd 9 K.

Rnd 10 *K3, kfb, rep from * to end. 30 sts.

Place marker.

Rnd 11 K.

Rnd 12 K3, M1, k to last 3 sts, M1, k3. 32 sts.
Rnd 13 K.
Rep last 2 rnds twice more. 36 sts.
Place marker at beg of next rnd.
Rnd 18 K.
Rnd 19 K2, skpo, k to last 4 sts, k2tog, k2. 34 sts.
Rnd 20 K.
Rep last 2 rnds twice more. 30 sts.
Rnd 25 *K4, k2tog, rep from * to end. 25 sts.
Rnd 26 K.
Rnd 27 *K3, k2tog, rep from * to end. 20 sts.
Rnd 28 K.
Rnd 29 *K2, k2tog, rep from * to end. 15 sts.
Rnd 30 K.
Stuff the mouse and cont to stuff it as you go.
Rnd 31 *K1, k2tog, rep from * to end. 10 sts.
Rnd 32 K.
Rnd 33 *K2tog, rep from * to end. 5 sts.
Cut yarn and thread end through rem sts. Pull up tight and secure.

WHEELS (MAKE 2)
Cast on 4 sts using **A** and size 2 (2.5mm) needles.
Row 1 (RS) Kfb, k to last st, kfb. 8 sts.
Row 2 P.
Rep last 2 rows once more. 16 sts.
Work st st for 5 rows.
Row 10 (RS) K2tog, k to last 2 sts, k2tog. 8 sts.
Row 11 P.
Rep last 2 rows once more. 4 sts.
Cut yarn and thread end through rem sts. Pull up tight, stuffing the wheel, and secure.
Following the manufacturer's instructions, snap one toy eye into center of each wheel. Alternatively, embroider French knots with yarn.

EARS (MAKE 2)
Cast on 3 sts, using **MC** and size 2 (2.5mm) needles.
Row 1 (RS) Kfb, k to last st, kfb. 5 sts.
Row 2 P.
Rep last 2 rows once more. 7 sts.
Work st st for 4 rows.
Row 9 (RS) K2tog, k to last 2 sts , k2tog. 5 sts.
Row 10 P2tog, p to last 2 sts, p2tog. 3 sts.
Cut yarn and thread end through rem sts. Pull up tight and secure.

MAKING UP

Sew the wheels to each side of the mouse.
Following the manufacturer's instructions, snap the eyes in the center of the eye markings. Alternatively, embroider the eyes with yarn.
Sew on a length of kitten **MC** (or any spare yarn) as a simple tail.

tortellini tortoise

Tortellini's shell is made in seven pieces, each knitted round and round.

Fascination and curiosity is what makes tortoises so desirable. Their ancient, almost dinosaur-like, and characterful faces, their intricately patterned shells, and their steady slow movements make them the perfect pet to watch and wonder over. This is Tortellini—and he is captivating in slow motion!

The choice of self-patterning yarn is so vast that each tortoise can be totally unique.

RATING * *

yarn

Fingering-weight (4-ply) yarn

- ½ x 1¾oz (50g) ball in blue/brown (**A**)
- Oddment in blue (**B**)

Lightweight (DK) yarn

- ½ x 1¾oz (50g) ball in beige (**C**)
- ½ x 1¾oz (50g) ball in grey (**MC**)

needles

- 4 x size 3 (3mm) double-pointed needles
- 4 x size 4 (3.5mm) double-pointed needles

notions

- 2 x ¼in- (6mm-) diameter toy safety eyes (or black yarn)

gauge

12 sts and 15 rows to 2in (5cm), using **MC** and size 4 (3.5mm) needles

Don't worry if the gauge is not exact—it doesn't matter if tortoise is a little bigger or smaller than shown.

finished size

Approx 18½in (47cm) diameter across the shell

People think I'm slow ...

Knitting notes

- Tortellini's shell is created with 7 hexagons.
- The tortoise is worked in the round (see page 327) on double-pointed needles.
- Do not use even safety eyes on toys for an infant, as they can be a potential choking hazard. Instead, embroider the eyes in place with yarn.

TORTOISE PATTERN

SHELL TOP HEXAGONS

Cast on 60 sts using **A** and size 3 (3mm) needles. Divide sts evenly over 3 needles. Work in the rnd (see page 327) as follows:

Rnd 1 (WS) K60.

Rep last rnd once.

Rnd 3 [K2tog, k6, skpo] 6 times. 48 sts.

Rnd 4 K48.

Rep last rnd once.

Rnd 6 [K2tog, k4, skpo] 6 times. 36 sts.

Rnd 7 K36.

Rep last rnd once.

Rnd 9 [K2tog, k2, skpo] 6 times. 24 sts.

Rnd 10 K24.

Rep last rnd once.

Cut **A**. Join **B**.

Rnd 12 K2tog 12 times. 12 sts.

Rnd 13 K12.

Cut yarn and thread end through sts. Pull up tight and secure.

Rep patt to make 6 more hexagons.

SHELL BASE

Cast on 2 sts, using **C** and size 4 (3.5mm) needles.

Row 1 K2.

Work as i-cord (see page 328) as follows:

Row 2 Kfb twice. 4 sts.

Row 3 Kfb 4 times. 8 sts.

Row 4 Divide sts: k3 onto n1, k2 onto n2, k3 onto n3.

With RS facing, work in the rnd as follows:

Rnd 5 [K1, kfb] 4 times. 12 sts.

Rnd 6 [K2, kfb] 4 times. 16 sts.

Rnd 7 [K3, kfb] 4 times. 20 sts.

Rnd 8 [K4, kfb] 4 times. 24 sts.

Cont to inc 4 sts on every rnd until last rnd has 11 sts before each inc. 52 sts.

Place marker at beg of rnd, k all sts onto circular needle, shaping as follows:

Next rnd [K12, kfb] 4 times. 52 sts.

Next rnd [K13, kfb] 4 times. 56 sts.

Next rnd [K14, kfb] 4 times. 60 sts.

Inc 4 sts on every rnd until last rnd has 31 sts before each inc. 132 sts.

Next rnd K132.

Place marker.

Rep last rnd 4 more times.

Bind off. Weave in ends.

HEAD

Cast on 4sts using **MC** and size 4 (3.5mm) needles.

Row 1 (RS) *Kfb, rep from * to end. 8 sts.

Row 2 P.

Rep last 2 rows once more. 16 sts.

Shape head

Row 5 (RS) K7, [M1, k1] twice, k7. 18 sts.

Row 6 P.

Row 7 Divide sts: k7 onto n1, k4 onto n2, k7 onto n3.

With RS of facing, keeping gauge fairly tight in first rnd, work in the rnd as follows:

Rnd 8 K18.

Rnd 9 K7, kfb, k2, kfb, k7. 20 sts.

Rnd 10 K20.

Rnd 11 K7, kfb, k4, kfb, k7. 22 sts.

Rnd 12 K22.

Rnd 13 Skpo, k5, kfb, k6, kfb, k5, k2tog.

Rnd 14 K22.

Rnd 15 Skpo, k4, kfb, k8, kfb, k4, k2tog.

Rnd 16 K22.

Rep last rnd 8 more times.

Rnd 25 *K2tog, rep from * to end. 11 sts.

Cut yarn and thread end through sts. Pull up tight and secure.

LEGS (MAKE 4)

Cast on 12 sts, using **MC** and size 4 (3.5mm) needles.

Row 1 (RS) P.

Row 2 K1, *M1, k1, rep from * to end. 23 sts.

Row 3 P.

Row 4 K1, M1, k8, [M1, k1] 6 times, k7, M1, k1. 31 sts.

He likes to stop for a rest now and again ...

... you'd be slow
if you carried your
home around.

You lead the way, Tortellini,
I'm never far behind!

Hey, am I picking up speed now!?

Another well deserved rest.

Work 3 rows in st st.
Row 8 (WS) K13, k2tog, k1, skpo, k to end. 29 sts.
Row 9 P.
Row 10 K12, k2tog, k1, skpo, k to end. 27 sts.
Row 11 P.
Row 12 K7, bind off next 13 sts, k to end. 14 sts.
Row 13 P14.
Row 14 Kfb, k to last st, kfb. 16 sts.
Row 15 P.
Row 16 K1, k2tog, k1, skpo, k3, k2tog, k1, skpo, k2. 12 sts.
Work 7 rows in st st.
Row 24 (WS) K1, k2tog, k1, skpo, k1, k2tog, k1, skpo. 8 sts.
Row 25 *P2tog, rep from * to end. 4 sts.
Cut yarn and thread end through sts. Pull up tight and secure.

MAKING UP

HEAD
Following the manufacturer's instructions, snap the eyes in place on each side of the nose. Alternatively, embroider the eyes with yarn.
Stuff the head and neck fairly firmly.
Mattress stitch (see page 329) the seam around the nose.

LEGS
With right side (reverse stockingette stitch) facing, fold the front leg in half at the bind-off edge and matching the row ends. Beginning at the top of the leg, work mattress stitch to join along the leg front. Mattress stitch the opening at the inside edge of the foot closed.
For claws, work three French knots (see page 331) or looped sts in **MC** along the narrower folded edge at the back of the foot. Repeat for the other feet.

SHELL
Press the hexagons, using a cool iron and pressing cloth.
Piece the shell together with six hexagons around a central one. With matching yarn, backstitch (see page 329) the edges together. Press.
Press the base, retaining the bowl shape created by the shaping.
Pin the top shell onto the upturned base, so that the top shell overhangs the base, stuffing it as you go. Sew in place.
Manipulate the stuffing to give a good shape to the shell.

HEAD
Create a hollow at the front in the base, just under the top shell, and sew the bind-off edge of the neck into it. Make the head look as if it's just popping out from under the shell.

LEGS
Sew the legs in place to the base, just under the shell.

bamber the labrador puppy

Bamber is quite easy to make, knitted in the round and with his i-cord tail.

Cute, floppy, cuddly, adorable … oh, and a lot less messy than the real thing! Bamber brings his own collar and lead—though be warned, this particular pup loves to snuggle up and stay in rather than 'go walkies'.

You could always try different colors if you want a yellow or a chocolate lab.

RATING * *

yarn

Lightweight (DK) yarn

- ½ x 1¾oz (50g) ball in ecru (**MC**)
- Oddment in light brown (**B**)

Fingering-weight (4-ply) yarn

- Oddment in brown (**A**)

needles

- 4 x size 2 (2.5mm) double-pointed needles

notions

- 2 x 1⁵⁄₁₆in- (8mm-) diameter toy safety eyes (or black yarn)

gauge

15sts and 19 rows to 2in (5cm) of st st, using **MC** and size 2 (2.5mm) needles

Don't worry if the gauge is not exact—it doesn't matter if the puppy is a little bigger or smaller than shown.

finished size

Approx 8in (20cm) long (not including the tail) x 6in (12cm) tall

Yum! I wonder if I could fit in a second helping?

Knitting notes

- The main part of the body is worked in one piece from the nose to the tail.
- The puppy is worked on double-pointed needles using the techniques i-cord (see page 328) and working in the round (see page 327). Kitchener stitch (see page 323) is used to make a 'seamless' join.
- If you are knitting for a very young child, embroider the eyes with yarn instead of using toy eyes. Even safety eyes can be a choking hazard.

PUPPY PATTERN

HEAD, BODY, LEGS AND TAIL

Cast on 3 sts using **A** and size 2 (2.5mm) needles.

Row 1 (RS) Kfb, k1, kfb. 5 sts.

Row 2 P.

Shape nose

Row 3 K4, turn.

Row 4 Sl 1, p2, turn.

Row 5 Sl 1, k1, turn.

Row 6 Sl 1, p2 to end.

Row 7 Cast on 5 sts, k5, k2tog, k to end. 9 sts.

Row 8 Cast on 5 sts, p5, p2 tog, p to end. 13 sts.

Row 9 K.

Row 10 P.

Cut yarn.

Shape jowls

Row 11 (RS) **MC** K1, kfb 3 times, k5, kfb 3 times, k1. 19 sts.

Row 12 P.

Row 13 K2, kfb 4 times, [k1, M1] twice, k3, [M1, k1] twice, kfb 4 times, k2. 31 sts.

Row 14 P.

Row 15 K10, [M1, k1] twice, k7, [M1, k1] twice, k10. 35 sts.

I take Bamber for a walk twice a day.

Row 16 Sl 35 sts p-wise and divide: 12 sts onto n1, 11 sts onto n2, 12 sts onto n3.

With RS facing, keeping gauge fairly tight on first rnd, work in the rnd (see page 327) as follows:

Rnd 17 K.

Rnd 18 [K2tog] 3 times, k8, M1, k2, M1, k3, M1, k2, M1, k8, [k2tog] 3 times. 33 sts.

Rnd 19 K.

Rnd 20 [k2tog] twice, k7, [M1, k2] twice, M1, k3, [M1, k2] twice, M1, k7, [k2tog] twice. 35 sts.

Rnd 21 K.

Rnd 22 K3, [M1, k2] 6 times, [M1, k1] 5 times, [M1, k2] 6 times, M1, k3. 53 sts.

Divide sts: 16 sts onto n1, 21 sts onto n2 (at top of nose), 16 sts onto n3.

Shape eyebrows

Rnd 23 K16, skpo, k2tog, k13, k2tog tbl, skpo, k16. 49 sts.

Place marker at beg of next rnd.

Rnd 24 K.

Rep last rnd 5 more times.

Shape chin

Rnd 30 [k2tog] twice, k41, [k2tog] twice. 45 sts.

Rnd 31 K.

Divide for ears

Cont to work st st.

Row 32 K30, turn.

Row 33 P15, turn.

Work 5 rows.

Cut yarn.

With WS facing, sl these 15 sts onto a stitch holder.

Sl rem 2 sts onto the adjacent needles, giving 15 sts on n1, 15 sts on n3.

Shape head sides

Rejoin **MC** to right side of head.

Row 39 (RS) K15 from n1, K15 from n2. 30 sts.

With WS facing, sl 30 sts p-wise, dividing them equally over 2 needles. Cont working st st with n3.

Row 40 (WS) P.

Row 41 K2tog, k to last 2 sts, k2tog. 28 sts.

Row 42 P.

Rep last 2 rows once more. 26 sts.

Row 45 K.

Shape ears

Row 46 Pick up and k13 along the row end from where you divided for the left ear. Turn and work on these 13 sts.

Work 3 rows st st.

Row 50 (RS) *Kfb, k to last st, kfb. 15 sts.

Row 51 P.

Rep last 2 rows, 5 more times. 25 sts.

Row 62 (RS) K2tog, k to last 2 sts, k2tog. 23 sts.

Row 63 P2tog, p to last 2 sts, p2tog. 21 sts.

Rep last 2 rows, 4 more times. 5 sts.

Bind off.**

Row 72 (RS) **MC** Pick up and k13 along the row end

Time for walkies, Bamber!

See? It's so much warmer in here!

from where you divided for the right ear.
Work 3 rows st st.
Rep from * to ** for the right ear.

Complete head

With RS facing, sl 15 sts p-wise from the stitch holder for the top of the head onto size 2 (2.5mm) needle.
Row 76 (RS) **MC** K15 across the back of the head.
Work in the rnd as follows:
Rnd 77 Pick up and k13 down the left side of the head, k13 up the right side of the head. 41 sts.
Without turning, join in the rnd as follows:

Shape back of head

Rnd 78 K7, sl1, k1, psso, k19. Place marker.
Rnd 79 K.
Rnd 80 K19, k2tog, k19. 39 sts.
Rnd 81 K18, k3tog, k18. 37 sts.
Rnd 82 K37.
Rnd 83 K1, M1, k16, k3tog, k16, M1, k1.
Rnd 84 K.
Rnd 85 [K1, M1] twice, k15, k3tog, k15, [M1, k1] twice. 39 sts.
Work 2 more rnds.

Shape neck

Rnd 88 [K3, M1] 12 times, k3. 51 sts.
Work 3 more rnds.

Divide for front

Rnd 92 K44, sl next 17 sts onto a safety pin. 34 sts.
Divide sts: 10 sts on n1, 14 sts on n2, 10 sts on n3.

Shape front legs

With WS facing, cont in st st and cast on 20 sts at beg of next 2 rows. 74 sts.

Shape feet

Row 95 (WS) *P5, turn.
Row 96 Sl 1, k3, turn.
Row 97 Sl 1, p2, turn.
Row 98 Sl 1, k1, turn.
Row 99 Sl 1, p to end.
Row 100 K5, turn.
Row 101 Sl 1, p3, turn.
Row 102 Sl 1, k2, turn.
Row 103 Sl 1, p1, turn.
Row 104 Sl 1, k to end.
Work 9 rows in st st.

Work inside front left leg

Row 114 (RS) K20, turn.
Work 9 rows in st st.

Shape inside left foot

Row 124 (RS) k5, turn.
Row 125 Sl 1, p3, turn.
Row 126 Sl 1, k2, turn.
Row 127 Sl 1, p1, turn.
Row 128 Sl 1, k17 to end.
Bind off.
Row 129 (RS) MC K. 54 sts.**

Work inside front right leg

Row 130 (WS) p20, turn.
Work 9 rows in st st on these 20 sts for the inside right leg.

Naughty Bamber hid his lead behind the sofa!

Shape inside right foot

Row 140 (WS) ***P5, turn.
Row 141 Sl 1, k3, turn.
Row 142 Sl 1, p2, turn.
Row 143 Sl 1, k1, turn.
Row 144 Sl 1, p17 to end.
Bind off. ****

Work body

Row 145 (WS) **MC** P. 34 sts.
Work 11 rows in st st.

Shape back legs

With WS facing, cast on 20 sts at beg of next 2 rows. 84 sts.
Work the back legs as the front legs from * to **.
54 sts.
Rejoin **MC**.

Divide for tail

Row 159 (RS) K13, sl next 8 sts onto a safety pin, k33 under the tail to end of row. 46 sts. (Keep gauge tight as you knit under the sts held on safety pin.)

Shape inside back right leg

Row 160 (WS) P20, turn.
Work 9 rows in st st.
Work as the inside front right leg from *** to ****.

Shape underbody

With RS facing, rejoin **MC** to 26 sts.
Next row (RS) *K2, k2tog, rep from * to last 2 sts, k2. 20 sts.
Next row *P2tog, rep from * to end. 10 sts.

You want a walk now it's sunny, do you?

Work 6 rows in st st.
Cut yarn, leaving sts on needle.

Work neck

Sl 17 sts for the neck off the safety pin onto size 2 (2.5mm) needle.
Next row (RS) **MC** K.
Work 35 rows in st st.
Cut yarn, leaving sts on needle.
Next row (RS) *K1, k2tog, rep from * to end. 11 sts.
Next row P.

Join seam under back legs

Cut yarn, leaving approx 20in (50cm) end.
With WS tog, hold needles parallel. Work Kitchener st (see page 323) to close the seam, taking off last st p-wise. Weave in end.

Shape tail

Sl 8 sts for the tail off the safety pin onto size 2 (2.5mm) needle.
Divide sts over 3 needles.
Cont working in the rnd.
Work 7 rnds.
Next row [K1, k2tog] 3 times. 5 sts.
Sl sts onto one needle.
Work as i-cord (see page 328) until the tail measures 2¾in (7cm).
Next row K2tog, k1, k2tog. 3 sts.
Work as i-cord until the tail measures 3in (8cm).
Cut yarn and thread end through rem sts. Pull up tight and secure.

MAKING UP

Weave in the end at the tail.

EYES

Following the manufacturer's instructions, snap the eyes in place just under the eyebrow shaping. Alternatively, embroider the eyes with yarn.

LEGS

Work mattress seam (see page 329) throughout to join the body parts. With wrong side facing, fold the front leg in half, joining the row ends and matching the foot shaping. Leaving the tops (bind-off edges) of the legs unsewn, sew the row ends to join the inside leg to the outer leg. Work running stitch around the bind-off edge at the foot, pull up tight to gather and secure. Stuff the leg fairly firmly, shaping the foot as you do so. Weave the end inside the foot. Repeat for all legs.

HEAD

Beginning at the tail end, join the seam along the sides of the body and tops of the legs up to the front leg/neck join, leaving an opening for stuffing.
Stuff the dog, working stuffing fairly firmly into the head and to shape the jowl, but less firmly into the body to allow it to be a bit floppy. Sew the opening closed.

FINISHING TOUCHES

Work straight stitches at the ends of the feet to create paws, pulling the yarn tightly to create four toes at the front of each foot.
Pinch the knitting at the back of the knees, approx 1in (2.5cm) from the feet, and then define this shaping with stitches.
Using black cotton thread, embroider three straight sts in an upside-down Y shape directly under the nose to define a mouth.
Manipulate the stuffing at the feet and along the neck and body to really give that puppy feel.

DOG LEAD PATTERN

Cast on 35 sts using **B** and size 2 (2.5mm) needles.
Turn, with WS facing.
Sl 35 sts p-wise and divide: 12 sts onto n1, 11 sts onto n2, 12 sts onto n3.
With RS facing, join to work in the rnd.
Place marker.
Rnds 1–5 K.
Rnd 6 Sl 1 st, bind off next 29 sts, k5.
Slide sts onto one needle.
Work as i-cord (see page 328) for 2 rnds.
Rnd 9 K2tog, k1, k2tog. 3 sts.
Work as i-cord until the lead measures 4in (10cm).
Bind off.
At this bind-off end, loop the end over your finger and sew the cast-off edge onto the length of the lead.
Weave in all loose ends.

I think Bamber prefers relaxing indoors to walking sometimes ...

ravenous rats

The rats' bodies are knitted in stockinette stitch, with simple shaping and i-cord legs and tails.

Tawny, Mouse (a rat called Mouse—I know—but she doesn't care!), and Whisker are three of the cleanest, most affectionate and lovable pets you'll ever own. Some say they are unsurpassed by even the cutest kitten or cuddliest puppy—and they'll only eat all your biscuits if you leave them lying around!

It's worth seeking out blue eyes to make your white rat look just right.

RATING * *

yarn

For each rat

Lightweight (DK) yarn

- Oddment in brown, grey or ecru (**MC**)

Fingering-weight (4-ply) yarn

- Oddment in pink (**A**)

needles

- 2 x size 2 (2.5mm) knitting needles
- 2 x size 0 (2mm) double-pointed needles

notions

For each rat

- 2 x ¼in- (6mm-) diameter toy safety eyes (or black/blue yarn)

gauge

15sts and 19 rows to 2in (5cm) of st st, using **MC** and size 2 (2.5mm) needles for st st

Don't worry if the gauge is not exact—it doesn't matter if the rats are a little bigger or smaller than shown.

finished size

Approx 4½in (11.5cm) long (not including the tail) x 2in (5cm) tall

This was left here for us ... right?

Knitting notes

- The main pattern is for the grey rat.
- The main part of the rat is worked in one piece from the head to the tail.
- The rats are worked on double-pointed needles and use the i-cord technique (see page 328).
- Even safety eyes can present a choking hazard for a very young child. So, instead of using toy eyes, embroider the eyes with yarn.
- If you want a tighter fabric, simply knit on needles that are one size smaller than specified.

GREY RAT PATTERN

HEAD, LEGS, BODY AND TAIL

Cast on 2 sts using **MC** and size 2 (2.5mm) needles.

Row 1 (RS) Kfb twice. 4 sts.
Row 2 *Pfkb, rep from * to end. 8 sts.
Row 3 Kfb twice, k4, Kfb twice. 12 sts.
Row 4 Pfkb, p to last st, pfkb. 14 sts.
Row 5 Kfb, k to last st, kfb. 16 sts.
Work 7 rows in st st, beg with a p row.

Shape top of head

Row 13 (RS) K11, turn.
Row 14 Sl 1, p5, turn.
Row 15 Sl 1, k4, turn.
Row 16 Sl 1, p3, turn.
Row 17 K.
Row 18 Pfkb twice, p to last 2 sts, pfkb twice. 20 sts.
Row 19 Kfb, k to last st, kfb. 22 sts.
Work 3 rows in st st, beg with a p row.

Divide for front legs

Row 23 (RS) Kfb 3 times, sl next 5 sts onto a safety pin, kfb 6 times, sl next 5 sts onto a safety pin, kfb 3 times. 24 sts. (Keep gauge tight as you knit under the sts held on safety pins.)
Work 3 rows in st st, beg with a p row.
Row 27 (RS) K12, M1, k12. 25 sts.
Row 28 P.
Row 29 K12, M1, k1, M1, k12. 27 sts.
Row 30 P.
Row 31 K13, M1, k1, M1, k13. 29 sts.
Row 32 P.
Row 33 K14, M1, k1, M1, k14. 31 sts.
Row 34 P.
Row 35 K15, M1, k1, M1, k15. 33 sts.
Row 36 P.
Row 37 K16, M1, k1, M1, k16. 35 sts.
Row 38 P.
Row 39 K16, k3tog, k16. 33 sts.
Row 40 P.
Row 41 K15, k3tog, k15. 31 sts.
Row 42 P.
Row 43 K14, k3tog, k14. 29 sts.
Row 44 P.
Row 45 K13, k3tog, k13. 27 sts.
Row 46 P.
Row 47 K12, k3tog, k12. 25 sts.
Row 48 P.

Divide for back legs

Row 49 (RS) K3, sl next 6 sts onto a safety pin, k7, sl next 6 sts onto a safety pin, k3. 13 sts. (Keep gauge tight as you purl in front of the sts held on safety pins.)
Row 50 P.

Divide for tail

Row 51 (RS) [k2tog] twice, k1, sl next 3 sts onto a safety pin, k1, [k2tog] twice. 6 sts. (Keep gauge tight as you knit under the sts held on safety pin.)
Cut yarn and thread end through rem sts. Pull up tight and secure.

Work front legs (make 2)

Sl 5 sts held on the safety pin for one front leg onto size 0 (2mm) needle.

My rats have the sparkliest eyes!

Do I have to share?

Whisker loves to snuggle up after a big lunch.

It must be tea time soon!

Row 52 (RS) **MC** K.
Work as i-cord (see page 328) for 6 more rows or until the leg measures ¾in (2cm).
Change to **A**, work as i-cord for 7 more rows or until the leg measures 1½in (4cm).
Bind off.

Work back legs (make 2)
Sl 6 sts held on the safety pin for one back leg onto size 0 (2mm) needle.
Row 66 (RS) **MC** K.
Work i-cord for 8 more rows or until the leg measures 1in (2.5cm).
Change to **A**, cont to work as i-cord for 2 more rows.
Row 77 K2, k2tog, k2. 5 sts.
Work i-cord for 6 more rows or until the leg measures 2in (5cm).
Bind off.

Work tail
Sl 3 sts from the safety pin onto size 0 (2mm) needle.
Row 84 (RS) **MC** K.
Work in i-cord for 2 more rows.
Join **A** and work tog with **MC** until the tail measures 4in (10cm).
Cut yarn and thread end through rem sts. Pull up tight and secure.

So that's where all my cheese went!

EARS (MAKE 2)
Cast on 5sts using **MC** and size 0 (2mm) needles.
Row 1 (RS) Kfb, k3, kfb. 7 sts.
Row 2 P.
Row 3 K2, k3tog, k2. 5 sts.
Row 4 P.
Row 5 K1, k3tog, k1. 3 sts.
Cut yarn and thread end through rem sts. Pull up tight and secure.

MAKING UP

HEAD
Following the manufacturer's instructions, snap the eyes in place on each side of the nose. Alternatively, embroider the eyes with yarn.
With right side facing and working backstitch, join the head and body, leaving an opening in the belly for turning through and stuffing. Turn through.
Stuff the head and neck without distorting the shaping or knitting. Sew the opening closed.
Sew an ear to each side of the rat's head and embroider a nose using yarn **A** and straight stitches.

BODY AND LEGS
Oversew to close any gaps under the arms, legs, or tail.
Sew a couple of stitches to bend the back legs so they sit alongside the belly.
If you wish, stitch the front feet together and sew the front legs to the sides of the body to bend them slightly.
Curl the tips of the feet under a little and hold in place with a couple of stitches to give the impression of tiny fists.

Knitting notes

- The brown rat is worked as the grey rat, but using yarn **MC** for the tail and ears.
- The white rat is worked as the grey rat, but using yarn **A** for the tail and ears.

biscuit the cat

Biscuit combines working in the round, i-cord, and self-patterning yarn.

How do you fancy a teeny tiny biscuit—a ginger one naturally—but a ginger cat, not a real biscuit! This Biscuit is a stay-at–home kind of cat, who likes nothing better than dozing in his very own knitted basket (see page 288–289). He'll only condescend to wake up if there's a whiff of fish in the air.

Use a tiny bead or tinkling bell for Biscuit's collar.

RATING * *

yarn

Fingering-weight (4-ply) yarn

- ½ x 1¾oz (50g) ball in ginger (**MC**)

needles

- 4 x size 3 (3mm) double-pointed needles
- Crochet hook (optional)

notions

- 2 x ¼in- (6mm-) diameter toy safety eyes (or black yarn)
- Pink yarn for nose
- Beige machine sewing thread for whiskers
- Oddment of yarn and 1 bead for collar (optional)

gauge

13 sts and 16 rows to 2in (5cm) of st st, using **MC** and size 3 (3mm) needles

Don't worry if the gauge is not exact—it doesn't matter if the cat is a little bigger or smaller than shown.

finished size

Approx 5in (13cm) long (not including the tail) x 4½in (11.5cm) tall (including the ears)

Mind you don't fall off the chair—only nine lives remember!

Knitting notes

- The main part of the cat is worked in one piece from the nose to the tail.
- The cat is worked on double-pointed needles using the techniques i-cord (see page 328) and working in the round (see page 327).
- Do not use even safety eyes on toys for an infant, as they can be a potential choking hazard. Instead, embroider the eyes in place with yarn.
- You can knit any yarn with needles one size smaller than the size recommended on the ball band to give a tight fabric that doesn't allow the stuffing to show through.

CAT PATTERN

HEAD, BODY, LEGS AND TAIL

Cast on 4 sts, using **MC** and size 3 (3mm) needles.

Row 1 (RS) *Kfb, rep from * to end. 8 sts.

Row 2 P.

Rep last 2 rows once more. 16 sts.

Shape front of head

Row 5 K7, [M1, k1] twice, k7. 18 sts.

Row 6 P.

Row 7 Divide sts: k7 onto n1, k3 onto n2, k8 onto n3.

With RS facing, keeping gauge fairly tight on first rnd, work in the rnd (see page 327) as follows:

Rnd 8 K18.

Rnd 9 [M1, k3] 6 times. 24 sts.

Rnd 10 K24.

Rnd 11 K6, [M1, k1] 12 times, k6. 36 sts.

Rnd 12 K36.

Place marker at beg of next rnd.

Rep last 2 rows.

Divide for ears

Rnd 15 K10, sl next 6 sts onto a safety pin, kfb 4 times, sl next 6 sts onto a safety pin, k10. 28 sts. (Keep tension tight to avoid gaps as you knit under the sts on safety pins.)

Shape side of head

Rnd 16 K3, bind off next 7 sts, k7, bind off next 7 sts, k2.

K next 3 sts so there are 6 sts for the neck on one needle.

Cut yarn. Leave sts on needle.

Work head back

Slip 8 sts for the head back off the safety pin onto size 3 (3mm) needle.

Row 17 (RS) **MC** K. turn.

Work 9 rows in st st.

Join head back to neck

Row 27 (RS) K8, k across 6 sts from the neck. 14 sts.

Row 28 P.

Work neck

Row 29 Divide sts: k8 onto n1, k3 onto n2, k3 onto n3.

With RS facing, keeping gauge fairly tight on first rnd, work in the rnd as follows:

Rnd 30 K14.

Rep last rnd once more.

Rnd 32 K4, M1, k5, kfb 4 times, k1. 19 sts.

Rnd 33 K19.

Rnd 34 K4, M1, k1, M1, k8, kfb twice, k4. 23 sts.

Rnd 35 K23.

Rnd 36 K16, kfb twice, k5. 25 sts.

Rnd 37 K25.

Divide for front

Rnd 38 K22, sl last 8 sts onto a safety pin. K17, turn.

With WS facing, back and forth on 2 needles as follows:

Shape front legs

With WS facing, cast on 18 sts at beg of next 2 rows. 53 sts.

Shape feet

Row 41 (WS) P5, turn.

Row 42 Sl 1, k3, turn.

Row 43 Sl 1, p2, turn.

Row 44 Sl 1, k1, turn.

Row 45 Sl 1, p to end.

Row 46 K5, turn.

Row 47 Sl 1, p3, turn.

Row 48 Sl 1, k2, turn.

Row 49 Sl 1, p1, turn.

Row 50 Sl 1, k to end.

Work 3 rows in st st.

Work inside front left leg

Row 54 (RS) K18, turn.

Work 3 rows in st st on these 18 sts for the inside left leg.

Shape inside left foot

Row 58 (RS) K5, turn.

Row 59 Sl 1, p3, turn.

Row 60 Sl 1, k2, turn.

Row 61 Sl 1, p1, turn.

Row 62 Sl 1, k15 to the end of the leg, turn.

Bind off 18 sts.

With WS facing, rejoin yarn to foot end of right leg.

Work inside front right leg

Row 63 (WS) P18, turn.

Row 64 K.

Shape inside right foot

Row 65 (WS) p5, turn.

Row 66 Sl 1, k3, turn.

Row 67 Sl 1, p2, turn.

Row 68 Sl 1, k1, turn.

Row 69 Sl 1, p15 to the end of the leg, turn.

Bind off 18 sts.

Leave 17 sts from the back on the needle and return to the front as follows:

Work front

Sl 8 sts at the neck off the safety pin onto size 3 (3mm) needles.

Row 70 (RS) **MC** K.

Work 7 rows in st st, ending with a WS row.

Join front to back

Row 78 (RS) K8, k8 from the back onto n2, k9 from the back onto n3.

With RS facing, keeping gauge tight across junctions, work in the rnd as follows:

Rnd 79 K25.

Shape back

Rnd 80 K16, M1, k1, M1, k8. 27 sts.

Rnd 81 K27.

Rnd 82 K17, M1, k1, M1, k9. 29 sts.

Rnd 83 K29.

Place marker and rep last rnd 3 more times.

Divide for back legs

Rnd 87 K8, sl last 8 sts onto a safety pin, cast on 3 sts, k to end. 24 sts.

Cont to work in st st, shaping the back as follows:

Row 88 (WS) Cast on 3 sts, p to end. 27 sts.

Row 89 Cast on 3 sts, k16, M1, k1, M1, k to end. 32 sts.

Row 90 Cast on 3 sts, p to end. 35 sts.

Row 91 Cast on 2 sts, k19, M1, k1, M1, k to end. 39 sts.

Row 92 Cast on 2 sts, p to end. 41 sts.

Work 4 rows in st st.

Row 97 (RS) K19, k3tog, k to end. 39 sts.

Row 98 P.

Divide for tail

Row 99 (RS) K17, sl next 5 sts onto a safety pin, k17 sts under the tail to end. 34 sts. (Keep tension tight to avoid gaps as you knit under the sts on safety pins.)

Row 100 P16, p2tog, p to end. 33 sts.

Row 101 K15, k3tog, k to end. 31 sts.

Row 102 P9, [p2tog] 3 times, p1, [p3tog] 3 times, p to end. 25 sts.

Shape inside back left leg

Row 103 (RS) Bind off 2 sts, k6, turn.

Row 104 P7.

Row 105 Bind off 3 sts, k3, turn.

Bind off 4 sts.

With WS facing, rejoin **MC** to the foot end of the right leg.

Shape inside back right leg

Row 106 (WS) Bind off 2 sts, p6, turn.

Row 107 K7.

Row 108 Bind off 3 sts, p3, turn.

Bind off 4 sts.

Row 109 (WS) Rejoin **MC** to rem 7 sts and k to end.

Work st st for 15 rows, so ending with a WS row.

Cut yarn, leaving approx 12in (30cm) tail.

Join seam under back legs

Sl 8 sts from the under body off the safety pin onto size 3 (3mm) needles.

With WS tog, hold needles parallel. Work Kitchener st (see page 323) to close seam, taking off last st p-wise.

Biscuit is getting very cosy with his new friend

It's good to stretch—
and then have
another nap ... purr

Weave in end.

Work lower left back leg

Row 125 *With RS facing, pick up and k8 along the row end at the end of the upper leg.

Row 126 (WS) P.

Divide all 8 sts evenly over 2 needles. With RS facing, work in the rnd as follows:

Rnd 127 K8.

Rep last rnd 9 more times.

Shape foot

Rnd 137 M1, k1, M1, k5, [M1, k1] twice. 12 sts.

Rnd 138 K12.

Rnd 139 M1, k1, M1, k9, [M1, k1] twice. 16 sts.

Rnd 140 K16.

Bind off. **

Work the lower right back leg from * to **.

EARS (MAKE 2)

Sl 6 sts for one ear off the safety pin onto size 3 (3mm) needle. With RS facing, rejoin **MC** and cont in st st.

Row 1 K across.

Row 2 (WS) P2tog, p to last 2 sts, p2tog. 4 sts.

Row 3 [k2tog] twice. 2 sts.

Row 4 P2tog. 1 st.

Fasten off.

TAIL

Sl 7 sts for the tail off the safety pin onto size 3 (3mm) needle.

Work as i-cord (see page 328) until the tail measures 3½in (9cm).

Cut yarn and thread end through rem sts. Pull up tight and secure.

MAKING UP

HEAD

Carefully turn the work to the wrong side. Backstitch (see page 329) the row ends at the side of the head. To join the nose, bring its tip (the bind-off end) down to the point where you began to work in the round. Join along the row ends, along two sides of the triangle you have created. Carefully turn right side out. Push out the shaping at the nose.

EYES

Following the manufacturer's instructions, snap the eyes in place on each side of the nose. Alternatively, embroider the eyes with yarn.

Stuff the head and neck fairly firmly.

NOSE AND WHISKERS

Embroider the tip of the nose, working a couple of stitches in pink yarn.

Cut short lengths of thread for the whiskers. Thread one length into a tapestry needle and pass it through a knitted stitch in the nose, so both ends are the same length. Make another stitch to secure. Work other strands into other knitted sts to create more whiskers. Trim.

EARS

Weave in the tail of yarn at the tip of the ear. Oversew the opening behind the ear closed, joining the back base of the ear to the head. Repeat for the other ear.

If your want to make the ears stand up, dampen them and gently press flat, using a pressing cloth. Alternatively, use the sugar solution method (see page 330).

FRONT LEGS

With wrong side facing, fold the front leg in half, joining the row ends and matching the foot shaping. Leaving the tops (bind-off edges) of the legs unsewn, mattress stitch (see page 329) the row ends to join the inside leg to the outer leg. Work a running stitch around the bind-off end at the foot, pull it up tight to gather and secure.

Stuff the leg fairly firmly—you may find tweezers helpful—and shape the foot. Weave in the end. Stuff and shape the other foot to match.

BACK LEGS

Stuff the feet. Attach the feet to the back legs, using mattress stitch and matching the front seam of the leg with the front of the foot.

BODY

Beginning at the tail end, join the seam along the sides of the body and around the tops of the legs, leaving an opening for stuffing.

Stuff the body quite lightly—the cat should be able to stand, but not be too stiff to sit down. Sew the opening closed. Manipulate the stuffing in the legs and feet and along the neck and body to get a good shape.

COLLAR

Crochet (see page 332) a chain of yarn and attaching a bead to create a collar and bell.

biscuit's basket

Biscuit's basket is easy to knit on nice big needles.

Where would Biscuit be without his basket? Left exposed on the hearth, that's where. This squishy squoshy basket gives Biscuit all the home comforts he needs.

Choose a two-toned yarn for a really handcrafted basket.

RATING *

yarn

Lightweight (DK) yarn

- ½ x 1¾oz (50g) ball (**A**)

needles

- 4 x size 5 (3.75mm) double-pointed needles

gauge

11 sts and 15 rows to 2in (5cm) of st st, using **A** and size 5 (3.75mm) needles

Don't worry if the gauge is not exact—it doesn't matter if the basket is a little bigger or smaller than shown.

finished size

Approx 4¾in (12cm) diameter x 1⅛in (3cm) high

BASKET PATTERN

BASE

Cast on 2 sts using **A** and size 5 (3.75mm) needles.

Row 1 K2.

Work as i-cord (see page 328) as follows:

Row 2 Kfb twice. 4 sts.

Row 3 Kfb 4 times. 8 sts.

Row 4 Divide sts: k3 onto n1, k2 onto n2, k3 onto n3.

With RS facing, work in the round as follows:

Rnd 5 [K1, kfb] 4 times. 12 sts.

Rnd 6 [K2, kfb] 4 times. 16 sts.

Did you see that mouse?

Rnd 7 [K3, kfb] 4 times. 20 sts.
Rnd 8 [K4, kfb] 4 times. 24 sts.
Cont to inc 4 sts on every rnd until there are 15 sts before each inc. 68 sts.
Place marker. Work 2 rnds without shaping.
Bind off. Weave in ends.
If necessary, press with a cool iron to flatten the base into a disk.

RIM
Cast on 8 sts using **A** and size 5 (3.75mm) needles.
Row 1 K2, p2, k2, p2.
Row 2 Rep last row.
Row 3 Rep last row.
Row 4 P2, k2, p2, k2.
Row 5 Rep last row.
Row 6 Rep last row.
Rep rows 1–6 until work measures the same as the circumference of the base.
Bind off.

MAKING UP

Oversew cast-on and bind-off edges on the rim. Then oversew the base to the rim. Fold the top of the rim to the inside of the basket and stitch in place if you wish.

reggie veggie the stegosaurus

Reggie's back plates are knitted with two strands of yarn to make them stiff enough to stand upright.

Can you imagine how crazy—but wonderful—it would be to have a little pet dinosaur. What would your friends think? Well meet Reggie Veggie! This little chap is second only to the real thing. And he's always on the look out for scraps of food—if he were any bigger, he'd eat you out of house and home, I'm sure!

Once you've knitted Reggie, try adapting the techniques to make other prehistoric monsters.

RATING * *

yarn

Lightweight (DK) yarn

- 2 x 1¾oz (50g) balls in green (**MC**)
- 1 x 1¾oz (50g) ball in dark green (**A**)

needles

- 4 x size 6 (4mm) double-pointed needles

notions

- 2 x ¼in- (6mm-) diameter toy safety eyes (or black yarn)
- Black cotton thread

gauge

11 sts and 14 rows to 2in (5cm) in st st, using **MC** and size 6 (4mm) needles

Don't worry if the gauge is not exact—it doesn't matter if the stegosaurus is a little bigger or smaller than shown.

finished size

Approx 13¼in (34cm) long (including the tail) x 7½in (19cm) tall

Did I grow or did the trees just get smaller?

Knitting notes

- The stegosaurus is worked in the round (see page 327) on double-pointed needles.
- If you are knitting for a very young child, embroider the eyes with yarn instead of using toy eyes. Even safety eyes can be a choking hazard.
- Once you've mastered the techniques, try knitting with one size smaller needles to give a tighter fabric that gives stuffing no chance to show through.

Stegosaurus pattern

HEAD, BODY, LEGS AND TAIL

Cast on 8 sts using **MC** and size 6 (4mm) needles.

Row 1 (WS) P.

Row 2 *Kfb, rep from * to end. 16 sts.

Work 7 rows in st st.

Shape head

Row 10 (RS) K2, [M1, k1] twice, k2, kfb 4 times, k2, ([k1, M1] twice, k1. 24 sts.

Row 11 P.

Row 12 Divide sts: k8 onto n1, k8 onto n2, k8 onto n3.

With RS facing, keeping gauge fairly tight on first rnd, work in the rnd (see page 327) as follows:

Rnd 13 K24.

Rnd 14 Skpo, k20, k2tog. 22 sts.

Rnd 15 K9, skpo, k2tog, k9. 20 sts.

Rnd 16 K8, skpo, k2tog, k8. 18 sts.

Rnd 17 K7, skpo, k2tog, k7. 16 sts.

Rnd 18 K16.

Rnd 19 Kfb, k14, kfb. 18 sts.

Shape first set of plates

Rnd 20 K8, [picot 1] twice, k8.

Rnd 21 K18.

Rnd 22 Kfb, k16, kfb. 20 sts.

Rnd 23 K9, [picot 3] twice, k9.

Rnd 24 K20.

Rep last rnd once more.

Rnd 26 K9, [picot 5] twice, k9.

Rnd 27 K20.

Rnd 28 Kfb, k18, kfb. 22 sts.

Rnd 29 Kfb, k8, kfb 4 times, k8, kfb. 28 sts.

Divide for plates

Row 30 K16, turn.

Row 31 (WS) P2, sl last 2 sts onto a safety pin, p26, working sts onto 3 needles. 26 sts.

Cont working back and forth around the sides and belly as follows:

Row 32 (RS) Kfb, k26, kfb. 28 sts.

Row 33 P.

Rep last 2 rows once more. 30 sts.

Divide for front legs

Row 36 (RS) Kfb, k18, sl last 8 sts onto a safety pin, k10, kfb.

Work right side

Row 37 (WS) P12.

Work right leg

Row 38 Cast on 12 sts, k23, kfb. 25 sts.

Row 39 P.

Shape foot

Row 40 (RS) K5, turn.

Row 41 Sl 1, p3, turn.

Row 42 Sl 1, k2, turn.

Row 43 Sl 1, p1, turn.

Row 44 Sl 1, k to last st, kfb. 26 sts.

Row 45 P.

Row 46 K to last st, kfb. 27 sts.

Row 47 P.

Work inside front right leg

Row 48 (RS) k12, turn.

Work 3 rows in st st on these 12 sts.

Shape inside right foot

Row 52 (RS) K5, turn.

Row 53 Sl 1, p3, turn.

Row 54 Sl 1, k2, turn.

Row 55 Sl 1, p1, turn.

Row 56 Sl 1, k9 to the end of the inside leg, turn.

Bind off 12 sts.

Row 57 With WS facing, rejoin **MC** to rem sts for the right side, k to last st, kfb. 16 sts.

Work 7 rows in st st.

Row 65 (RS) K2tog, [k1, M1] twice, k12. 17 sts.

Row 66 P.

Work right back leg

Row 67 (RS) Cast on 14 sts, k15, [M1, k1] 3 times, k13. 34 sts.

Row 68 P.

Shape foot

Row 69 (RS) K5, turn.

Row 70 Sl 1, p3, turn.

Row 71 Sl 1, k2, turn.

Reggie just can't stop eating

Careful Reggie—you'll soon outgrow this forest!

I'm going to need more
leaves soon ...

Row 72 Sl 1, p1, turn.
Row 73 Sl 1, k to end.
Work 5 rows in st st.
Work inside back right leg
Row 79 (RS) K14, turn.
Work 5 rows in st st on these 14 sts for the inside right leg.
Shape inside right foot
Row 85 (RS) K5, turn.
Row 86 Sl 1, p3, turn.
Row 87 Sl 1, k2, turn.
Row 88 Sl 1, p1, turn.
Row 89 Sl 1, k11 to the end of the inside leg, turn.
Bind off 14 sts.
Leave rem 20 sts from the right side on a needle.
Work left side
With RS facing, rejoin **MC** to 12 sts from the left side.
Row 90 (RS) Kfb, k to end. 13 sts.
Work left leg
Row 91 (WS) Cast on 12 sts, p to end. 25 sts.
Row 92 Kfb, k to end. 26 sts.
Shape foot
Row 93 (WS) P5, turn.
Row 94 Sl 1, k3, turn.
Row 95 Sl 1, p2, turn.
Row 96 Sl 1, k1, turn.
Row 97 Sl 1, p to end.
Row 98 Kfb, k to end. 27 sts.
Row 99 P.
Row 100 Kfb, k to end. 28 sts.
Work inside front left leg
Row 101 (WS) P12, turn.
On these 12 sts for the inside right leg, work 3 rows in st st.
Shape inside left foot
Row 105 (WS) P5, turn.
Row 106 Sl 1, k3, turn.
Row 107 Sl 1, p2, turn.
Row 108 Sl 1, k1, turn.
Row 109 Sl 1, p9 to the end of the inside leg, turn.
Bind off 12 sts.
Row 110 (WS) Rejoin yarn to rem 16 sts for the left side, p across.
Work 6 rows in st st.
Row 117 (RS) K12, [M1, k1] twice, k2tog. 17 sts.
Row 118 P.
Row 119 P14, [M1, k1] 3 times. 20 sts.
Work left back leg
Row 120 (WS) Cast on 14 sts, p to end. 34 sts.
Row 121 K.
Shape foot
Row 122 (WS) P5, turn.
Row 123 Sl 1, k3, turn.
Row 124 Sl 1, p2, turn.
Row 125 Sl 1, k1, turn.
Row 126 Sl 1, p to end.
Work 5 rows in st st.
Work inside back left leg
Row 132 (WS) P14, turn.
Work 5 rows in st st on these 14 sts for the inside left leg.
Shape inside left foot
Row 138 (WS) P5, turn.
Row 139 Sl 1, k3, turn.
Row 140 Sl 1, p2, turn
Row 141 Sl 1, k1, turn.
Row 142 Sl 1, p11 to the end of the inside leg, turn.
Bind off 14 sts. Cut yarn.
Leave rem 20 sts from the left side on a needle.
Work neck/gusset
With RS facing, rejoin **MC** to 8 sts on the safety pin from the neck.
Row 143 (RS) K.
Work 25 rows in st st.
Join gusset to sides
Row 169 (RS) K8 from the gusset, [k1, k2tog, k17] from the left side, turn. 27 sts.
Row 170 P2tog, p24, [p1, p2tog, p15, p2tog] from the right side. 44 sts.
Row 171 K2tog, k15, k2tog, k6, k2tog, k15, k2tog. 40 sts.
Row 172 P2tog, p13, p2tog, p6, p2tog, p13, p2tog. 36 sts.
Row 173 K2tog, k11, k2tog, k6, k2tog, k11, k2tog. 32 sts.
Shape tail
Row 174 (WS) P2tog, p9, p2tog, p6, p2tog, p9, p2tog. 28 sts.
Row 175 K2tog, k7, k2tog, k6, k2tog, k7, k2tog. 24 sts.
Row 176 P2tog, p5, p2tog, p6, p2tog, p5, p2tog. 20 sts.
Row 177 Divide sts: k7 onto n1, k6 onto n2, k7 onto n3.
With RS facing, keeping gauge fairly tight on first round, work in the rnd as follows:
Rnd 178 K20.
Rnd 179 K19, Sl 1, k1 (from beg of next rnd), pass slipped st over. 19 sts.
Rnd 180 Picot 6, k16, picot 6, k1.
Rnd 181 K19.
Rnd 182 K2tog, k18, k2tog. 17 sts.
Rnd 183 K5, k2tog, k3, k2tog, k5. 15 sts.
Rnd 184 K15.
Rnd 185 Picot 4, k12, picot 4, k1.
Rnd 186 K15.
Rnd 187 K2tog, k11, k2tog. 13 sts.
Rnd 188 K13.
Rnd 189 Picot 2, k10, picot 2, k1.
Rnd 190 K13.
Rep last rnd 5 more times.
Rnd 196 Picot 8, k9, picot 8, k2.
Rnd 197 K13.
Rep last rnd 5 more times.
Rep last 7 rnds once more.
Rnd 210 K1, [k2tog, k1] 4 times. 9 sts.

Rnd 211 K9.
Rnd 212 K1, [k2tog, k2] twice. 7 sts.
Rnd 213 K7.
Cut yarn and thread end through sts. Pull up tight and secure.

PLATES (MAKE 2 SETS, A and B)
Cast on 3 sts, using double strand of **A** and size 6 (4mm) needles.
For set A only:
Work 5 rows: K.
For both sets, A and B:
Plate 1
Row 1 (RS) K2, yon, k1. 4 sts.
Row 2 K.
Row 3 K2, yon, k2. 5 sts.
Row 4 K.
Row 5 K2, yon, k3. 6 sts.
(Rows 1–5 form patt for each triangular plate.)
Row 6 K.
Row 7 K2, yon, k4. 7 sts.
Row 8 K.
Row 9 Bind off 4 sts, k2. 3 sts.
K 4 rows.
Plate 2
Patt 5 rows.
Row 19 (RS) K.
Row 20 K2, yon, k4. 7 sts.
Row 21 K.
Row 22 K2, yon, k5. 8 sts.
Row 23 K.
Row 24 K2, yon, k6. 9 sts.
Row 25 Bind off 6 sts, k2. 3 sts.
K 4 rows.
Plate 3
Patt 5 rows.
Row 35 (RS) K.
Row 36 K2, yon, k4. 7 sts.
Row 37 K.
Row 38 K2, yon, k5. 8 sts.
Row 39 K.
Row 40 K2, yon, k6. 9 sts.
Row 41 K.
Row 42 K2, yon, k7. 10 sts.
Row 43 Bind off 7 sts, k2. 3 sts.
K 4 rows.
Plate 4
Patt 5 rows.
Row 53 (RS) K.
Row 54 K2, yon, k4. 7 sts.
Row 55 K.
Row 56 K2, yon, k5. 8 sts.
Row 57 Bind off 5 sts, k2. 3 sts.
K 4 rows.
For Set A only: Bind off 3 sts.
For Set B only: Cont with plate 5.
Plate 5
Patt 5 rows.
Row 67 Bind off 3 sts, k2. 3 sts.
K 4 rows.
Bind off.
Sew one set of plates to the inside of each side of the opening along the back.
Backbone
Rejoin **MC** to 2 sts on the safety pin where the back divides for the plates.
Next row K2.
Work as i-cord (see page 328) until the backbone measures the length of the opening between the plates.
Cut yarn and thread end through sts. Pull up tight and secure.

MAKING UP

HEAD
Working mattress stitch (see page 329), join the seam under the nose and chin. Embroider a couple of straight sts in black thread at the tip of the nose for nostrils.

EYES
Following the manufacturer's instructions, snap the eyes in place on each side of the nose. Alternatively, embroider the eyes with yarn.
Stuff the head and neck fairly firmly, manipulating the stuffing into the shaping at the top of the head.

FRONT LEGS
With wrong side facing, fold the front leg in half, joining the row ends and matching the foot shaping. Leaving the tops (bind-off edges) of the legs unsewn, mattress stitch the row ends to join the inside leg to the outer leg. Work a running stitch around the bind-off end at the foot. Stuff the foot. Pull the thread up tight to gather and secure. Weave in the thread.

BACK LEGS
Join the back legs along the row ends, leaving the cast-on and bind-off edges unsewn.

BODY
Mattress stitch the short seams at the front and back legs along the sides of the body and around the tops of the front and back legs.
Stuff the tail quite lightly.
Join the backbone to each side of the plates to close the opening, stuffing the body as you do so.
Manipulate the stuffing to shape the head and feet.

Okay, i'll try to be good

pip and pop ponies

It's very easy to secure embroidery floss to make glamorous swishy tails and manes.

Pip and Pop are tiny pocket ponies to pamper and play with. I can just imagine these equine buddies galloping wildly around a lush green field—manes flopping, tails flicking—having a wonderful frolick.

Work the white pony without the change of yarn given for the grey pony.

RATING * *

yarn

Lightweight (DK) yarn

For the white pony

- ½ x 1¾oz (50g) ball in white (**MC**)

For the grey pony

- ½ x 1¾oz (50g) ball in grey (**A**)
- Oddment in white for muzzle (**MC**)

For both ponies

- Oddment in pink (**B**)

needles

- 4 x size 4 (3.5mm) double-pointed needles

notions

For each pony

- 2 x ¼in- (6mm-) diameter toy safety eyes (or black yarn)
- 1 x skein stranded embroidery floss in grey/beige for mane
- Black thread for nostrils and eyelashes

gauge

12 sts and 15 rows to 2in (5cm) in st st, using **MC** and size 4 (3.5mm) needles

Don't worry if the gauge is not exact—it doesn't matter if the ponies are a little bigger or smaller than shown.

finished size

Approx 5½in (14cm) long (not including the tail) x 9in (23cm) tall (including the ears)

It's so good to feel the wind in your hair!

knitting notes

- The main part of the pony is worked in one piece from the nose to the tail.
- The ponies are worked on double-pointed needles using the techniques i-cord (see page 328) and working in the round (see page 327).
- Even safety eyes can present a choking hazard for a very young child. So, instead of using toy eyes, embroider the eyes with yarn.
- If you want a tighter fabric, simply knit on needles that are one size smaller than specified.

PONY PATTERN

HEAD, EARS, BODY, LEGS AND EARS

Cast on 7 sts, using **MC** and **B** tog, and size 4 (3.5mm) needles.

Row 1 (RS) Kfb, k to last st, kfb. 9 sts.

Row 2 P.

Cut **B** and cont in **MC**.

Rep last 2 rows once more. 11 sts.

Shape sides of head

Row 5 (RS) Kfb twice, k to last 2 sts, kfb twice. 15 sts.

Row 6 P.

Rep last 2 rows once more. 19 sts.

Work 4 rows in st st.

Row 13 Divide sts: k6 onto n1s, k7 onto n2, k6 onto n3.

With RS facing, keeping gauge fairly tight on first rnd, work in the rnd (see page 327) as follows:

Rnd 14 K19.

Rnd 15 [M1, k1] twice, k15, [M1, k1] twice. 23 sts.

White pony: Cont in **MC**.

Grey pony only: Cut **MC** and cont in **A**.

Rnd 16 K8, place marker for the outer edge of one ear, k7, place marker for the outer edge of the other ear, k8.

Shape back of head

Rnd 17 K19, skpo, turn.

Row 18 (WS) Sl 1, p15, p2tog, turn.

Row 19 Sl 1, k14, skpo, turn.

Row 20 Sl 1, p13, p2tog, turn.

Row 21 Sl 1, k12, skpo, turn.

Row 22 Sl 1, p11, p2tog, turn.

Row 23 Sl 1, k14 to beg of rnd, keeping gauge tight across dec, turn.

Row 24 Sl 1, p16, turn.

Row 25 K17. Join for working in rnd.

Rep last rnd once more.

Shape neck

Rnd 27 Kfb, k6, k3tog, k6, kfb.

Rnd 28 K17.

Rep last 2 rows once more.

Rnd 31 Kfb twice, k5, k3tog, k5, kfb twice. 19 sts.

Rnd 32 Divide sts: k5 onto n1, k9 onto n2, k5 onto n3.

Rnd 33 Kfb twice, k6, k3tog, k6, kfb twice. 21 sts.

Rnd 34 K21.

Place marker.

K 7 rnds.

Shape shoulders

Rnd 42 K1, [M1, k1] 3 times, k14, [M1, k1] 3 times. 27 sts.

Rnd 43 K27.

Divide for front

Rnd 44 K4, sl last 8 sts onto a safety pin, k6, M1, k7, M1, k6, turn. 21 sts.

With WS facing, work back and forth as follows:

Shape front legs

With WS facing, cast on 22 sts at beg of next 2 rows. 65 sts.

Shape feet

Row 47 (WS) P5, turn.

Row 48 Sl 1, k3, turn.

Row 49 Sl 1, p2, turn.

Row 50 Sl 1, k1, turn.

Row 51 Sl 1, p to end.

Row 52 K5, turn.

Row 53 Sl 1, p3, turn.

Row 54 Sl 1, k2, turn.

Row 55 Sl 1, p1, turn.

Row 56 Sl 1, k to end.

Work 3 rows in st st.

Work inside front left leg

Row 60 (RS) K22, turn.

Work 3 rows in st st on these 22 sts.

Shape inside left foot

Row 64 (RS) K5, turn.

Row 65 Sl 1, p3, turn.

Row 66 Sl 1, k2, turn.

Row 67 Sl 1, p1, turn.

Row 68 Sl 1, k19 to the end of the inside leg, turn.

Bind off 22 sts.

With WS facing, rejoin **MC/A** to the foot end of the right leg.

Work inside front right leg

Row 69 (WS) P22, turn.

Row 70 K.

Shape inside right foot

Row 71 (WS) P5, turn.

Row 72 Sl 1, k3, turn.

Row 73 Sl 1, p2, turn.

Row 74 Sl 1, k1, turn.

Row 75 Sl 1, p19 to the end of the inside leg, turn.

Bind off 22 sts.

Leave rem 21 sts from the back on the needles.

Work front

Sl 8 sts at the neck off the safety pin onto size 4 (3.5mm) needles. Rejoin **MC/A**.

Row 76 (RS) K.

Work 9 rows in st st.

Join front to back

Row 86 (RS) K8, K13 from the back onto n2, k8 from the back onto n3. 29 sts.

With RS facing, keeping gauge tight across junctions, work in the rnd as follows:

Shape tummy

Rnd 87 (RS) K8, [k2, M1] 3 times, k9, [M1, k2] 3 times. 35 sts.

Rnd 88 K35.

Shape back

Rnd 89 K8, [k1, M1] 3 times, k9, k3tog, k9, [M1, k1] 3 times. 39 sts.

Pip is such a free spirit.

Rnd 90 K39.
Rnd 91 K23, M1, k1, M1, k15. 41 sts.
Rnd 92 K41.
Rnd 93 K8, skpo, k14, M1, k1, M1, k14, k2tog.
Rnd 94 K41.
Rep last 2 rnds 3 more times.
Divide for back legs
Rnd 101 K8, sl last 8 sts onto a safety pin, K33. 33 sts.
With WS facing, work back and forth as follows:
Cast on 3 sts at beg of next 2 rows. 39 sts.
Rep last 2 rows once more. 45 sts.
Cast on 4 sts at beg of next 2 rows. 53 sts.
Shape bottom
Row 108 (RS) K25, k3tog, k to end. 51 sts.
Row 109 P.
Row 110 K24, k3tog, k to end. 49 sts.
Row 111 P.
Row 112 K23, k3tog, k to end. 47 sts.
Row 113 P.
Row 114 K22, k3tog, k to end. 45 sts.
Shape inside back right leg
Row 115 (WS) P10, turn.
Row 116 K.
Row 117 Bind off 4 sts, p5, turn.
Row 118 K6.
Row 119 Bind off 3 sts, p2, turn.
Bind off 3 sts.
With RS facing, rejoin **MC/A** to the foot end of the back left leg.
Shape inside back left leg
Row 120 (RS) Bind off 4 sts, k5, turn.
Row 121 P6.
Row 122 Bind off 3 sts, k2, turn.
Bind off 3 sts.
With WS facing, rejoin **MC/A** to rem 25 sts. Bind off.
Work front
Sl 8 sts from the underbody, where work divided for the back legs, off the safety pin onto size 6 (4mm) needles.
Row 123 (RS) **MC/A** K.
Work 17 rows in st st.
Row 141 (RS) K2tog, k to last 2 sts, k2tog. 6 sts.
Row 142 P.
Rep last 2 rows once more. 4 sts.
Row 145 [k2tog] twice. 2 sts.
Bind off.
Work left lower back leg
Row 146 *(RS) pick up and k10 along the row end at the end of the upper leg.
Row 147 (WS) P.
Row 148 Divide sts: k3 onto n1, k4 onto n2, k3 onto n3.
With RS facing, work in the rnd as follows:
Rnd 149 K10.
Rep last rnd 4 more times.
Shape hoof
Rnd 154 K4, k2tog, k4. 9 sts.
Rnd 155 Kfb twice, k5, kfb twice. 13 sts.
Rnd 156 Kfb twice, k9, kfb twice. 17 sts.
Rnd 157 K17.
Rep last rnd twice more.
Rnd 160 Skpo 4 times, k1, [k2tog] 4 times. 9 sts.
Cut the yarn and thread the end through the rem sts. **
Work lower right back leg as left one from * to **.
Shape ears
Beg at one of the markers at the top of the head:
Row 161 (RS) **MC/A** *Pick up and k3 towards the center top of the head. Break yarn on WS and tie loose ends tog.
Row 162 Rejoin **MC/A** to 3 'picked up' sts, k. 3sts.
Work i-cord (see page 328) as follows:
Row 163 Kfb, k1, kfb. 5 sts.
Row 164 K.
Row 165 Kfb, k3, kfb.
Row 166 K2tog, k to last 2 sts, k2tog. 5 sts.
Row 167 K2tog, k1, k2tog. 3 sts.
Row 168 K3tog.** 1 st.
Fasten off. Weave the end to the WS.
Beg at the other marker, rep from * to ** for other ear.

MAKING UP

TAIL
Cut 10in (25cm) lengths of embroidery floss to make a tail. Thread one length into a tapestry needle and pass it through a knitted stitch at the horse's rear end, so both ends are the same length. Make another stitch to secure. Work other lengths into other knitted stitches to create a tail. Trim.

MANE
Cut shorter lengths of embroidery floss and attach them between the ears and down the neck in the same way as for the tail.

HEAD
Carefully turn the work to the wrong side. Work backstitch (see page 329) to join around the muzzle.

EYES
Following the manufacturer's instructions, snap the eyes in place on each side of the nose. Alternatively, embroider the eyes with yarn.

HEAD
Join any gaps at in the head shaping with mattress stitch (see page 329).
Stuff the head and neck fairly firmly.
Weave in the end at the tip of the ear along one row end to the base of each ear.

FRONT LEGS

With wrong side facing, fold the front leg in half, joining the row ends and matching the foot shaping. Leaving the tops (bind-off edges) of the legs unsewn, mattress stitch the row ends to join the inside leg to the outer leg. Work a running stitch around the bind-off end at the foot. Stuff the foot. Pull the thread up tight to gather and secure. Weave in the thread. Repeat for the other front foot.

Start to fill the legs, putting a little stuffing into the knees and thighs.

BACK LEGS

Sew up and stuff as for the front legs.

BODY

Mattress stitch the short seams at the front legs along the sides of the body and around the tops of the front legs, easing the fullness to fit the shapings.

Mattress stitch the gusset at the back legs up to the back tail in the same way, leaving an opening for stuffing.

Stuff the body quite lightly. Sew the opening closed.

Manipulate the stuffing at the legs, feet, neck and body to create the correct shapes.

FACE

For nostrils, work a couple of stitches over each other near the end of the nose, in contrasting yarn, to pinch the muzzle in a little. Work a few stitches of black thread around the top edge of the yarn to create a shadow.

Embroider eyelashes around the eyes.

Charlie the Chameleon

Despite his delicate legs and bug eyes, Charlie is created with i-cord and working in the round—barely more difficult than the other pets.

I've often wondered—as chameleons change color to blend with their surroundings—what would happen if one sat on a bright piece of Fair Isle? Well, this is Charlie and he certainly is a bright little chap. If you make him your pet, make sure there are plenty of bugs for his supper packed away in your freezer...

Charlie's psychedelic colors are easy to create using self-striping yarn.

RATING * * *

yarn

Lightweight (DK) yarn

- 1 x 1¾oz (50g) ball of sock/self-striping yarn (**MC**)

needles

- 2 x size 2 (2.5mm) double-pointed needles
- 4 x size 0 (2mm) double-pointed needles

notions

- 2 x ¼in- (6mm-) diameter toy safety eyes (or black yarn)

gauge

15 sts and 19 rows to 2in (5cm) of st st, using **MC** and size 2 (2.5mm) needles

Don't worry if the gauge is not exact—it doesn't matter if the chameleon is a little bigger or smaller than shown.

finished size

Approx 4in (10cm) long (with the tail curled up) x 2in (5cm) tall

So much for camouflage!

knitting note

- The main part is worked in one piece from the tail to the head.
- The chameleon is worked on double-pointed needles using the techniques i-cord (see page 328) and working in the round (see page 327).
- If you are knitting for a very young child, embroider the eyes with yarn instead of using toy eyes. Even safety eyes can be a choking hazard.
- You can knit any yarn with needles one size smaller than the size recommended on the ball band to give a tight fabric that doesn't allow the stuffing to show through.

CHAMELEON PATTERN

TAIL, LEGS, BODY AND HEAD

Cast on 4 sts using **MC** and size 2 (2.5mm) needles. Work as i-cord (see page 328), until the tail measures 3in (8cm). Slide sts to other end of needle without turning. Keeping gauge tight, pull working yarn across the back of i-cord. (Row numbers start from 1 now, although the tail is already started.)

Row 1 K2, M1, M2. 5 sts.

Work as i-cord for a further 3 rows. Don't turn.

Shape tail

Row 5 K2, M1, k1, M1, k2. 7 sts.

Row 6 K7.

Row 7 Kfb, k2, M1, k1, M1, k2, kfb. 11 sts.

Row 8 K11.

Row 9 [Kfb, K4] twice, kfb, turn. 14 sts.

Row 10 (WS) P.

Row 11 Divide sts: K4 sts on n1, 6 sts on n2, 4 sts on n3.

With RS facing, keeping gauge fairly tight on first rnd, work in the rnd (see page 327) as follows:

Rnd 12 Kfb, k6, M1, k6, kfb. 17 sts.

Rnd 13 K.

Rnd 14 [Kfb, k7] twice, kfb. 20 sts.

Divide for back legs

Rnd 15 [K1, M1] twice, sl next 5 sts onto a safety pin, kfb 6 times, sl next 5 sts onto a safety pin, [M1, k1] twice. 20 sts. (Keep gauge tight as you knit under the sts held on safety pins.)

Rnd 16 K.

Shape back

Rnd 17 Kfb, k9, M1, k9, kfb. 23 sts.

Rnd 18 K.

Rnd 19 K11, picot 1, k11.

Rnd 20 K.

Rnd 21 K11, M1, k1, M1, k11. 25 sts.

Rnd 22 K.

Rnd 23 K12, picot 2, k12.

Rnd 24 K.

Rnd 25 K12, M1, k1, M1, k12. 27 sts.

Rnd 26 K.

Rnd 27 K13, picot 2, k13.

Rnd 28 K.

Rnd 29 K13, M1, k1, M1, k13. 29 sts.

Rnd 30 K.

Rnd 31 K14, picot 2, k14.

Rnd 32 K.

Rnd 33 K13, k3tog, k13. 27 sts.

Rnd 34 K.

Rnd 35 K13, picot 2, k13.

Rnd 36 K.

Rnd 37 K12, k3tog, k12. 25 sts.

Rnd 38 K12, picot 2, k12.

Rnd 39 K11, k3tog, k11. 23 sts.

Rnd 40 K11, picot 2, k11.

Rnd 41 K10, k3tog, k10. 21 sts.

Rnd 42 K10, picot 2, k10.

Rnd 43 K2, kfb twice, k13, kfb twice, k2. 25 sts.

Divide for front legs

Rnd 44 Kfb twice, k2, sl next 3 sts onto a safety pin, k5, M1, k1, M1, k5, sl next 3 sts onto a safety pin, k2, kfb twice. 23 sts.

(Keep gauge tight as you knit under the sts held on safety pins.)

Rnd 45 K.

Rnd 46 K.

Stuff the body lightly.

Shape head

Rnd 47 K10, [M1, k1] 4 times, k19. 27 sts.

Rnd 48 K13, kfb, k13. 28 sts.

Rnd 49 K7, skpo, k10, k2tog, k7. 26 sts.

Rnd 50 K8, skpo, k6, k2tog, k8. 24 sts.

Rnd 51 K9, skpo, k2, k2tog, k9. 22 sts.

Rnd 52 K10, k2tog, k10. 21 sts.

Rnd 53 K9, k3tog, k9. 19 sts.

Rnd 54 K.

Rnd 55 Skpo, k6, k3tog, k6, k2tog. 15 sts.

Rnd 56 Skpo, k4, k3tog, k4, k2tog. 13 sts.

Rnd 57 K5, k3tog, k5. 10 sts.

Bind off.

Stuff the head.

Mattress stitch (see page 329) the bind-off edge closed.

Back legs (make 2)

With RS facing, sl one set of 5 sts off the safety pin and onto size 0 (2mm) needle. Rejoin **MC**.

Work as i-cord (see page 328) until the leg measures 1½in (4cm).

Next row K2, skpo, k1. 4 sts.

Divide for toes

K2, then using n3, work i-cord on these 2 sts for 3 rows.

Bind off.

Rejoin yarn to rem 2 sts and work to match the first toe.

Front legs (make 2)

With RS facing, sl one set of 3 sts off the safety pin onto size 0 (2mm) needles. Rejoin **MC**.

Work as i-cord until the leg measures 1½in (4cm).

Next row K1, skpo. 2 sts.

Divide for toes

Kfb in next st, then using 3rd needle, work i-cord on these 2 sts for 2 rows.

Bind off.

Rejoin yarn to rem 1 st and work to match the first toe.

EYES (MAKE 2)
Cast on 4 sts using **MC** and size 0 (2mm) needles.
Row 1 (RS) *Kfb, rep from * to end. 8 sts.
Row 2 (WS) P.
Rows 3–5 st st.
Row 6 (WS) *P2 tog, rep from * to end. 4 sts.
Cut yarn and thread end through rem sts. Pull up tight and secure.
Following the manufacturer's instructions, snap one toy eye into the center of the work with wrong side facing or alternately embroider the eye using black yarn.
Run gathering stitch around the edges of the knitting. Pull up the stitches to gather, enclosing the back of the toy eye. Stuff the eye with spare yarn and stitch the opening closed.

Making Up

Weave the yarn end into the tail.
Following the manufacturer's instructions, snap the eyes in the center of the eye pieces. Alternatively, embroider the eyes with yarn.
With a couple of stitches, sew the legs to the side of the body to bend the knees slightly.
Curl the tips of the feet under a little to give the impression of tiny fists and sew them in place with a couple of stitches.
Sew up any gaps left under the arms and legs.
Curl the end of the tail slightly and stitch in place.

zoom the greyhound

Working to a tight tension will keep this greyhound in good shape.

Zoom by name, but not necessarily by nature. This pocket-sized little greyhound pal won't be chasing rabbits, but he might give the odd spider or beetle a run for its money. Of course, Zoom would win in his 'go-faster' speedy red coat (see pages 314–315)!

Zoom's limbs are quite fine, so stuff them with care to give them a good greyhound shape.

RATING * * *

yarn

Lightweight (DK) yarn

- 1 x 1¾oz (50g) ball in grey (**MC**)

needles

- 4 x size 3 (3mm) double-pointed needles

notions

- 2 x ¼in- (6mm-) diameter toy safety eyes (or black yarn)
- Black yarn for nose

gauge

13 sts and 16 rows to 2in (5cm) of st st, using **MC** and size 3 (3mm) needles

Don't worry if the gauge is not exact—it doesn't matter if the dog is a little bigger or smaller than shown.

finished size

Approx 8in (20cm) long (not including the tail) x 5in (13cm) tall

I wonder if I could catch one of those rabbits?

Knitting notes

- The main part of the dog is worked in one piece from the nose to the tail.
- The dog is worked on double-pointed needles using the techniques i-cord (see page 328) and working in the round (see page 327).
- Do not use even safety eyes on toys for an infant, as they can be a potential choking hazard. Instead, embroider the eyes in place with yarn.
- If you want a tighter fabric, simply knit on needles that are one size smaller than specified.

Are you ready, steady ...?

DOG PATTERN

HEAD, BODY, LEGS AND TAIL

Cast on 4 sts using **MC** and size 3 (3mm) needles.

Row 1 (WS) P.

Row 2 Kfb, k to last st, kfb. 6 sts.

Row 3 Pkfb, p to last st, pkfb. 8 sts.

Rep last 2 rows once more. 12 sts.

Work 6 rows in st st.

Shape front of head

Row 12 (RS) K4, kfb 4 times, k4. 16 sts.

Row 13 P.

Shape jaw

Row 14 (RS) Kfb, k to last st, kfb. 18 sts.

Row 15 P.

Row 16 Divide st: k6 onto n1, k6 onto n2, k6 onto n3.

With RS facing, keeping gauge fairly tight on first rnd, work in the rnd (see page 327) as follows:

Rnd 17 K9, M1, k9. 19 sts.

Shape back of head

Rnd 18 K16, skpo, turn and work the head back and forth as follows:

Row 19 (WS) Sl 1, p13, p2tog, turn.

Row 20 Sl 1, k11, skpo, turn.

Row 21 Sl 1, p8, p2tog, turn.

Row 22 Sl 1, k4, skpo, turn.

Row 23 Sl 1, p2, p2tog, turn.

Row 24 Sl 1, k8 to beg of rnd.

Join to work in the rnd as follows:

Rnd 25 (RS) K13.

Rep last rnd once more.

Shape neck

Rnd 27 Kfb, k4, k3tog, k4, kfb.

Rnd 28 K13.

Rep last 2 rnds once more.

Divide sts: 3 sts onto n1, 7 sts onto n2, 3 sts onto n3.

Rep last 2 rnds once more.

Rnd 31 Kfb twice, k3, k3tog, k3, kfb twice. 15 sts.

Rnd 32 K15.

Rnd 33 Kfb twice, k4, k3tog, k3, kfb twice. 17 sts.

Rnd 34 K17.

Place marker. Work 5 rnds without shaping.

Divide for front

Rnd 40 K4, sl last 8 sts onto a safety pin. K9, turn.

With WS facing, work back and forth as follows:

Shape front legs

Cast on 22 sts at beg of next 2 rows. 53 sts.

Shape feet

Row 43 (WS) P5, turn.

Row 44 Sl 1, k3, turn.

Row 45 Sl 1, p2, turn.

Row 46 Sl 1, k1, turn.

Row 47 Sl 1, p to end.

Row 48 K5, turn.

Row 49 Sl 1, p3, turn.

Row 50 Sl 1, k2, turn.

Row 51 Sl 1, p1, turn.

Row 52 Sl 1, k to end.

Work 3 rows in st st.

Work inside front left leg

Row 56 (RS) K22, turn.

Work 3 rows in st st on these 22 sts for the inside left leg.

Shape inside left foot

Row 60 (RS) K5, turn.

Row 61 Sl 1, p3, turn.

Row 62 Sl 1, k2, turn.

Row 63 Sl 1, p1, turn.

Row 64 Sl 1, k19 to the end of the inside leg, turn.

Bind off 22 sts.

With WS facing, rejoin **MC** to the foot end of the right leg.

Work inside front right leg

Row 65 (WS) P22, turn.

Row 66 K.

Shape inside right foot

Row 67 (WS) P5, turn.

Row 68 Sl 1, k3, turn.

His get up and go seems to have got up and gone!

Do not disturb!

Row 69 Sl 1, p2, turn.
Row 70 Sl 1, k1, turn.
Row 71 Sl 1, p19 to the end of the inside leg, turn.
Bind off 22 sts.
Leave 9 sts from the back of the dog on the needle and return to the front as follows:
Work front
Sl 8 sts at the neck off the safety pin onto size 3 (3mm) needles. With RS facing, rejoin **MC**.
Row 72 K.
Work 7 rows in st st.
Join front to back
Row 80 (RS) K8, K4 from the back onto n2, k5 from the back onto n3. 17 sts.
With RS facing, keep gauge tight across junctions, work in the rnd as follows:
Shape tummy
Rnd 81 (RS) K8, [k2, M1] twice, k1, [M1, k2] twice. 21 sts.
Rnd 82 K21.
Rnd 83 [K2, M1] 6 times, k2, kfb, k2, [M1, k2] twice, M1. 31 sts.
Rnd 84 K31.
Rep last rnd 6 more times.
Rnd 91 K2tog, k7, k2tog, k20. 29 sts.
Rnd 92 K2tog, k5, k2tog, k20. 27 sts.
Rnd 93 K2, k3tog, k2, k2tog, k2, k2tog, k8, k2tog, k2, k2tog. 21 sts.
Rnd 94 K21.
Rnd 95 K1, k3tog, k17. 19 sts.
Rnd 96 K19.
Rnd 97 K3tog, k17. 17 sts.
Rnd 98 K17.
Rep last rnd 8 more times.
Divide for back legs
Rnd 107 K17, sl last 4 sts onto a safety pin.
Rnd 108 Cast on 25 sts, k to end. 38 sts.
Work in st st as follows:
Row 109 (WS) Cast on 25 sts, p to end. 63 sts.
Shape feet
Row 110 (RS) K5, turn.
Row 111 Sl 1, p3, turn.
Row 112 Sl 1, k2, turn.
Row 113 Sl 1, p1, turn.
Row 114 Sl 1, k to end.
Row 115 P5, turn.

Row 116 Sl 1, k3, turn.
Row 117 Sl 1, p2, turn.
Row 118 Sl 1, k1, turn.
Row 119 Sl 1, p to end.
Shape back
Row 120 (RS) K30, k3tog, k to end. 61 sts
Row 121 P.
Row 122 K29, k3tog, k to end. 59 sts.
Divide for tail
Row 123 (WS) P28, sl next 5 sts onto a safety pin, p28 sts under the tail to end. 54 sts. (Keep tension tight to avoid gaps as you purl above the sts on safety pins.)
Work inside back left leg
Row 124 (RS) K25, turn.
Work 3 rows in st st on these 25 sts for the inside left leg.
Shape inside left foot
Row 128 (RS) K5, turn.
Row 129 Sl 1, p3, turn.
Row 130 Sl 1, k2, turn.
Row 131 Sl 1, p1, turn.
Row 132 Sl 1, k22 to end of inside leg, turn.
Bind off 25 sts.
With WS facing, rejoin **MC** to the foot end of the right leg.
Work inside back right leg
Row 133 (WS) P25, turn.
Work 3 rows in st st on these 25 sts for the inside right leg.
Shape inside right foot
Row 137 (WS) P5, turn.
Row 138 Sl 1, k3, turn.
Row 139 Sl 1, p2, turn.
Row 140 Sl 1, k1, turn.
Row 141 Sl 1, p22 to the end of the inside leg, turn.
Bind off 25 sts.
Sl 4 sts on the safety pin at the tail end onto size 3 (3mm) needles.
Row 142 (RS) **MC** K across.
Work st st for 5 rows, so ending with a WS row.
Cut yarn and leave sts on needle.
Join seam under back legs
Sl 4 sts from the safety pin at the under body onto size 3 (3mm) needle.
With WS tog, hold needles parallel. Work Kitchener stitch (see page 323) to close the seam. Weave in end.
Shape tail
Sl 5 sts off the safety pin at the tail onto size 3 (3mm) needle.
Work as i-cord (see page 328) for 7 rows.
Next rnd K2tog, k1, k2tog. 3 sts.
Work as i-cord until the tail measures 4in (10cm).
Cut yarn and thread end through sts. Pull up tight and secure.

EARS (MAKE 2)
Cast on 3 sts using **MC** and size 3 (3m) needles.
Row 1 (WS) P.
Row 2 Kfb, k to last st, kfb. 5 sts.
Rep last 2 rows once more. 7 sts.
Row 5 P.
Row 6 K2tog, k to last 2 sts, k2tog. 5 sts.
Rep last 2 rows once more. 3 sts.
Row 9 P3tog. 1 st.
Fasten off. Weave in end.

MAKING UP

HEAD
Carefully turn the work to the wrong side. Backstitch (see page 329) the row ends at the side of the head and along the nose. Carefully turn right side out. Use your finger to push out the shaping at the nose.

EYES
Following the manufacturer's instructions, snap the eyes in place on each side of the nose. Alternatively, embroider the eyes with yarn.
Stuff the head and neck fairly firmly.

NOSE
Embroider the top of the nose with a few long stitches in black yarn.

EARS
Join the bind-off end of each ear to each side of the head where the shaping decreases.

FRONT LEGS
With WS facing, fold the front leg in half, joining the row ends and matching the foot shaping. Leaving the tops (bind-off edges) of the legs unsewn, mattress stitch (see page 329) the row ends to join the inside leg to the outer leg. Work a running stitch around the bind-off end at the foot, pull it up tight to gather and secure.
Using tweezers, stuff the leg fairly firmly. Shape the leg and foot. Weave in the end. Stuff and shape the other leg and foot to match.
Join the seam around the front leg. Then stuff the body quite firmly.

BACK LEGS
Sew up, stuff and shape the back legs as for the front legs.
Join the seam around the back legs. Then stuff the back of the body quite firmly. If necessary, backstitch any opening under the tail.
Take time to really sculpt your dog to give it a greyhound shape.

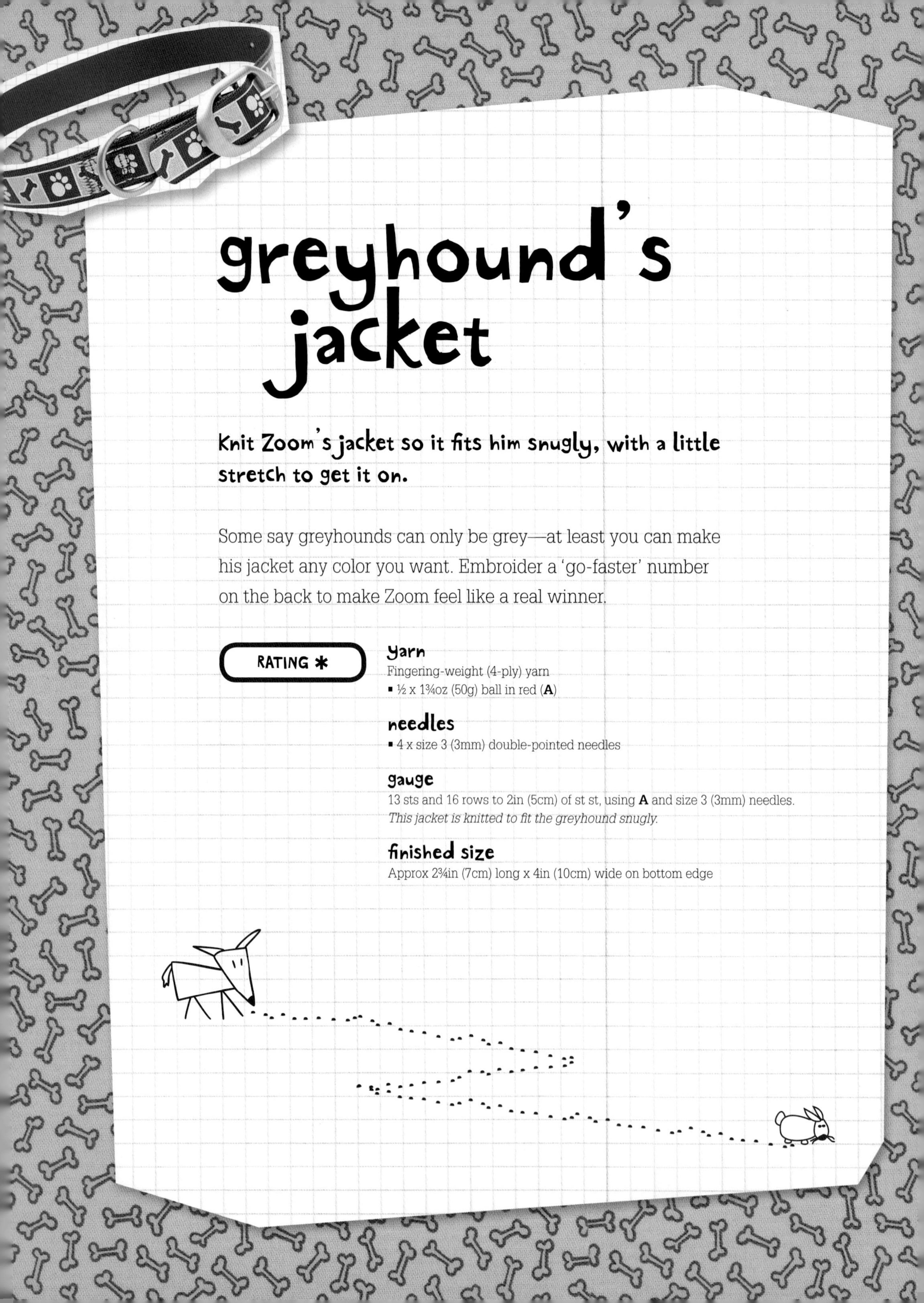

greyhound's jacket

Knit Zoom's jacket so it fits him snugly, with a little stretch to get it on.

Some say greyhounds can only be grey—at least you can make his jacket any color you want. Embroider a 'go-faster' number on the back to make Zoom feel like a real winner.

RATING *

yarn

Fingering-weight (4-ply) yarn
- ½ x 1¾oz (50g) ball in red (**A**)

needles

- 4 x size 3 (3mm) double-pointed needles

gauge

13 sts and 16 rows to 2in (5cm) of st st, using **A** and size 3 (3mm) needles.
This jacket is knitted to fit the greyhound snugly.

finished size

Approx 2¾in (7cm) long x 4in (10cm) wide on bottom edge

Zoom's jacket makes him look the part, even if he's not really keen on chasing rabbits ...

JACKET PATTERN

Cast on 25 sts using **A** and size 3 (3mm) needles.
Row 1 (RS) Kfb, k to last st, kfb. 27 sts.
Row 2 Pkfb, p to last st, pkfb. 29 sts.
Work 2 rows st st.
Row 5 Divide sts: k10 onto n1, k9 onto n2, k10 onto n3.
With RS facing, keeping gauge fairly tight on first rnd, work in the rnd (see page 327) as follows:
Rnd 6 K29.
Rep last rnd 5 more times.

Shape armholes

Rnd 12 K3, bind off next 6 sts, k10, bind off next 6 sts, k2. 17 sts.
Rnd 13 K next 3 sts to give 6 sts on one needle.
Turn and work back and forth on these 6 sts for the underside of the jacket.
Row 14 (WS) P.
Work 2 rows in st st. Cut yarn and leave sts on needle.
With WS facing, rejoin **A** to 11 sts (slide onto one needle) for the top of the jacket.
Row 17 P, turn.
Work 2 rows in st st. Cut yarn and leave sts on needle.

Join upper to underside

Rnd 20 K11, k2tog from 6 sts at the underside, k2, k2tog, k1 from upper again to join in the rnd. 15 sts. (Keep tension tight across junctions.)
Rnd 21 K15.
Rep last rnd 3 more times.
Bind off.
Weave in all ends, neatening around the armholes.

Techniques

All the projects in this section are quick—some take less than a day—and easy to knit, once the basic techniques have been mastered. The pets are all, or in part, knitted using four double-pointed needles—a fairly new approach to toy knitting. This can seem a little daunting to the uninitiated—I was one of those half a year ago. But sock knitting had been re-invented and I thought I should try to master the technique. Now, for me, it's the only way to knit! The very act of going round and round is pure meditation and fun—and the knitted creation is 'sculptured' in three-dimensional form as you work, so you can instantly see how your work is progressing.

If you are new to knitting or need to brush up on your past skills, there are basic techniques over the next few pages, from how to cast on, knit and purl, knit in the round, and bind off. There is also advice on special design techniques and finishing touches.

My advice is to have fun choosing your yarn, enjoy the process of knitting, and take your time to achieve your perfect pet. Be fussy!

Abbreviations

All knitting patterns use abbreviations to save time and space. These may seem a bit daunting if you are not familiar with the terms, but you'll quickly pick up the language. Below is a list of all the abbreviations used in the patterns for this section.

The rows and rounds in the patterns in this section are numbered sequentially throughout each pattern piece so that you can easily identify your place.

approx approximately
beg beginning
cm(s) centimetre(s)
cont continue
dec decrease
DK double knitting
g gram(s)
in(s) inch(es)
inc increase
k knit
k2tog knit the next two stitches together (decrease by one stitch)
k3tog knit the next three stitches together (decrease by two stitches)
kfb knit into front and back of the same stitch (increase by one stitch)
MC main color
mm millimetre(s)
n needle (with the needle number: needle 1, needle 2, etc.)
oz ounce(s)
p purl
p2tog purl the next two stitches together (decrease by one stitch)
p3tog purl the next three stitches together (decrease by two stitches)
patt pattern
pfkb purl into front and knit into back of the same stitch (increase one stitch)
picot cast on one/more stitches, then bind off the same number of stitches (the number of stitches is given as picot 2, picot 5, etc.)
psso pass the slipped stitch over (decrease by one stitch)
rem remaining
rep repeat
rnd round
skpo slip one, knit one, pass the slipped stitch over (decrease by one stitch)
sl slip
sl 1 slip one stitch
st(s) stitch(es)
st st stockinette stitch (stocking stitch)
tog together
yon yarn over/yarn over needle (increase by one stitch in lace pattern)

Basic equipment

Of course, you'll need a selection of knitting needles. Most of the patterns use double-ended needles, but some use single-ended ones and circular needles. If you wish to make a collar for Biscuit the Cat, you'll require a crochet hook. You'll also need a selection of safety pins and stitch holders for holding stitches and markers to indicate the start of rounds. A large-eyed tapestry or darning needle will be handy for making up your pets. Use a good quality toy stuffing and, if you wish, a pair of tweezers for stuffing the narrower shapes.

My little pony—knitted in the round

My most colorful pet!

Gauge

On the band or sleeve of every ball of yarn there is information on the gauge (what European knitters call 'tension') of the yarn. This tells you how many stitches and rows you should aim to achieve over 4in (10cm) square. The gauge will differ depending on the size of the needles you use and the thickness of the yarn. However, we all knit differently. Some people are naturally loose knitters and others knit more tightly. The beauty about toys is that the gauge doesn't really matter in most cases. If your pet is a little bit bigger or smaller than mine, no-one will know!

Casting on

All projects start with getting the first stitches onto the knitting needles—in other words, casting them on. There are various methods of casting on, but I find the knitting-on method is simple and versatile. Of course, if you have a favorite method, use that.

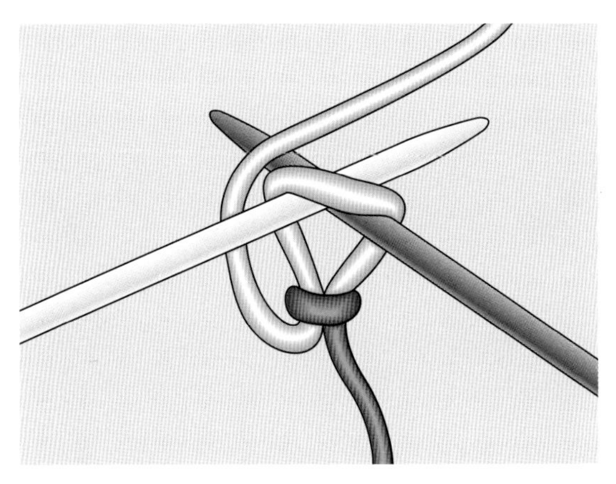

1 Make a slipknot in the working end of your yarn, leaving an end of approx 12in (30cm). Place the slipknot on the left-hand needle. Insert the right-hand needle into the loop of the slipknot and wrap the yarn around the tip of the needle, from back to front.

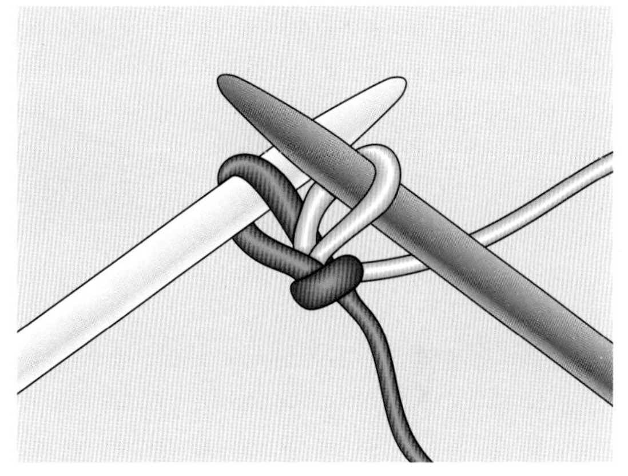

2 Slide the tip of the right-hand needle down to catch this new loop of yarn.

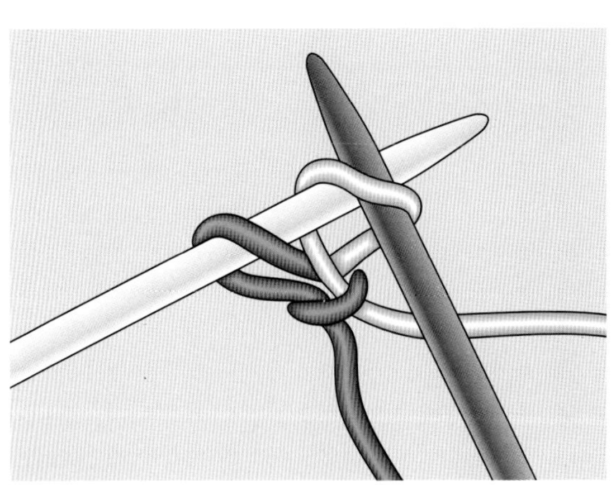

3 Place the new loop on the left-hand needle.

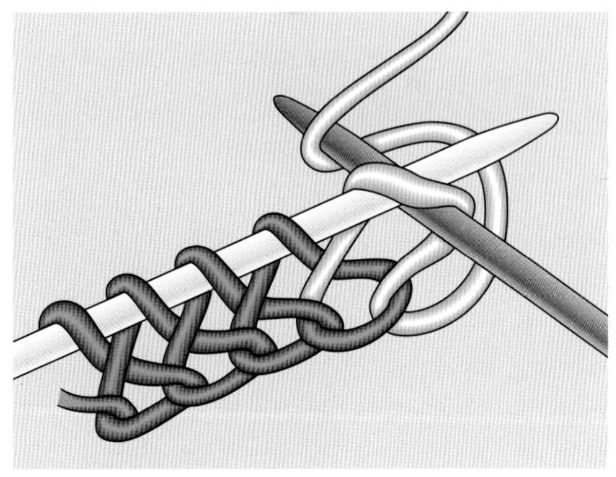

4 Repeat this process until you have cast on as many stitches as the project requires.

The knit stitch

The most basic stitch in knitting is called, not surprisingly, the knit stitch. It can be used completely on its own, when knitting in the round (see page 327), to produce stockinette stitch (also known as stocking stitch, see page 322). When it is used on its own for working back and forth along rows, it produces garter stitch (page 322).

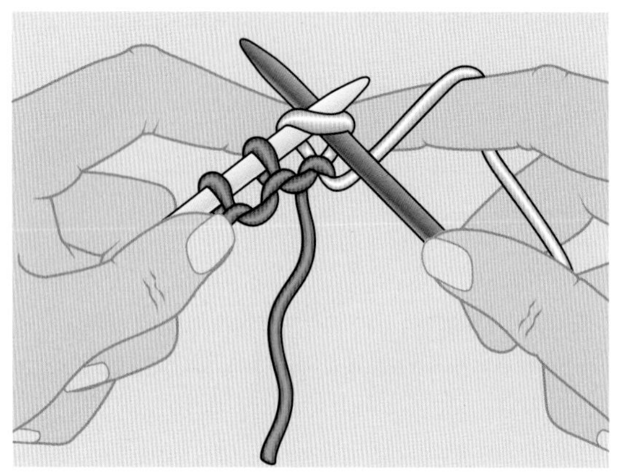

1 The working stitches will be on the left-hand needle. Take the right-hand needle and insert the tip from right to left into the first loop on the left-hand needle.

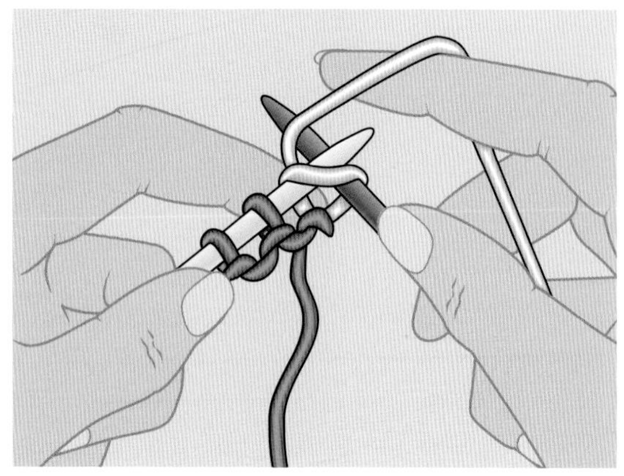

2 Wrap the yarn from back to front around the tip of the right-hand needle.

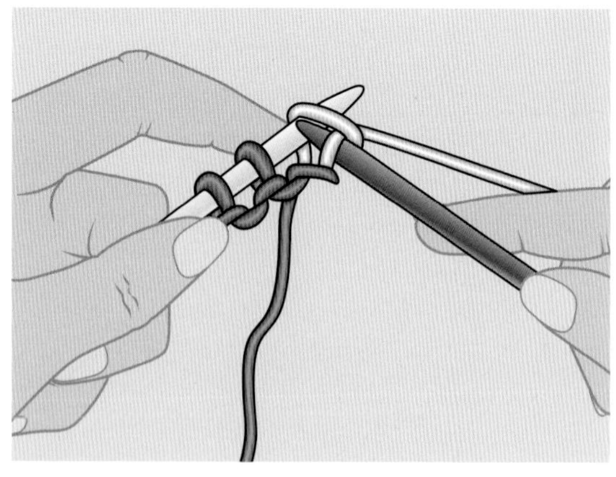

3 Slide the needle down to catch this new loop of yarn. Slip the loop off the left-hand needle and onto the right-hand needle. This is your first stitch. Repeat the process until all the stitches have been knitted off the left-hand needle onto the right-hand one.

Most of the pets use knit stitch, knitted in the round.

The purl stitch

The perfect complement to the knit stitch is the purl stitch. The right side of each looks like the reverse side of the other. If purl stitch is used when working back and forth, alternating rows with knit stitch, the combination produces stockinette stitch (see page 322).

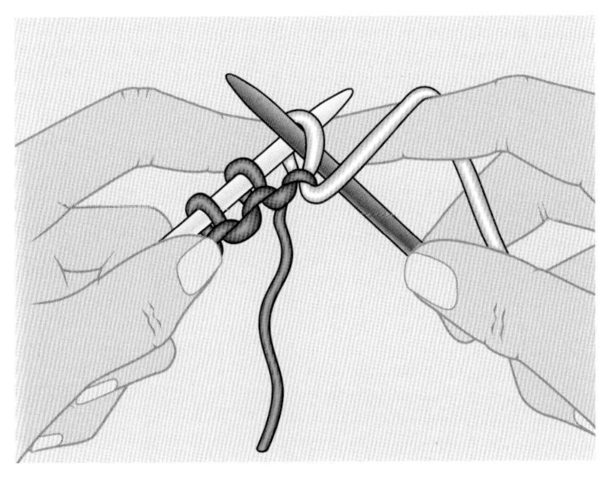

1 The working stitches will be on your left-hand needle.

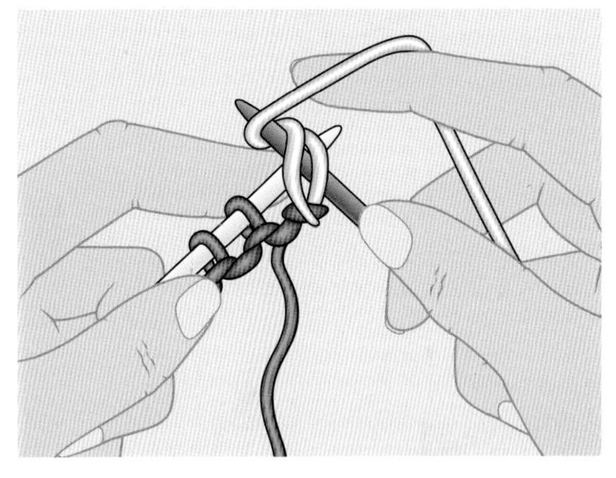

2 Wrap the yarn counterclockwise around the tip of the right-hand needle.

Biscuit's basket uses purl stitch, with knit stitch, to create an interwoven look

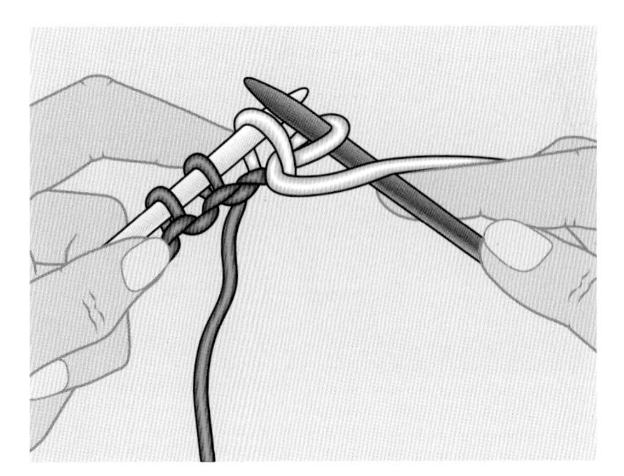

3 Use the tip of the right-hand needle to pick up the new loop of yarn. Slide the loop off the left-hand needle and onto the right-hand needle. This is your first stitch. Repeat the process until all the stitches have been knitted off the left-hand needle onto the right-hand one.

Basic stitch patterns

Only the very basic stitch patterns are used to make the knitted pets in this section. They are mostly knitted in stockinette stitch, with a few details knitted in reverse stockinette stitch and garter stitch.

Stockinette Stitch

Stockinette stitch (also referred to as stocking stitch by Europeans) is the knitted fabric that features most often in this section. It is created by knitting one row and purling the next row when knitting back and forth, or by knitting every row in the round. The knitted side forms the 'right side'; the purl side forms the 'wrong side'.

Stockinette stitch gives a smooth texture—just right for a velvety rabbit.

Textured legs for better traction!

Reverse Stockinette Stitch

Reverse stockinette stitch is made in the same way as stockinette stitch, but the purl side forms the right side. I have used reverse stockinette stitch to give Tortellini Tortoise's legs (see pages 264–267) a more wrinkled-looking texture.

Garter Stitch

Garter stitch is made by knitting every row when knitting back and forth. This creates quite a dense fabric that looks the same on both sides. The hens' tail feathers (see page 235) are knitted in garter stitch to help them stand up.

Their tails are so pretty!

Binding off

Before you can make up your pets, you'll need to bind off your knitting so that the stitches don't work loose. Below are instructions for the standard binding off of one edge. On some pets, you'll need to bind off (graft) two edges together, for which you can use Kitchener stitch (grafting).

Standard Bind Off

1 Work the first stitch on the left-hand needle as if making a regular knit stitch. Then knit the second stitch. Insert the left-hand needle into the first stitch on the right-hand needle.

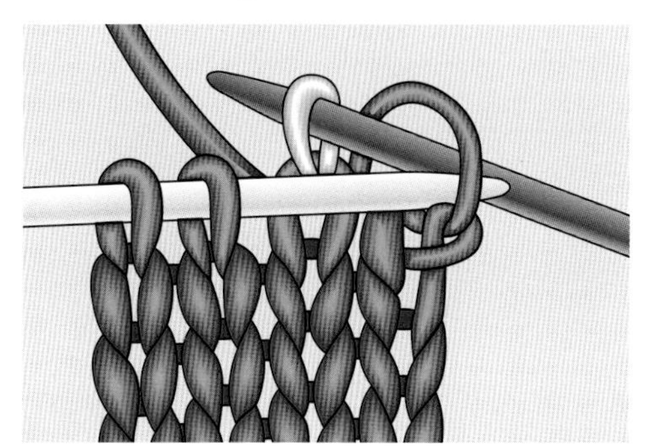

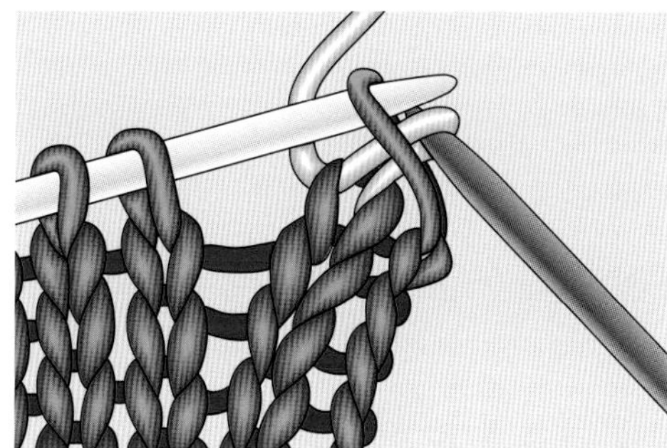

2 Pass this stitch over the second loop on the right-hand needle and drop it off the needle. This makes the first bind-off stitch. To continue, knit the next stitch. Use your left-hand needle to pass the new first stitch over the second stitch and drop it off the needle. Carry on until all the stitches in the row have been bound off.

Kitchener Stitch

1 Cut the working yarn, leaving a long end, and thread it into a tapestry needle. Hold the double-pointed needles, each with the same number of stitches, parallel in your left hand. Insert the tapestry needle purl-wise into the first stitch on the closest knitting needle. Pull the yarn through, leaving the stitch on the knitting needle.

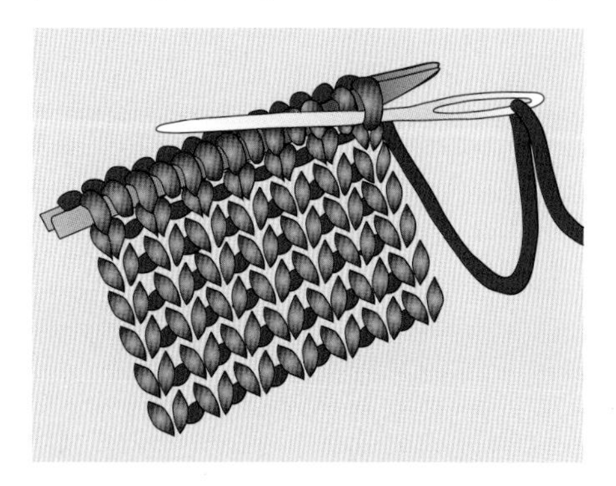

2 Insert the tapestry needle knit-wise into the first stitch on the back knitting needle. Pull the yarn through, leaving that stitch on the knitting.

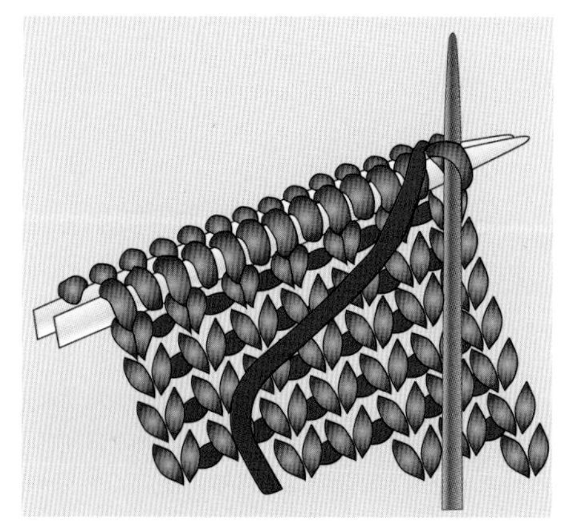

3 Insert the tapestry needle into the same front stitch as before, this time knit-wise, and slip that stitch off the knitting needle onto the working yarn.

4 Insert the tapestry needle purl-wise through the next front stitch, leaving it on the knitting needle. Pass the tapestry needle purl-wise through the same stitch as before on the back knitting needle, slipping it off the needle and onto the working yarn. Insert the tapestry needle knit-wise through the next backstitch, leaving it on the knitting needle. Repeat steps 3 and 4 until there are no stitches left on the needles.

Colorwork

One of the main ways to knit designs using two or more colors—intarsia—is used to give the short-haired guinea pig (is that Itty or Bitty?) the pale patch on his forehead (see pages 238–243). Many of the other pets, such as Silkysoft Snake (see pages 226–229), Tortellini Tortoise (see pages 262–267) and Biscuit the Cat (see pages 282–267), cleverly use variegated yarn to find their colorful selves.

INTARSIA

Intarsia knitting is used for designs where there are blocks of color. You'll need a separate ball of yarn for each color, and you'll often have to change colors in the middle of a row.

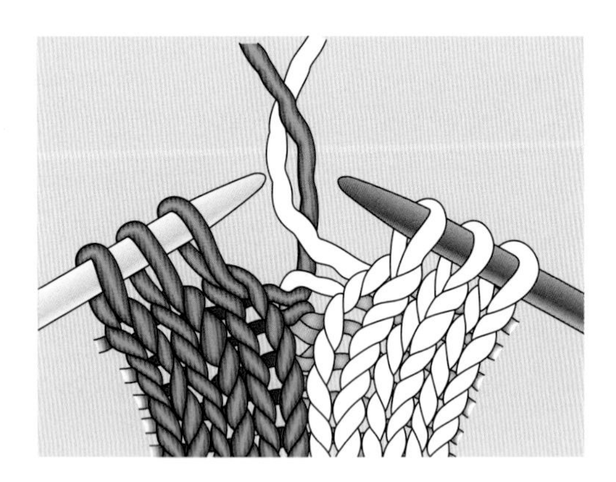

Knit along the row until the new color is needed. Drop the first color and pick up the second color underneath the first one, crossing the two yarns over before knitting the next stitch in the second color. The crossing of the stitches ensures that no holes are created between colors.

So sweet with his little patch!

Adding color is easy with space-dyed yarn.

Shaping

The pets in this section have been created by shaping the knitting (increasing and decreasing stitches), as well as by knitting in the round (see page 327) and with the i-cord technique (see page 328). This means you can see your pets developing their three-dimensional shape as you knit and there is much less sewing up to do after you finish knitting. The different shaping techniques are explained below.

Decreasing Stitches

Decreasing stitches is where you lose stitches, in these patterns usually one at a time. This can be achieved in several ways.

SKPO (SLIP ONE, KNIT ONE, PASS THE SLIPPED STITCH OVER)

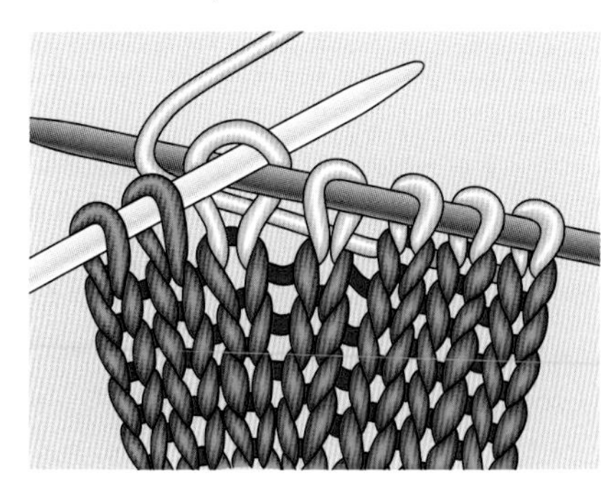

1 Knit along the row until you reach the area you want to decrease. Slip the stitch (unknitted) onto the right-hand needle. Knit the next stitch.

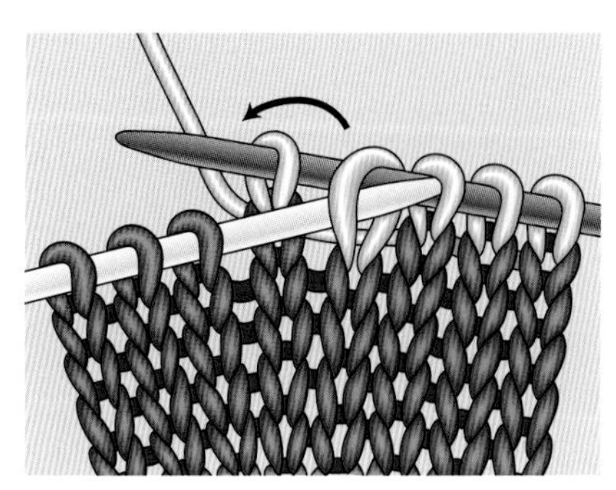

2 Lift the slipped stitch over the knitted stitch and off the needle. This decreases by one stitch.

K2TOG (KNIT TWO STITCHES TOGETHER)

Knit along the row until you reach the area you want to decrease. Knit through the next two stitches as though they were one stitch. This decreases by one stitch.

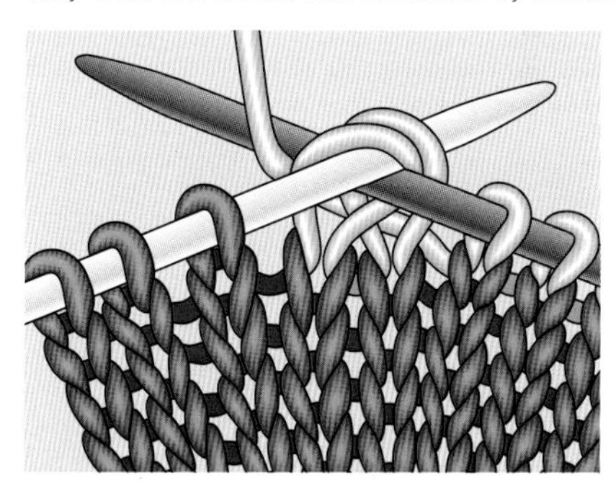

P2TOG (PURL TWO STITCHES TOGETHER)

Purl along the row until you reach the area you want to decrease. Purl through the next two stitches as though they were one stitch. This decreases by one stitch.

MULTIPLE DECREASES

You can also decrease by more than one stitch at a time. Some of the pattern instructions ask you to k3tog or p3tog, for example. Work these decreases as explained above; you'll just need to insert your working needle through three stitches and knit or purl them together as though they were one stitch. K3tog and p3tog decrease by two stitches.

Increasing Stitches

Increasing stitches is where you make a stitch.

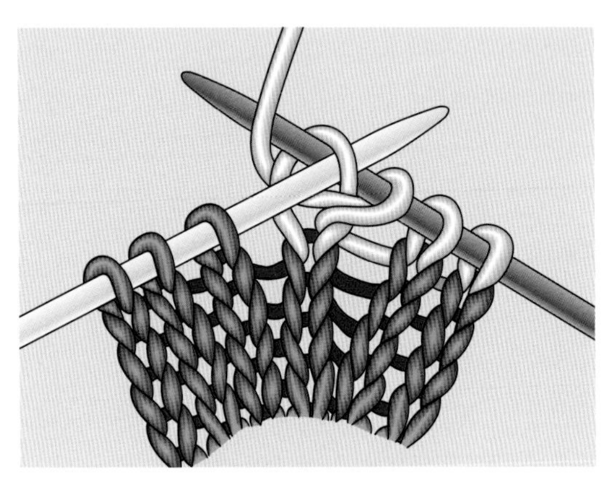

KFB (KNIT INTO THE FRONT AND BACK)
Knit along the row until you reach the area you want to increase. Knit into the front of the next stitch on the left-hand needle. Instead of removing it from the needle, knit into it again through the back loop. Then slip the original stitch off the left-hand needle.

PFKB (PURL INTO THE FRONT, KNIT INTO THE BACK)
Purl along the row until you reach the area you want to increase. Purl into the front of the next stitch on the left-hand needle. Instead of slipping it off the needle, take the working yarn to the back of the work and knit into the stitch through the back loop. Slip the original stitch off the left-hand needle.

Reggie's upright back plates make him feel very brave when he's exploring.

YON (YARN OVER/YARN OVER NEEDLE)
Wrapping the yarn over the needle makes an additional stitch and a hole in knitted lace and textured patterns. I have used this technique to create tiny holes in the hens' feathers (pages 232–233) and to shape Reggie Veggie's triangular plates (page 296).

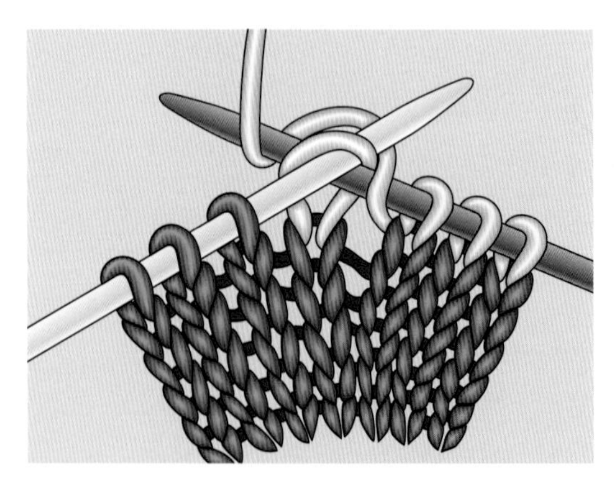

Bring the yarn over between the two needles. Knit the next stitch, taking the yarn over the right needle.

Knitting in the round

Most of the pets in this section have parts that are knitted in the round on double-pointed needles. Some of the pets use the i-cord technique, which also produces tubular pieces—this time like a thin knitted string—for the legs and tails. Knitting in this way is great because it saves you having to sew up fiddly seams later.

The rounds are numbered straight on from any preceding row or round, although sometimes you need to knit part of a round to get to the correct place to start knitting the next part of your pet. Often you'll want to place a marker to show the beginning of the round.

The pony's agile body is knitted in the round.

Pink i-cord makes a picture-perfect tail

KNITING I-CORD

Using two double-pointed needles, cast on the number of stitches you need and knit across them. Instead of turning your knitting, slide the stitches to the opposite end of the needle with the knit side facing you. Take the working yarn, from the left-hand edge, across the back of the work and knit across the stitches. Slide the stitches to the opposite end of the needle as before and knit across the stitches, drawing the knitting into a tube. Pull the yarn quite tightly when knitting the first stitch.

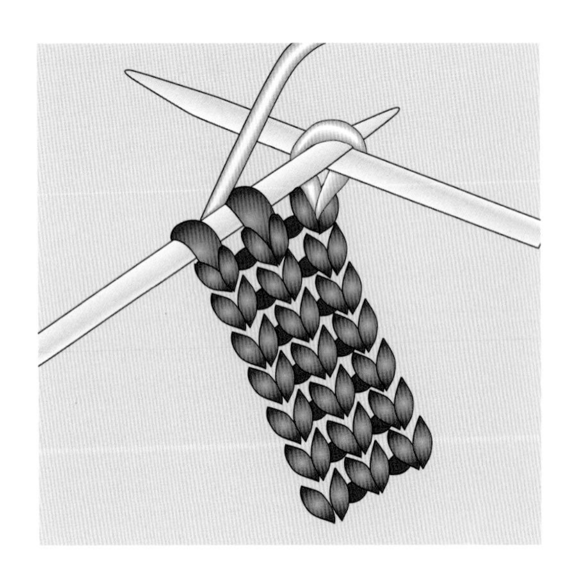

KNITTING ON DOUBLE-POINTED NEEDLES

Double-pointed needles are shorter than standard needles and easier to handle than a circular needle when you have only a few stitches to work in the round.

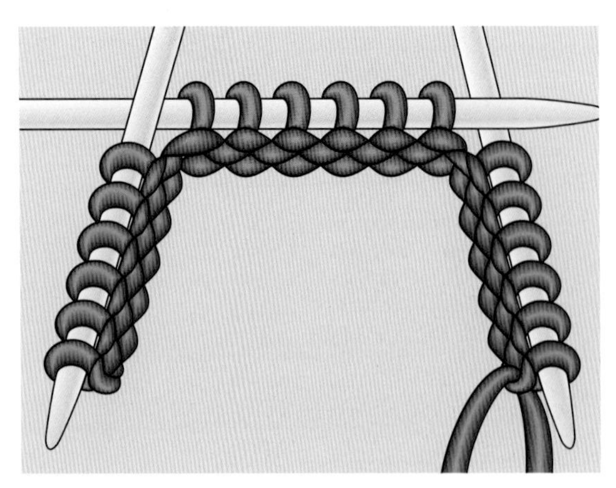

1 Cast on as you would normally and distribute the stitches equally over three double-pointed needles.

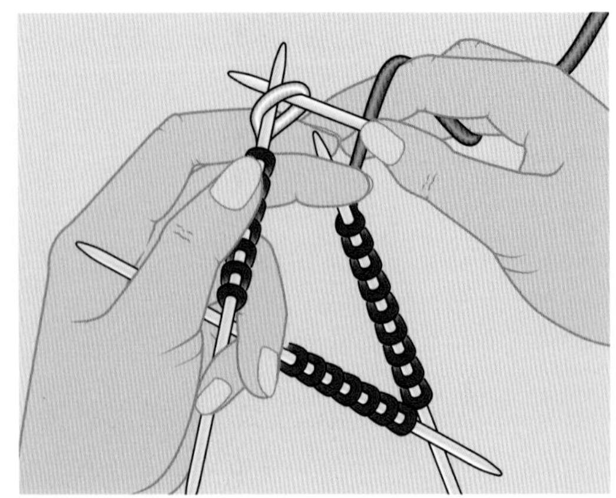

2 Continue knitting round, transferring the stitches so that you have an equal number of stitches on each needle.

Making up

There are various ways of sewing up knitting, so use whichever you like or suits the occasion best. Always use the same yarn you knitted with so the stitches are less visible. Often you'll be able to use the long end you left when you cast on. It's best to use a tapestry or darning needle with a large eye and blunt end so that you don't split the yarn.

Weaving in ends

You'll have some loose yarn ends from casting on and binding off, so weave these in first. One of the best ways to weave in the loose ends so they will be invisible is to thread the yarn end through a tapestry needle and sew it into the seam by passing the needle through the 'bumps' of the stitches on the wrong side of the work. Sew them in for approx 1–2in (2.5–5cm) and then snip off any excess yarn.

Backstitch (reverse sides out)

Put both knit sides (right sides) together so the wrong sides are facing you. Carefully make small stitches along the edge, taking the needle down for each stitch behind the end of the previous stitch. Make sure you are sewing in a straight line as close to the edge as possible. It might sound obvious, but it is very easy to pick up stitches that are further away from the edge than you think. You want the sewing to be as invisible as possible.

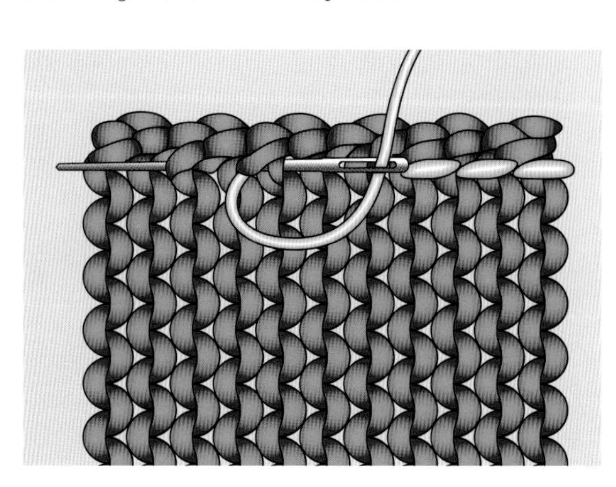

Mattress stitch (knit sides out)

Put the two pieces of knitting next to each other, knit sides up and seams matching. Run the yarn through the center of the first stitch on one piece of knitting, then down through the center of the first stitch on the other piece of knitting. Next go through the second stitch on the first piece of knitting and down through the center of the second stitch on the other piece. Continue in this way along the row, pulling up the stitches fairly tightly.

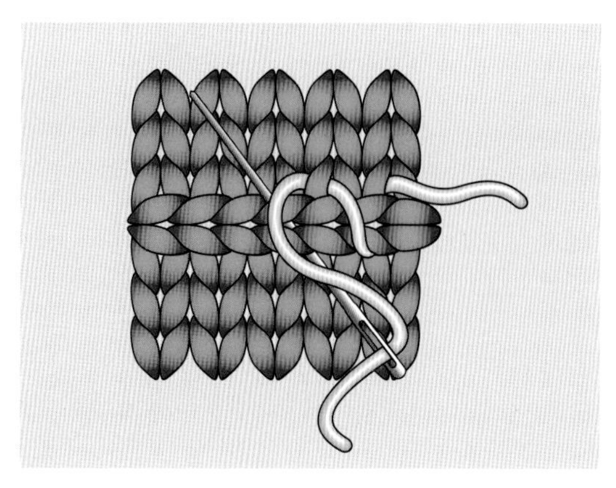

Biscuit's ears are all attentive!

Standing your pets up

I have designed these pets to look as much like the bird or animal they represent as I can, but yarn being yarn it can have its own mind about whether it wants to stand up or which way it wants to lie. So, if you feel it necessary, a little gentle persuasion may be needed.

To make Biscuit's ears (page 287) extra perky, tame a pony's mane (page 302) or give the little birds' legs (page 225) standing power, for example, try a 50:50 solution of sugar (or PVA adhesive) and water. Make the solution with hot water to dissolve the sugar and then leave it to cool. Dab or paint the solution onto the knitted part you want to stiffen and then leave it to dry in the desired position.

To make sure a knitted pet will stand easily every time, insert a drinking straw into each leg before you sew it up. Stuff gently around the straw and particularly at the ends to stop it from poking through the knitting.

Stuffing your pets

Toy stuffing is an essential component for your knitted pets. You'll be able to find a suitable brand at haberdashery and craft stores. Use stuffing that is specifically designed for toys so you can be sure it is safe for children. Check the safety logo before you buy it.

Don't stuff toys too fully or they will become solid and have no movement. You want your pets to be cuddly. You'll probably find that your fingers are all you need to push stuffing into small or fiddly pieces, but you might also find tweezers useful.

Sewing in final ends

Once you have stuffed the toy, you'll need to close the small opening in the middle of the seam. I knot together the two ends of the yarn used for sewing the seams, then thread the ends through the toy so that the knot is hidden and the ends are kept long. You don't want to cut the ends too short to avoid the knot coming undone.

Just the right amount of stuffing will keep your kitten cuddly.

Finishing touches

The smallest details can really bring your pets to life and give them their very own character. A small scrap of fabric will add color and pattern, and simple embroidered features will create a most endearing face. All animals have different markings, like the white rabbit (see pages 244–251), so add your own finishing touches to create a bespoke pet. You can also give your pets accessories like Biscuit's crocheted collar (see page 287).

EMBROIDERING DETAILS

Spend time making the facial features perfect and full of character. You can use any sewing stitches to create these features, although simple straight stitches are as effective as any. You can adapt them to make eyelashes for a pony (page 303), a mouth for a puppy (page 274), a nose for a kitten (page 258) or eyes for any of the pets. You could use French knots to make the eyes on the smaller toys or claws for a tortoise (page 267). Choose what works best for you. Just remember, you need the stitches to look neat and be as firm as possible so that they don't undo.

STRAIGHT STITCH

This is the simplest of stitches. Thread a tapestry needle with the new color of yarn and insert it from the back of the work to the front where you want the stitch to start. Take the yarn over at least a couple of knitted stitches and insert it back through the knitting where you want the stitch to end. Work as many stitches as you wish and then secure the ends at the back of the work. You can adapt these stitches endlessly, for example sewing them close together, on top of each other or splayed apart.

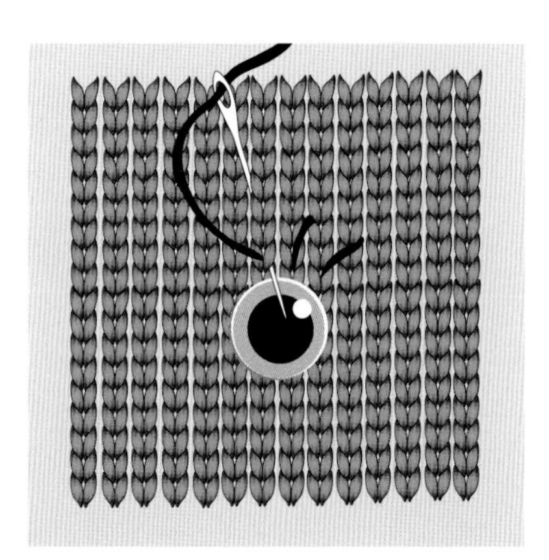

FRENCH KNOT

Bring the needle from the back to the front of the work and wind the yarn twice around the needle. Pull the needle through the twists, bringing the yarn through too. This creates the knot. You can twist the yarn round the needle more times if you want a bigger knot and once only for a smaller knot.

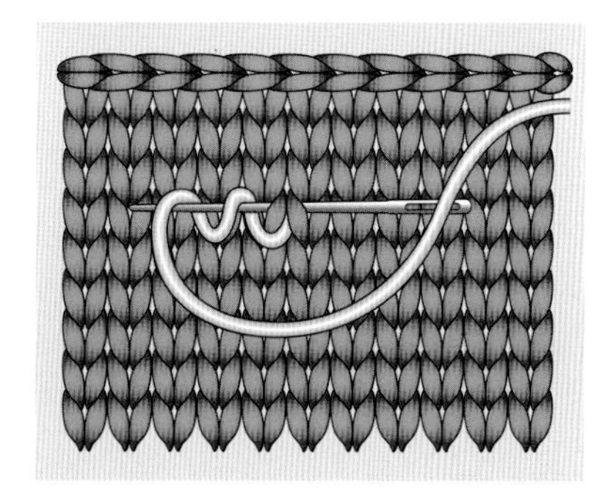

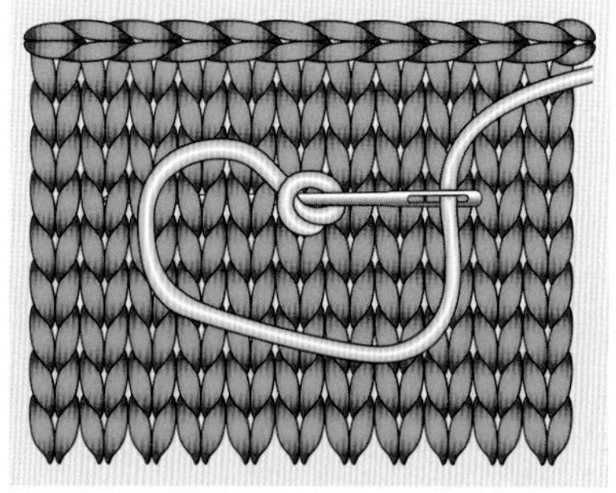

DUPLICATE STITCH (SWISS DARNING)

This is a simple way of adding small areas of contrasting color and forms duplicate stitches over the knitted stitches. Thread a tapestry needle with yarn and bring it up from the back of the work to the front through the middle of a knitted stitch where you want the contrast patch to be. Weave the contrasting thread to duplicate and cover the knitted stitch. Repeat, to cover as many knitted stitches as you wish. Secure the ends of yarn at the back of the contrasting patch.

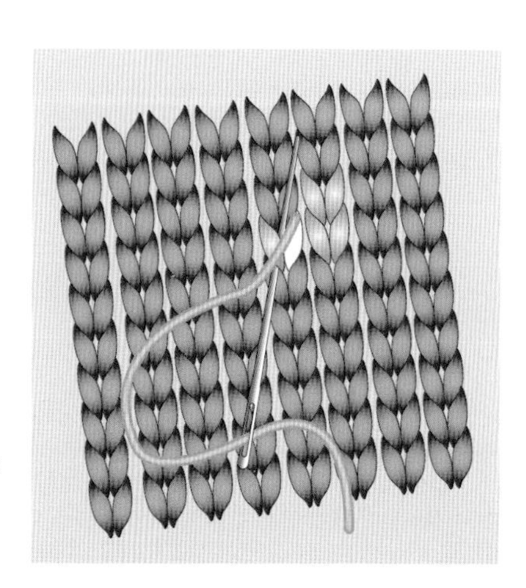

APPLIQUÉ

The Little Feathered Friends (pages 220–225) combine knitting with fabric appliqué and give the birds truly unique characters. You can add a touch of nostalgia by using treasured scraps of old fabric to really personalize your work.

SEWING APPLIQUE ON

There are several ways you can sew fabric details onto the knitting. I have simply used straight stitches to attach the edges of fabric to the knitting. Use normal sewing thread rather than yarn. Try to get your stitching as neat as possible and be creative with the color of thread you use. The most important thing to ensure is that the fabric is sewn securely to the knitting.

This little song bird looks even prettier with a red patterned breast.

Biscuit doesn't realize the bell warns the birds!

CROCHET

Crochet is very handy for making collars, leads and reins for pets. You just need to make a chain, which is easy to do.

CROCHETING A CHAIN

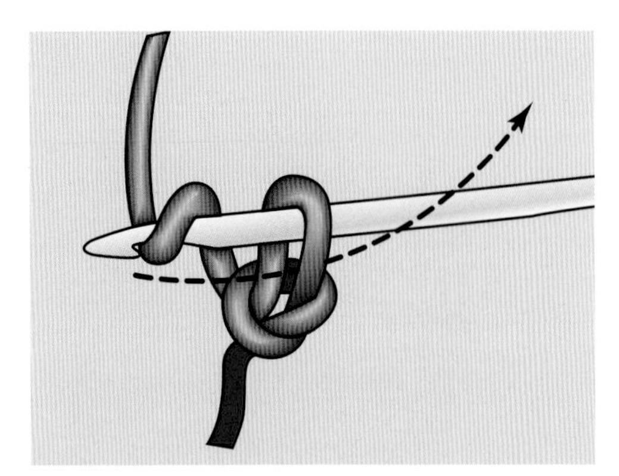

1 Tie a slipknot in the working end of the yarn and place the loop on your crochet hook. Wrap the yarn clockwise over the hook.

2 Pull the yarn through the loop on the hook to form a new loop. This is the first chain. Repeat the process until the chain is as long as you want it.

Yarns

Each of the project instructions gives a generic description of the yarn that was used. The specific yarns I used are listed below if you want to recreate the project exactly.

Yarn companies frequently update their lines and may discontinue certain yarns or colors. If the yarns below are not available, or if you want to use a substitute yarn, you'll need to work out the yardage (meterage) needed, as yarns vary. Details will be on the ball band or on good yarn suppliers' websites so that you can make comparisons.

PAGE 220 **LITTLE FEATHERED FRIENDS**
PINK BIRD
Claudia Hand Painted Yarns: ½ ball in shade Strawberry Latte (**MC**)
Rowan Pure Wool 4-ply: oddment in shade 416 Hessian (**A**)

YELLOW BIRD
Rowan Pure Wool 4-ply: ½ ball in shade 032 Gilt (**MC**)
RYC Classic 4-ply in shade 448 Sweetcorn (**C**)
Rowan Pure Wool 4-ply: oddment in shade 417 Mocha (**A**)

BLUE BIRD
Rowan Pure Wool 4-ply: ½ ball in shade 445 Chalk (**MC**)
Rowan Pure Wool 4-ply: oddment in shade 410 Indigo for contrast face (optional)
Rowan Pure Wool 4-ply: oddment in shade 417 Mocha (**A**)

PAGE 226 **SILKYSOFT SNAKE**
Claudia Hand Painted Yarns: ½ ball in shade Eat Your Veggies (**MC**)

PAGE 230 **HAUGHTY HEN TRIO**
WHITE HEN
Rowan Organic Wool DK: ½ ball in shade 600 Natural (**MC**)
Sirdar Escape DK: oddment in shade 182 Grey, Black and White (**A**)
Debbie Bliss Rialto 4-ply: oddment in shade 22009 Red (**B**)
Rowan Pure Wool 4-ply: oddment in shade 433 Honey (**C**)

BLACK/WHITE/GREY HEN
Sirdar Escape DK: ½ ball in shade 182 Grey/Black/White (**MC**)
(**B**) and (**C**) as WHITE HEN

BROWN SPECKLED HEN
Wendy Skye DK: ½ ball in shade 2802 Hazel (**MC**)
(**B**) and (**C**) as WHITE HEN

PAGE 236 **EGG-STRA GOOD LAYERS**
Sublime Extra Fine Merino Wool: oddment in shade 445 Salty Grey
Sublime Baby Cashmere Merino Silk: oddment in shade 120 Lambie
Sublime Baby Cashmere Merino Silk 4-ply: oddment in shade 05 Waterlily

PAGE 238 **ITTY BITTY GUINEA PIGS**
SHORT-HAIRED GUINEA PIG
Rowan Organic Wool DK: ½ ball in shade 600 Natural (**MC**)
Rowan Purelife British Sheep Breeds DK: oddment in shade 780 Ecru (**C**)

LONG-HAIRED GUINEA-PIG
Stylecraft Eskimo DK: ½ ball in shade 5067 Chocolate (**MC**)
Rowan Organic Wool DK: oddment in shade 607 Onion (**A**)

PAGE 244 **MITTENS & SOCKS**
BROWN SPECKLED RABBIT
Stylecraft Kon-Tiki DK: 2 balls in shade 1460 Charcoal Marble (**MC**)
Rowan Classic Baby Alpaca DK: oddment in shade 208 Southdown (**B**)

WHITE RABBIT
Patons Pompero: 2 balls in shade 02 (**MC**)
Rowan Purelife British Sheep Breeds DK: oddment in shade 785 Mid Brown Jacob (**A**)

PAGE 252 **SPECKLE THE KITTEN**
KITTEN
Rowan Purelife British Sheep Breeds DK: 1 ball in shade 785 Mid Brown Jacob (**MC**)
Rowan Purelife British Sheep Breeds DK: oddment in shade 780 Ecru (**A**)

PAGE 260 **TOY MOUSE**
Rowan Pure Wool DK: oddment in shade 032 Gilt (**MC**)
Rowan Pure Wool DK: oddment in shade 002 Shale (**A**)

PAGE 262 **TORTELLINI TORTOISE**
Claudia Hand Painted Yarns: ½ ball in shade Donna's Favorite (**A**)
RYC Baby Alpaca: oddment in shade 210 Lagoon (**B**)
Rowan Organic Wool DK: ½ ball in shade 606 Alder Buckthorn (**C**)
Sublime Organic Merino Wool DK: ½ ball in shade 0190 Pod (**MC**)

PAGE 268 **BAMBER THE LABRADOR PUPPY**
Sublime Baby Cashmere Merino Silk DK: ½ ball in shade 03 Vanilla (**MC**)
Sublime Baby Cashmere Merino Silk DK: oddment in shade 105 Treacle (**B**)
RYC Bamboo Soft: oddment in shade 105 Bamboo (**A**)

PAGE 276 **RAVENOUS RATS**
BROWN RAT
Rowan Purelife British Sheep Breeds DK: oddment in shade 782 Mid Brown (**MC**)
Sublime Baby Cashmere Merino Silk 4-ply: oddment in shade 0001 Piglet (**A**)

MOTTLED BROWN RAT
Rowan Purelife British Sheep Breeds DK: oddment in shade 783 Marl (**MC**)
(**A**) as BROWN RAT

WHITE RAT
Rowan Purelife British Sheep Breeds DK: oddment in shade 780 Ecru (**MC**)
(**A**) as BROWN RAT

PAGE 282 **BISCUIT THE CAT**
Claudia Hand Painted Yarns: ½ ball in shade Honey (**MC**)
Sirdar Super Nova Super Chunky: ½ ball in shade 889 Cream (**A**)

PAGE 290 **REGGIE VEGGIE**
RYC Cotton Jeans: 2 balls in shade 361 Jute (**MC**)
King Cole Mirage DK: 1 ball in shade 864 Greens (**A**)

PAGE 298 **PIP AND POP PONIES**
WHITE PONY
Sublime Organic Merino Wool DK: ½ ball in shade 0112 Chalk (**MC**)
Sublime Baby Cashmere Merino Silk 4-ply: oddment in shade 0001 Piglet (**B**)

GREY PONY
Sublime Organic Merino Wool DK: ½ ball in shade 0113 Twine (**A**)
Sublime Organic Merino Wool DK: oddment in shade 0112 Chalk (**MC**)
(**B**) as WHITE PONY

PAGE 304 **CHARLIE THE CHAMELEON**
Adriafil Knitcol Trends: 1 ball in shade 051 Green/Blue/Purple/Pink/Orange (**MC**)

PAGE 308 **ZOOM THE GREYHOUND**
Sublime Organic Merino Wool DK: 1 ball in shade 0115 Pumice (**MC**)
Debbie Bliss Rialto 4-ply: ½ ball in shade 22009 Berry Red (**A**)

Suppliers

ADRIAFIL
www.adriafil.com
(USA) Yarnmarket, LLC
12936 Stonecreek Drive, Unit D
Pickerington, OH 43147
Tel: +1 888 996 9276
www.yarnmarket.com
(UK) Angel Yarns
Angel House
77 North Street
Portslade
East Sussex BN41 1DZ
Tel: +44 (0)871 288 7358
www.angelyarns.com
(AUS) Wool N Things
Shop 9, Rowens Arcade
Princes Highway
Ulladulla NSW 2539
Tel: (02) 4455 2501
email: woolnthings@rowens.com.au

CLAUDIA HAND PAINTED YARN
www.claudiaco.com
(USA) Claudia Hand Painted Yarns
40 West Washington Street
Harrisonburg, VA 22802
Tel: +1 540 433 1140
www.claudiaco.com

DEBBIE BLISS
www.debbieblissonline.com
(USA) Knitting Fever Inc.
315 Bayview Avenue
Amityville, New York
NY 11701
Tel +1 516 546 3600
www.knittingfever.com

(UK) Designer Yarns Ltd
Units 8–10, Newbridge Industrial Estate,
Pitt Street
Keighley BD21 4PQ
Tel: +44 (0)1535 664222
email: david@designeryarns.uk.com
www. designeryarns.uk.com
(AUS) Prestige Yarns Pty Ltd
PO Box 39
Bulli NSW 2516
Tel: +61 02 4285 6669
email: info@prestigeyarns.com
www. prestigeyarns.com

KING COLE
www.kingcole.co.uk
(UK) King Cole Ltd
Merrie Mills, Elliott Street
Silsden
Keighley BD20 0DE
Tel: + (0)1535 650230
email: lance.martin@kingcole.co.uk
www.kingcole.co.uk

PATONS
www.makeitcoats.com
(USA/CAN) Patons
320 Livingstone Avenue South
Listowel, ON
Canada
N4W 3H3
Tel: +1 888 368 8401
email: inquire@patonsyarns.com

(UK) Coats Crafts UK
PO Box 22, Lingfield House
Lingfield Point, McMullen Road
Darlington DL1 1YJ
Tel: +44 (0)1325 394237
email: consumer.ccuk@coats.com
www.coatscrafts.co.uk
(AUS) Patons
PO Box 7276, Melbourne Victoria 3004
Tel: +61 (0)3 9380 3888
email: enquiries@auspinners.com.au

ROWAN, including **RYC**
www.knitrowan.com
(USA) Westminster Fibers Inc
165 Ledge Street, Nashua
New Hampshire 03060
Tel: +1 603 886 5041/5043
email: info@westminsterfibers.com

(UK) Rowan
Green Lane Mill, Holmfirth HD9 2DX
Tel: +44 (0)1484 681881
email: info@knitrowan.com
www.knitrowan.com
(AUS) Australian Country Spinners Pty Ltd
Level 7, 409 St Kilda Road
Melbourne, Victoria 3004
Tel: +61 (0)3 9380 3888
email: tkohut@auspinners.com.au
www. ausyarnco.com.au

SIRDAR, including **SUBLIME**
www.sirdar.co.uk
(USA) Knitting Fever Inc.
315 Bayview Avenue
Amityville, NY 11701
Tel: +1 516 546 3600
www.knittingfever.com

(UK) Sirdar Spinning Ltd
Flanshaw Lane, Alvethorpe
Wakefield WF2 9ND
Tel: +44 (0)1924 371501
email: enquiries@sirdar.co.uk
www.sirdar.co.uk
(AU) Creative Images Crafts
PO Box 106
Hastings, Victoria 3915
Tel: (03) 5979 1555
email: creative@peninsula.starway.net.au

STYLECRAFT
www.stylecraft-yarns.co.uk
(UK) Stylecraft
PO Box 62, Goulbourne Street
Keighley BD21 1PP
Tel: +44 (0)1535 609798
email: info@stylecraftltd.co.uk
www.stylecraft-yarns.co.uk

WENDY
(UK) KnitAndSew
Knitandsew
21/22 Park Street
Swansea SA1 3DJ
Tel: +44 (0)845 0940835
email: sales@knitandsew.co.uk

About the author

Claire Garland's early memories of deliberating over her favorite toy-making book as a seven-year old, before cutting and sticking wondrous creations and designing clothes for her teenage dolls, live on in the toys she designs today.

The grown-up Claire studied art and design in Cardiff, Wales, and a year after finishing her studies started designing needlepoint kits for the internationally renowned company Primavera.

For her own young children, Claire first tried her hand at embroidering bed linen before rekindling her interest in knitting. The knitted dolls she designed, with their characterful looks and fashionable clothes, captured the imagination of many so much that their own special blogger website was created.

Today Claire lives with her husband and three children (and no real, only knitted, pets) in a pretty cottage in Cornwall where she writes and illustrates her books on sewing, knitting, and crochet, makes toys and runs her online mail order company www.dotpebbles.com for her own brand knitted doll kits.

Acknowledgments

Special thank yous to Jenny and the team at David & Charles for the sandwiches and cakes, and for supporting this project. Special thanks also to Karen for her time and patience. And finally an appreciative thanks to Lorna Yabsley for her superb wow-factor photography—these little guys really have come alive!

Index

A SEWANDSO BOOK

SewandSo is an imprint of F&W Media International, Ltd
Pynes Hill Court, Pynes Hill, Exeter, EX2 5AZ, UK

F&W Media International, Ltd is a subsidiary of F+W Media, Inc
10151 Carver Road, Suite #200, Blue Ash, OH 45242, USA

First published in the UK and USA in 2019
Previously published as *My Knitted Doll* (2016), *Knitted Toy Tales* (2009) and *Knit & Purl Pets* (2010)

A catalogue record for this book is available from the British Library.

ISBN-13: 978-1-4463-0751-9 paperback

Printed in China by RR Donnelley for:
F&W Media International, Ltd
Pynes Hill Court, Pynes Hill, Exeter, EX2 5AZ, UK

10 9 8 7 6 5 4 3 2 1

Acquisitions Editors: Sarah Callard and Jennifer Fox-Proverbs
Editors: Bethany Dymond, Kate Nicholson, James Brooks, Emma Gardner and Emma Fletcher
Project Editors: Jane Trollope, Karen Hemingway and Nicola Hodgson
Art Editors: Anna Wade, Prudence Rogers and Sarah Clark
Designers: Courtney Kyle, Jodie Lystor, Sabine Eulau and Sarah Underhill
Illustrator: Ethan Danielson
Photographers: Jason Jenkins, Sian Irvine, Jack Kirby and Lorna Yabsley
Production Manager: Beverley Richardson

F&W Media publishes high quality books on a wide range of subjects.
For more great book ideas visit: www.sewandso.co.uk

Layout of the digital edition of this book may vary depending on reader hardware and display settings.